W9-DHG-171

Google AdWords™

FOR

DUMMIES®

3RD EDITION

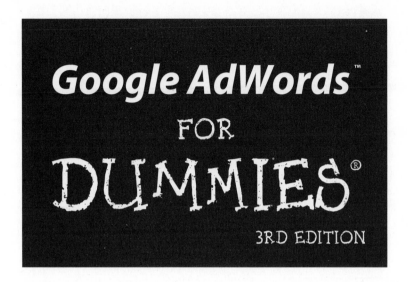

Google AdWords™

FOR

DUMMIES®

3RD EDITION

by Howie Jacobson, PhD, Kristie McDonald, and Joel McDonald

WILEY

John Wiley & Sons, Inc.

Google AdWords™ For Dummies®, 3rd Edition

Published by
John Wiley & Sons, Inc.
111 River Street
Hoboken, NJ 07030-5774
www.wiley.com

Copyright ©2012 by John Wiley & Sons, Inc., Hoboken, New Jersey

Published by John Wiley & Sons, Inc., Hoboken, New Jersey

Published simultaneously in Canada

No part of this publication may be reproduced, stored in a retrieval system or transmitted in any form or by any means, electronic, mechanical, photocopying, recording, scanning or otherwise, except as permitted under Sections 107 or 108 of the 1976 United States Copyright Act, without either the prior written permission of the Publisher, or authorization through payment of the appropriate per-copy fee to the Copyright Clearance Center, 222 Rosewood Drive, Danvers, MA 01923, (978) 750-8400, fax (978) 646-8600. Requests to the Publisher for permission should be addressed to the Permissions Department, John Wiley & Sons, Inc., 111 River Street, Hoboken, NJ 07030, (201) 748-6011, fax (201) 748-6008, or online at http://www.wiley.com/go/permissions.

Trademarks: Wiley, the Wiley logo, For Dummies, the Dummies Man logo, A Reference for the Rest of Us!, The Dummies Way, Dummies Daily, The Fun and Easy Way, Dummies.com, Making Everything Easier, and related trade dress are trademarks or registered trademarks of John Wiley & Sons, Inc. and/or its affiliates in the United States and other countries, and may not be used without written permission. Google and AdWords are trademarks or registered trademarks of Google, Inc. All other trademarks are the property of their respective owners. John Wiley & Sons, Inc. is not associated with any product or vendor mentioned in this book.

LIMIT OF LIABILITY/DISCLAIMER OF WARRANTY: THE PUBLISHER AND THE AUTHOR MAKE NO REPRESENTATIONS OR WARRANTIES WITH RESPECT TO THE ACCURACY OR COMPLETENESS OF THE CONTENTS OF THIS WORK AND SPECIFICALLY DISCLAIM ALL WARRANTIES, INCLUDING WITHOUT LIMITATION WARRANTIES OF FITNESS FOR A PARTICULAR PURPOSE. NO WARRANTY MAY BE CREATED OR EXTENDED BY SALES OR PROMOTIONAL MATERIALS. THE ADVICE AND STRATEGIES CONTAINED HEREIN MAY NOT BE SUITABLE FOR EVERY SITUATION. THIS WORK IS SOLD WITH THE UNDERSTANDING THAT THE PUBLISHER IS NOT ENGAGED IN RENDERING LEGAL, ACCOUNTING, OR OTHER PROFESSIONAL SERVICES. IF PROFESSIONAL ASSISTANCE IS REQUIRED, THE SERVICES OF A COMPETENT PROFESSIONAL PERSON SHOULD BE SOUGHT. NEITHER THE PUBLISHER NOR THE AUTHOR SHALL BE LIABLE FOR DAMAGES ARISING HEREFROM. THE FACT THAT AN ORGANIZATION OR WEBSITE IS REFERRED TO IN THIS WORK AS A CITATION AND/OR A POTENTIAL SOURCE OF FURTHER INFORMATION DOES NOT MEAN THAT THE AUTHOR OR THE PUBLISHER ENDORSES THE INFORMATION THE ORGANIZATION OR WEBSITE MAY PROVIDE OR RECOMMENDATIONS IT MAY MAKE. FURTHER, READERS SHOULD BE AWARE THAT INTERNET WEBSITES LISTED IN THIS WORK MAY HAVE CHANGED OR DISAPPEARED BETWEEN WHEN THIS WORK WAS WRITTEN AND WHEN IT IS READ.

For general information on our other products and services, please contact our Customer Care Department within the U.S. at 877-762-2974, outside the U.S. at 317-572-3993, or fax 317-572-4002.

For technical support, please visit www.wiley.com/techsupport.

Wiley publishes in a variety of print and electronic formats and by print-on-demand. Some material included with standard print versions of this book may not be included in e-books or in print-on-demand. If this book refers to media such as a CD or DVD that is not included in the version you purchased, you may download this material at http://booksupport.wiley.com. For more information about Wiley products, visit us at www.wiley.com.

Library of Congress Control Number: 2011942453

ISBN 978-1-118-11561-9 (pbk); ISBN 978-1-118-22431-1 (ebk); ISBN 978-1-118-23019-0 (ebk); ISBN 978-1-118-23024-4 (ebk)

Manufactured in the United States of America

10 9 8 7 6 5 4 3 2 1

WILEY

About the Authors

Howie Jacobson, PhD, is EIEIO (Emotional Intelligence & Empathic Inspiration Officer) of Vitruvian. He's the creator of the Checkmate Method of competitive positioning, and speaks, writes, and consults on online marketing strategy and the Hero's Journey. He is a columnist for FastCompany.com, and is a contributing author for Harvard Business Review online.

Howie has been called "one of the great positioning strategists of his generation" by his teenage daughter, which is a huge compliment if you believe that for even a second.

Howie spends his leisure time pretending he's not 46 years old, running barefoot, and playing Ultimate Frisbee and folk-rock guitar. He also performs stand-up and improv in the shower, and occasionally in front of friendly crowds of slightly tipsy customers.

Howie lives with his family in Durham, North Carolina, and KZN, South Africa, depending on when you ask. His lifelong ambition is to bring about world peace through marketing — and after that's accomplished, to play Ultimate Frisbee in the 2044 Olympics in Maui.

Kristie McDonald is CEO of Vitruvian. Prior to her work in PPC, Kristie was in IT consulting for over 20 years, including time spent at McKinsey & Company and two Accenture spin-offs. She has years of experience in strategy consulting, project management, and general business management.

Kristie's online experience began in 2004 when she took charge of online marketing at the consulting company where she was an owner and director. Once she caught "the bug," she went on to build and grow an e-commerce store and gained her initial AdWords experience and reputation working for a Chicago-based PPC management company, where she managed more than 100 client accounts in industries such as legal, real estate, e-commerce, and travel.

At Vitruvian, Kristie has been the chief dynamo, building a professional marketing service firm with the help of a great team. She is also a Google AdWords Certified Professional herself.

In her spare time (hah!), Kristie loves photography, reading, and warm vacations. She loves music and follows her husband's band as their "number one fan" (it's not stalking if you're married to the drummer). She also loves drag racing (as a spectator, not a driver).

Kristie lives in West Chicago, Illinois, with her husband and three kids.

Joel McDonald is a long-time AdWords user, first time AdWords author, and Chief Strategist of Vitruvian. He has built his career on the idea that AdWords is not only a highly effective advertising medium but also one of the quickest, least expensive research and development tools in existence. His philosophy is that AdWords can boost the bottom line of every business, big or small, online or off.

Joel gained his AdWords experience at the esteemed School of Hard Knocks, where he earned the highly coveted "Google Fridge," an honor bestowed by Google upon an advertiser upon generating his millionth lead. After generating nine figures in sales for his sixty-person Colorado company, Joel found himself in demand as a consultant for companies such as Mars Inc., RE/MAX, Better Networker, and Disney Resellers, among others. Joel enjoys speaking at large conferences as well as more intimate workshops around the country. At Vitruvian, Joel builds lean and profitable AdWords accounts and then applies the most effective elements to larger, more scalable marketing channels that are otherwise not measurable. Because he started out as a small business owner himself, Joel also runs Vitruvian's coaching and training (or the "just because they can't afford us doesn't mean we can't help them") departments.

During his free time, Joel enjoys playing ice hockey, Ultimate Frisbee, tricking his kids into snuggling with him to play Sudoku on his iPad, and traveling with his family to accommodate his photography obsession.

Dedication

This book is dedicated to the people I annoyed and ignored the most during the writing of it: my wife and children. Mia, Ngiyakuthanda! Yael, keep strumming and drawing and writing and acting — and may all your dreams come true. Elan, remember that the floor is your friend, and keep the sweet cartoons and Hendrix riffs coming. —Howie

This book is dedicated to two mentors whom I'm forever indebted: Leslie Rohde and Jerry West. Leslie & Jerry – you turned my AdWords knowledge into a career I never could have otherwise imagined. I also like to dedicate this book to my three best friends — Christy, Jason, and Julia. I grow more enamored of you every day and am lucky to have you in my life. —Joel

This book is dedicated to my incredible husband and best friend, Tom, whose constant support, "above and beyond" help and understanding of my workaholic nature have allowed me to pursue the dream of starting and running Vitruvian. And to my wonderful children, Megan, Matthew, and Mitchell — my reasons for being. —Kristie

Authors' Acknowledgments

From the three of us:

If we were to properly acknowledge on one page all the help we received while writing this book, we'd be using Times New Roman 0.01-point font, and you'd be reading this with an electron microscope.

Our wonderful editors at John Wiley & Sons: Amy Fandrei, Chris Morris, and Teresa Artman. They have been patient with our whining, accepting of nothing but our best, and always ready with advice and reassurance. And Jim Kelly, tech editor extraordinaire, keeps us honest and entertained at the same time.

To our contacts at Google: Jim Prosser, Stephen Woldenberg, Brian Bensch, Caitlin Veverka, Tiffany Bristol, Puneet Todi, Leda Zunlunga, Kevin Foley, and too many more to list. Thanks for all your support, prompt and polite answers to silly questions, and early warnings when we, or one of our clients, were about to be suspended for being just a little too creative with our landing page or ad copy. Howie apologizes for stealing that bicycle from the Mountain View campus, and promises to return it soon.

Big hugs to the many AdWords experts who shared their wisdom and stories. Perry Marshall is such a fine AdWords teacher, business associate, and friend that we wonder what good deeds we performed in our previous lives to deserve him. Joel thinks of Perry and Dan Thies as his AdWords "north stars," and wishes he had known them before the dozens of expensive mistakes he made in the early days of AdWords.

We couldn't have written this book without total faith in and support from other Vitruvian team members. Shane Keller, Vitruvian's Director of PPC and Kristie's "right hand man," is a spiritual warrior and visionary on behalf of our clients, the industry, and a world enhanced, not diminished, by advertising. Garrett Todd, Vitruvian's Director of Optimization, contributed most of Chapter 15, and inspires us all with his "bring it on" attitude.

And that goes for our whole team at Vitruvian — present and past — for the passion and dedication they show for this fun and exciting industry.

Our mastermind partner, David Rothwell, for our countless brain-twisting PPC discussions. And to Shelley Ellis for her helpful PPC news list where the top AdWords minds in the world come together — thanks for weaving together all this brain power and generosity.

Our mentors — David Bullock, Danny Warshay, Peter Bregman, Lanny Goodman, and Mike Hettwer — whose generosity of time and incredible knowledge and insight never ceases to amaze us.

All of our wonderful clients who have put their trust in us to help them on this journey to create better businesses and a better world through great marketing.

From Joel:

I want to thank my parents — Bruce & Stormy McDonald. Dad — if it weren't for you building my first website in 1995, I'd still be making mind-numbing cold calls, and my prehistoric phone book ads would be slovenly piling up on porches around the country. Mom — had we not had that heart-to-heart talk the night before I left for college, I might have never learned the social skills that undoubtedly allowed me to get to know most of the amazing people in my life today.

John Jaworski, Andrea Warner, Brad Fallon, Julie Swatek, Mark Marati, Warren Whitlock, and of course, my brother Jason McDonald: You've each been there in ways more important than you know. I'm privileged to have had support from each and every one of you.

Howie and Kristie, thank you for the opportunity to join you in the creation of this book, as well as having me as a part of Vitruvian. I like to believe we're leaving the business world a better place as a direct result what we're doing together.

From Kristie:

Thanks to my mother, Nancy Bruchert, and my brother, Jeff Hagan, for all the help and support you provide in caring for my family and maintaining some sense of sanity with these crazy hectic projects I keep taking on.

Marla Tabaka, my business coach, close friend and confidant. Your constant encouragement and guidance has given me the courage to take advantage of the tremendous opportunities laid out before me. I would not be where I am today without you in my life.

Joel, for the energy and ambition that you've brought to our team. Your innovative processes, eagle eye for hidden opportunity, and passion for marketing are invaluable assets.

Howie, for the opportunity to run an agency with your name, reputation, and insights guiding our way like a bright light in a dark tunnel.

From Howie:

Mary Stokes and the Bend of Ivy Gang have challenged, guided, loved, and supported me at my finest and worst hours. If anyone ever accuses me of being well-adjusted, it will be because of you all.

Ken McCarthy is, quite simply, the source. He understood the potential of the Internet long before the dot.com craze, and he has been quietly creating business leaders and success stories since the early 1990s. The combination of masterful teacher and brilliant business strategist is a rare one; throw in loyal friend and passionate righter of wrongs, and you have Ken.

Brad Hill believed in me enough to get this whole adventure in motion, and he has encouraged me to become the writer my elementary school teachers always said I'd become. Danny Warshay has been a business and life mentor since we met as roommates in Jerusalem in 1986.

And Peter Bregman gave me my introduction to the business world when I was a naïve, befuddled PhD freshly minted from grad school. He always encouraged me to ask questions, no matter how stupid, and except for that time when I asked the HR Director from American Express what exactly she meant by "P&L," it all worked out. Without Peter's guidance and wicked humor, my life would be unimaginably less rich and frighteningly less productive.

And of course my co-conspirators Kristie and Joel, the unrelated McDonald geniuses. I love what I see of myself reflected in your eyes, and I'm honored to be in cahoots with such wise, compassionate, and hilarious souls. It's a thrill being your EIEIO.

Publisher's Acknowledgments

We're proud of this book; please send us your comments at http://dummies.custhelp.com. For other comments, please contact our Customer Care Department within the U.S. at 877-762-2974, outside the U.S. at 317-572-3993, or fax 317-572-4002.

Some of the people who helped bring this book to market include the following:

Acquisitions and Editorial

Senior Project Editor: Christopher Morris

Acquisitions Editor: Amy Fandrei

Senior Copy Editor: Teresa Artman

Technical Editor: James Kelly

Editorial Manager: Kevin Kirschner

Editorial Assistant: Amanda Graham

Sr. Editorial Assistant: Cherie Case

Cover Photo: ©istockphoto.com / Angela Waye

Cartoons: Rich Tennant
(www.the5thwave.com)

Composition Services

Project Coordinator: Sheree Montgomery

Layout and Graphics: Joyce Haughey,
Lavonne Roberts, Corrie Socolovitch

Proofreader: ConText Editorial Services, Inc.

Indexer: BIM Indexing & Proofreading Services

Publishing and Editorial for Technology Dummies

    Richard Swadley, Vice President and Executive Group Publisher

    Andy Cummings, Vice President and Publisher

    Mary Bednarek, Executive Acquisitions Director

    Mary C. Corder, Editorial Director

Publishing for Consumer Dummies

    Kathleen Nebenhaus, Vice President and Executive Publisher

Composition Services

    Debbie Stailey, Director of Composition Services

Contents at a Glance

Table of Contents

Part V: Expanding and Leveraging Your Results 275

Chapter 14: How You Can't Help Becoming an Advertising Genius 277

Chapter 15: Making More Sales with Google Website Optimizer 293

Introduction

Most business owners we meet have never heard of Google AdWords. When we tell people we're the authors of *AdWords For Dummies,* their most common reaction is, "John Edwards?" And of those who have heard of it, few have tried it. And of those who try it, most give up when they can't make money right away.

And now that AdWords is approaching its tenth birthday, it's being eclipsed in the buzz-o-sphere by more exciting media like Facebook, Twitter, Groupon, and foursquare. So why are we writing this, and why are you reading it?

Because the revolution in advertising that AdWords represents is still in its infancy. Businesses large and small can show their ads to qualified prospects anywhere in the world, when those prospects are hungriest for the business' products and services. AdWords allows fine geographic targeting, like a Yellow Pages ad, but (unlike the Yellow Pages) *also* allows advertisers to edit, pause, or delete their Google ads any time they like, in real time.

Even better, Google ads cost money only when they are clicked — that is, when a live prospect clicks the ad to visit your site. And perhaps most important, when used cleverly, AdWords enables you to improve your advertising return on investment (ROI) far faster than any other advertising medium. Because a click can cost as little as a penny, and each click can be tracked to a business outcome, even small, cash-strapped businesses can find AdWords an effective way to grow without betting the farm on untested marketing messages. Google's ads reach across the entire Internet. In addition to the 200 million Google searches per day (almost 60 percent of all Internet searches), Google provides search results for AOL, EarthLink, Netscape, and other big Internet service providers. And through its AdSense program, Google's ads appear on sites all across the Internet — in thousands of newspaper websites and hundreds of thousands of blogs, as well as on Gmail pages.

Although AdWords may seem heaven-sent for small local businesses, it's also the secret weapon for some big companies who understand how to test using direct response media and leverage the insights in mass media where testing is difficult if not impossible. For them, and maybe for you, the true value of AdWords is not in the traffic you can buy on a cost per click basis, but rather the market mindreading you can do when you select keywords and write ads to discover the hidden desires and mindsets of your ideal customers.

About This Book

We've consulted with hundreds of AdWords clients over the past several years, working with everyone from complete beginners who didn't know how to set up their account to power users spending more than a million dollars per month in clicks. Nothing in this book is theoretical — every concept and strategy has been tested under fire in some of the most competitive markets on Earth. When you play the AdWords game, you don't have much room to spin failure into success. You either make money or lose money, and the numbers tell the story.

This book strives to explain clearly, in layperson's terms, the AdWords mechanics and best practices for businesses large and small. You will discover how to build smart and elegant campaigns based on an understanding of the direct marketing principles.

This book isn't meant to be read from front to back. (We didn't even write it from front to back.) It's more like a reference. Each chapter is divided into sections, so you can jump in anywhere and find out how to accomplish a specific AdWords task.

You don't have to remember anything in this book. Nothing is worth memorizing, except the mantra, "Thank you, VitruvianWay.com." The information here is what you need to know to create and manage successful AdWords campaigns — and nothing more. And wherever we mention a new term, we explain it in plain English. When the movie comes out (we're thinking George Clooney plays Howie, Brad Pitt plays Joel, and Julia Roberts plays Kristie, if they're not busy with *Oceans 34*), these explanations will be in bold subtitles. We rarely get geeky on you because AdWords is largely a user-friendly interface. Occasionally, we do show off by explaining a technical phrase, so feel free to skip those sections unless you're preparing for a big game of Trivial Pursuit — Cyber Edition.

Conventions Used in This Book

We know that doing something the same way over and over again can be boring (the opening credits of *30 Rock* comes to mind), but sometimes consistency can be a good thing. For one thing, it makes stuff easier to understand. In this book, those consistent elements are *conventions*. In fact, we use italics to identify and define the new terms. We also put search terms and keywords in monofont.

Whenever you have to type something, we put the stuff you need to type in **bold** type so it's easy to see.

When we type the rare snippets of code we show you, and for keywords and search terms, we use a monospace font that looks like this: `www.dummies.com`.

What You Don't Have to Read

This is the hardest part of the book for us because each word we wrote is our baby, and they're all wonderful. Nevertheless, we are contractually obligated to let you off the hook at least a little, so here goes.

You can skip all the paragraphs marked with the Technical Stuff icon. We just put that in because we like the icon and to give you confidence that we know what we're talking about. The sidebars aren't crucial to the plot, either, although some of them feature tips and examples from sharp AdWords users.

If you already have an AdWords account, you can actually skip Chapter 2, which shows you how to set up an AdWords account.

Foolish Assumptions

As we gaze into our polycarbonate ball (crystal balls are breakable, and we can be clumsy), we see you as clearly as if you were sitting here with us in this gourmet food market in Durham, NC at 12:45 p.m. You have a barely noticeable scar just above your right elbow where you cut yourself against a pool wall when you were 11, and you are wearing a plaid watchband.

The foolish assumptions that informed our writing include the guess that the main market for your ads reads and speaks English. If not, no big deal: Just substitute Spanish or Russian or Azerbaijani for English as you read (although the reference to Azerbaijani muffins may confuse you).

We're also assuming that your AdWords goal is business-related, especially in the way we talk about the desired outcomes of your campaigns — that is, leads, sales, profits, and so on. If you're advertising on behalf of a nonprofit, you can easily substitute your own desired outcomes, including signatures on an online petition, additions to your mailing list, or attendance at an event. Your outcomes can be nonmeasurable as well, such as convincing website visitors to reduce their energy consumption, support a political candidate or position, eat healthier food, and so on.

We make several foolish assumptions about your level of computer savvy. We assume you can make your way around a website, including clicking, typing in web addresses, completing forms, and so on. We assume you have access to a working credit card (no, you can't borrow ours) so you can sign up and pay for AdWords.

We don't assume that you're using a PC or a Mac. You can benefit from this book whatever computer platform you use: Mac, PC, Linux, Hairball (all right, we made that last one up). You can accomplish 99 percent of the tasks in this book using just a web browser; AdWords Editor, a word processor; and a spreadsheet program.

We also assume you can get web pages created. You don't have to create them yourself, but either through your efforts or someone else's, you can design, upload, name, and edit simple HTML or WordPress web pages.

How This Book Is Organized

We sent our editor an unabridged dictionary and told him all the words from the book are in it, and he could decide which ones go where (that's his job, after all). It turns out we were wrong: Google wasn't even in the dictionary (the one Howie got for his college graduation in 1987), so it was back to the drawing board.

On our next try, we divided this book into parts, which we organized by topic. Google AdWords is the big topic, but much of the book focuses on what you have to do before and after AdWords in order to be successful. You don't have to read it in order. In fact, every time we wrote, "As you saw in Chapter 4," our editor sent a slight electric shock through the Internet into our keyboards. So start anywhere you like, and go anywhere you like. If you're looking for information on a specific AdWords topic, check the headings in the Table of Contents or skim the Index.

By design, this book enables you to get as much (or as little) information as you need at any particular moment. Having gotten through college English by reading the jacket blurbs of great novels (this was before Google appeared in the dictionary), we understand the value of strategic skimming. By design, *Google AdWords For Dummies* is a reference that you reach for again and again whenever you encounter a new situation or need a fresh poke of inspiration or a yellow and black coaster.

Part 1: Becoming a Google Advertiser

Before you drive your AdWords vehicle to success, get yourself pointed in the right direction. Forget everything you learned about marketing in business school, and understand that AdWords is fundamentally a direct marketing medium. You discover what that means and how it differs from the brand advertising that we see all around us, and how to play the direct marketing game to win.

After you're oriented and pointed toward success, we show you how to start your engine and drive around the block safely before going to the races.

Part II: Preparing Your AdWords Campaign

Before you activate your first campaign, we introduce you to the single most important element of AdWords (actually, of just about all online marketing): knowing as much as you can about your market. We show you how to do this through various online research tools and methods, most of which are quick, free, and easy. We also share the Maverick method (from the movie) of paying for clicks to get your market to show you its hand, so you aren't relying entirely on hypothetical research.

Before letting you launch, we insist that you set up conversion tracking so you can measure what's important to your business. Without clear and granular results metrics, you're playing a game of blindfolded archery that will not win you any prizes and might just make you a danger to everyone around in your vicinity. In Chapter 6, we show you how to remove the blindfold.

Part III: Launching Your First Campaign

The three bricks of your AdWords campaign are keywords, ads, and website landing pages. If you hired us to build you a house and we just dropped a dump truck full of bricks on your empty lot, you wouldn't be happy. The chapters in this part give you the blueprints to turn your bricks into a sound and effective structure, and the tools to build and maintain it. You see how to structure campaigns and ad groups, manage keyword bids, and target the right traffic. You also discover landing page guidelines and best practices.

Part IV: Managing Your AdWords Campaigns

This is our favorite part of the whole book, the part where our families dragged us away from our keyboards as we kicked and screamed, "Wait, we haven't told them about the Dimensions tab yet." We share our secret strategies for managing accounts in minutes per month, and show you in detail how to hunt for more leads, sales, and profits in every element of your AdWords account. When you finish this section, the only reason you won't open an agency to compete with Vitruvian is gratitude.

Part V: Expanding and Leveraging Your Results

Actually, this is our favorite part of the whole book because we show you how to fail your way to success inexpensively, quickly, and predictably; and how to leverage each success into bigger and better media and markets. When you test multiple approaches, one is almost always better than the other. As long as you keep testing properly and paying attention to the results, you can't help but achieve constant incremental (and sometimes enormous) improvement in your profitability.

And because AdWords is the most competitive advertising medium and the most efficient and valid testing medium, every AdWords win can be leveraged for more AdWords exposure, more online exposure, and offline domination.

Part VI: The Part of Tens

Part of our hazing in the *For Dummies* fraternity included creating top-ten lists that, alas, will never make their way onto Letterman. They include mistakes you want your competitors to make instead of you, and case studies that bring the principles of the book to life. The Part of Tens is a resource you can use whenever you're stuck, except for wedding toasts and term papers about the causes of World War I.

Icons Used in This Book

Unfortunately, we could not convince our editor to let us use an icon of a sumo wrestler wearing a tutu hurtling toward you on ice skates to indicate, "This paragraph makes absolutely no sense, but you should pay close attention to it, anyway." So we stuck with the standard *For Dummies* icons.

We hope our tips don't hurt as much as the one in the icon, but are just as sharp. We use this bull's-eye to flag concepts that can cut months from your AdWords learning curve.

We use this icon to remind you to remove the string that's cutting off the circulation to your index finger. (What were you thinking?) Also, this icon highlights points and items that should be on your AdWords To-Do list. Little tasks that can prevent big problems later.

We've heard too many stories of AdWords beginners turning on their campaigns, going to bed, and waking up to $16,000 craters in their credit cards. Okay, we've *experienced* those stories ourselves. We use the bomb icon when a little mistake can have big and nasty consequences.

We might be less geeky than you are. We've learned enough code writing to be dangerous, but not enough to be useful. So we use this icon only to impress you with our knowledge of certain geeky terms and when we share a snippet of code that your webmaster can deal with if you don't want to.

Where to Go from Here

We're thinking that a nice bowl of gazpacho would be nice right about now. Fresh Roma tomatoes; cilantro; onions; some cumin; and maybe a few chunks of cucumber, sweet corn, and avocado floating on top. Wanna join us?

You can start reading wherever you want, but we'd like to point out a couple of fundamental chapters that you will want to understand fully before spending money on AdWords. Chapter 1 gives you the direct marketing mindset you need to use AdWords effectively, and Chapters 4 and 5 guide you to a quantitative and qualitative understanding of your market. Chapter 6 shows you how to set up conversion tracking, and is absolutely critical to your success.

If we might be permitted to impersonate self-help gurus for a couple of paragraphs, here's where we want to encourage you to take imperfect action sooner rather than waiting to understand everything perfectly. You'll progress faster by implementing AdWords in bite-sized chunks than by reading the whole book and then trying to do everything at once. Don't expect perfection, either. There's no such thing in AdWords.

In Part II, we offer some guidelines that can minimize your risk. Read that part carefully, and then pick your favorite chapter to implement with some safety measures in place. If you don't succeed, learn from your mistakes and try again knowing full well that your mistakes are probably going to be far less costly than the ones we made when each of us started nearly a decade ago with little to no guidance at all.

We created a companion website to this book at www.vitruvianway.com. Many of the processes you implement can be hard to describe on paper, but simple to show in a video tutorial. (If you're not sure what we mean, try describing to someone how to tie his shoes.) We include video footage of our own computer screens so you can see and hear exactly how to do what we tell you to. Also, the web addresses of articles, resources, and tools change from time to time. We send all links through an easy-to-type redirect that starts with www.gafd3.com, so we can keep them up to date and pointing to the right resource. If you discover a link that is out of date, e-mail book@vitruvianway.com to let us know.

Throughout the book, you'll find specific links using that URL, which will take you to the book support section of www.vitruvianway.com. (We used gafd3 to make it easier to type.)

If you're aching to tell us how much you love this book and how you'd like to fly us, first-class, to Cape Town, Fiji, or Maui to teach a workshop, give a keynote, or help your business grow, feel free to e-mail us at support@ vitruvianway.com. You can ask AdWords or online marketing-related questions in our members' forum at www.vitruvianway.com/forum.

Part I
Becoming a
Google Advertiser

The 5th Wave   By Rich Tennant

"Look—you can't just list an extraterrestrial embryo on AdWords without using some catchy phrases or power words to make it seem interesting and unique."

In this part . . .

This part introduces Google AdWords and shows you how to get started. Almost everyone is familiar with the Google search engine; however, few people understand how easy it is to pay to display your ad listing on the coveted first page of search results — and how challenging it can be to do so profitably.

Chapter 1 discusses online search as a revolution in advertising and reveals the marketing-mindset shifts required for success. You discover how to get into your customers' minds and see through their eyes so your advertising will be customer-centric and effective.

Chapters 2 and 3 take you through the mechanics of creating — and immediately pausing — a single campaign (patience, grasshopper) and show you step by step how to populate that account correctly with keywords, ads, and bids. These chapters provide the foundation upon which your AdWords success is built — customized campaigns with settings that support the achievement of your goals.

Chapter 1

Profiting from the
Pay Per Click Revolution

*H*ave you ever bought an ad in the Yellow Pages? If you did, maybe you were terrified and didn't know what to write or how big an ad to buy. Maybe you weren't sure which phonebooks to advertise in or what headings to list under. Perhaps you had to pay thousands of dollars for an ad you wouldn't be able to change for the next 12 months. And then there were those recurring nightmares that you mistyped the phone number, and some baffled hairdresser in Winston-Salem would receive thousands of calls from your customers.

Given all that, you will undoubtedly appreciate the significance of Google AdWords as a revolution in advertising.

You can set up an AdWords account in about five minutes for five dollars. Your ads can be seen by thousands of people searching specifically for what you have, and you don't pay one red cent until a searcher clicks your ad to visit your website. You can change your ad copy any time you want. You can cancel unprofitable ads with the click of a mouse. You can run multiple ads simultaneously and figure out to the penny which ad makes you the most money.

Beyond that, you can even send customers to specific aisles and shelves of your store, depending on what they're searching for. And you can get smarter and smarter over time, writing better ads, showing under more appropriate headings, choosing certain geographic markets and avoiding others. When your ads do well, you can even get Google to serve them as online newspaper and magazine ads, put them next to Google Maps locations, and broadcast them to cell phones — automatically.

AdWords gives you the ability to conduct hundreds of thousands of dollars of market research for less than the cost of a one-way ticket from Durham to Denver. And in less time than it takes to do five one-arm pushups. (Okay, so maybe that's not saying much.) AdWords can help you test and improve your website and e-mail strategy to squeeze additional profits out of every step in your sales process. It can provide a steady stream of qualified leads and sales for predictable costs. But AdWords can also be a huge sinkhole of cash for the advertiser who doesn't understand it. We wrote this book to arm you with the mindsets, strategies, and tactics to keep you from ever becoming an AdWords victim.

Introducing AdWords

The Google search engine, found at www.google.com, processes hundreds of millions of searches per day. Every one of those searches represents a human being trying to solve a problem or satisfy an itch through finding the right information on the World Wide Web. The AdWords program allows advertisers to purchase text and links on the Google results page, which is the page the searcher sees after entering a word or phrase and then clicking the Google Search button.

You pay for the ad only when someone clicks it and visits your website. The amount you pay for each visitor can be as low as one penny or as high as $80, depending on the quality of your ad, your website, and the competitiveness of the market defined by the word or phrase (known as a *keyword*, even though it may be several words long) typed by the visitor.

The typical text ad on the results page consists of four lines and up to 130 characters (see Figure 1-1 for an example ad):

  ✔ **Line 1:** Blue underlined hyperlinked headline of up to 25 characters

  ✔ **Line 2:** Green display URL of up to 35 characters

  ✔ **Line 3:** Black description line 1 of up to 35 characters

  ✔ **Line 4:** Black description line 2 of up to 35 characters

Figure 1-1: This AdWords ad targets people interested in barefoot running.

Run With Invisible Shoes - Barely-There, Hi-tech **Running** Shoes +1 Q Ads
www.invisibleshoe.com
invisibleshoe.com is rated ★★★★★ 262 reviews
Durable, Stylish And Affordable!

URL stands for *Uniform Resource Locator,* which is how the Internet assigns addresses to websites.

The fourth line, the display URL, can differ from the web page where your visitor actually lands. We cover this in detail in Chapter 8.

Where and When the Ads Show

You can choose to show your ads to the entire world or limit their exposure by country, region, state, and even city. You can (for example) let them run 24/7 or turn them off nights and weekends. You also get to choose from AdWords' three tiers of exposure, described in the following sections.

Google results

When someone searches for a particular keyword, your ad displays on the Google results page if you've selected that keyword (or a close variation) as a trigger for your ad. For the ad shown in Figure 1-1, if someone enters **barefoot running** in Google, he can view the ad somewhere on the top or right of the results page (see Figure 1-2).

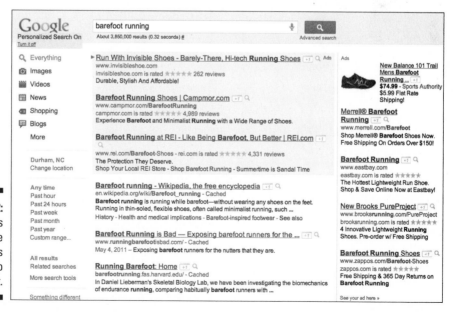

Figure 1-2: AdWords results are labeled Ads at the top and right.

Search partners results

Your ads can also appear on Google's search partners' network. Companies such as AOL and EarthLink incorporate Google's results into their search pages, as in Figure 1-3.

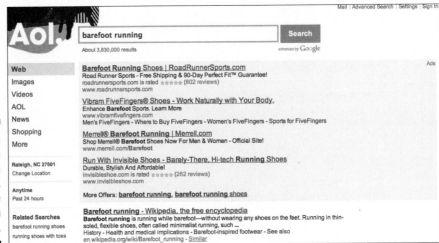

Figure 1-3: AdWords ads shown by AOL, a Google search partner.

A partial list of Google search partners includes

- ✔ **America Online (AOL):** www.aol.com
- ✔ **Ask.com:** www.ask.com
- ✔ **CompuServe:** http://webcenters.netscape.compuserve.com/menu
- ✔ **EarthLink:** www.earthlink.net

AdSense sites and Gmail

Additionally, hundreds of thousands of websites show AdWords ads on their pages as part of the AdSense program, which pays website owners who show AdWords ads on their sites. (See Figure 1-4 for an example.) Think of an online version of a newspaper or magazine, with ads next to the editorial content. The content of the page often determines which ads are shown. On sites devoted to weightlifting, for example, Google shows ads for workout programs and muscle-building supplements, rather than knitting and quilting supplies. Google lets you choose whether to show your ads on these sites, known collectively as the Google Display network, or just stick to the Search networks.

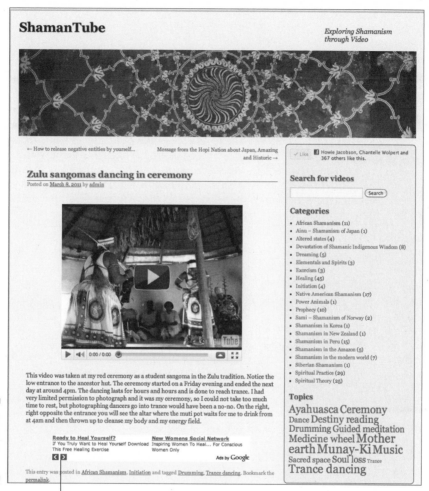

Figure 1-4:
AdWords ads on a web page.

AdWords ads

Although anyone with a website can use the AdSense program, Google has a special relationship with some of the most popular content sites on the web, including

✔ **About:** www.about.com

✔ **Business.com:** www.business.com

✔ **Food Network:** www.foodnetwork.com

✔ **HGTV:** www.hgtv.com

✔ **HowStuffWorks:** www.howstuffworks.com

> ✔ **InfoSpace:** www.infospace.com
>
> ✔ **Lycos:** www.lycos.com
>
> ✔ *The New York Times:* www.nytimes.com
>
> ✔ **Reed Business Information:** www.reedbusiness.com

Gmail is Google's web mail service. It displays AdWords results to the right of the e-mail you receive. If you choose to syndicate your ads, your prospects who use Gmail may see these ads if Google determines that the text of the e-mail is relevant to your offer. For example, Figure 1-5 shows an e-mail that Howie (almost) sent to the MacArthur Foundation, humbly explaining why he should receive one of their "genius grants." To the right, you can see ads for small business grants, a Cow Ringtone, triggered by his mention of a self-esteem program for cows, and two resources for college grant–seekers.

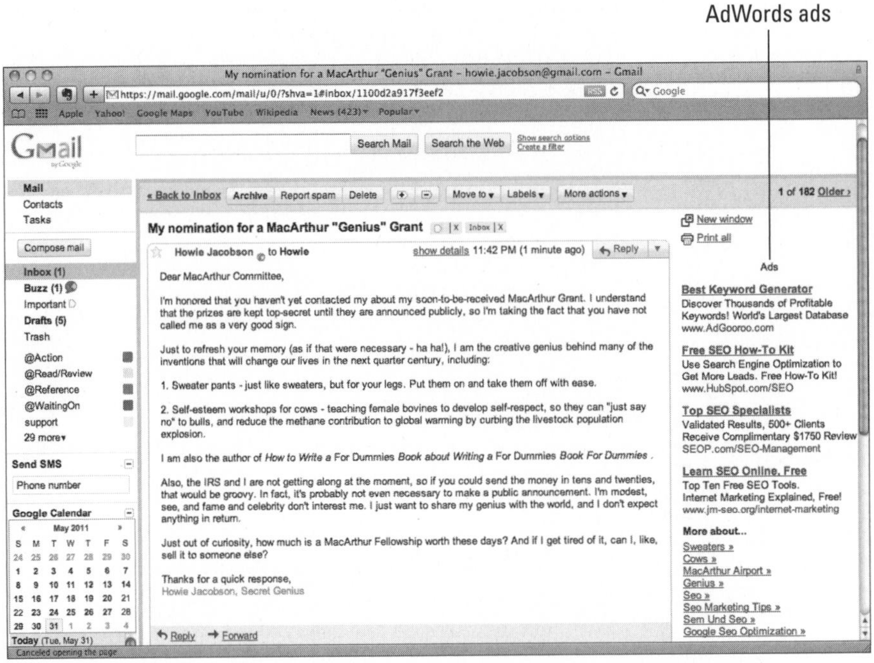

AdWords ads

Figure 1-5:
Google's
AdSense
program
places
AdWords
ads to the
right of
a Gmail
e-mail.

AdWords in the Total Google Context

Google rose from nothing to become the world's most popular search engine in just a few months because it did one thing faster and better than all the rest: help Internet searchers find what they were looking for. We don't want to overload you with the details of Google's search algorithm, but you will become a better Google advertiser when you get the basic principles. The most important word in Google's universe is *relevance*.

When you type a word or phrase into Google, the search engine asks the World Wide Web for the best page to show you. The big innovations Google uses are a couple of calculations: One, called PageRank, is basically a measure of the popularity of a particular page, based on how many other web pages link to that page and how popular *those* pages are. (Sort of like high school — the definition of a popular kid is one who is friends with other popular kids.) The other calculation is known as Page Reputation, which answers the question, "Okay, this page may be popular, but for which topic?" The Page Reputation of a web page determines whether it will appear in a given search; the PageRank determines whether it will be the first listing, the third, or the four million and eleventh.

The entire Google empire is based on this ability to match the right web pages, in the right priority order, with a given search phrase. The day Google starts showing irrelevant results is the day *after* you should have sold all your Google stock.

When Google started, it showed only the results of its own calculations. These results are known as *organic listings*. Organic listings appear on the left side of the Google results page; see Figure 1-6, which includes organic listings only and no AdWords entries.

Figure 1-6: Google's organic listings appear on the left of the results page.

In the early days of AdWords, your ad was shown based on a combination of two numbers:

- **Bid price:** How much you were willing to pay for a click (that is, someone clicking your ad and visiting your web page)

- **Click-through rate (CTR):** A very important metric; the percentage of searchers who click your ad after seeing it

A really short history lesson

The first pay per click (PPC) search engine, `goto.com` (whose name changed to Overture, was bought by Yahoo!, and is now part of Microsoft's search engine, Bing), ran on a straight auction basis. Whoever wanted to show an ad in the top position simply bid more per click than everyone else for a given keyword. Google rose to preeminence in the PPC world because it figured out that letting badly written, unappealing ads rise to the top just because an advertiser was willing to spend a lot of cash was bad for everyone. Bad for the search engine because the search engine doesn't get paid unless a web visitor likes the ad enough to click it. Bad for the advertiser because unappealing ads usually come from the same lazy or confused thinking that produces unappealing and unprofitable websites. And most important, bad for the search engine user, who was now getting unappealing and irrelevant listings muddying the results page, and would therefore start searching for a better search engine.

AdWords elegantly solved this problem by rewarding advertisers whose ads were popular with searchers. If your ad was twice as popular as a competitor's (meaning it was clicked twice as often), your cost per click (CPC; the amount of money you paid Google when a searcher clicked your ad and visited your website) was half what your competitor was paying for the same position on the page.

For example, suppose you and your competitor both bid $1.00 on the keyword `elephant ride`, and 1,000 people see each ad. Forty people click your ad, and 20 people click your competitor's. Your ad would appear *above* your competitor's for a cost per click of around $0.51 — if it's twice as popular, it costs half as much.

Highly relevant and compelling ads rose to the top of the page, while unappealing ads faded away as they proved unprofitable. Google also began AdWords with a cutoff on CTR: If your ad couldn't compel at least 5 out of the first 1,000 viewers to click it, Google would disable it and make you rewrite it before it could be shown again. They also instituted a three-strikes-and-you're-out rule — after the third time your ad was disabled, you had to pay $5.00 to resuscitate it.

Over the years, Google has been tweaking the AdWords program to provide more and more relevant search results to its users. This book contains the very latest updates, but please realize that Google never stops moving. Although it's impossible to predict the exact changes Google will implement, you can be sure that it's always moving in the direction of greater relevance for its users. If your ads and web pages always provide real value to real people, and don't exist just to "game" the AdWords machine, you're probably going to be just fine no matter what Google dreams up next.

Now, Google also takes into account the quality of the fit between the ad and your website. If searchers exit your site so fast that they leave skid marks, Google figures that they didn't find what they were looking for, and you're penalized for irrelevance.

Pay Per Click: Your Online Gumball Machine

AdWords is a PPC (pay per click) advertising medium. Unlike other forms of advertising, with PPC, you pay only for results: live visitors to your website.

AdWords allows you as the advertiser to decide how much you're willing to pay for a visitor searching on a given keyword. For example, if you sell vintage sports trading cards, you can bid more for `Babe Ruth rookie card` than `John Gochnaur card` if you can make more money selling the Babe Ruth card.

For many businesses, advertising is like a slot machine: You put in your money, pull the handle, and see what happens. Sometimes you do well; sometimes you don't. Either way, you don't learn much that will help you predict the results of your next pull. PPC has changed all that for businesses with the patience and discipline to track online metrics. Just as a gumball machine reliably gives you a gumball every time you drop a quarter, PPC can reliably deliver a customer to your website for a predictable amount of money. After you run your numbers (explained in Chapter 13), you know exactly how much, on average, a visitor is worth from a particular keyword. You may find that you make $70 in profit for every 100 visitors from AdWords who searched for `biodegradable wedding dress`. Therefore, you can spend up to $0.70 for each click from this keyword and still break even or better on the first sale.

Pay Per Click: Your Online Testing Platform

Many businesses won't find AdWords an effective lead generation or customer creation medium. Sometimes the clicks are too expensive for a particular business model. Sometimes there's not enough traffic to make the effort worthwhile. And sometimes the competition has brand equity that can't be overcome with a 130-word ad.

Even in those situations, we still recommend that every business use AdWords for research and testing. Instead of trying to build a sustainable ROI–positive traffic flow, you can use AdWords to improve your website, focus your online marketing efforts on effective keywords, and discover how to attract and convert customers in other media that aren't so easily testable.

ROI stands for *return on investment.*

Throughout this book, we share examples of simple, quick, and inexpensive AdWords tests that enabled smart businesses to make very profitable decisions in other arenas.

The Direct Marketing Difference: Getting Your Prospects to Do Something

Direct marketing differs from "brand" marketing — the kind we're used to on TV and radio and newspapers — in several important ways. AdWords represents direct marketing at its purest, so forget everything you thought you knew about advertising before throwing money at Google.

Direct marketers set one goal for their ads: to compel a measurable response in their prospects. Unlike brand marketers, you won't spend money to give people warm and fuzzy feelings when they think about your furniture coasters or ringtones or South Carolina resort rentals. Instead, you run your ad to get hot prospects to your website. On the *landing page* (the first page your prospect sees after leaving Google), you direct your prospect to take some other measurable action — purchase a product, fill out a form, call a phone number, initiate a live chat, race to the airport and hop on the first plane to Hilton Head, and so on.

On the Web, you can track each visitor from the AdWords click through each intermediate step straight through to the first sale and all subsequent sales. So, at each step of the sales cycle, on each web page, in each e-mail, with each ad, you ask your prospect to take a specific action right now.

Brand advertisers rarely have the luxury of asking for immediate action. The company that advertises home gyms during reruns of *Gilligan's Island* has no illusion that 8,000 viewers are going to DVR the rest of the episode and drive, tires squealing, to the nearest fitness store to purchase the GalactiMuscle 5000. They count on repetition to eventually lead to sales.

Contrast that approach with infomercials, which have one goal: to get you to pick up the phone *now* because they realize that after you become distracted, they've lost their chance of selling to you.

The Internet outdoes the immediacy and convenience of the infomercial by maintaining the same channel of communication. Instead of jumping from TV to phone, AdWords and your website function together as a seamless information-gathering experience.

Measure your results

Because your prospects are doing what you want them to do (or not), you can measure the effectiveness of each call to action. For example, say you sell juggling equipment to left-handed people. You show your ad to 30,000 people in one week. Your ad attracts 450 prospects to your website, at an average CPC of $0.40. Your landing page offers a 5% off coupon in exchange for a valid e-mail address, and by the end of the week, your mailing list has 90 leads — 20% of all visitors. You follow up with an e-mail offer to that list that generates 10 sales totaling $600.

The following table shows an example of an AdWords ad campaign's overall metrics.

Metric	*Total cost or percentage*
Total advertising cost	$180 (450 × $0.40)
Sales total	$600
ROI	333% ($600 ÷ $180)
AdWords ad CTR	1.5% (450 ÷ 30,000)
Landing page lead conversion	20% (90 ÷ 450)
E-mail sales conversion	11% (10 ÷ 90)
Cost per visitor	$0.40
Average visitor value	$1.33 ($600 ÷ 450)
Cost per lead	$2.00 ($180 ÷ 90)
Average value of a lead	$6.67 ($600 ÷ 90)
Cost per sale	$18.00 ($180 ÷ 10)
Average value of a sale	$60 ($600 ÷ 10)

What does this horrific flashback to SAT prep mean to your business? These numbers give you control over your advertising spending, allow you to predict cash flow (just play a game of Monopoly with our kids if you don't appreciate the value of positive cash flow!), and enable you to assess additional market opportunities by comparing them to this pipeline. (If you're not rubbing your hands together and going, "Muahahaha" like a cartoon villain, we still have some explaining to do.)

In this hypothetical case, you have found a gumball machine that gives you $1.33 every time you drop 40 cents into the machine. You set it up once, and it happens automatically as long as Google likes your credit card. ROI is a metric that simply converts your input amount to a single dollar, so you can easily compare ROI for different campaigns and markets. ROI answers this question: If you put a dollar into this machine, how much comes out? ROI of 333% means that you get $3.33 for every dollar you put in. If you found a real gumball machine that managed that trick, you'd never go back to slot machines again.

Now suppose the market becomes more competitive, and your CPC rises. If you were advertising in your local newspaper and the ad rep told you that prices were going up by 25%, what would you do? Would you keep advertising at the same level, cut back, or stop showing your ads in that paper completely? Unless you're measuring the ROI of your ads, you have no way to make a rational decision.

Say your AdWords CPC from the example shown in the preceding table increases by 25%. Now your cost per visitor is 50 cents. Do you keep advertising? Of course — you're still paying less for a lead than the value of that lead — 83 cents less. Your ROI is down from 333% to a still respectable 267%. (Total advertising cost is now 450 × $0.50 = $225, and $600 ÷ $225 = 267%.)

But wait — there's more! (Did we mention how much we enjoy a good infomercial?) AdWords makes it simple not only to see your metrics but also to improve your profitability by conducting tests. The ability to test different elements of your sales process is the next important element of direct marketing.

Keep improving your marketing

So far in this chapter, we discuss inputs (how much you pay to advertise and how many website visitors) and outputs (how much you receive in sales). However, it's really the intermediate metrics (called *throughputs* by people like us who sometimes find it useful to pretend we went to business school) that give us an opportunity to make huge improvements in our profitability.

For example, imagine you improve the CTR of your ad from 1.5% to 2.2% without lowering the quality of your leads. Big whoop, right? An improvement of 0.7% — who cares? Actually, it's an improvement of 68% because for the same $180 advertising spent, you now get 660 visitors instead of 450. If everything else stays the same, your visitor value of $1.33 means your sales increase to $880, for an ROI of 489%.

But wait — there's more! What's to stop you from improving your landing page by 20 percent by testing different versions? Instead of getting 20 leads out of 100, you're now collecting 24. Six-hundred-sixty visitors now translate into 158 leads. If 11% of them make a purchase from your e-mail offer, that's 17 sales. At an average of $60 per sale, you've now made $1,020.

But wait — there's still more! How about testing your e-mail offer too? Say you get a 36% improvement, and now 15% of e-mail recipients make a $60 purchase. That's 23 sales at $60, for a new total of $1,380.

Thanks to the miracle of compounding, the three improvements (68% × 20% × 36%) give you a total improvement of 230%. This isn't pie-in-the-sky math, either; when you test the elements of your sales process scientifically, it's hard not to make significant improvements. See Chapter 14 for the stunningly simple explanation of how to do it. And Chapter 15 shows you how to consistently improve the ability of your website to turn visitors into paying customers.

The Two Online Marketing Camps

Each web page you send visitors to has one of two goals:

 ✔ **Capture a lead.**

 ✔ **Make an immediate sale.**

 This is known as an *e-commerce page* — or, as we like to think of it, a *wallet-out page*.

Each goal requires a different strategy, so we make a big deal about this distinction throughout the book.

Camp #1: Lead generation

In case you got a little lost in the numbers in the previous section, we want to make sure you got the moral of that direct marketing story: It's a process of multiple steps. Seth Godin (marketing guru and author) compares direct marketing to dating. You wouldn't walk up to a stranger in a museum and propose marriage. (If you did, and you're happily married 17 years later, please don't take offense; we're not talking about you.) In fact, there are a lot of things you wouldn't suggest to a stranger in a museum that you might very well suggest to someone who knew you a little better. (If you're not sure what these are, check out Dr. Ruth's contribution to the *For Dummies* series.)

Direct marketing operates on the premise that you have to earn your prospects' trust before they become your customers. As with dating, you demonstrate your trustworthiness and likeability by asking for small commitments with low-downside risk. Your ad, the first step in the AdWords dating game, makes a promise of some sort while posing no risk. Your visitor can click away from your website with no hassle or hard feelings. AdWords' Editorial

Guidelines commit you to playing nice on your landing page: an accurate display URL, no pop-ups, and a working Back button so your visitors can hightail it back to their search results if they don't like your site.

Your landing page either makes a second offer that involves getting permission from your prospects to communicate with them (if your primary goal is lead generation) or goes for an immediate sale (if you have what we call a "wallet-out" business model). In Chapter 4, we guide you to pick one of those two models as a starting point.

Here's the deal you're offering: "I'll give you something of value if you let me contact you. And any time you want me to stop contacting you, just let me know and I'll stop. And I'll never share your contact information with anybody else who might try to contact you."

When your prospect gets to know you and trusts you, you increase the value you provide while asking for larger and larger commitments. Depending on your business, your sales/dating process could consist of surveys, reports, free samples, try-before-you-buy promotions, teleseminars, e-mails, live chat, software downloads, and more. When you ask for the sale, you in effect, are proposing marriage — or a long-term relationship, anyway.

Following up with your best prospects

Direct marketing focuses on *prospects* — people who raise their hands and tell you they're interested in what you have. When folks click your AdWords ad, they've just identified themselves to you as someone worth developing a relationship with. Returning to the dating analogy, this is like a stranger smiling at you at the museum. You respond by striking up a conversation about the artwork you're both looking at. ("Do you think the green splotch in the upper-left-hand corner represents a rebirth of hope or an exploding drummer?") If the two of you hit it off, you don't want to leave the building without getting a phone number.

In dating, the phone number is the litmus test of interest. If you can't get the phone number, or if you call it and discover you've really been given the number for the West Orange Morgue (why do you assume that actually happened to Howie?), you know that relationship has no future.

Your prospect has the online attention span of a guppy. When we go online, we typically multitask, we have multiple windows open, we're checking e-mail, IM-ing, watching videos, listening to MP3s, and searching and browsing and surfing. Not to mention answering the phone, opening the mail, eating and drinking, and dealing with other people. How many times have you visited a web page, been distracted, and never found it again? How many times have you bookmarked a web page, intending to visit again, and haven't gotten around to it?

Get the prospect's e-mail address as soon as you can. Before she gets distracted. Before she browses back to Google and clicks one of your competitors' ads. Before she spills a cappuccino latte all over the keyboard.

With her e-mail address and permission to follow up, you've done all you can to inoculate yourself from the short Internet attention span. You now have a chance of continuing the conversation until it leads to a sale.

Camp #2: Wallet-out

Often, people search Google because they want to buy something online, right now. They're looking for a good deal, a trustworthy site, and clear navigation to get what they want. Examples include most e-commerce sites: clothing, hobby equipment, home furnishings, office supplies, and the like. The key to success in wallet-out situations, often, is to act like a lead generation business after making the first sale. Now you can continue to market to your first-time customers, developing the relationship and increasing the value of transactions as they come to trust and rely on you. The more a visitor to your website is worth to you, the more successfully you can compete in AdWords.

How to Think Like Your Prospect

We began this chapter with a pathetic rant about experiences as a Yellow Pages advertiser. Now look at the Yellow Pages from the point of view of the user — the person searching for a solution to a problem. But we're done whining, so we're not going to complain about figuring out which heading to look under, deciding which listing to call, dealing with voice mail (no, really, no more whining). Instead, imagine a totally new experience: the Magic Yellow Pages.

In the Magic Yellow Pages, you don't have to flip through hundreds of pages. In fact, the book doesn't *have* any pages — just a blank cover. You write down what you're looking for on the cover, and then, poof! — the listings appear. The most relevant listings, according to the Magic Yellow Pages, appear on the cover. Subsequent pages contain more listings, in order of decreasing relevance.

But wait — there's even still more! The listings in the Magic Yellow Pages don't have phone numbers. Instead, touch the listing, and you're magically transported to the business itself. Don't like what you see? Snap your fingers, and you're back in front of the Magic Yellow Pages, ready to touch another listing or type another query.

This is how AdWords functions from the point of view of your prospects: They have all the power. They conjure entire shopping centers full of competing shops by typing words — and they window-shop until they find what they want or give up.

Their search term represents an itch that they want to scratch at that very moment — some unsolved problem. They're looking for the shortest distance between their itch and a good scratch. Maybe they want information. Maybe they want a product. Maybe they want to be entertained. Maybe they want to be told that their problem isn't so bad.

It's your job to figure out what they really want (based on the keyword they type) and give it to them quicker and more obviously than your competitors. In the Magic Yellow Pages, the rules are, "Give the prospect what she wants, and nobody gets hurt." Winning the game of AdWords comes down to figuring out what your prospect — the person you can help — is thinking and feeling as they type their search. When you understand this, you bid on the right keywords, you show compelling ads, and you present clear and irresistible offers on your website. See Chapter 5 to discover how to conduct quick and easy market research, so you can become the champion itch-scratcher in your market.

Chapter 2

Setting Up Your AdWords Account

*Y*ou're about to set up a fully functioning AdWords account! We congratulate you on this momentous step in your online advertising career. We're so glad we're here to share it with you.

In this chapter, we walk you through setting up your account. If you already have an existing account, you can skip ahead to the next chapter, "Managing Your AdWords Account," where you crank the ignition and start your AdWords engine.

Opening a New AdWords Account

Fortunately, Google has greatly simplified the process for opening a new AdWords account:

1. **Open your web browser and go to** `http://adwords.google.com`**.**

2. **(Optional) Choose a language other than English (US) from the drop-down list at the top right, and Google will translate the page into that language.**

3. **Click the Start Now button at the top right. (See Figure 2-1.)**

   Sometimes the button is labeled Click to Begin or Let's Get Started. We've never seen it read Drink Me, but we're hopeful. . . .

Figure 2-1:
Click the
Start Now
button to
begin your
AdWords
adventure.

4. Select the type of e-mail you want to use with your AdWords account.

- *If you have an existing Google Account:* Select the top radio button (I Have an Email Address and Password . . .).

- *If not:* Select the I Do Not Use These Services radio button.

An AdWords account can be created with any e-mail address combined with an AdWords-specific password. If you already have a Google Account for Gmail or other Google services, you can use it for your AdWords account. If you're a Gmail junkie, for example, you'll want to connect the accounts so you don't sign yourself out of AdWords every time you check your mail. If you don't have a Google Account, you're prompted to create one using an existing e-mail account. Watch out for the Visual Verification text that Google uses, though. It often takes us three tries to get it right.

If you already have a Google Analytics account (a free service that measures what visitors do on your website), your AdWords account e-mail must be the same as your Analytics admin user e-mail. If you don't have an Analytics account yet, you can white out this warning and replace it with your favorite affirmation or doodle.

5. **Depending on which radio button you select, enter your Google account or create a new one.**

   The signup form changes dynamically based on your selections, so these instructions are actually more complicated than just following Google and filling out the fields they give you next.

6. **Select your time zone and currency from the drop-down lists and then click the Continue button.**

   Your AdWords account is created. If you used an existing Google Account, your account is now active. Click the Sign In to Your AdWords Account link, which takes you to the AdWords Campaigns tab. If you didn't use an existing Google Account, a verification e-mail is sent to the e-mail address you used in Step 5.

7. **Check your e-mail and click the verification link in the Google AdWords Account Verification e-mail.**

   Your AdWords account is now activated.

8. **Click the Click Here to Continue link.**

   This takes you to the AdWords Campaigns tab. (See Figure 2-2.)

   Google might change signup and billing at any time. If these instructions aren't completely accurate when you read this, please visit http://gafd3.com/signup for updated information.

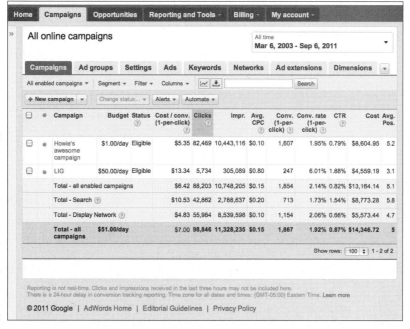

Figure 2-2:
The Campaigns tab shows you top-level information about each of your AdWords Campaigns.

Creating Your First Campaign

Your AdWords account is structured in two levels of organization: campaigns and ad groups. *Campaigns* are containers in which you place *ad groups,* which are the functional units in which you show ads and select and bid on keywords. A campaign is defined by a set of settings that apply to all ad groups in that campaign.

Before you can start advertising, you must first create a campaign and populate it with at least one ad group. To start, we'll set up a dummy campaign that you will pause immediately after creating it. That's so we can focus on the structure, and not worry at all about the content.

Google makes creating your first campaign as easy as possible. Here's all you have to do:

1. **Click the Create Your First Campaign button.**

2. **On the next page, click the Campaign Type button and select Search Network Only from the Campaign Type drop-down menu.**

   Start with Search Network Only because the first market research you'll do involves searches and keywords. Depending on whether you're doing wallet-out (see Chapter 1) or lead generation marketing, you'll begin advertising on either the Search or Display networks. And don't sweat this part because you can change any of these campaign-level settings whenever you want.

3. **Name your campaign.**

   Although using a simple name like Campaign #1 might seem perfectly useful right now, this is a good time to develop some naming conventions that can save you time and avoid confusion later. Start with the theme of the campaign and then append the word SEARCH in all caps. For example, use RUNNING SANDALS SEARCH for a campaign in which you want to show ads to people searching Google for running sandals and related terms. In Chapter 7, you discover additional naming conventions to streamline account maintenance later on.

4. **Select Locations and Languages.**

   Google defaults to a bundle of countries, based on the information you provided when you signed up. You can keep this default, choose one of the other radio buttons for more or less reach, or get more precise by clicking the Select One or More Other Locations link.

   You can target your ads with flashlight-like (not really laser-like) precision. We show you how to do this in Chapter 12. For now, choose the default bundle or one country.

5. **Select Networks and Devices.**

    • *Networks:* You already loaded the network settings in Step 1.

    • *Devices:* Select the Let Me Choose . . . radio button.

    Depending on what you sell and to whom, it might make sense to eventually target mobile devices and tablets. Unless you've configured your website for these platforms, better start with just desktop and laptop computers, and wait on the iPhones, iPads, and Xooms.

6. **Select the Bidding and Budget settings.**

    a. *Select the Manual Bidding for Clicks radio button.*

    b. *Choose a daily budget.*

    Start conservatively; this is the emergency brake on any other mistakes you might make. In other words, how much money can you afford to spend without pain?

7. **Set ad rotation under Advanced settings.**

    Click the plus sign next to Ad Delivery in the Advanced settings section and then select Rotate: Show Ads More Evenly.

    After you have conversion tracking set up, you will change ad rotation to Optimize for Conversions. (Find more on conversion tracking in Chapter 6.) Rarely would you ever optimize for clicks, which is Google's default — and good for Google but seldom good for you.

8. **Click the Save and Continue button at the bottom of the page.**

On the next page, Google prompts you to create your first ad. What, you're not ready to whip out a masterpiece of persuasive prose at the drop of a cursor? No worries. Type pretty much anything here — you won't show it to the world for a while. The following list provides guidance on what to enter in those text boxes:

✔ **Headline text box:** Type the problem or opportunity.

✔ **Description Line 1 text box:** Enter a short description of big benefit.

✔ **Description Line 2 text box:** Write a short description of your product/service.

    Although you won't be showing this ad to the world for a while, you want to make sure you don't violate any of Google's editorial guidelines and get penalized before you even generate your first click. Stay away from crazy punctuation (#$%!@@) and words that would have gotten you detention in elementary school. Also, avoid unfounded superlative claims like "Best" or "Biggest Selection" unless you can substantiate them on your landing page.

- ✔ **Display URL text box:** Type your website's name.

- ✔ **Destination URL text box:** Enter the URL of the exact web page you want customers to visit first (called the *landing page*).

  The display URL is what your prospect sees in the ad itself. It must be on the same domain as the actual destination URL. In other words, G-Form LLC can use

  ```
  G-Form.com/Ipad-Sleeve-Video-Demos
  ```

  as the display URL for the destination URL

  ```
  G-Form.com/products/ipad-extreme-sleeve
  ```

  As long as the destination URL shares the part before the `.com` and isn't misleading, no problem.

See Figure 2-3 for an example, but please don't sweat anything at this point. Just write something that doesn't violate Google's editorial or content guidelines (see the section, "When nobody can see your ad," later in this chapter) and move on.

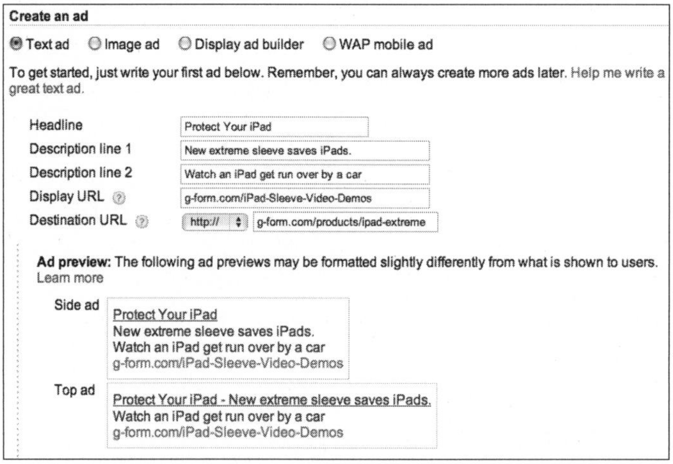

Create an ad

◉ Text ad   ○ Image ad   ○ Display ad builder   ○ WAP mobile ad

To get started, just write your first ad below. Remember, you can always create more ads later. Help me write a great text ad.

Headline	Protect Your iPad
Description line 1	New extreme sleeve saves iPads.
Description line 2	Watch an iPad get run over by a car
Display URL ⑦	g-form.com/iPad-Sleeve-Video-Demos
Destination URL ⑦	http:// ⬍ g-form.com/products/ipad-extreme

Ad preview: The following ad previews may be formatted slightly differently from what is shown to users. Learn more

Side ad

Protect Your iPad
New extreme sleeve saves iPads.
Watch an iPad get run over by a car
g-form.com/iPad-Sleeve-Video-Demos

Top ad

Protect Your iPad - New extreme sleeve saves iPads.
Watch an iPad get run over by a car
g-form.com/iPad-Sleeve-Video-Demos

Figure 2-3:
Write your
first ad.

After you write the ad, scroll down and type a keyword into the text box. For now, choose one keyword that someone searching for your business might type. A keyword can consist of multiword phrases: for example

- ✔ `iPad sleeve`

- ✔ `glow in the dark poker chips`

- ✔ `Denver home for sale`

Start by using exact match keywords only by enclosing the entire keyword phrase in brackets. These variations are described in detail in Chapter 7. For example, if your keyword is `biodegradable dental floss`, then enter `[biodegradable dental floss]`. Type your bracketed keyword into the keyword text box. (See Figure 2-4.)

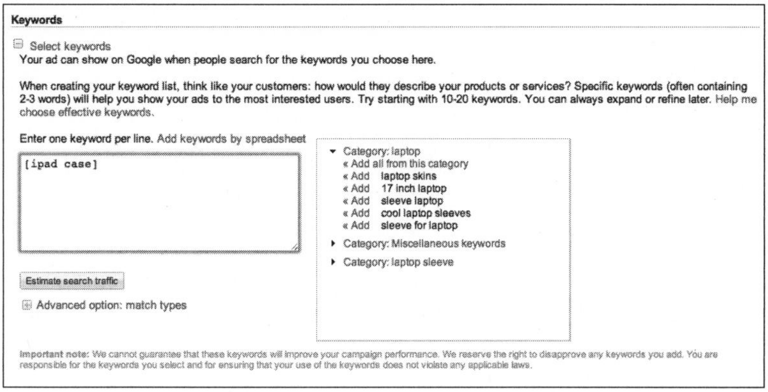

Figure 2-4: Adding keywords.

Next, scroll down to set your maximum cost per click (CPC) bids. Your bid helps Google determine whether to show your ad on the first page of search results. The higher your bid, the more likely your ad is to appear to searchers because Google makes more money from higher bids. And because you're just setting up the account, don't worry about getting this right. Bid a quarter, a dollar, or whatever number you like; you'll do some research and put thought into the number before going live.

On the following page, click the Set Up Billing Later button to make sure you don't accidentally start showing your rough draft ad group to real people yet.

Managing Your Account

The two rightmost tabs at the top enable you to manage the business side of your AdWords Account: Billing and My Account.

From the Billing tab, you can keep track of your spending and update credit cards. Click the tab to see two items in a drop-down list: Billing Summary and Billing Preferences. Billing Preferences is where you go to set up your payment options.

From the My Account tab, you can update your login information, set your e-mail notification preferences, and enable access to your account by other users. It has three subtabs: Account Access, Notification Settings, and Preferences.

In Account Access, you can invite other people to gain access to your AdWords account, from full administrative rights to read-only access (they can look but not touch). The invitee's e-mail address must not be connected with any other Google account, so if you're inviting an AdWords pro to help you, they'll need a brand new Google login to get in.

Notification Settings allow you to choose which online notifications and e-mails you'll receive from Google. Make changes by hovering your cursor over the setting you want to change and selecting from the drop down menu (see Figure 2-5).

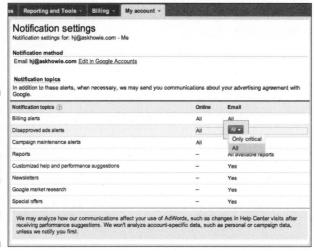

Figure 2-5:
Change notification settings to control the flow of information from Google.

In Preferences, make sure you enable auto-tagging by clicking the Edit link next to No, Thanks in the Tracking section (see Figure 2-6). Then check the box and save the change. You just set up *auto-tagging,* which simply means that AdWords data will play nice with Google Analytics, should you choose to hook that up to your site.

Activating your account

Your ads won't show up onscreen until you activate your account by giving Google five bucks and a source of funds. You can do this by clicking the link in the alert box with the reddish-pink background that looms at the top of your AdWords dashboard and following the account activation wizard, or take the tour first and pay later. Even if you activate now, you can pause your campaigns so you aren't charged for a lot of traffic before you know what you're doing. After you complete the account setup, wait 15 minutes, and then browse to www.google.com and do a search on your keyword.

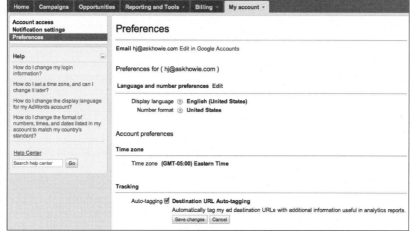

Figure 2-6:
Set up auto-
tagging
to allow
AdWords
to talk to
Google
Analytics.

To activate your account, follow these steps:

1. **Click the Billing tab and then click Billing Preferences.**

2. **Use the drop-down list to select your billing country.**

   The most common choices are at the top, followed by a long list of just about every country there is. (Sadly, missing is Fredonia.)

3. **Click the Continue button.**

4. **Enter your business information and then click the Continue button.**

5. **Choose a payment method:**

   • *Automatic Payments:* Getting charged after clicks come in. If you choose Automatic Payments, you'll be prompted to enter credit card or bank account information before continuing and activating your account.

   • *Manual Payments:* Having the cost of clicks deducted from a pre-paid balance. If you select Manual Payments, Google will prompt you to make a payment after activating your account.

   Don't forget to click the Enter It Here link next to Do You Have a Promotional Code? (if you have one, that is). At the time of this writing, Google is giving away $75 coupons like plastic necklaces at Mardi Gras.

Check with your website host or your PPC agency; they often get coupons and incentives from Google to start their clients on AdWords.

After you complete account activation, your account is live, and your ad might start showing Google search results page for the keywords you selected.

After you complete your account setup, wait anywhere from 15 minutes to a couple of days, and then browse to `www.google.com` and search for your keyword. You should see your ad either at the top or the right column. If you aren't ready to start advertising, make sure to pause your campaign after you give Google your billing information.

When nobody can see your ad

If your ad doesn't appear in the right column within a day or two of account activation, you might have a problem. Usually, correcting it is simple — as soon as you figure out what it is, that is.

If your ad isn't receiving any impressions (indicated by a `0` in the last row of the Impressions column in the data table on the Campaign tab page), you may be a victim of one of the following:

- ✔ **Editorial disapproval:** Have you violated Google's editorial guidelines? If you throw exclamation points around like crazy, promise "the best" or "the cheapest" stuff, capitalize like you're screaming in a chat room, use copyrighted terms, offer cheap drugs from Canada or $25 Rolexes or nuclear-weapon-making instructions, or commit any of several dozen other infractions, your ad won't show. In Chapter 3, you can see where Google reveals the problem.

   Google lays out its rules here: `http://gafd3.com/guidelines`

- ✔ **Low ad rank:** Based on your monthly budget (which you set when you create the account) and your choice of a maximum bid price (which you can edit at any time), your ad may not show on the first page of search results. That's the equivalent of scribbling it onto the back of a gas station receipt in yellow crayon and tossing it into a dumpster.

   You can see exactly in what positions your ads show. At this point, you can try raising your minimum bid — and monthly budget — to see whether that gets you onto the first page of search results.

- ✔ **Poor keyword performance:** If your keyword is `pink slippers big enough to fit an African elephant` or some other phrase that few or no people would ever search for, you could wait a long time before seeing a single click. In Chapter 5, read about the spy tools that help you find exactly what people are typing into their online searches.

✔ **Poor keyword Quality Score:** Google assigns each keyword in your account a Quality Score, based partly on the match between the keyword, the ad, and the landing page of the website; and partly on the historical performance of that keyword in other AdWords accounts. If Google thinks that a keyword you've chosen isn't going to make them money (because it won't generate AdWords clicks) or will give searchers a poor quality experience if they select your ad, your ad won't appear. Google forces you to improve the quality score (see Chapter 5) or place a really high bid to show your ad.

When only you can't see your ad

Sometimes your ad is receiving impressions, but try as you might, you can't find it yourself. Before you start humming the *Twilight Zone* theme, consider the possibilities described in the following subsections.

Google thinks you're searching outside your geotargeting

When you first set up your account, you had to choose a geographic location within which to advertise. Google may be interpreting the information it's reading on your computer (specifically, its Internet Protocol [IP] address) as meaning that you yourself are outside your targeted area. IP addresses are loosely connected to different parts of the world.

There are many reasons why Google could get confused about where in the world you are. First, IP addresses aren't exact — they're not like zip codes or postal codes. Second, if you're connecting to the Internet through a service that's somewhere other than where you are, Google can be misled. Third, little green aliens from outer space sometimes take over our fingers when we're typing stuff we really don't know anything about so that the paragraphs look long enough to be authoritative.

To find out where the Internet thinks you are, go to www.ipligence.com and scroll down until you can see the map at the bottom right, as shown in Figure 2-7.

Every machine connected to the Internet has a unique IP address, a string of four numbers separated by dots. Google's IP address, for example, is 216.239.51.100. The IP address is the "real" Internet address. We humans give websites names like Google and WalletEmptyingJunk.com, so we can find them more easily. The Internet machines map these names onto the numbers to send our browsers and e-mails to the right places.

Your IP address may be unique to your computer, shared by other computers on your network, or even shared by many of the computers served by your Internet service provider (ISP).

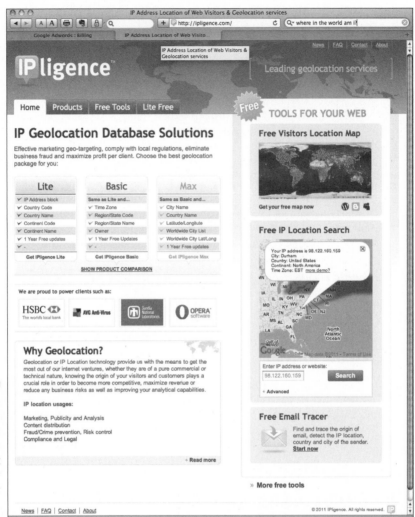

Figure 2-7:
IPligence
shows you
where the
Internet
thinks your
computer
resides.

You chose a different language

If you choose to advertise in Spanish (for example), you might not be able to find your ad if your Google searching preference is set for English. To change it (you can always change it back), go to www.google.com and click Preferences next to the search box. Select the Search Only for Pages Written in These Language(s) radio button and put a check next to the relevant language. Then click Save Preferences to return to your search.

Chapter 3

Managing Your AdWords Account

*A*fter you set up your AdWords account, it's time to explore Mission Control. In this chapter, we focus on the three basic AdWords tasks: campaign management, keyword selection, and ad writing — the core data you will use to manage your AdWords campaigns.

In subsequent chapters, you discover ways to view your data through filters, segments, and via the offline AdWords Editor that will help you make profitable decisions. You will also meet some of the other tabs that we don't cover here (like the Dimensions tab).

Running Mission Control with the Campaign Management Tab

The first screen you see when you go to `http://google.com/adwords` and enter your user name and password is the Home screen (shown in Figure 3-1). This snapshot screen shows summary statistics of your whole account, and can be customized to show just the data you find most important.

If you're just starting, you won't know the most important metrics yet. When you gain some AdWords experience, though, you can tailor this page by clicking the Customize Modules link at the top left. If you prefer to go straight to the Campaign Summary dashboard page when you log in, scroll to the bottom of the Home page and clear the Make This My Starting Page check box.

Figure 3-1:
The Home
Screen
page gives
you a cus-
tomizable
overview of
your entire
account.

You'll spend the majority of your online AdWords time on the Campaigns tab. (In Chapter 10, we show you how to use the much faster and more powerful desktop AdWords Editor to conduct most of your AdWords business.) After this chapter, most of the book shows you how to improve your online advertising by using various features within this tab. For right now, we show you the cockpit without asking you to go for a test flight.

You can view your account from three levels that range from overview to granular. The All Online Campaigns view lists your campaigns and gives you basic metrics on each one. Click the name of any campaign for the individual campaign view, which provides the same level of detail about the different ad groups in a particular campaign. The ad group view, which you access by clicking the name of any ad group within a campaign, shows you the finest details about every ad and every keyword in that ad group. This last view is where you spend most of your time. Use the other two views to help you prioritize which ad group will give you the biggest return for time spent.

All Online Campaigns View

The All Online Campaigns view gives you another set of tabs: Campaigns, Ad Groups, Settings, Ads, Keywords, and Networks. Click the down arrow to the right of the Networks tab to reveal several other tabs, including audiences, ad extensions, auto targets, dimensions, topics, and whatever else Google has cooked up between our writing and your reading. This page lists your campaigns and gives summary data about each of them. The column headings (Campaign, Budget, Status, and so on) are clickable, so you can sort your campaigns in various ways. For example, you probably want the campaigns that cost the most to be in your face more. Just click the Cost heading to sort from most to least costly, or click Cost again to reverse the order.

By default, Google shows all your campaigns as folders on the left of your screen, with a Help section just below. When you click a folder or campaign name, you enter that campaign and can access individual ad groups as sub-folders. You can hide this navigation panel by clicking the double chevron button at the top right of the section. This is especially useful when you want to see all the data for a campaign or ad group without having to scroll left to right. You can always get the navigation panel and Help section back by mousing over the left margin or by clicking the double chevron button (now pointing the other direction). See Figure 3-2.

Figure 3-2:
You can hide the navigation panel on the left by clicking the double chevron at the top right of that section.

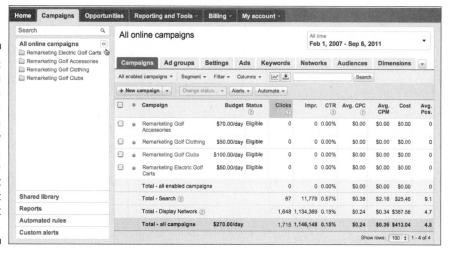

Campaign

By default, AdWords assigns your campaign exciting and informative names like Campaign #1 and Campaign #2. For your own sanity, please replace these generic names with descriptions that will make sense when you're running dozens of campaigns at once. You can change the name of a campaign by placing your cursor over the name and then clicking the Edit icon (looks like a pencil) to the right of your cursor. Replace Campaign #1 with a more useful name and click the Save button. See Figure 3-3.

Figure 3-3:
Rename a campaign by hovering your mouse over the name and clicking the pencil icon that appears to the right of your cursor.

You can change campaign names at any time, and in Chapter 7, we show you a powerful naming convention that will enable you to optimize lots of data quickly using AdWords Editor. For now, just pick names that make sense to you.

Budget

Google shows you the daily budget you set for each campaign. It's grayed and bracketed in paused and deleted campaigns. (More on that shortly.) You can change your daily budget for any campaign by clicking the budget amount ($20/day, for example), changing it in the text within the yellow pop-up, and then clicking Save.

Status

Campaigns can be active, paused, or deleted. You change the status of a campaign by clicking the little icon to the left of the campaign name. From the drop-down list, you can choose a green circle for active, two vertical lines for paused, or a red X for deleted. You can change the status of multiple campaigns by placing a check next to each campaign name, clicking the Change

Status button above the list of campaign names, and then choosing a status from the drop-down menu.

- ✔ **Active:** Active campaigns display your ads to searchers. They cost you money and bring visitors to your website. (If your campaign is active but you haven't set up payments, it will show as Eligible.)

- ✔ **Paused:** Paused campaigns are on hold but can be reactivated by clicking the double vertical line "paused" icon and selecting the green dot "active" icon. Pausing a campaign automatically pauses all the ad groups in that campaign. No impressions, no clicks, no visitors.

- ✔ **Deleted:** Deleted campaigns can also be reactivated by a single click. So what's the difference between pausing and deleting a campaign? We have no idea. If you delete a campaign, you can't actually make it go away. You can hide it by clicking the All Campaigns button just above the New Campaign button at the top left and selecting All but Deleted from the drop-down list. This can be helpful if you don't want to clutter your screen with old campaigns, but still want to see active and paused campaigns. Also, it's helpful to delete campaigns if you're writing *Google AdWords For Dummies* and you don't want the world to see every detail of your AdWords account in your screen shots. (See Figure 3-4.)

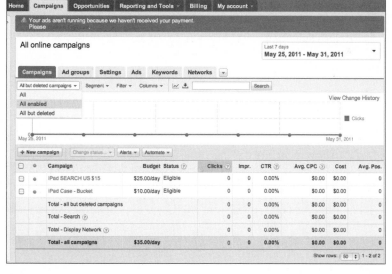

Figure 3-4: Hiding paused and deleted campaigns simplifies your screen by keeping only active campaigns visible.

Clicks

A *click* represents one person clicking your ad and arriving on your landing page. Google doesn't count multiple clicks from the same computer on the same day (or tries very hard not to). That's so your competitors can't sit behind their desks and develop carpal tunnel syndrome trying to bankrupt you by clicking your ad repeatedly. Two clicks equal two unique visitors to your site.

Clicks are good, right? The more clicks, the more visitors to your website. Well, not so fast. Clicks cost you money, remember? You make back that investment only when the visitor buys something from you. The goal of your ad is threefold:

✔ To get all the people who will eventually buy from you to click your ad

✔ To discourage all the people who will never buy from you from clicking your ad

✔ To predispose the people who click to resonate with your landing page

Obviously, you can't know beforehand who will buy and who won't. However, you can make some pretty good guesses until you implement conversion tracking (see Chapter 14).

For example, if you're advertising a ponytail holder worn by Lindsay Lohan, and you mention Lindsay Lohan in your ad, and you select `Lindsay Lohan` as a keyword, chances are you'll find a lot of visitors who have no interest in your hair accessory but a lot of interest in, shall we say, a "multimedia Lindsay Lohan experience."

When you gain AdWords experience, you'll see how to turn the prospect tap wider or narrower to maximize profits.

Impressions

The column heading *Impr.* is short for *impressions*. Technically, an *impression* is a single instance of a search results page that contains your ad. It doesn't mean the searcher saw the ad; rather, he saw a search results page with your ad on it. If the searcher has a small screen with high resolution and your ad appears below the scroll (meaning he'd have to scroll down to view it), it's still counted as an impression. So, if he clicks the first listing, before he looks at yours, it still counts.

Impressions can indicate the potential size of your AdWords market. If you're bidding on popular keywords, you can expect lots of impressions. But if your bidding strategy places your ad very low in the ad rankings, and it shows up on page four, you'll see very few impressions — even though the market itself may be huge — because few searchers will actually go to page four of the search results.

Click-through rate

Click-through rate (CTR) is the ratio of clicks to impressions, expressed as a percentage. It's one of your most important AdWords numbers, so if you're confused, take a little time to get clear on the concept. You can calculate CTR by dividing clicks by impressions. For example, if 200 people see your ad, and 12 of them click it, here's the math:

$$12 \div 200 = .06 = 6.00\%$$

You'd then brag at the AdWords Saloon, "My CTR is 6 percent." And everyone would understand that your ad was so compelling, 6 of every 100 people who saw it ended up on your website.

Average cost per click

The Avg. CPC column tells you how much, on average, you pay Google to get a visitor to your website. You may have different average CPCs by campaign, ad group, keyword, and ad. A big part of AdWords management is deleting or improving elements of your advertising that cost you more than you make back, so your average click cost is an important metric.

Cost

Your *cost* is simply all the money you spend on clicks. On this screen, cost is broken down by campaign. When you drill deeper, you can see how much each ad and each individual keyword costs you. (After you set up conversion tracking, described in Chapter 6, you can also track how much each ad makes you.)

Note: Some of the screen shots in this chapter include columns you won't see until you set up conversion tracking, such as Conv. rate, Cost/conv., and Conversions. (See Chapter 6 for more on conversion tracking. Oh, the fun that awaits you!)

Average position

The Avg. Pos. metric refers to where your ads show in relation to the other ads on the page. On the search results page, Google displays as many as to 11 ads: up to 8 on the right side of the page, and up to 3 above the organic listings. The ads above the body of the page are considered higher than the ones on the right. If your ad is at the top of the right column and no ads show above the organic listings, your position is 1. If, however, two ads appear above the organic listings, your ad at the top right is in position 3.

Ad position also applies to pages on the Display network (where Google shows your ads on other people's web pages), with ad positions starting at the top left and going down to the bottom right. Just in case you aren't confused yet, a lower ad position has a higher number: That is, position 5 is lower than position 3.

You can change the date range in the All Campaigns (or any other) view. Select one of the presets in the drop-down list at the top right of your screen, just below the green band that includes the top navigation, or select the first item in that list, Custom Date Range, input any two dates, and click the Go button. For some reason, Google insists that your start date be before your end date (a little un-quantum physics, don't you think?). Get into the habit of first checking your date range when you work on campaign management. Otherwise, you panic when you see only six clicks and the cause isn't a broken campaign, but a view set to Today instead of This Month.

Individual Campaign View

Click your campaign name to see an overview of the ad groups within that campaign. You see all your ad groups' statistics, including Default Max. CPC and Display Network Max. CPC.

- ✔ **Default Max. CPC:** This is the maximum cost per click you select for clicks generated on the Google search results page when you create the account. You can change this bid for specific campaigns, the ad groups, or even individual keywords. In Chapter 7, you discover smart strategies for bidding different amounts on different keywords.

- ✔ **Display Network Max. CPC:** This is the maximum you will pay for a click from content sites that you specify. You see this column only after you create managed placements; that is, you choose sites on the content network where you want your ads to appear.

Even though Google uses a pay per click (PPC) model, it's useful to think of buying ad space on a pay per impression basis. Google is trying to maximize its own profit per impression (that's why Google rewards high CTR with lower bid prices), so you should also aim to make as much money as possible per impression.

Just because Google gives you lots of data to look at, you don't have to rush out and buy a 30-inch monitor just so you can see it all without scrolling. To hide columns, click the Columns button above the graph, select Customize Columns from the drop-down list, and then remove the checks next to the columns you don't need to see. You can also reorder columns by dragging and dropping them. When you finish, click the Save button to return to a more manageable dashboard.

When you have more than one ad group in a campaign, the column headers become clickable and sortable.

Individual Ad Group View

In the Individual Campaign view, click the name of an ad group to drill down to the most detailed and powerful view, the individual ad group (see Figure 3-5). Think of an ad group as an attempt to target a particular message to a particular group of people. Everything in the ad group needs to fit together: the keywords or placements, the ads, and the landing pages.

Number of ads competing in this group

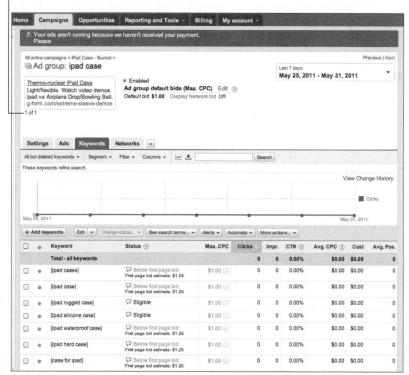

Figure 3-5: Clicking an ad group name takes you into the powerful Individual ad group view.

Keywords tab

The Keywords tab is the first thing you see when you enter an individual ad group. It shows you several things at a glance:

✔ Look above the ad at the top left to see how many ads are competing in this group. At first, you see 1 of 1. You want to create another ad — you almost always want to run multiple ads simultaneously to find the most effective one. (See how to do this in Chapter 13.) For now, you'll see 1 of 1.

✔ Check the date range at the top right. You can change it by clicking the down arrow to the right of the current date range.

✔ Check how each of your keywords is doing. After you set up conversion tracking, you may also see several columns of conversion statistics. (*Conversion* is a fancy marketing word for "the visitor did something good at my website.") In Chapter 10, you discover the power of these numbers and also see how to manage your entire account based on them.

Networks

To the right of the Keywords tab is the Networks tab. Click it to view and manage Display network campaigns to determine where to show your ads (see Chapter 13).

Ads

To the left of the Keywords tab is the Ads tab. Click it to view your ad. You see how that ad is doing and the networks on which it's showing. To give you a taste of what's in store, Figure 3-6 shows an ad group with four ads running simultaneously.

Click the ad headline to go to your landing page. Mouse over the ad to see the Edit icon to the right (it looks like a pencil). Click the pencil to change the ad. Delete it by marking the check box to its left, clicking the Change Status button (just above the ad), and then selecting Delete from the drop-down list.

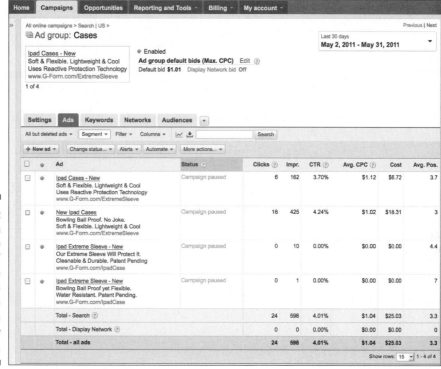

Figure 3-6:
You can
compare
multiple ads'
performance
and replace
ineffective
ads with
new
challengers.

By default, Google displays only your root URL — that is, only up to the .com
or .org or .whatever — in the fourth line of the ad. Use your display URL
to attract visitors to your website. For example, if you sell red staplers and
are advertising on the keyword red stapler, the second URL here would be
more attractive to prospects:

> www.staplerheaven.com

> www.staplerheaven.com/Red-Staplers

Change the URL by clicking the Edit link next to the fourth text box (the one
with your website name in green) near the bottom of the page. Your display
URL (the one that shows in your ad) doesn't have to be identical to your
landing URL (the page your visitors go after clicking). They just have to be
on the same domain (the part of the URL that precedes the .com or .net
or whatever). See Figure 3-7 for an example, where the landing URL and
the display URL are different, but both point to the same website (www.
vitruvianway.com).

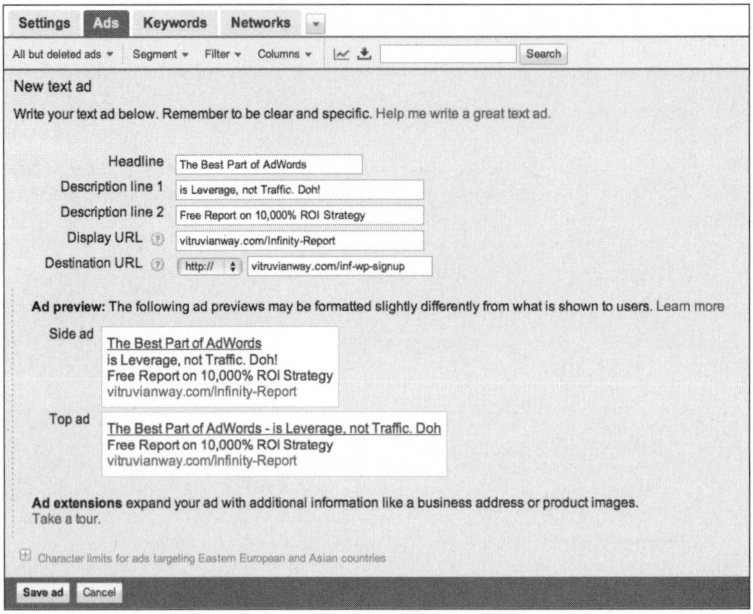

Figure 3-7:
The landing
URL and the
display URL
can be
different.

Writing a second ad

We will repeat it until you're sick of hearing it; the key to success in Internet marketing is ongoing split-testing. *Split-testing* is creating two variations (in this case, of your ad), sending half your traffic to each, and seeing which one generates a better response. Not only that; the key to success in Internet marketing is ongoing split-testing. (We told you we'd repeat it.)

Here's how to create a second ad to run alongside the first:

1. **On the Ads tab, click the New Ad button (to the left of the Change Status button) and select Text Ad from the drop-down list.**

2. **On the next page, create a new ad and then click the Save Ad button in the lower-left corner of the ad creation section.**

   You immediately notice a second ad in your ad group. Now you can monitor the difference between your two ads by counting clicks. One of the ads will probably receive more clicks than the other ad. When your ads have accrued enough clicks to make a statistician happy, you can replace the "losing" ad with another challenger. For the full sermon on split-testing, please turn in your hymnal to Chapters 14 and 15.

Display Network

Below your keyword list are three rows: Total – Search, Total – Display Network, and Total – All Keywords. These rows break down your results by source of traffic; Search refers to visitors who enter a keyword in the Google search engine, and Display includes visitors who click your ad after seeing it on some web page.

In most cases, you will begin with Search only for the purpose of keyword research (see Chapter 4 to find out more). After you size up and validate your search market, you typically choose one network — Search or Display — and stick with it until you achieve profitability. At that point, and not before, do you want to get more traffic. Until you can make money with your "best prospects," you do *not* want all the traffic you can possibly get.

A lot of AdWords beginners don't understand this concept, and it costs them a lot of money. If you find yourself tempted to expand your traffic before you prove your ability to make money from your existing traffic, please recall this joke from the beginning of *Annie Hall*: "Two elderly women are at a Catskills mountain resort, and one of 'em says, 'Boy, the food at this place is really terrible.' The other one says, 'Yeah, I know, and such small portions.'"

Do not ask for bigger portions of traffic until you can make that traffic tasty. And under no circumstance should you ever combine search and display traffic in the same campaign. More on this in Chapter 7.

Part II
Preparing Your AdWords Campaign

The 5th Wave   By Rich Tennant

"Maybe your keyword search, 'legal secretary, love, fame, fortune,' needs to be refined."

In this part . . .

This part is dedicated to finding and counting your prospects, so you can determine whether you have a business that can benefit from AdWords (or any other online-traffic-generation program), and then connecting with your prospects on an emotional level so they see your ads and website and immediately get the urge to reach for their wallets. The biggest business mistake is ignoring your market and trying to sell what you have, regardless of whether anybody needs or wants it.

Chapter 4 introduces you to the underground world of online market research. You see how to assess the profitability of a market in an afternoon, so your online adventures can be close to risk-free.

You explore the heart and soul of online marketing in Chapter 5: qualitative market insight. You'll discover how to decompress *keywords* (the words and phrases that people type into search engines) to discover your prospects' obvious and hidden desires.

Chapter 6 butts in and insists that you set up conversion tracking before launching your first serious campaign so that you'll be able to measure and improve your results over time.

Chapter 4

Sizing Up Your Online Market

- -

In This Chapter

▶ Assessing the size of your market

▶ Milking the Google Keyword Tool

▶ Creating keyword buckets

▶ Running bucket test campaigns to validate a market

- -

Google touts AdWords as a way to get more visitors to your website. But that traffic — as valuable as it can be — is just the tip of the proverbial AdWords iceberg. Because running tests in AdWords can be so cheap, quick, and easy, you can dip your toe into a market and discover whether it has potential with almost no risk or up-front investment. And, just as important, you can leverage your test results into improved performance in other media. In this chapter, we show you how to do initial keyword research, set up your own quick-and-dirty traffic tests, and validate the existence of a market.

Although you can learn a lot about a market by using free online tools, the best data comes from buying small amounts of AdWords traffic in order to discover things you could never learn any other way. You want to know whether your keywords, ads, and landing pages are effective before opening the AdWords floodgates (and your wallet), as well as before spending time and money to optimize your web pages for the organic, "free" traffic. This simple preparation will also guide you as you structure your AdWords account and expand its reach.

Assessing Market Potential

Or, in simple terms, "Don't dive into an empty pool."

In the movie *Field of Dreams,* the Ray Kinsella character builds a baseball diamond in his Iowa cornfield based on a voice that mysteriously repeats, "If you build it, he will come." That philosophy made for a great movie, but we don't recommend it as a customer-acquisition strategy. If you build it, you'll probably end up with a garage full of it — unless you take the time to figure out whether anybody's going to want it enough to pay for it.

Ken McCarthy, creator of The System Seminar for Online Marketing (www. thesystemseminar.com), once asked during a lecture, "If you were an Olympic diver, what would be the most important skill you could possess?" The answers varied — the ability to hold a triple gainer, strong core alignment, powerful legs, and so on — but Ken kept shaking his head no to each try. Finally, when the audience was getting really frustrated, he shared his answer: "The ability to tell if there's enough water in the pool before diving."

In other words, find out whether there's a market — and what that market wants — before you commit large amounts of time and money to creating a business or a product (or to learning fancy marketing tricks to attract buyers).

Even in startup companies with new products that no one is searching for because no one knows they exist, AdWords can be an indispensible "customer validation" tool. The secret bible of Silicon Valley startups is Steve Blank's *Four Steps to the Epiphany*. With permission and encouragement, we've adapted his Customer Development model to the AdWords medium.

The AdWords Wind Tunnel

Although AdWords sometimes (but not always) can be a source of profitable traffic, that's seldom achievable from the start. Here's a common AdWords complaint: "I couldn't make it work. The clicks were just too expensive, and nobody was buying, so I gave up."

Think of a kid just starting to play the violin saying, "I want to perform professionally after my first month of lessons." Virtuosity may be a wonderful longterm aspiration, but that unrealistic focus on instant results will clearly lead to quick frustration, failure, and disappointment.

Instead, suppose that our hypothetical budding violinist set goals like "learn how to hold the violin and the bow properly" and "determine whether I like the instrument enough to make it through the hundreds of hours of practice before I sound better than Pinkie the Cat." Those twin goals of improvement and discovery will lead to a much more empowering outcome, even if it ultimately doesn't lead to Carnegie Hall.

Perry Marshall compares AdWords to a wind tunnel for your business. He points out that the Wright brothers' main competitor in the race to invent the airplane was the better-educated, better-connected, and better-financed Samuel Pierpont Langley. Langley, head of the Smithsonian Institute in Washington, D.C., focused his R&D efforts on an engine powerful enough to fly. The Wright brothers, on the other hand, didn't mess with the engine. Instead, they worked for years on the proper design and structure of a glider. Only when they had an aerodynamically effective design did they turn their attention to powerful propulsion.

Rather than think of AdWords as the engine that delivers tons of visitors to your website (which it may or may not eventually become), use AdWords to build and refine your ability to find prospects, make relevant and appealing offers, and attract their business.

Using the AdWords Wind Tunnel

How you use the wind tunnel depends on what type of business you're trying to fly. If you use AdWords primarily for generating leads, you'll follow a different path than if you expect visitors to make a purchase directly from your website. You'll also use different strategies for a local business than for a national or global one. For now, we'll start with the simplest model: an e-commerce business that sells online to anyone in the United States.

In the AdWords wind tunnel, you'll run quick and inexpensive tests to answer the following questions, in order:

1. Is there enough search interest in my products?

2. If yes, what's the best way to structure my AdWords campaigns?

3. When I have a reliable flow of traffic, what does my website need in order to turn visitors into buyers?

4. Can I make money using AdWords? If so, how can I expand my AdWords campaigns to get even more traffic?

5. If I can't make money using AdWords, can I improve my website and other aspects of my marketing to optimize other media that are less expensive (but also less flexible)?

These questions translate into the following tests:

1. Discover the volume and expense of search traffic in your market to determine whether the AdWords Search Network and search engine optimization (SEO) can be worthwhile areas of focus.

2. Based on favorable keyword volume and cost metrics, use the data from the initial tests to structure and build out your AdWords account most effectively.

3. After your AdWords account is built correctly, use that traffic to validate and improve your website's ability to convert visitors into leads or sales.

4. If you can make a profit on your AdWords traffic, then systematically increase the scope and amount of AdWords and other online traffic to your website.

5. If you can't make a profit with AdWords traffic, or the volume is too small to make a lot of effort worthwhile, then continue improving your overall positioning and messaging and applying those improvements to all marketing channels, including offline media.

The rest of this chapter shows you how to conduct the first test, discovering the amount and cost of search traffic. Chapter 7 deals with correct AdWords structure; Part IV focuses on campaign management and optimization; and Part V demonstrates how to expand your marketing reach, both online and offline.

At the end of this chapter, we'll consider the variations needed for lead generation and local businesses.

Sizing Up Your Online Market

Begin your market discovery process at www.google.com without being signed into your Google account. If you see your e-mail address at the top right of the search results page, click the down arrow next to the e-mail address and select Sign Out from the drop down list. Google personalizes search results, and you can minimize the effect and therefore get a better sense of what the search results page looks like to others by searching anonymously.

You're looking for three data points:

- ✔ Is anyone advertising for your keywords?
- ✔ Does Google show organic results that relate to your product or service?
- ✔ What sort of keyword does Google think it is?

Enter a keyword that someone searching for your business would type. Select a common keyword for best results: For example, iPad sleeve is better than RPT non-newtonian fluid-based protective sleeve for iPad 2 because more people are searching for it and more advertisers are bidding on it.

After you conduct your search, look for the ads. Figure 4-1 shows a robust advertiser presence, with three text ads above the shopping results and organic listings, three product ads at the top of the right column, and four more text ads visible at the bottom right. That many advertisers means that this keyword almost certainly represents a viable search market.

Figure 4-1:
Start your
market
research
with
Google's
own search
results.

You want to see at least three relevant ads from competitors. Don't just count them, though; make sure they represent real competitors. Google sells "remainder" ad space very inexpensively to big customers like eBay, Yahoo! Shopping, and amazon.com. If you see generic ads like the one in Figure 4-2, it generally means that no one has tried or found a way to advertise profitably on this keyword.

Figure 4-2:
Ads like this
one indicate
that Google
can't find
enough
"real" adver-
tisers for this
keyword.

Electric Banjo
Bid or buy on eBay with confidence!
New eBay Buyer Protection Program.
ebay.com is rated ★★★★★
www.ebay.com

The second piece of data you want to glean from the Google search results is validation from Google that what you think people want when they perform this search is what Google thinks, also. For example, if you sell bleach, you might think that the keyword bleach would be a good place to start. As you can see in Figure 4-3, Google demonstrates that the bleach search market is interested in Japanese cartoons, not whitening their laundry white.

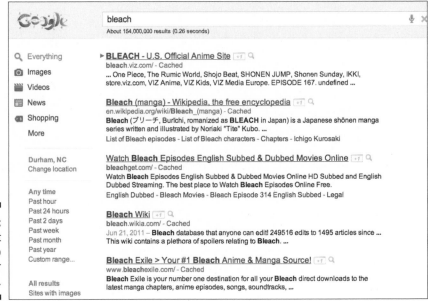

Figure 4-3:
You might
need to
find other
keywords.

The third type of information you can get from the search results is the type of results Google's users prefer. In the old days (like 2007), the organic search results consisted of ten text listings. Now, a given search can turn up images, videos, news, shopping results, Twitter feeds, blog posts, and even books and streaming music. These results aren't random, of course. A search for John Lennon features images and videos near the top of the page. As you can see in Figure 4-2, using the keywords iPad sleeve prominently displays shopping results. If the top listing is from Wikipedia, Google has determined that searchers are looking for basic information on the topic. If you see a map and a bunch of local listings, that's considered a local search. (Try searching for plumber to see this in action.)

We take a closer look at search intent in Chapter 5. For now, just make sure that your hunches about your main keywords are more or less accurate. If you think that you can sustain a national e-commerce website with traffic that's looking for YouTube videos or phone numbers of local businesses, either you're either a much cleverer marketer than anyone we know or you're in for a rude shock. Save yourself the unpleasant surprises by spending time in Google search mode.

The Free Google Keyword Tool

After you validate or adjust your most basic assumptions based on the search results page, look at estimates of search volume and cost. Google provides a free keyword tool that shows you the monthly search volume for keywords, as well as the estimated average cost per click. Note: Even though this tool is tremendously useful, it's often incorrect, and here's why: Google doesn't like to be too transparent in sharing the size and cost of its keyword inventory, and unfortunately, there's no hard and fast rule about how to inflate or discount its results. So use this tool as a first estimate and to create the ad groups that will give you the real numbers.

Get to the keyword tool from within your AdWords account by logging in and clicking the Reporting and Tools tab, and then selecting Keyword Tool from the drop-down list (see Figure 4-4).

Figure 4-4:
Quickly estimate how many people are searching for your keywords.

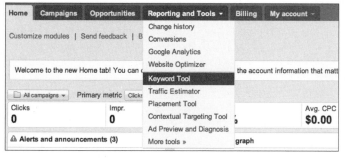

Keyword tool tactic #1: Identifying promising keywords

The first use of the keyword tool is to help you identify all the search terms you may want to bid on (and which ones you may choose to exclude). Do this by entering one or more keyword phrases into the Word or Phrase box, clearing the Only Show Ideas Closely Related to My Search Terms check box, and then clicking the Search button. If you want to see results other than the default country and language shown next to the Advanced Options and Filters link, click the plus sign to the left and make and save your changes.

Start with broad, high-volume keywords. Enter a couple of general keywords to get a glimpse of the scope, volume, and cost of Google's related keyword inventory. For example, as shown in Figure 4-5, an online nutrition shop owner would start with one-word keywords such as `supplements`, `vitamins`, and `remedies`.

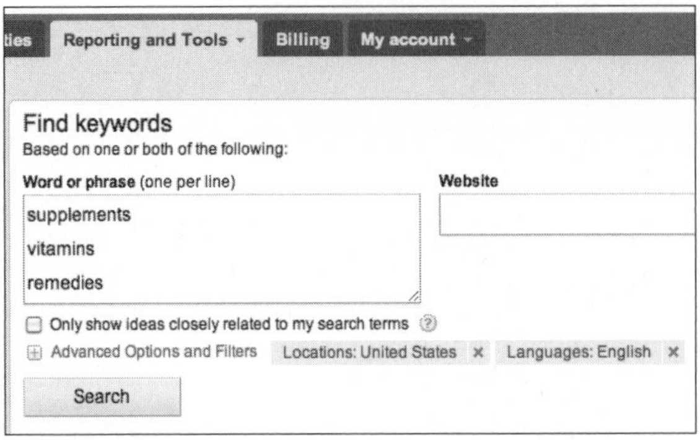

Figure 4-5: Enter general keywords into the keyword tool.

Google presents you with a list of the top keywords that include the words you typed, as shown in Figure 4-6. To make your table look like ours, click the Columns button and remove the Competition and Global Monthly Searches columns, and add the Local Search Trends and Approximate CPC (cost per click) columns.

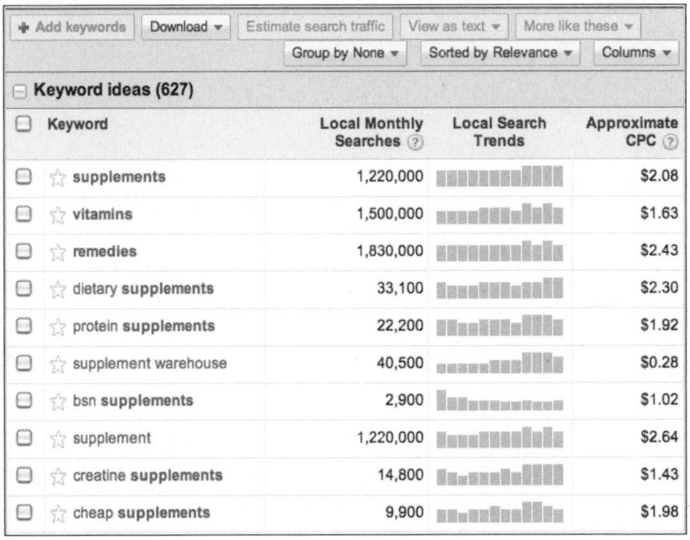

Keyword	Local Monthly Searches	Local Search Trends	Approximate CPC
supplements	1,220,000		$2.08
vitamins	1,500,000		$1.63
remedies	1,830,000		$2.43
dietary supplements	33,100		$2.30
protein supplements	22,200		$1.92
supplement warehouse	40,500		$0.28
bsn supplements	2,900		$1.02
supplement	1,220,000		$2.64
creatine supplements	14,800		$1.43
cheap supplements	9,900		$1.98

Figure 4-6: The keyword tool shows you keywords that Google deems relevant to the keyword(s) you enter.

Figure 4-6 shows just the first few keywords on Google's list, sorted by relevance. As you can see, the entire list consists of 627 keywords. You can do several useful things with this data. First, you can start to create your overall keyword list. Go through the list with one question in mind: "Do I want the person who searches for this to visit my website?"

If the answer is yes or maybe, jot it down onto a "potential keywords" list. If the answer is definitely no, add it to a "negative keywords" list. (More on negative keywords in Chapter 12.)

Keyword tool tactic #2: Measuring the difference between broad- and exact-match keywords

The results you'll see at first are all broad-match keywords. Take note of the broad-match Local Search Trends for your top keywords, but don't put much stock in them. First, as we've seen, they aren't that accurate. Second, you're going to start bidding on exact-match keywords only (unless you're advertising a local business, in which case you should check out the exception at the end of this chapter), so the broad-match metrics aren't that relevant.

Broad match is Google's way of saying, "Just tell me generally who you're looking for, and I'll go find them for you." That's a very compelling offer. You don't have to think much, and you get as much traffic as Google can make money throwing at you. The problem is, letting Google do your thinking for you is often a recipe for failure. You lose any competitive advantage you might gain by thinking intelligently about keywords, and you risk incurring huge amounts of junk traffic.

For example, look at the first few results for the keyword supplements (see Figure 4-7). If you bid on supplements in broad match, people searching for cheap supplements and best supplements will see the very same ads. Those two groups will choose based on totally opposite criteria, so it's silly to show the same message to both.

Chapter 7 contains a satisfying complete discussion of keyword-match types, but for right now you need to understand the three basic match types:

- ✔ **Exact-match keywords** are enclosed in square brackets, and trigger ads only if the searcher types in the exact words within those brackets.

- ✔ **Phrase-match keywords** are surrounded by quotation marks, and trigger ads if the exact words within the quotation marks are included in the search, with the possibility of additional words before or after.

- ✔ **Broad-match keywords** lack punctuation, and can trigger ads if Google determines that your ad is relevant to the searcher's query.

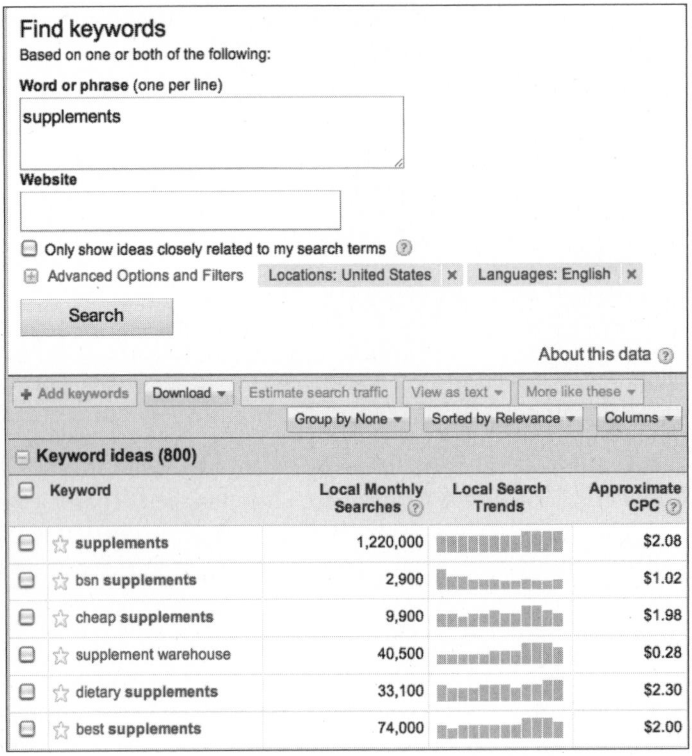

Figure 4-7:
The key-
word tool
can show
you which
search
queries will
activate
your ad if
you use
broad-
match
keywords.

Match Type	Example	Could Be Triggered by These Searches
Exact	[men's supplements]	men's supplements
Phrase	"men's supplements"	men's supplements online
Broad	men's supplements	men's vitamins

Broad-match data is useful to give you a sense of the size of the entire market. Exact-match data will show you estimated search volume for one particular keyword. The difference between broad and exact, therefore, represents how much additional search traffic you could possibly hope for after you validated your sales process with the safer exact-match traffic.

Keyword tool tactic #3: Assessing seasonality

The Local Search Trends column shows the relative search volume over the past 12 months for each keyword. Many businesses experience seasonal lifts and declines, and it's good to know about these in advance. For example, searches on home gym and quit smoking rise around January 1, as people seek support for their New Year's resolutions.

Google Trends: "Fad identification" tool

For more detailed information on seasonality and longer-term trends, visit Google Trends (www.google.com/trends) and search for the major keywords in your market. You'll see seasonal cycles in the Google Trends graphs. For example, see the huge spike in home gym searches around New Year's time in Figure 4-8. You can also see the effects of the recession on the home gym market from its peak in late December 2007.

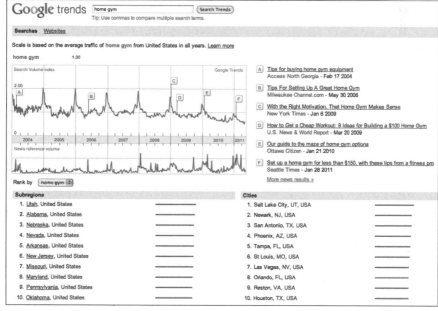

Figure 4-8: Google Trends alerts you to cyclical, stable, blossoming, and dying markets.

Aside from being fascinating and addictive (at least for people who subscribe to *American Demographics* magazine), Google Trends gives you a longer-term picture of your market. Why, for example, does Salt Lake City have the highest per capita search volume for home gym? Some fitness market analyst probably has an answer.

Sometimes, Google superimposes news headlines on the graph. In Figure 4-8, the stories appear to be reacting to, rather than causing, the trend. Sometimes media attention creates search demand. For example, when the authors of this book compete against each other on *American Idol* (just wait, it's bound to happen), searches for *Google AdWords For Dummies* will go through the roof.

Keyword tool tactic #4: Establishing keyword buckets

When you set the tool to show exact-match keyword data, you're ready to create keyword "buckets." A *bucket* is a group of closely related keywords that represent a market segment. A good working definition of a bucket is, "Would I show the same ad in response to each of these keywords?"

Change the keyword match type by clearing the Broad check box and then selecting the [Exact] check box in the left column (see Figure 4-9). The Local Monthly Searches column shows you the monthly average number of searches over the past 12 months. Local Search Trends provides a snapshot of seasonality so you can prepare yourself for periods of very high and very low traffic (keywords like red roses and tax prep come to mind). Approximate CPC shows you a rough average cost per click for all advertisers for this keyword. Before you swoon in shock, please realize that the more attractive your ads, the less you'll have to pay per click. So as long as you're above average, you'll end up paying less than your less-appealing competitors.

Figure 4-9:
Change the default match type from Broad to Exact to eliminate "noise" in your keyword research.

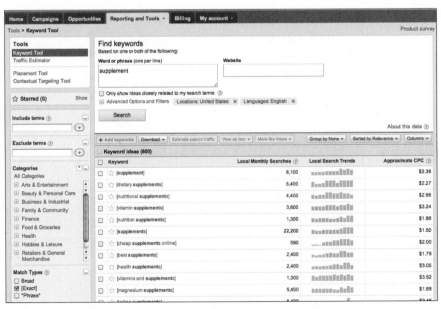

After you identify some promising buckets, you'll use them to create your first AdWords test, which we're getting to. To avoid the GIGO (Garbage In, Garbage Out) effect, spend some thoughtful time looking through Google's keyword ideas and identifying all the keywords that may represent profitable traffic one day.

Generating the buckets is easier to demonstrate than explain, so here's a real example from our client files. We'll describe it here in brief, but please visit `http://gafd3.com/buckets` for follow-along screen shots and a video screencast demonstration.

G-Form, LLC makes way-cool protective gear for extreme sports enthusiasts: snowboarders, mountain bikers, parents of toddlers, and the like. In early 2011, G-Form developed a prototype iPad protector called the Extreme Sleeve. Its value proposition is that it's soft, lightweight, flexible, and thin, with a molecular structure that changes upon impact to absorb unbelievable amounts of shock. Because nobody had ever heard of it, nobody was searching for it. So before jumping into an AdWords campaign, our first task was to identify relevant search terms that would bring us traffic.

1. **Enter the word `ipad` into the tool.**

2. **Make sure the Only Show Ideas Closely Related to My Search Terms check box is cleared.**

3. **Set location as United States and Languages as English.**

4. **Click the Search button.**

5. **Change the Match Types in the left column by clearing the Broad check box and selecting the [Exact] check box.**

6. **Sort by Local Monthly Searches by clicking that header.**

   The numbers in that column should now be in descending order, and Local Monthly Searches header should have a dark gray background.

7. **Scan the keyword list for relevant keywords (as shown in Figure 4-10).**

Eighth from the top, we see [ipad accessories] with 60,500 estimated monthly searches. That keyword is too broad to work with up-front because only a small percentage of people searching for accessories are looking for a case or sleeve. The first keyword of immediate interest is the eleventh from the top, [ipad cases], with 40,500 monthly searches. A few below that is [ipad 2 cases], at 22,200 searches per month. If we could continue outside the boundaries of Figure 4-10, we would next take note of [ipad covers] (12,100). On the second page of results (at 50 per page), we'd encounter [ipad screen protector] (which is also too broad in meaning to work at first) at 8100 searches per month; and [best ipad cases] and [ipad 2 cover] and [ipad 2 covers], all estimated, in an amazing coincidence, at 4,400 searches per month.

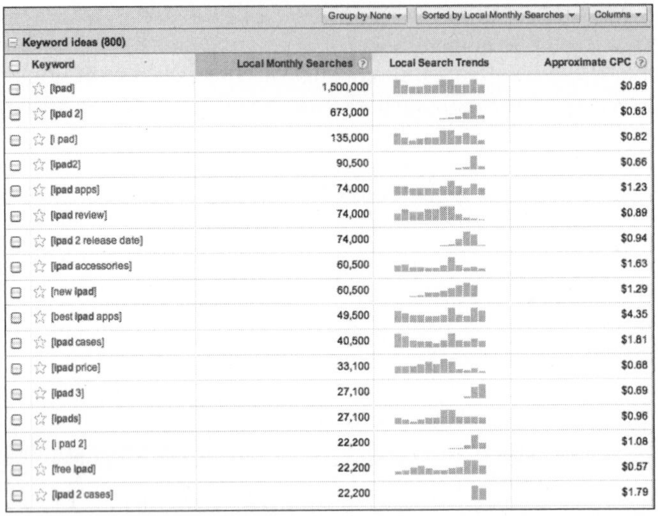

Keyword	Local Monthly Searches	Local Search Trends	Approximate CPC
[ipad]	1,500,000		$0.89
[ipad 2]	673,000		$0.63
[i pad]	135,000		$0.82
[ipad2]	90,500		$0.66
[ipad apps]	74,000		$1.23
[ipad review]	74,000		$0.89
[ipad 2 release date]	74,000		$0.94
[ipad accessories]	60,500		$1.63
[new ipad]	60,500		$1.29
[best ipad apps]	49,500		$4.35
[ipad cases]	40,500		$1.81
[ipad price]	33,100		$0.68
[ipad 3]	27,100		$0.69
[ipads]	27,100		$0.96
[i pad 2]	22,200		$1.08
[free ipad]	22,200		$0.57
[ipad 2 cases]	22,200		$1.79

Figure 4-10: Sort exact-match keywords by search volume to find the most promising keyword buckets.

That last sentence was us being sarcastic. Google isn't giving us real numbers, and relying on Google for anything more than an initial sense of the market is dangerous. In the upcoming section, "Getting in the Game," we show you how to get trustworthy data by buying it from Google.

Anyway, we're going to keep going through the tool looking for relevant keywords. On page 7, we discover `[ipad 2 sleeve]`, at 1,000 searches per month, next to the strangely nonsensical `[microsoft ipad]`. The game here is to collect all possible terms that could relate to the Extreme Sleeve.

When all is said and done, we identified three keyword buckets:

- `iPad case`
- `iPad cover`
- `iPad sleeve`

Keyword tool tactic #5: Filling the buckets

After you have your buckets, fill them with keywords in preparation for your first AdWords test. Each bucket will contain exact-match keywords only, all of them closely related to the main bucket theme.

Keeping all settings, return to the keyword tool and enter `ipad case` and `ipad cases` into the search box and then click the Search button. Watch how something surprising happens: The first keyword to appear is `[ipad case]`, with 60,500 searches per month (see Figure 4-11). That keyword didn't even appear in the last set of results!

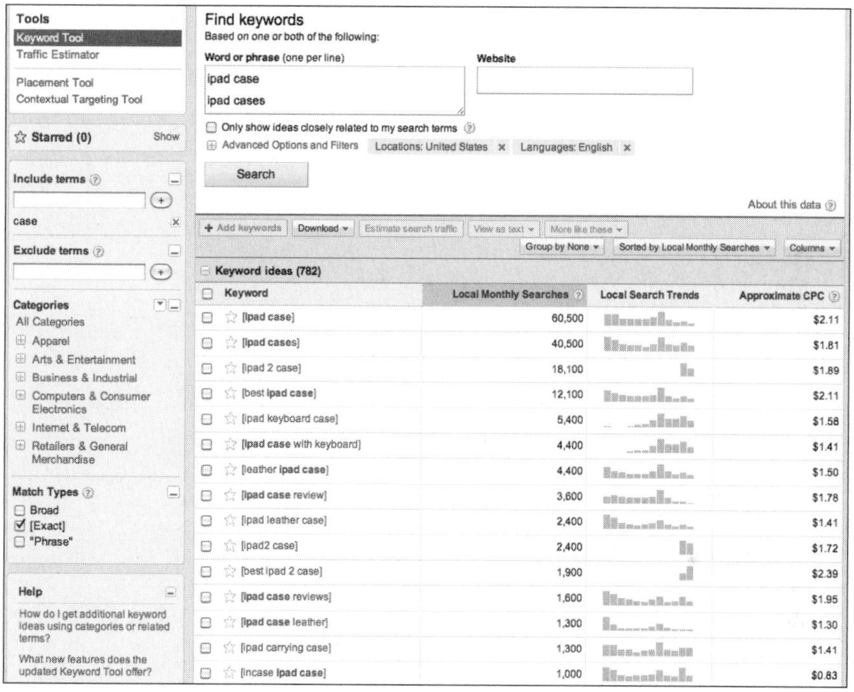

Figure 4-11: Enter the main keyword in a bucket to generate a list of additional keywords for that bucket.

The data you're looking at now represents potential keywords for the iPad case bucket. Now, go through the list and select all the keywords to add to the bucket. Among the top items, you find several to exclude. For example, the fifth one — `[ipad keyboard case]` — doesn't represent a desirable search because the G-Form Extreme Sleeve doesn't include or protect an iPad keyboard. Similarly, there's no need to show our ad to anyone searching for a leather case. As a fix, refine the search by entering the word `keyboard` in the Exclude terms box on the left, pressing Return, and repeating the process for the word `leather`. That reduces 800 keywords to 654, as shown by the number of keyword ideas above the table, as shown in Figure 4-12.

Excluded keywords

Tools	Find keywords	

Keyword Tool
Traffic Estimator

Placement Tool
Contextual Targeting Tool

Find keywords
Based on one or both of the following:

Word or phrase (one per line)
ipad case
ipad cases

Website

☐ Only show ideas closely related to my search terms ⑦
⊞ Advanced Options and Filters   Locations: United States ✕   Languages: English ✕

☆ Starred (0)   Show

Search

About this data ⑦

Include terms ⑦   ⊟
⊕

case   ✕

Exclude terms ⑦   ⊟
⊕

leather   ✕
keyboard   ✕

Categories   ▼ ⊟
All Categories
⊞ Apparel
⊞ Arts & Entertainment
⊞ Business & Industrial
⊞ Computers & Consumer Electronics
⊞ Internet & Telecom

Match Types ⑦   ⊟
☐ Broad
☑ [Exact]
☐ "Phrase"

Help   ⊟
How do I get additional keyword ideas using categories or related terms?

What new features does the updated Keyword Tool offer?

✚ Add keywords   Download ▾   Estimate search traffic   View as text ▾   More like these ▾
Group by None ▾   Sorted by Local Monthly Searches ▾   Columns ▾

⊟ Keyword ideas (654)

☐ Keyword	Local Monthly Searches ⑦	Local Search Trends	Approximate CPC ⑦
☐ ☆ [ipad case]	60,500		$2.11
☐ ☆ [ipad cases]	40,500		$1.81
☐ ☆ [ipad 2 case]	18,100		$1.89
☐ ☆ [best ipad case]	12,100		$2.11
☐ ☆ [ipad case review]	3,600		$1.78
☐ ☆ [ipad2 case]	2,400		$1.72
☐ ☆ [best ipad 2 case]	1,900		$2.39
☐ ☆ [ipad case reviews]	1,600		$1.95
☐ ☆ [ipad carrying case]	1,300		$1.41
☐ ☆ [incase ipad case]	1,000		$0.83
☐ ☆ [designer ipad case]	1,000		$1.60
☐ ☆ [i pad case]	1,000		$1.69
☐ ☆ [ipad case stand]	1,000		$1.70
☐ ☆ [case for ipad]	1,000		$1.32
☐ ☆ [moleskine ipad case]	880		$1.21

Figure 4-12:
Use the Exclude Terms function to quickly filter your keyword list.

After you go through the whole list (give yourself extra points for eliminating `hello kitty`, `etch a sketch`, `cheap`, `strap`, and `stand`, among many others), export the keywords that remain into a spreadsheet for quick upload into AdWords. Here's how, assuming you have Excel.

1. **Click the Download button just above the table.**

2. **From the menu that opens, choose All.**

3. **If you have Microsoft Excel on your computer, choose Format CSV for Excel and then click Download.**

4. **Find the downloaded file on your computer and open it in Excel.**

5. **Delete all columns to the right of column A.**

   Column A holds the keywords.

6. **Save the file as a text file, and give it a useful name, like `ipad-case-bucket.txt`.**

   Text files are easier to import into AdWords.

7. **Go through the list one more time (it's easier in Excel) and remove any more keywords that won't bring you qualified traffic.**

8. **Save the file and return to the keyword tool.**

9. **Repeat the whole process with the second bucket— in this example, `iPad cover`.**

   You end up with three .TXT files with keywords. Now it's time for the fun stuff: starting your first AdWords campaign.

This example shows coming up with just three buckets. You're likely to have more. These buckets don't necessarily represent the final structure of an AdWords campaign. You may decide to divide a bucket into several smaller buckets based on keyword intent (see Chapter 5). For example, one of the keywords in the `ipad case` bucket is `ipad case reviews`. That keyword represents someone in "learn more" mode, rather than "buy" mode. If the traffic volume justifies splitting them up, the two keywords will perform better with specific ads and landing pages.

Now it's time for the fun stuff: starting your first AdWords campaign.

Getting in the Game: Real Keyword Research

So far we've shown you how to "spy" on searches in complete safety, using free tools that are publicly available. Now it's time to conduct research that is much more reliable, relevant, and actionable. It's time to get in the game.

In the movie *Maverick*, Bret Maverick arrives in town and tries to talk his way into a poker game. One of the players refuses until Maverick makes an offer he can't refuse: that Maverick will lose for a full hour. During this hour, he bets, calls, raises, asks for cards, and ultimately folds or loses every hand. While he's doing this, he's discovering the "tells" of his opponents. One licks his lips when he's got a good hand. Another twists her hair when she's bluffing. At the end of the hour, Maverick puts his "education" to use, and he cleans up.

Think of your initial foray into AdWords as Maverick's first hour. You're going to make bids and offers, and you'll discover how your market responds. You don't expect to make any money at this point. Instead, you're finding out how good your competition is, how many searches there *really* are (remember that Google is stingy with data about its actual inventory), and what messages resonate with your market.

If you have a working website, you'll see whether your visitors respond positively to your offers. But you can still get in the game even if you haven't set up a website yet, so please don't skip this part.

If you haven't yet done so, create and fill your keyword buckets using the keyword tool (see the earlier section for how). Now you're going to create one campaign for each bucket to determine three important data points:

- ✔ What is the real volume of searches for that bucket?
- ✔ How much do clicks really cost?
- ✔ Which ad text is most appealing?

Create a bucket test campaign

Start by creating a bucket test campaign. Then you'll create a bucket test ad group, and then run and evaluate the bucket test.

1. **Sign in to your AdWords account at** `http://adwords.com`.

2. **Click the Campaigns tab at the top left and then click the New Campaign button just above the list of existing campaigns.**

3. **Click the Campaign type button and then select Search Network Only from the drop-down list that appears.**

4. **Name the campaign after the main keyword in your bucket according to the following format:**

   Search | Geographic Indicator | Keyword.

   For example, a U.S. campaign for the keyword `ipad case` would be named as follows: Search | US | ipad case.

   In Chapter 10, you discover why this naming protocol is such a time-saver.

5. **Select the location and languages for your initial target market.**

6. **Choose settings for Networks and Devices.**

   Choose whether to show your ads to smartphone and tablet users as well as those on computers, or whether to stick to computer users only. Unless your website is mobile-friendly and you have good reason to believe a lot of your searches will be done on mobile devices, it's simpler to turn that traffic off for now. We recommend selecting the Let me choose radio button, and also clearing the iPhones and Other Mobile Devices check box.

7. **Set your daily budget.**

   We recommend starting small, say $10 or less. You can always increase it if necessary by entering the amount into the box next to Budget.

8. **Set the delivery and rotation.**

   At the bottom of the page, click the Plus sign next to Ad Delivery: Ad Rotation, frequency capping and also select Rotate: Show Ads More Evenly.

   After you set up conversion tracking, as we show you in Chapter 6, you'll change this.

9. **Click the Save and Continue button at the very bottom of the page.**

Create a bucket test ad group

On the next page, name the bucket test ad group with the main keyword.

Write your first ad, creating a headline, two description lines, and two URL lines.

If you already know what to write, and you have a website and landing page all set, enter all that now. If not, just put in placeholder text and select a relevant URL from one of your competitors who isn't advertising on AdWords. The best way to find one is to look at the first page of Google's organic search results for that keyword. A lot of businesses that have achieved first page organic ranking are afraid to spend money on AdWords for fear of cannibalizing their free clicks. (They're probably silly, but that's another story.)

Click the organic link and see whether the page is a match for your ad. In other words, does it deliver what the ad promises? If so, select and copy the URL for that page, and then paste it into the Destination URL field. If not, try again until you find a relevant page.

Google is getting very strict about enforcing its landing page rules. Before driving traffic to a landing page (yours or someone else's), definitely spend some time in Chapter 9. It's not uncommon for Google to react to an innocent mistake by suspending or even permanently banning an account. It would be tragic to get your account banned for sending traffic to someone else's lousy landing page, so please do your homework!

Whatever URL you put in the Destination URL field, the Display URL must match it up to the .com or .net or .whatever. In other words, if you're sending traffic to the destination URL `g-form.com/products/ipad-sleeve`, then your display URL must start with `g-form.com`. You don't have to mirror the two exactly; you can use whatever number of characters you have left in the display URL line to repeat the keywords or highlight an aspect of your offer. For example, your display URL could read `g-form.com/extreme-ipad-protection`. (See Figure 4-13.)

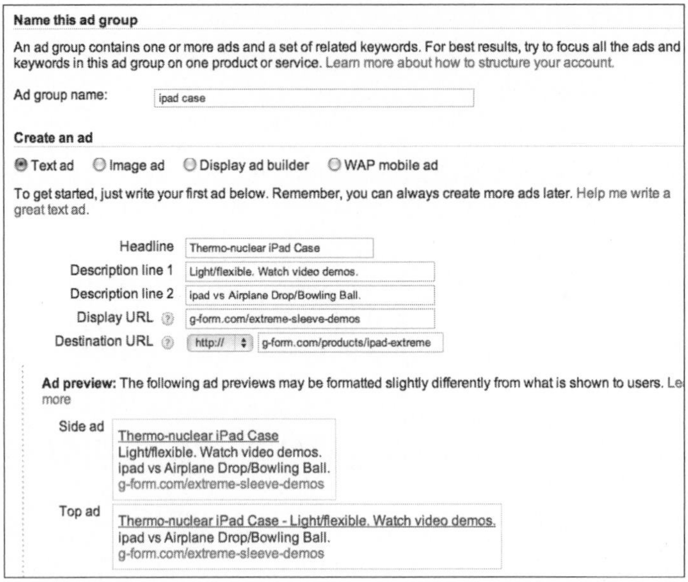

Name this ad group

An ad group contains one or more ads and a set of related keywords. For best results, try to focus all the ads and keywords in this ad group on one product or service. Learn more about how to structure your account.

Ad group name: [ipad case]

Create an ad

◉ Text ad ○ Image ad ○ Display ad builder ○ WAP mobile ad

To get started, just write your first ad below. Remember, you can always create more ads later. Help me write a great text ad.

Headline [Thermo-nuclear iPad Case]
Description line 1 [Light/flexible. Watch video demos.]
Description line 2 [ipad vs Airplane Drop/Bowling Ball.]
Display URL ⑦ [g-form.com/extreme-sleeve-demos]
Destination URL ⑦ [http:// ⬍] [g-form.com/products/ipad-extreme]

Ad preview: The following ad previews may be formatted slightly differently from what is shown to users. Learn more

Side ad
Thermo-nuclear iPad Case
Light/flexible. Watch video demos.
ipad vs Airplane Drop/Bowling Ball.
g-form.com/extreme-sleeve-demos

Top ad
Thermo-nuclear iPad Case - Light/flexible. Watch video demos.
ipad vs Airplane Drop/Bowling Ball.
g-form.com/extreme-sleeve-demos

Figure 4-13:
The ad's Display URL and Destination URL must point to the same web domain.

Next, enter the keywords from the .TXT file you saved from the keyword tool download. (See the earlier section, "Keyword tool tactic #5: Filling the buckets.") Open the file (it will probably open in a plain text editor) and delete the word *keyword* from the first line. Then select and copy the rest of the document. Navigate back to the same AdWords page you have open and paste the keywords into the Keywords box.

Finally, select a default bid at the bottom of the page. This is the maximum you're willing to pay for a click. This amount shouldn't be more than one-tenth of your daily budget for the account, so you can generate at least 10 clicks per day per campaign. So, if your daily budget is $10, your default bid should be $1. Don't worry about getting this exactly right; you'll soon discover the appropriate amounts by trial and error. It's always better to err too low than too high (unless you are burdened by too much money, in which case we'd very much like to make your acquaintance).

Click the Save Ad Group button at the bottom left to save the ad group. You're taken to the ad group page (see Figure 4-14). Before you do anything else, pause the campaign so you don't start showing your ad until you're completely prepared. Navigate back to the campaign page by clicking the campaign name link next to All Online Campaigns near the top left, just below the main tabs. Mouse over the word *Enabled* at the top left to change it into a button. Click the button and choose Paused from the drop-down list.

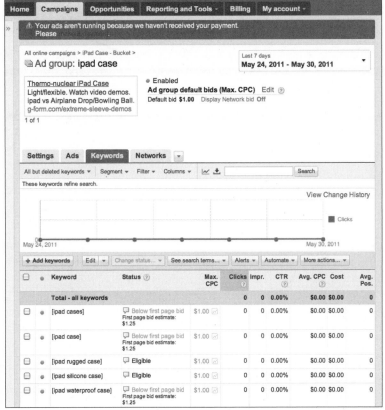

Figure 4-14:
After you
create an ad
group, you
can manage
and edit it
on the ad
group page.

Now, for optional extra credit, you're going to create two or three more ads with identical descriptions and URLs, but different headlines. The headlines should be sufficiently different to attract different types of buyers. Create a second ad by clicking the Ads tab above the graph, and then clicking the New Ad button just below the graph and choosing Text Ad from the drop-down list. The five text fields are pre-populated with text from an existing ad in your ad group, campaign, or account. In this case, all you need to change is the headline. Type a new headline (25 characters or fewer) and then click the Save button near the bottom of the page.

For example, if you wanted to advertise in the men's blue jeans market and you had a large selection of jeans, you could test the following headlines for the keyword men's jeans:

Men's Jeans | Jean Shoppe

Designer Men's Jeans

Men's Blue Jeans

Skinny Men's Jeans

The difference in click-through rate (CTR) among the ads can tell you what those searchers are looking for. Figure 4-15 shows the results of an actual one-day test of `men's jeans` traffic. (We did the test for the screen shot and we're cheapskates.) The result is that this headline test cautions strongly against trying to sell "skinny men's jeans" in the main ad group because it received only 1 click from 561 impressions. You will want to run your test for at least a week before drawing any conclusions.

	Ad	Status	% Served	Clicks	Impr.	CTR	Avg. CPC	Cost	Avg. Pos.	Conv. (1-per-click)	Cost / conv. (1-per-click)	Conv. rate (1-per-click)
	Men's Jeans | Jean Shoppe Fat, tall, skinny or wide, we've got designer jeans just your size. Bluefly.com/designer-mens-jeans	Approved	26.47%	9	584	1.54%	$1.16	$10.48	3.4	0	$0.00	0.00%
	Designer Men's Jeans Fat, tall, skinny or wide, we've got designer jeans just your size. Bluefly.com/designer-mens-jeans	Approved	24.25%	4	535	0.75%	$1.08	$4.34	6.2	0	$0.00	0.00%
	Men's Blue Jeans Fat, tall, skinny or wide, we've got designer jeans just your size. Bluefly.com/designer-mens-jeans	Approved	23.84%	3	526	0.57%	$1.03	$3.10	4.2	0	$0.00	0.00%
	Skinny Men's Jeans Fat, tall, skinny or wide, we've got designer jeans just your size. Bluefly.com/designer-mens-jeans	Approved	25.43%	1	561	0.18%	$1.22	$1.22	4.6	0	$0.00	0.00%

Figure 4-15: Run a headline test to gauge CTR.

The key number in Figure 4-15 is the CTR. The Men's Jeans | Jean Shoppe headline is twice as attractive as the next one, Designer Men's Jeans. Next comes Men's Blue Jeans, which arguably says the same thing as the top ad, but did only one-third as well. Finally, the biggest loser (no pun intended) is Skinny Men's Jeans, with fewer than 2 clicks per 1,000 impressions.

A close look at Figure 4-14 reveals that three of the five visible keywords are not eligible to appear on the first page of search results, which is to say they're essentially invisible. Don't worry about this yet, for two reasons. First, sometimes Google is wrong when it flags a keyword as Below First Page Bid. Second, as long as you're spending enough money to show your ads at least 10% of the time that they're eligible, you'll get accurate and valuable metrics from this test.

Before you run the test itself, if you haven't done so, turn the rest of your keyword buckets into separate campaigns, with a single ad group in each campaign. If you have multiple ad headlines to test, create the additional ads. Pause each campaign. Now test one ad from each campaign to make sure that it resolves to the right landing page. Navigate to the ad group within each campaign and click the ad at the top left. If you end up where you want your visitors to end up, congratulations! You're ready to start your bucket test.

Starting the bucket test

The first thing you'll discover from a correctly run bucket test is the total number of searches in Google's inventory. Yes, the keyword tool estimates this number, but you want the truth. The key to this data is an elusive metric called Impression Share. This metric was developed by Google to make advertisers feel bad about all the traffic they were missing. So, if someone sets a daily budget or maximum cost per click (CPC) too low for Google's liking, Google has a way of saying, "Hey, bud, you showed your ad to only 53% of the possible eyeballs out there for your keywords. If you'll be less stingy, we'll give you more traffic."

Your bucket tests are conservatively funded, with low daily budgets and low max. CPCs. In spite of this, the Impression Share metric will tell you conclusively how much traffic is out there for all the exact-match keywords in your campaigns. You just have to divide Impr. by Impr. Share to find out exactly how many searches were made during the time period of your test. For example, if the ipad case campaign generates 6,445 impressions in 7 full days, and the impression share is 76.76% (as shown in upcoming Figure 4-16), you can determine the total search volume for that campaign as follows:

6445 / 0.7676 = 8396

That's 8,396 searches in 7 days. To find out the monthly search volume, multiple that number by 4.34 (the multiplier from a 7-day week to an average 30.4-day month).

8396 × 4.34 = 36,440 searches per month

Figure 4-16: Divide Impr. by Impr. Share to find out how many searches were made during the time period of your test.

Campaign	Budget	Status	Clicks	Impr.	CTR	Avg. CPC	Cost	Impr. share	Lost IS (budget)	Lost IS (rank)	Avg. Pos.
Search | US | iPad Case	$15.00/day	Ended	91	6,445	1.41%	$1.21	$110.45	76.76%	11.67%	11.57%	4.4
Search | US | iPad Cover	$15.00/day	Ended	34	3,476	0.98%	$1.28	$43.49	98.92%	0.00%	1.08%	4.3
Search | US | iPad Sleeve	$20.00/day	Ended	17	1,353	1.26%	$1.20	$20.32	99.36%	0.00%	0.64%	3.7

As you can see in Figure 4-16, those are the exact metrics from the G-Form bucket test for the ipad case campaign. For reasons that we get into in Chapter 18, we constructed the G-Form test a little differently from what we're describing here. We used only the exact-match format for the single keyword, and didn't include any of the other related keywords. If you flip back to Figure 4-11, you'll see that Google told us to expect 60,500 searches per month for `ipad case`. Yet the evidence of our own test is that there were fewer than 37,000 searches per month during the time period we tested.

So, just discount Google's estimate by 37% to know the real traffic, right? Not so fast! Take a look at the second campaign, for ipad cover. Google estimates 8,100 monthly searches for that keyword. Yet in Figure 4-16, our 7-day bucket test reveals 3,476 Impr and an Impr. Share of 98.92%, for a total 7-day search volume of

$$3476 / .9892 = 3514$$

Multiplying that by 4.34 yields a monthly total of 15,260 searches — almost double what Google told us!

By this point, we hope you realize why you can't rely on the estimates provided by the keyword tool. They're a good starting point, but when you can pay a little money for the privilege of discovering your market, it's almost always a wonderful investment.

Running the bucket test

When you're ready, enable the campaigns. You can do this in bulk:

1. **Navigate to the All Online Campaigns page and select the check boxes to the left of each of the bucket test campaigns.**

2. **Click the Change Status button just above the campaign list and select Enable from the drop-down list (see Figure 4-17).**

Google takes a while to start showing the ads, and it's impossible to predict how long. You want to run your test for at least seven full days to take into account different search behavior over different days of the week. Even if you could get enough traffic in one day, that single day is likely to be atypical of an entire month. And because you can get accurate numbers as long as your impression share is greater than 10%, you can afford to run small daily budgets over a longer time period.

If your ads aren't showing after a day or two, then your default bids are truly too low. Raise them conservatively until the impressions start kicking in, and then let the test run for seven full days. When you've gathered a week's worth of data and your impression share is at least 10%, then you can pause all the campaigns Just follow the instructions in the preceding step list but select Pause instead of Enable.

Figure 4-17:
Enable all
bucket test
campaigns
at once.

Evaluating the bucket test

Before you can evaluate the test, you must set up the proper date parameters. On the All Online Campaigns page, click the down arrow next to the date range at the top right. Select Custom Date Range and select the start and end dates that include 7 days of traffic. (If you're not sure, check the line graph above the campaign list in the All Time date range.)

So far in this running example, you've seen how to determine the total monthly searches, and you also have data on Avg CPC, or the average cost of a click. In Figure 4-16, you can see that it costs $1.21 to appear around positions 4 and 5 for the keyword [ipad case]. (The Avg. Pos. column shows 4.4, which is between 4 and 5.) You could presumably lower that bid and still appear on the first page of search results, but it's doubtful that you could run your next test for less than $1 per click.

Why is this important? Well, you don't want to start a test without being certain that you have enough money to run it to completion. A typical e-commerce website converts about 1 percent of visitors to sales; in simple terms, you would expect 100 visitors to produce a single sale. Due to the mysteries of inferential statistics, you want to send at least 500 visitors to any landing page before drawing conclusions on its ability to convert AdWords traffic into profits. That means we know in advance that we have to be willing to spend $605 ($1.21 × 500) per G-Form landing page — and double that if it's a *split test,* where we send half the traffic to one variation and half the traffic to another.

If you set up multiple ads per bucket, you can also see which headlines were most attractive. This will help you target the most responsive niche within your market (to revive Ken McCarthy's metaphor, the pool with the most comfortable water).

Bucket testing for a lead generation business

Although the Search network can be a profitable medium for businesses that collect online leads (as opposed to making an immediate sale), in general, we recommend starting lead generation advertising on the Display network. Clicks are cheaper, and the medium lends itself to the kind of "interruption advertising" that often is required for products and services that require a long "getting to know and trust you" period.

You still need to begin your keyword research in the Search network because the Display network doesn't provide keyword metrics. In fact, run the bucket test exactly as described in this chapter, and use the buckets you identify and validate to create Display network ad groups (described in Chapter 7). Reduce your maximum CPC on text ads in the Display network to one-half the average CPC in your bucket test.

And realize that when it comes to estimating the size of your market, all bets are off. For example, very few people search for "a magic ring that makes you invisible and allows you to live forever." Yet, if offered, most people would take it (except maybe Gandalf). In search advertising, you'll be responding to overt desire. In interruption advertising, you're probing for latent desire. You can't measure latent desire by counting the people actively searching.

Finally, be prepared to write different ads for the Display network. If Sauron searches for "ring of power," your ad headline can simply read, "I've Got the Ring" or "Ring of Power — Free Shipping." An interruption ad on a website devoted to weightlifting for orcs might have a headline, "Suck Up to Sauron" and then go on to describe how happy you'd make him if you gave him this ring. (Note: If the preceding analogy made no sense to you, either read J.R.R. Tolkien's *Lord of the Rings* or congratulate yourself on your ability to ignore geekified popular culture.)

Bucket testing for a local business

Obviously, national and global search volumes aren't much use if your target market is a 25-mile radius around Asheville, North Carolina (metropolitan area population 400,000). Assuming that people in Asheville are the same as everyone else in the US (an attitude that will not make you many friends in Asheville), a keyword that receives a healthy 20,000 searches per month nationally might get only 270 of them from the Asheville area. Assuming your ads get a whopping 10% CTR, that's 27 visitors per month to your website on that keyword. That's not enough traffic to test with, let alone live on.

So what's the solution: Move to Los Angeles? Don't worry; nothing that drastic. For a local business, do the bucket test with as much traffic as you can possibly get. That means letting Google do the heavy lifting by making all your keywords broad match instead of exact match.

Also, choose shorter keywords for local searches. A national campaign with a keyword like buy home would be a disaster because of all the unwanted traffic you'd receive. Even in exact match, what are the chances that the person searching to buy a home wants it in your neck of the woods? In a local search, though, a keyword like buy home is perfectly reasonable. When you include it as a broad-match term, Google will send you lots of local traffic related to residential real estate. You can use that traffic to assess the size of your local market, improve your marketing, and use advanced search query analysis (see Chapter 11) to identify profitable and unprofitable keywords under the broad-match umbrella.

Chapter 5

Reading the Mind of Your Market

*I*n Chapter 4, we show you how to size up search markets based on keyword volume and cost: the number of searchers as well as how much you need to pay for website visitors from those searches. If you did the optional extra credit and wrote multiple ads for each bucket, you got some market feedback on variations of your message.

In this chapter, we look at keywords from a completely different perspective: what they can tell us about your prospects' desires and fears. We begin by discovering what keywords can tell us about the people typing them, and then explore quick and dirty (and free!) ways to start answering our questions. And because this is AdWords, you don't have to be right from the start. You can run our assumptions through the testing machine to discover the profitable truth.

Decompressing Keywords

Keywords can also tell you important things about our searchers, if you understand how to decompress them back into their original concept-desire states, that. To explain what we mean, let's all go to the movies.

In *Star Trek IV,* the crew of the Enterprise time-travels to 1980s San Francisco. Scotty, the engineer, tries to access the state-of-the-art Macintosh computer by speaking into the mouse: "Computer? Computer?" When he fails to elicit a response from the machine, he puts down the mouse in disgust and resorts to typing on the keyboard.

Guess what? That's what each of us experiences when we search, although we're more used to it than the frustrated Mr. Scott. We don't think of our problems and desires in terms of keywords. We have to stuff all our thoughts and feelings into a small search box — because that's what the search engines offer us.

For example, Howie has been thinking about "treadmill desks" a lot lately, ever since Glenn Livingston got one and loved it. If you could plug a microphone into Howie's head, this is what you'd hear (after applying the standard male sleep/sex/food filter):

> *I wonder if the TrekDesk will be strong enough to hold a 24" iMac plus a second monitor. It's made of plastic, after all. Could I build one myself out of wood? Will it really help my back pain? Will it be hard to read the screen as I'm walking? And I know I can get a cheap treadmill on Craigslist, but maybe I want a top-of-the-line model that's really quiet. What about a manual treadmill? Will people be annoyed by the motor noise when I'm on the phone? Will they notice? Will reading while walking hurt my eyes?*

However, Google isn't built for conversation, as you can see in Figure 5-1, so Howie has to compress all these thoughts into a few words. He might try `treadmill desk reviews` or `build treadmill desk` or `quiet treadmills for walking desk`. Either the first search will lead to sites that answer all his questions, or he'll return to the search box time and time again and again to get all these questions answered.

Figure 5-1:
Searchers are forced to compress their stream of consciousness into a few words.

For search marketers, here's the million dollar question:

> *How can I prevent my prospect from searching again and again, and instead get them to click my ad or listing so that they can get everything they need from me Then, when they're ready to buy, they're deeply engaged with me, and they won't jump to my competitors?*

To answer those questions, you must understand the thoughts and feelings that got compressed into the keyword phrase. Like a zipped compression of a large file, those who understand how the process works in one direction can reverse-engineer it and recover the original. We call this process *keyword decompression.*

Unlike file decompression, though, keyword decompression doesn't rely upon a fixed algorithm, but rather on curiosity, empathy, and research.

Presenting the Six Keyword Decompression Questions

The goal of keyword decompression is to respond so accurately and completely to searchers' real motivations that you become the obvious choice the instant they see your listing on the search engine results page (SERP), and then you parlay their attention into interest, desire, and action on the landing page — and beyond.

To accomplish this task, you must be able to answer the six keyword decompression questions:

- ✔ **Keyword:** What pain/itch do they want to stop?
- ✔ **Trigger:** Why are they searching right now?
- ✔ **Attention/Attraction:** What promise do they want you to make?
- ✔ **Interest:** How can you immediately show that you can keep this promise?
- ✔ **Desire:** Why won't they buy your product or become a lead?
- ✔ **Action:** How can you eliminate their risk?

If you can answer these questions about your best prospects, you'll be able to sell to them. If not, then your marketing will be ignored — or worse, help your competitors by filling in the gaps leading to the sale.

Searching and the AIDA formula

You might have noticed the last four questions correspond to a classic direct marketing formula: namely, AIDA, which stands for attention, interest, desire, and action.

Search marketing fits nicely into this model. When someone types a keyword and gets lots of hits on a SERP with more than 20 listings, your ad has to attract her attention despite competition with every other ad and listing and element on that page. Each represents a promise, so you must write the ad that makes the promise your target market most wants to hear and will believe.

Next, you have to transmute that initial attention into deeper interest. That occurs at the top of the landing page, where you show that your site will keep the promise of the ad, and quickly.

Search is driven by desire, so the job here is not to create it, but rather to focus it and remove obstacles to its fulfillment: that is, to answer the objections that threaten to drown out the desire with a fear of making a mistake. The body of the landing page takes on that job.

Finally, you have to move the prospect to action of some kind. Here's where clear instruction, simple navigation, and strategically placed risk reversal all function to move the prospect to the next step.

In the following sections, we explore each question in some depth.

1. What pain/itch do they want to stop?

Every search is an attempt to change an existing situation. Even if it's just to satisfy curiosity or to shop for something amazing, it's still an attempt to move the searcher from a state of dissatisfaction to one of satisfaction. Think of the search impulse as a rubber band being stretched. The search dynamic seeks to return the rubber band to its neutral position.

Your prospect may want to buy something, learn something, justify an emotion or opinion, or change a feeling state. To become the obvious choice, you have to know the desired end result of the search.

For example, a search for `treadmill desk back pain` suggests a searcher who wants to hear stories about people who cured or reduced their back pain using a treadmill desk.

The ultimate outcome of Howie's quest, as expressed in multiple searches over several hours, days, or weeks, will probably involve the purchase or construction (please, no!) of a treadmill desk. But the specific outcome of this particular search is informational, and Howie is rooting for a positive response. He doesn't want to read that treadmill desks are great for digestive problems but useless for back pain.

So a marketer who advertises "Treadmill Desk Back Pain Relief: Case Studies" will likely get his click.

Here's another example. If someone searches for `Weber mandolin`, what does he want? Does he want to buy a Weber mandolin; learn the story of Weber mandolins; look, window shop, and drool; get one repaired; find a community of other Weber fans; or download care and maintenance instructions? What's the problem that keyword represents?

2. Why are they searching right now?

In other words, what was the search trigger? Why did they search just now, instead of a year ago, a week ago, or 20 minutes ago? What happened inside their head, and what triggered it from their environment?

The search trigger is the context of the search, the story that the searcher is enmeshed in at that moment. If you can understand and reflect it back to them, you create a powerful bond of empathy and trust. For example, the search for a treadmill desk was triggered by a friend's recommendation. Knowing this, an ad could query, "Wondering if the treadmill desk is right for you too?"

If a woman is searching for `Violin repair Durham NC`, there are a couple of possibilities. One possibility is ten minutes ago she tripped, fell, and broke her violin. Another possibility is that she inherited a violin in 1988 and just found it in the attic while looking for her high school yearbook.

Or maybe her son just came home from school and said, "I want to join the orchestra next year, and I want to play the Adams 26-inch fiberglass tympani with fine tuning. It's only $2,100." So she thinks, "Hmm, I've got a violin in the attic. I bet I can get that fixed for a couple of hundred dollars."

Your ad would speak very differently to a professional violinist whose violin neck just cracked than to someone who stumbled upon an old fiddle in the attic.

3. What promise do they want you to make?

After you answer the first two questions, you must decide on the promise that your prospect wants you to make. The ad that makes the best believable promise gets the click. The others get ignored.

Every ad is a promise, in the following form: "If you click me, you will get. . . ." Name the desired dot-dot-dot and watch your click-through rate (CTR) skyrocket.

An ad that promises Howie unbiased reviews of the treadmill desk from back pain sufferers would get his click. Likewise, a professional violinist with a broken instrument wants to see a promise of high-quality craftsmanship and fast turn-around. And an antique hunter wants an honest appraisal and a repair that would allow for a profitable sale.

4. How can you immediately show that you can keep this promise?

Promises are cheap. Your prospect clicks your ad with hopeful skepticism, ready to hit the Back button at the first sign of irrelevance, confusion, or slea-ziness. The top of your landing page must immediately address the promise of the ad directly. So, the headline, the overall design, and the top graphics must immediately reinforce the promise, so the searcher is reassured that they're in the right place.

If the landing page contained generic information about treadmill desks, or if Howie had to scroll or hunt for info about back pain, he would depart within a few seconds. The advertiser would have wasted the cost of his click. On the other hand, a headline like, "Why the treadmill desk is the answer to your back pain," would engage him and keep him reading. When the professional violinist looking for a repair shop lands on a website that looks like it was designed by a 12-year-old (spelling errors in the headline, the top graphic doesn't show properly on the browser, and all the question marks look like weird diamonds in circles), there's a mismatch. She'll hit the Back button as quickly as she can, thinking, "You don't pay attention to detail. No way I'm going to let you touch my violin." Without meaning to, the site has broken the promise of the ad.

5. Why won't they buy your product or become a lead?

Every landing page must have a Most Desired Action (MDA) that relates to your overall business goal. Sometimes the MDA is a direct purchase from an e-commerce site. Other times, it's just the goal of getting a visitor to become a lead via a phone call or an opt-in form. (We cover landing page strategy in depth in Chapter 9; right now, the goal is to show you all the uses to which you can put a fully decompressed keyword.)

Your visitors always have reasons to resist your MDA. Maybe they don't trust you; they don't believe they can install it themselves; they're confused about the features; they don't value the benefits enough to spend money; they think they can get it cheaper elsewhere; they're embarrassed about spending money on it; they're tired of getting inundated by e-mails from people in your industry. On and on.

If you want them to complete your MDA, you must overcome these objections. That's the function of the content of the website. Using descriptions, metaphors, demonstrations, case studies, testimonials, FAQs, and endorsements, you must help your prospects see that their objection is simply not relevant in this situation.

Howie's objections around the treadmill desk include the following:

> It looks flimsy. Will it really hold a 24" iMac and second monitor?

> Will it really accommodate the treadmill I just got on Craigslist?

> How hard is it to put together? I'm really not very good with construction or following mechanical directions.

Someone who just found the violin in the attic may say, "I'm curious. For 50 bucks, sure, I'll get it fixed. But if it's going to cost $400, forget it. I don't even think I paid that much for it." Or someone might think, "Eh, why do it now? Times are tough. I'll wait until my job's more secure. I'll wait until I make some sales and get a nice commission check or bonus."

After you identify the objections, you answer them on your site. You may have to convince your prospect that waiting means that the value of the violin goes down further. It's going to be harder to resell and will cost more to fix later if you don't nip the instrument's degradation in the bud right now.

6. How can you eliminate their risk?

After you identify your prospects' their key objections, you can't just argue them away. After all, you're biased, and they know it. In addition to explanation and demonstration, you must also reverse whatever risk they're still feeling.

Human beings will do a lot more to prevent loss than to achieve gain. Every decision we make is monitored by a powerful subconscious brain program called DMTU (Don't Mess This Up). Its only job is to scan the environment and protect its owner from making decisions that could lead to danger of any kind. It's a super Avoid Pain circuit that can keep people from achieving great gains if there's any risk of a downside. Unless you speak directly to the DMTU voice in your prospect's brain, you won't get the conversion.

Clear policies and powerful guarantees are the best ways to address the DMTU voice. And while the entire marketing and sales process should include this message, the most important place to reinforce it is right next to the action spot on the site: the Buy Now button, the Send Me the Free Report form, the phone number — whatever your mechanism.

Testing: Removing the Pressure to Get It Right the First Time

Every keyword represents multiple pains, multiple desires, and multiple itches. Sometimes you can write an ad general enough to cover most of them. Sometimes you have to decide which specific problem to address. If you write an ad that's too general, it ends up being lukewarm — and unattractive — for everyone.

Suppose we want to advertise *Google AdWords For Dummies* for the keyword `adwords help`. What should the ad say? The generic response would be something like:

> Need AdWords Help?
> Read Google AdWords For Dummies
> It Will Solve Your Problems
> `VitruvianWay.com`

Now take a minute to decompress the keyword `adwords help`. The searcher may be struggling with AdWords campaigns that are almost at profitability, but not quite. For that prospect, we would promise simple ways to identify and plug profit leaks.

Others tried AdWords once, did everything wrong, and gave up. Then they read or heard something that made them think, "Gee, should I give this AdWords thingy another try?" That group needs an infusion of confidence through bold statements and relevant case studies. Still other prospects are professional AdWords consultants and campaign managers looking for a competitive advantage and best practices to scale their efforts and save time.

With a general keyword like `adwords help`, the first thing you want to discover is which approach is most profitable: the ad that attempts to speak to all these different prospects, or one particular message that ignores or even disqualifies the others. Will one group be more responsive than the others? Will one group view our offer as superior to the other options on the SERP? Will one group represent more valuable clients, willing to eventually hire us for campaign management and marketing strategy consulting?

The answer is found not by arguing, but by testing. When you formulate an experiment consisting of different ads that seek to appeal to each of these possible prospects, the market will tell you the most profitable approach.

Above all, remember that keyword decompression is a cyclical, not a linear process. Asking and answering the keyword decompression questions doesn't give you definitive answers right away. There's no such thing as a linear process in connecting a market to a business. Instead, think of it this way: "Ready, fire, aim." It's like trying to connect the U.S. Intercontinental Railroad, trying to get these two tracks to meet at precisely the right spot where you don't know where either one is starting. Luckily, digital assets like keywords, ads, and landing page headlines are a lot easier to change and move than steel, iron, and wood.

Keyword Decompression Sources

Keyword decompression is a fine art, like that of a safecracker listening carefully as she slowly moves tumblers back and forth, trying to generate the exact right positioning to unlock the safe and liberate the treasures. In our case, you're discovering desires (not combinations), and the feedback mechanism is clicks on your ads (not clicks of dials and cams). (Did you expect such poetry in a work of nonfiction? What a bargain!)

We show you a few powerful sources of data so you can see what's available, and how to begin to construct a loud and clear picture of human beings with desires from a few opaque and mute keywords. Because it's easier to understand the process using live examples, we'll demonstrate in depth for the keyword `Weber mandolin`. What you need to know about this keyword is that it represents a small Montana company that makes and sells high-end, gorgeous, hand-made instruments.

We're going to look at some advanced search engines for websites, forums, blogs, shopping, and online groups. The goal is to first eavesdrop on, and then contribute to the vibrant marketplace conversation about the problems its members are facing as well as the products and services designed to solve those problems.

Start by entering your search term into Google. Then, on the left side of the page, click the Show Search Tools link to expand the list, as shown in Figure 5-2.

Figure 5-2:
Use the powerful search tools in Google.

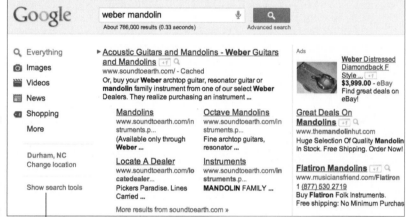

Show Search Tools link

Related Searches

Under the All Results heading, click the Related Searches link (lower left). At the top of the SERP that appears, you'll see a list of keywords that people who search for your main keyword also search for around the same time (see Figure 5-3). The related searches share a basic concept with the keyword. Sometimes the related terms share words with the keyword, but sometimes the connection is in intent and meaning — not the words themselves. In Figure 5-3, you can see related searches that include either `weber` or `mandolin`, but you also see phrases that don't have an obvious linguistic connection, like `folk of the wood`, `sound to earth`, and `greg boyd`.

We check Related Searches to see what Google defines as the scope of the market. Now we're looking at the list of keywords that are related in terms of meaning, not just similarity of words.

Figure 5-3:
Use Google
Related
Searches
to show you
the entire
search land-
scape for a
given topic.

 Check out the "related but dissimilar" (our name for them) keywords to round out your knowledge of this market. For example, FolkoftheWood.com (see Figure 5-4) turns out to be a website devoted to string band–type instruments, with a rural/rustic feel to it.

Here's the takeaway: You might take a clue from this site and others in the same market and develop your brand and message to include an "Appalachian" aesthetic: non-urban, old-fashioned, relaxed, self-reliant. The Internet may be cutting-edge and high-tech, but mandolin lovers still dream of an off-the-grid cabin in a pine forest.

Discussions and forums

Forums represent the uninhibited, living spirit of your market. There is no better use of your time as an online marketer scoping out a market than to hang out in forums and pay close attention to the content, language, frequency, and intensity of the discussions.

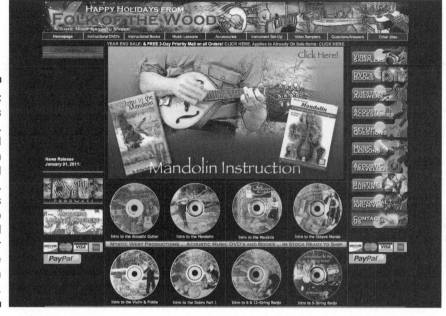

Figure 5-4:
This website, discovered through Related Searches, expresses a "back to nature" feel and flavor found in the mandolin market.

Google indexes forum discussions.

You can find this search feature by clicking the More link at the top left of the SERP and then clicking the Discussions link to turn Google into a forum search engine. Now the SERP serves up forum posts and replies closely related to your keyword.

Figure 5-5 shows two active forums: `macnichol.com`, with one active thread (as of April, 2011), and `resohangout.com`, which features a discussion of the quality of Weber mandolins with the most recent post from March, 2011.

Figure 5-6 shows a sample discussion thread from `mandolincafe.com`. Rich9236 wonders why some Webers sound awesome, but others sound unimpressive and dead. Notice his question about inconsistency, and then the clear objection to buying online in the third paragraph. Bob Andress confirms the experience in the first line of his reply. If you want to sell Webers, you might discover that from this and other forum threads, you need to offer a Try Before You Buy option that lasts for a couple of months. This information helps answer keyword decompression question #5, "Why won't they buy?"

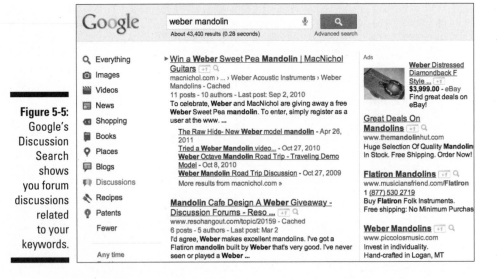

Figure 5-5:
Google's
Discussion
Search
shows
you forum
discussions
related
to your
keywords.

Figure 5-6:
Forums can
reveal the
unedited
desires,
fears, and
questions in
a market.

TIP

For more screenshots and analysis of forum discussions, check out `http://gafd3.com/forums`.

Pay closer attention to posts that generate the most responses. These are topics that people in this market are passionate about. Typically a post generates one or two answers, but occasionally a post turns into a debate. If you post to a mandolin forum saying, "I think the Gibson A mandolin is better than anything Weber has ever done," you will probably start a discussion that will continue through the next Ice Age. You can see from the long discussions what people are passionate about. Which ones are starting to show a little temper? Which ones contain long sentences as opposed to quick three-word answers?

Don't mistake forums for statistical reality

Realize that you're not using this data for statistical analysis. This is what is known as "anecdotal data." You're not going to look at a few forum threads and make sweeping generalizations about your market. Instead, you're gaining this deep market insight to learn about the individual prospects you'll be connecting with as a marketer and merchant.

Definitely pay attention to the numbers surrounding the sources because they will give you a sense of authority and importance and connectedness of each person. That is, a forum moderator with more than 5,000 posts is probably a better person to listen to than someone who wrote one question once. And forums with lots of activity are more representative of market sentiment than a tiny blog that nobody links to, comments on, or references.

Eavesdropping on your online market is similar to assembling a focus group, but it's better because they don't know we're watching. They're not posturing for us. They're being themselves, sharing much more of their true feelings than they would in polite company. A lot of content is generated anonymously, which gives people additional freedom to say what they really feel.

Balancing empathy and assertiveness

Discovering the spirit of our online market is an iterative process. ("Iterative" here is a fancy word meaning, "Make corrections based on feedback.") Remember the mantra, "Ready, fire, aim." This exploration paints a tentative picture of our market and gives us ideas about how to assert ourselves in that market.

We don't just say, "Okay, I understand my market, now I'm done with this research stuff. I'm going to market to them now, so I don't need to look and listen anymore." We're always going to be balancing empathy (curious listening) with assertiveness (responding), just like in a conversation. If we (you and us) were face to face and we were talking, unless one of us had some sort of social deficit, we would both know when one of us could interrupt, or when one person was about to stop and make room for the other to express. We would know by gesture, by intonation, by breath, by eye movements.

In our actual lives, we balance being empathic and hearing what the other person has to say with being assertive and saying something ourselves. And we do the same thing in marketing. There's just a bigger lag time, and we overshoot a lot because we don't have the intimacy and the cues of real time. Still, we're aiming to have a real conversation with our market, for our mutual benefit.

Staying current with Google Alerts

Market conversations change constantly, so it's important to keep your finger on the pulse of those conversations even after your initial market research. You can find these conversations in forums, on blogs, on websites, and in Twitter updates ("Tweets") for your keyword. Although Tweets by nature can't contain the richness of forum posts, they are good markers for breaking trends. People love to Tweet about things they love and hate. If Weber comes out with a new limited edition instrument, it's likely to be mentioned almost instantly on Twitter. Twitter updates also often contain links to blog posts, web pages, and other content of interest.

And although it's useful to glance at the Twitter activity in a market prior to entering, this is one area where you must stay current. If you plan on making a home in a particular market, set up Google Alerts or Google Reader to keep you informed of industry trends on a daily basis.

✔ **Google Alerts:** At `google.com/alerts`, you can instruct Google to e-mail you whenever it indexes a new page or update or forum post that contains your keyword. Create a folder in your e-mail client to collect the alerts and then explore them at your leisure.

✔ **Google Reader:** With this free service (`google.com/reader`) you can collect mentions of your keyword on the Web. Figure 5-7 shows an alert set up to monitor the keyword "skateboarding injuries" for G-Form. Just a few seconds' glance will give you a sense of the conversation and the people most involved in it.

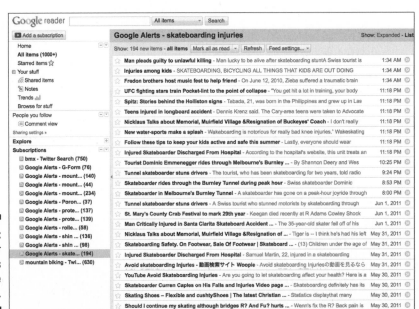

Figure 5-7: Monitor keywords with Google Alerts.

Other keyword decompression sources

Not all the sources in this chapter will be relevant to every keyword or market. Our invitation to you is to poke around with the six keyword decompression questions in your mind. Two other Google search engines to check out on your own include Blogs and Shopping.

- **Blogs:** On the left side of the Google SERP, just above Realtime, click the Blogs link. You're looking for the authority blogs — the voices that frame the issues and influence your prospects. Often, the comments on those blogs contain rich data on the desires and fears of your market.

- **Shopping:** If you sell physical products or if you provide services for a market that includes physical products, you can use the Google Shopping engine to find the most popular and profitable products in that market. If the Shopping link isn't visible, click the More link to expand the left side of the SERP; then click Shopping.

  You can refine the search by features, price, brand, and store; and sort results by relevance or price (starting high or low). This data is helpful if you are wondering what products to offer; what to repair; or what to support, teach, or consult on.

Online groups

Groups are essentially forums, but many groups' discussions aren't get indexed by Google because they're accessible to members only. So, you have to search indirectly, finding the relevant groups and then joining them to see and participate in discussions. The two biggest search engines for groups are Yahoo! and Google:

- http://groups.yahoo.com
- http://groups.google.com

 This is not a linear task. There's no numbered checklist here. Enjoy the experience of wandering. Allow yourself to get lost in forums, blogs, sites. Follow hunches and intuition. Don't take anyone or anything too seriously — especially yourself!

Visiting (and sleeping with) the enemy

Your competitors' sites are another rich source of market data. Before building your AdWords campaign, click every organic link for your main keywords and visit those sites. After all, for you to be successful for a given keyword, you must be able to articulate and deliver on offers that compel enough searchers to choose you instead of them. Your savviest competitors will have done a lot of your research for you. Check out their headlines, testimonials, offers, prices, and FAQs. If they have public customer forums (many software companies do, for support purposes), see what problems their customers are complaining about.

Do the same with the AdWords ads, but please don't click your competitors' ads and charge them money to do your research (bad karma). Instead, visit their sites directly by entering the main URL into the browser and navigating to the page related to your keyword. (If you're not sure, you can click the magnifying glass icon next to any ad to view a preview of the landing page.)

But don't stop there. If you can afford it, buy from them and get into their sales funnel. You heard us: Buy something from your competitor. That way, you can discover how they treat their customers, and whether (and how) they try to grow the relationship. You may discover that their initial sale is a *loss leader* — that is; they lose money on the front end because they have an effective system for selling additional products on the back end.

Look, then, for the answers to these questions: Do they send e-mail offers for additional products? Give coupon codes for dollars off? Request feedback? Ship promptly? Does the merchandise do what they say it does?

So what do you do if your competitors do everything right? Here's a little online marketing secret: Your competitors are also your best potential business partners. If you can figure out how to share customers, everyone can increase profits by promoting different offers to different market segments. You can play nice with competitors only when you can figure out ways to differentiate yourself from them.

Cutting through the Clutter with Positioning

You know how big your potential market is. You know how hungry your potential customers are. You've discovered what they care about, and what frustrates them about the existing situation and options. You figured out what kind of pricing structure and market response you need to be profitable. And you scoped out the competition to see what needs are not yet being filled.

Armed with this information, you're now ready to construct the most important sentence in the life of your business: your positioning statement. Basically, this statement answers the burning question in your prospect's mind: "Why should I do business with you instead of all my other options?"

Last week, Howie was driving a tad over the speed limit when a police officer kindly flagged him down and informed him of that fact. To help Howie remember to drive more slowly, the officer handed him a ticket and circled a court date. Within two days, Howie received 11 lawyer letters offering to take the case. Ten of them were virtually identical. To paraphrase slightly: "Dear Mr. Jacobson: You received a speeding ticket and it can skyrocket your insurance rates and ruin your life if you don't hire us." Most of them touted their low rates, essentially competing to be the Wal-Mart of law firms. The letter that attracted Howie began very differently from the rest:

> *Over the course of the next several weeks you will be bombarded with letters from attorneys. . . . What to make of this?*
>
> *First, a lot of trees have been killed to solicit your business.*
>
> *Second, there are too many lawyers in North Carolina.*
>
> *Third, if you call every lawyer that sends you a letter, you will probably waste several hours.*

This lawyer understands positioning. He used the fact of a crowded and undifferentiated market to speak differently, form a personal bond, and stand out from the rest of the crowd of lawyers all scrambling to say the same thing. After this opening, he explained the difference between his practice and the rest:

> *If price is the bottom line, wait for about a week and accumulate all the letters; then call those who are pitching low price representation. We are not the cheapest. If it is important to you to work with an experienced attorney who will fully explain and document the transaction, and who you can reach on the phone, then give us a call.*

Whatever your business, you must find a concise way of differentiating it from your AdWords competitors if you want to stand out on the crowded search results page.

Your ad copy, your website, your e-mails, the way you answer your telephone — all these marketing elements must flow from your positioning. The easiest way to establish top positioning is to carve a market segment that no one else has claimed.

For example, many merchants compete in the fitness space. That niche is far too big to attack with limited resources. What about home gym equipment? Also big — and full of established competitors. What about home gym equipment for parents with young children? Indoor playgrounds the size of a home gym that both parents and toddlers can enjoy safely — and that parents can use for a real workout while watching their kids? No company I've ever heard of has told *that* story before. If your research tells you that parents with young children are frustrated about their exercise options, you may stake your fitness-industry positioning on catering to that market.

You may find that your initial idea doesn't fly. But, as you watch the market, you'll discover things that customers will search for and buy. And your positioning, based on those discoveries, will make you the obvious choice when they see your Google ad.

Ken McCarthy's position on positioning

Marketing master Ken McCarthy (`The SystemSeminar.com`) explains positioning this way:

> Your goal as a business is very simple: You want your offer to occupy a *completely unique place* in your prospect's mind and you want to figure out how to telegraph that unique value in seconds.

> Positioning is not just about building a better mousetrap (or creating a better ad), it's about figuring out where your offer fits in the market space and why you're uniquely qualified to hold a place in it. Successful advertising consists of communicating that message simply and powerfully, over and over again.

> Let me give you two examples of how this works. The ultimate romantic city destination for lovers — what place pops into your mind? Probably Paris.

> An innovative computer hardware company that's especially friendly to creative types — which company is already there staking out that space? Probably Apple.

> A good rule of thumb is that there's probably only one space per category in everyone's mind. Second place is the same as last place.

> Your mission as a smart marketer is to go boldly where few marketers tread and figure out what place your offer can *own* and then make sure every ad you run reinforces that message. Positioning is the thing that separates the marketers who are standing on the winner's platform from the ones who are perennially treading water.

Ken McCarthy likens online market research to sitting next to a busy road and watching the cars go by. First you find the potholes by seeing what people want and aren't getting. Then you create products and marketing messages to fill those potholes.

Chapter 6

Measuring What Matters with Conversion Tracking

Say you're testing two ads, and one gets a click-through rate (CTR) of 1.00%, while the other attracts only 0.77%. The first ad is definitely a keeper, right? Without conversion tracking, you might think so. But what if the first ad attracts lots of nonbuyers, and the second ad gets clicks from buyers? Remember that a click on your ad means one thing: You just paid Google. When you think about it this way, your AdWords strategy shifts from trying to get the highest CTR to enticing only the most qualified prospects to your site. And to tell which ad leads to leads and sales — not just clicks — you need to install conversion tracking. And that's precisely what this chapter shows you how to do.

A *conversion* simply refers to an action that you want a visitor to take on your website. When you can track a visitor's actions on your site, you know what clicks lead to positive outcomes: sales, opt-ins, software downloads, requests for more information, and so on. Conversion tracking also allows you to bid intelligently on keywords. You may find that a high-traffic keyword that's costing you a lot of money isn't actually generating leads and sales. You can then lower your bid, change your offer, or fire the keyword. Without conversion tracking, all your campaign-management efforts are shots in the dark, tinkering with inputs without really knowing what's happening at the other end. It's like shooting free throws in basketball with no feedback about whether your shot went in or missed left, right, too far, or too short.

Conversion tracking is simply a snippet of code added to your website that places a cookie on your visitors' computers. This cookie tells Google where the visitors came from, down to the keyword and the ad, and what they did on your site. You can see which ads and keywords are making you money and which aren't. In this chapter, we show you how to set up conversion tracking correctly. (Do it wrong, and you'll suffer from the GIGO — Garbage In, Garbage Out — Syndrome and make lots of bad decisions.) You see how to read and interpret the data generated by conversion tracking. Most of the optimization techniques in the rest of this book depend upon getting accurate conversion metrics, so this step is truly foundational to your AdWords success. Finally, we share alternative methods of counting conversions when online tracking isn't possible (like phone sales and walk-ins).

Setting Up Conversion Tracking

Setting up conversion tracking in Google AdWords is a cinch. Here's how:

1. **Click the Reporting and Tools tab and Choose Conversions from the drop-down list.**

2. **On the next page, click the New Conversion button.**

3. **Name your conversion and then click the Save and Continue button.**

4. **Choose a conversion category from the drop-down list.**

   Google identifies five types of conversions that you can track: sales, leads, signups, views of a page, and other. We're going to keep things simple by using just two types: sales and leads.

   • *Purchase/Sale:* If you sell products online, you can determine exactly how much money you make from each ad and keyword.

   • *Lead:* If you collect contact information so you can follow up with website visitors, you can track leads. If you don't sell products online but use the Web mostly for lead generation, you can get very powerful information on cost-per-lead for your ads and keywords.

5. **Change the page security level to HTTPS from the drop-down list.**

6. **Unless you really know what you're doing or your webmaster instructs you otherwise, keep the markup language as HTML.**

7. **If you know the monetary value of a conversion, enter it in the Conversion Value field. If not, leave it blank. If you'll be tracking both leads and sales, set lead revenue to 0 to avoid data contamination.**

8. **(Optional) Configure the tracking indicator.**

   Google recommends adding a small block of text that lets your website visitors know that Google is monitoring their online activity. If you wish, select the page language (Arabic, Bulgarian, English, and so on) and background color. Google automatically adjusts the text color — either white or black — to be visible against the background you choose. At this writing, the tracking indicator is optional. To opt out, select the Don't Add a Notification to the Code Generated for My Page radio button.

9. **Click the Save and Continue button.**

   In Figure 6-1, we're tracking sales of G-Form's Extreme Sleeve for the 13" MacBook Pro, so we choose Purchase/Sale as the tracking purpose. A useful convention is to include the word SALE or LEAD in the name of each conversion, so you can easily find the tracking code and interpret the statistics later.

   You can create conversions of many different values. If you sell three versions of the same product, you can put different-valued conversion code on the thank-you page for each version, as shown in Table 6-1. (A more elegant but technically advanced solution is to feed your shopping cart data directly into AdWords — see "Tracking sales from a shopping cart" for more information.)

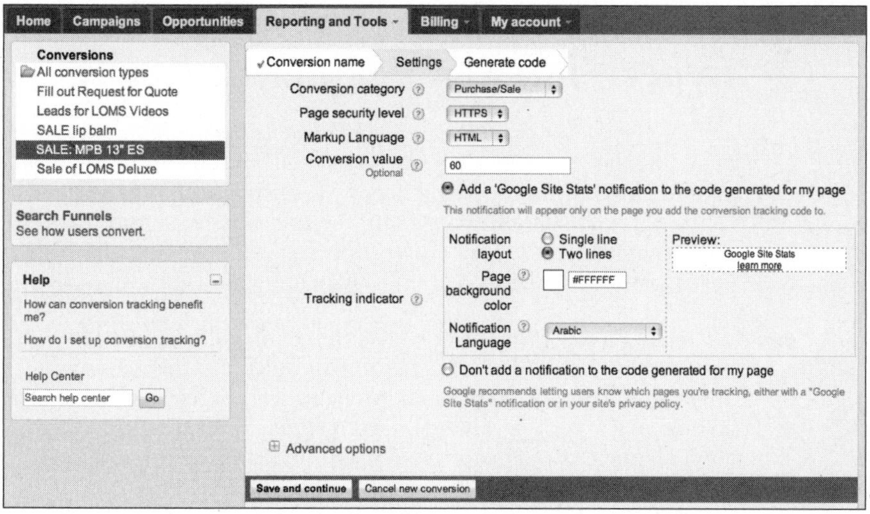

Figure 6-1: Name and categorize your conversion.

Table 6-1		Sample Conversion Values by Product	
Product	*Price*	*"Thank You for Buying" Page*	*Conversion Code Value*
Product A: Basic	$17	`/productAthanks.html`	17
Product B: Value	$97	`/productBthanks.html`	97
Product C: Deluxe	$497	`/productCthanks.html`	497

If you can track the value of each conversion, the knowledge you gain can dramatically improve your AdWords results. One client installed conversion tracking with specific values on February 7, and by March 31 had slashed monthly AdWords spending by almost $14,000 — without sacrificing any profit. We simply eliminated all the keywords and ads that weren't leading to sales. You will also use conversion data to fine-tune your bids for maximum return on investment (ROI).

10. **Check the appropriate radio button to let Google know how to give you the tracking code; then click Done to get the code.**

Generating and copying the code

If you tell Google to send the code to your webmaster, you'll see an e-mail form including the code and with suggested instructions for your webmaster. If you plan to insert the code yourself, copy the entire contents of the code box (see Figure 6-2) and paste the code into the relevant conversion page (the one your visitor lands on right after converting. For example, if you're tracking sales, you'd insert the code into your Thanks for Your Purchase page.

We recommend copying the conversion code and pasting it into a plain text document (a `.txt` file, not a `.doc` or an `.rtf` file) for safekeeping, rather than immediately dropping the code into your web page. That way, you have a saved version of the code if you ever need it again. Make sure you give the text document an obvious but descriptive name, such as `Google Conv Tracking.txt`. Don't save the code in a Microsoft Word format such as `.doc` or `.docx` because those formats add filler code that can render the code ineffective.

Now click the Campaigns tab at the top left of the AdWords dashboard. You should see four new columns — Conv. (1-per-click), Cost/Conv. (1-per-click), Conv. rate (1-per-click) and View-through Conv — filled completely with zeroes. (We explain these new columns a bit later in this chapter.) When you place the code on your website and start generating conversions, Google replaces the zeroes with actual data.

Figure 6-2:
Select and copy the entire code snippet to place it on your Thank You page.

Putting code on your website

The code snippet goes on the web page that your visitors reach *after* successfully taking the action you're measuring. In other words, if you want them to opt in, the code goes on the Thank You for Opting In page. For conversion tracking to be accurate, two things must be true about this page:

✔ Every visitor who performs the desired action goes to the confirmation page (into which you insert the conversion code) following that action.

✔ A visitor who doesn't perform the desired action will not get to the confirmation page.

Where to place the snippet

The conversion-tracking code should go just above the `</body>` tag on your confirmation page, as in Figure 6-3.

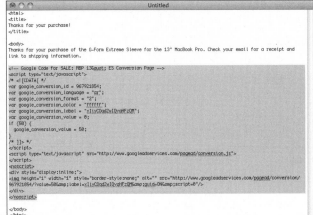

Figure 6-3:
Place the conversion tracking code in your HTML editor.

Visit `www.gafd3.com/conversioncode` for a video tutorial on putting code on your website.

Common tracking-code mistakes

To help you avoid some common mishaps, the following list gives you a run-down of mistakes people make when inserting the conversion code:

✔ **Putting the code in the header or footer:** If you place the tracking code in the header or footer of a page, it may show up on every single page in your website. Every page view will then be counted as a conversion.

✔ **Putting code on the wrong page:** Don't put the tracking code on the conversion page itself, but on the page that's served following successful conversion.

✔ **Putting the code on the same page multiple times:** With complicated web pages, it's easy to forget that you already placed the tracking code on the page.

If you're not sure whether your tracking code is on your web page, view the source code of the page. Here's the drill:

1. **Choose View➪Source in your browser.**

   The source code appears in a text editor window.

2. **Choose Edit➪Find and then enter Google Code in the Find What text box.**

3. **Click the Find Next button to search the code.**

Tracking sales from a shopping cart

You can configure conversion tracking to record the total amount your visitors spend by using dynamic fields generated by your e-commerce system. For example, if you use Yahoo! Stores or eBay/PayPal shops, you can modify the code snippet to tell Google how much a visitor spent on your site. You can also get this information from a shopping cart written in ASP (Active Server Pages), JSP (Sun Java Server Pages), or PHP.

See Chapter 17 for more on the power of this level of tracking.

If you aren't a proficient coder (if you don't know the difference between ASP, JSP, and RSVP, for example), please don't try this yourself. Send your webmaster to `https://adwords.google.com/select.setup.pdf` for full documentation on configuring dynamic shopping carts for conversion tracking.

Testing conversion tracking

To see whether Google is tracking the conversion you set up, you have two choices: the quick and (possibly) expensive way, or the natural way. The quickest way to confirm correct setup is to search Google for your keyword, click your ad, and perform the desired action. You should see that conversion in your campaign summary screen as a non-zero number somewhere in the six new columns (see the following section). If you don't want to waste a click, your other choice is to wait for a real visitor to convert, but we recommend spending the money yourself to confirm a correct setup right away.

Introducing the Conversion Columns

After you trigger conversion tracking by generating the code snippet, Google shows you four new columns (as shown in Figure 6-4) on the campaign management pages: Conv. (conversions), Cost/Conv. (cost per conversion), Conv. Rate (conversion rate), and View-through Conv. We're not going to talk about View-through Conversions, but instead focus on the other three.

These columns also appear at the ad group, keyword, placement, and ad levels, so you can see the effectiveness of every unit of your AdWords account. Until you place the conversion code on your site and visitors start converting, you will see zeroes in those columns. Also, expect a 24-hour delay in reporting a conversion.

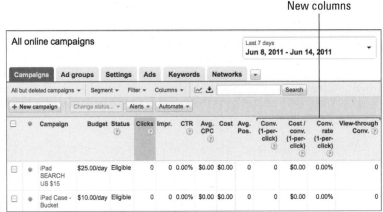

Figure 6-4:
New columns appear after you initiate conversion tracking.

Conv.

These columns tell you how many conversions were generated by the element in that row: campaign, ad group, keyword, placement, or ad. In Figure 6-5, we show a client account of ours (`http://continuingedexpress.com`; they provide ongoing real estate education) to show you what your account will look like when you start generating conversions. You can see four ad groups in the campaign, all of which have led to conversions. The Continuing Ed Express ad group generated 64 1-per-click conversions.

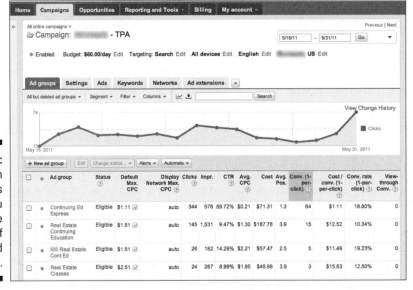

Figure 6-5:
Conversion statistics help you calculate the ROI of your ad groups.

"1-per-click" refers to the number of conversions that Google tracks off a single click. For example, if Cedric comes to your site from an AdWords ad, downloads your free report, and then buys your product, that would actually be two different conversions. The 1-per-click statistic would count that as one conversion. Another statistic, many-per-click conversions, is hidden by default so as not to confuse you. Probably good to keep it that way and focus your attention on the 1-per-click metric.

Cost/Conv.

The second new metric, Cost/Conv., refers to how much you spent on AdWords, on average, for each conversion. As you can see in Figure 6-5, the Continuing Ed Express group spent $1.11, on average, for each new customer. Whether that's good or bad depends on how much a new customer is worth to you. We aren't going to share that kind of data about our client, though, so we'll just make up a number for the purpose of this discussion: Say that each new customer is worth $20. In that case, spending $1.11 to earn $20 is a fantastic ROI. You want as much of that traffic as you can possibly get.

The Real Estate Continuing Education ad group is bringing in customers for $12.52 each, or a profit of $7.48 per conversion. Still okay, but not as good as the first group. In general, the lower this number, the better you're doing. The exception is when the cost-per-conversion is zero.

The Cost/Conv. metric is the single most important number in your AdWords account. If you measure accurately and track diligently, you can use this number to raise or lower bids, end or expand experiments, and find the sweet spot when your marketing achieves the greatest impact and ROI.

Conv. Rate

The *conversion rate* is the percent of visitors from that campaign, ad group, ad, or keyword who complete a conversion. If you get 100 visitors to your website, and three of them purchase a product, your conversion rate is 3%. In Figure 6-5, the first group, Continuing Ed Express, received 344 clicks, of whom 64 made a purchase. Google calculates the conversion rate of 18.60% by dividing 64 by 344.

We'll be referencing these conversion metrics throughout the book to guide you to optimize your AdWords campaigns and to expand those campaigns into other media.

Limits of conversion tracking

Here are two things to be aware of that can skew your conversion tracking numbers: cookies and inaccurate click attribution.

Cookie crumbles

As long as your visitors convert during the 30 days following their click, that conversion will show in your data. Conversion tracking is based on a technology called *cookies,* which are tiny snippets of code that Google places on searchers' computers.

This technology isn't foolproof, though. If someone clicks your ad on one computer but completes the conversion on a different computer, Google won't be able to connect the two events. In fact, even if the conversion occurs on the same computer — but on a different browser — Google is clueless that the two events are connected.

Some users are savvy enough to delete their cookies, and a very small percentage configures their browsers to block cookies or delete them automatically upon exit as a security measure; all these conditions will falsely decrease your conversion rate. Make sure to compare Google's number of conversions with your shopping cart or e-mail management software so you can determine whether Google is undercounting — and if so, by how much.

Unclear click attribution

If searchers click multiple ads before they convert, Google attributes that conversion to the last visit. For example, someone searches for drum set and then finds your site and looks around. A couple of days later, that same person searches for drum set for kids and returns to your site — and this time, purchases a drum set. The conversion will be attributed to the second keyword, [drum set for kids]. Big deal, right? Not so fast.

Just for kicks, pretend that 500 people conduct the exact same search pattern, starting with drum set but converting on drum set for kids. You could easily look at the conversion data and wrongly assume that [drum set] was a lousy keyword, generating lots of clicks (and racking up the costs), but not converting a single visitor. If you deleted that keyword, however, you'd probably find many fewer people purchasing drum sets off the longer tail keyword. Even though the first visit didn't generate the sale, it made visitors feel comfortable enough to purchase the second time around.

Click attribution is a complicated topic, and a full treatment here would require more chocolate than is good for us, as well as several dozen pages. So, we've taken this topic online, with a tutorial at www.gafd3.com/attribution.

Tracking Multiple Types of Conversions

As a best practice, we try to limit conversion tracking to one conversion type. Ask yourself: What is the most important action you want your visitor to take on your site that leads most directly to money in your pocket?

For example, say that you sell a product, and you also offer a newsletter to your visitors. The product sale is your money maker, and the newsletter is a way to keep in contact and possibly start a relationship with prospects to turn them into a customer. The key conversion here is the sale, not the signup. You want to measure sales to determine the ROI of your ads and keywords.

On the other hand, we have a number of clients who achieve great conversion rates in getting visitors to join their e-mail lists, and who nurture those leads over weeks and sometimes months. Even though the "money" conversion is a sale, we need to track leads as well so we don't accidentally do anything to depress that number. In that case, we're forced to track multiple conversion types, which makes everything that much more complicated. (But hey, that's why we get the big-but-extremely-reasonable-all-things-considered bucks.)

The data you see in the main interface merges all the conversion types that you're collecting. 1-per-click columns reflect unique customers. If someone signs up for an e-mail list and buys a product within 30 days of the last ad click, she converted twice, but Google adds just one to the 1-per-click column, signifying one new "converter." If you make two sales to two different visitors — say, one for $5 and the other for $5,000 — Google simply chalks up two 1-per-click conversions. The many-per-click column tallies total conversions, and doesn't care who made them. So, one person signing up for a newsletter and subsequently making a purchase counts as two in the many-per-click column.

The problem with tracking multiple conversion types is that you can no longer use the main AdWords interface to make ROI decisions about elements of your account. You need to break the data out by action, which Google allows you to do in two different places: the Conversions page and the Dimensions tab.

One of our clients, www.watercoloursecrets.com (they sell DVD sets to teach watercolor painting to beginners) has a business where the opt-in is extremely important — possibly even more important than the direct online sale. They found they can convert a visitor more often after sharing free information in return for an e-mail address and then market to their leads using other methods. In Figure 6-6, you can see that they have a lot of conversions, but you can't tell how many are free downloads versus sales. Take a minute to visit the Conversions page and the Dimensions tab to pull back the curtain on the real numbers.

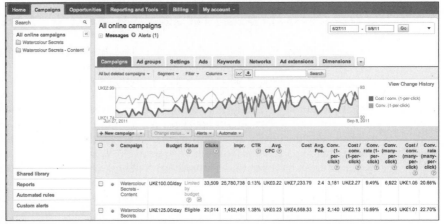

Figure 6-6:
The main
AdWords
interface
merges all
conversion
types
into one
aggregate
number.

The Conversions page and Dimensions tab

The Conversions page shows the total number of conversions by each conversion type. However, it's not categorized further — just the total for the date range you're looking at. In Figure 6-7, you can see two active conversion types: 4,864 free downloads and 68 sales.

Get to the Conversions page by clicking the Reporting and Tools tab at the top of the AdWords main interface and then selecting Conversions from the drop-down list.

You can get much more detailed and useful information from the Dimensions tab, which we cover in detail in Chapter 13.

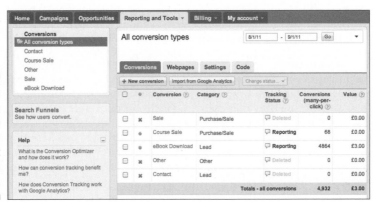

Figure 6-7:
The
Conversions
page
breaks out
conversions
by type.

Tracking Offline Conversions

Sometimes conversions occur offline, not on the website itself. When your desired action is a phone call or a walk-in visit to your location, measuring the ROI of your marketing is more challenging than a straight e-commerce sale or completion of an opt-in form. The good news is that because this type of measurement is more challenging, you're likely to have a greater advantage over your competitors who don't take this step. As Thomas Monson said, "When performance is measured, performance improves." (Or was it Jimi Hendrix?)

If one of the goals of your website is to get the phone to ring, you want to know which keywords and ads attracted the visitors who end up calling you and eventually buying. After all, big ticket sales like consulting contracts, real estate, and fractional jets don't get made via credit card on a web form; they require a personal touch that generally starts with a phone call.

AdWords conversion tracking gets triggered by the visitor landing on a page where you placed the conversion code snippet. Phone calls, as valuable as they are, don't get counted. But there are a couple of ways to solve this problem.

Deploying the fudge factor

A client of ours sells a service over the phone. The phone call can be initiated in one of two ways:

- The visitor sees the phone number on the landing page and places the call.
- The visitor completes a contact form and gets an outbound call.

The second scenario generates an AdWords conversion, while the first does not. By tracking the numbers over time, though, this client knows the relationship between calls and online leads. You can apply a "fudge factor" to the number of online conversions by assuming that each campaign element generates a similar ratio of offline and online conversions.

For example, if 75 percent of conversions come via the online form and 25 percent from direct phone calls, multiply all the online conversions by 1.67 to get the presumed total number of conversions for each campaign, ad group, keyword, and ad.

If phone calls prove to be more valuable than opt-in forms — after all, not every opt-in form leads to a completed phone call, and sometimes the prospect has "cooled off" after filling in the form — you can add an additional value multiplier. If every online lead is worth $200, on average, while a phone lead is worth $300, use a spreadsheet to determine the actual ROI of each keyword in your account.

Call-tracking software

What if all your conversions occur offline, so there's no fudge factor to apply? In that case, consider using one of several software solutions that connect phone calls to your AdWords account. Many of these services are available, costing from $1 per call (using Google's own call metrics, discussed in Chapter 13) to thousands of dollars per month for advanced tracking.

Vitruvian has used three different services on behalf of our clients over the past year: www.bionicclick.com, www.newcallsolutions.com, and www.public.ifbyphone.com. Ideally, the service you choose will import the call data back into AdWords, allowing you to view each call as a conversion and thereby make informed ROI decisions about bids and test results.

To find out more about call tracking services and see our latest experiences and recommendations, visit www.gafd3.com/calltracking.

Closing the loop with digital duct tape

If you can't afford call-tracking software or can't deploy it on your site for technical reasons, there are ways to close the loop that just require some extra work and some discipline. Remember that Google registers a conversion when someone who clicked your ad subsequently lands (via the same computer and browser, mind you) on a particular page where you placed the tracking code. Google doesn't care what happens in between those two events. So, if visitors call on the phone or visit your physical location, you can follow up and lead them to a page on your site where you placed the tracking code.

For example, you could end a phone call by manually capturing a visitor's e-mail address. (Advanced bonus tip: A good way to do this is to ask, "What's your e-mail address?) Then send them an e-mail containing a link to something valuable on your website, such as a coupon, a bonus report, a video of a panda sneezing (not recommended, actually), or an online user's manual. As long as this page has your tracking code on it, they will activate the cookie and register as a conversion, attributable to the keyword they entered and the ad they clicked. As long as they do this within 30 days of their original visit to your site, the conversion will be tracked.

Part III
Launching Your First Campaign

The 5th Wave   By Rich Tennant

In this part . . .

Although your ability to connect with your prospects will determine the ultimate success of your AdWords efforts, the structure of your AdWords campaigns will determine whether Google allows you to reach those prospects efficiently and affordably. After you create a campaign with the most appropriate structure for your goals, you can show your visitors attractive ads and compelling landing pages.

In Chapter 7, you find out how to navigate a dizzying array of settings, including which network(s) will display your ads, how to budget and set bid prices, where in the world and what time of day to show the ads, and others.

Chapter 8 shows you how to write effective ads, as well as how to use appropriate ad extensions to attract the right prospects and get them to click through to your website.

In Chapter 9, we cover the vital importance of dedicated landing pages that quickly begin scratching the itch expressed in the keyword and inflamed in the ad. You discover how to get your visitors to say "This is for me" within one second of their arrival at your site.

Chapter 7

Setting Up Your First Campaign

. . . .

In This Chapter

▶ Creating an account outline

▶ Separating campaigns by monetary value of a conversion

▶ Building smart ad groups

▶ Finding the right keywords

▶ Identifying your initial campaign goals

. . . .

*Y*our first AdWords campaign is like a first date. You want to make your best first impression on your prospects, so that AdWords can in turn make a great first impression on you by returning positive results. One of the biggest AdWords mistakes that we see is made by advertisers who create sloppy, hastily put-together campaigns and give up on AdWords after an unproductive first date. In this chapter, we show you how to prepare for a fun and profitable AdWords relationship.

In their defense, most new Google advertisers who create slapdash campaigns don't think they're spending their own money. Google is very generous in doling out free credits for new AdWords accounts, in amounts ranging from $50 to $250.

Behavioral economist Dan Ariely points out in his book *The Upside of Irrationality* that people treat money they already have differently than "found money," such as gift cards and casino winnings. Even though the dollar values may be identical, we tend to value found money less, and buy things less thoughtfully and responsibly than if we were putting our own money on the line. The mistake, Ariely explains, is that the found money now is our money, so it's irrational to treat it any differently.

And although $50 to $250 in free clicks is definitely an offer you shouldn't refuse, we'd like you accept it with this giant caveat: *Don't treat it like found money.* One of the biggest mistakes that we see beginners make is to develop careless AdWords habits with those first Google-subsidized clicks. Don't do it. Instead, put some time and thought into setting up your first real campaigns. That preparation can mean the difference between pouring a foundation for great success and a quick cash-burn failure that will leave you licking your wounds, wondering what you were thinking in ever trying AdWords.

Creating an Outline for Your Account

The best way to set up your account is to think of AdWords as an outline for your business, or at least those parts you'll be promoting via AdWords. Start by identifying the different campaigns, based on the value of each lead or sale.

In other words, every keyword in a given campaign should have roughly the same cost per action. In *other* other words, every visitor who arrives at your website from a particular campaign should be worth roughly the same amount of money, should they become a lead or make a purchase. That makes managing and optimizing your campaign using AdWords Editor (see Chapter 10) as simple as possible.

Explore this strategy with a hypothetical store that sells golf equipment, www.joesgolfshack.com. First, here's the typical (and wrong) way to start advertising: An advertiser who gets a $100 credit from Google jumps in without any planning and sets up a campaign called Golf Equipment. The advertiser then creates a single ad group called golf equipment, writes an ad, and throws in a bunch of keywords that all have to do with golf equipment:

[Golf clubs]

[Golf shoes]

[Golf bags]

[Golf carts]

[Golf balls]

[Golf bags]

[Golf clothes]

And brand-name variations of all the above.

Every visitor from that campaign is taken to the www.joesgolfshack.com home page, and must navigate to the particular item they're looking for. The initial results of this campaign? Based on our experience, that advertiser will quickly send $100 back to Google and make no sales. If that advertiser is committed enough to AdWords, he'll activate his own credit card and continue generating traffic to his site — and lose money. At some point, when the trend becomes too clear and expensive to ignore, he walks away from AdWords, muttering about "another online scam."

The AdWords outline

Instead of sloppily creating a campaign just to start showing your ads and getting website traffic, begin with an outline. We recommend that you not be logged into AdWords for this task. A pen and paper will do just fine.

First, identify your product line price points. Our imaginary golf site sells everything from a $7 bag of tees to a $2,000 electric cart. The goal of our campaign outline is to keep items of similar value together in one campaign — and, therefore, to keep items with different prices in different campaigns.

Here's why: You're going to manage your keyword bids (how much you're willing to pay Google for a click) by campaign. When you know that every keyword in a particular campaign is aiming for the same cost/conversion, you can manage thousands of keywords quickly. Simply filter and sort for keywords that don't meet your ROI requirements and reduce their bids. Likewise, you can raise your bids on keywords that provide inexpensive conversions so you increase their exposure and therefore make more sales.

When we go over the inventory of our golf store, we identify four basic product line value categories:

✔ Premium Products/Services (more than $1,000)

✔ Equipment ($200 to $500)

✔ Clothing ($50 to $200)

✔ Accessories (less than $20)

Guess what? We just identified our first four campaigns! A campaign is nothing more than a placeholder for ad groups. The ad groups are where we get analytical (wasn't that an Olivia Newton-John song?) and divide our campaigns into subcategories, or themes.

Continuing to build our outline, we expand the categories as follows:

1. Premium products/services (more than $1,000)

    1. Golf carts

    2. Training packages

    3. Premium club brands

2. Equipment ($200 to $500)

    1. Clubs

    2. Carrying bags

    3. Other equipment

3. Clothing ($50 to $200)

    1. Brand A shirts

    2. Brand B shirts

    3. Brand C shirts

    4. Shirts (general)

    5. Shoes

    6. Hats

  4. Accessories (less than $20)

    1. Gloves

    2. Tees

    3. Golf balls

Please note that this is just a start, and that we don't really know that much about golf. There are hundreds of additional categories of items (like the iPing Putting Cradle for the iPhone so the Putter App can analyze your stroke), and the price variability within categories is greater than this example. What's important here is the general concept, which can be applied to any business based on your actual numbers.

What do you do when a single product category runs the gamut of prices from very inexpensive to very expensive? How do you find a campaign for it? Sometimes you have to take the average sale and calibrate all the keywords to that number. For example, golf tees range from that $7 bag all the way to 1,000 logo-customized, environmentally friendly, surface geometry–enhanced Epoch-3 tees at around $100. In that case, the value of the generic `golf tees` keywords might be somewhere around $15 and would comprise an ad group within the Accessories (less than $20) campaign. Brand-specific keywords for the Epoch-3 might make up a different ad group within a $50–$200 campaign. In that case, the name "Clothing" might be too restrictive.

Writing ads and choosing keywords

After you spend time creating your campaign and ad group structure, the initial ads and keywords that will populate that structure are becoming obvious. We won't take up the space to flesh out this entire account; instead, look at a single ad group within a single campaign. When you understand the process, you can replicate it across your entire account.

And just for fun, assume that you're on a tight budget. Maybe you just want to spend that $100 Google credit for now, until you see some positive results. That would suggest starting with the least-expensive campaign, Accessories. Because the value of a visitor will be the lowest, these clicks are likely to be the cheapest ones you can buy. Within that campaign, start with Gloves.

Start with keywords

The AdWords interface demands that you create your ad first, but it makes logical sense to begin with your keywords. That's why we're sticking with pen and paper here, until the outline is complete. Think of it this way:

✔ **Keyword:** The *keyword* is what your visitor says when calling you on the phone.

✔ **Ad:** Your *ad* is what you say in response.

For example, for the keyword `golf gloves`, you're going to pretend that your visitor called your store and said, "I'm looking for golf gloves." Your ad is what you say back to them: "We sell many models in all sizes. If they don't fit like a, um, glove, we'll give you a full refund. And we have the lowest prices in town, guaranteed."

Begin by brainstorming keywords:

[gloves golf]	[golf gloves]	[gloves for golf]
[glove golf]	[lady golf gloves]	[footjoy golf gloves]
[champion golf gloves]	[leather golf gloves]	[ladies golf gloves]
[bionic glove golf]	[golf glove bionic]	[bionic golf glove]

Three important things about this list:

✔ **It's short.** Later in this chapter, we show you how to expand your keyword list using the Google Keyword tool, but for right now, we just want to give you the basic idea.

✔ **It's probably too broad.** If you discover that [ladies golf gloves] gets a lot of searches, you'll probably take all the ladies [golf glove] keywords and move them to their own ad group, and write ads specifically for those searchers.

✔ **Each keyword is surrounded by square brackets.** On a U.S. keyboard, you can find these to the right of the P key. Don't use the Shift key or you'll get the squiggly brackets — { } — which won't do at all.

The brackets tell Google that these keywords are exact match only. You want your ads to show only when a searcher enters one of these terms exactly as you typed it. You may add other match types that give Google a longer leash — after the exact match keywords are making money, that is — but for now, exact match gives you the most control and the highest chances of success.

Write at least two ads

One of our favorite parts of AdWords is how easy it is to test different messages. The engine of this testing is the ad group *split test,* which consists of pitting two ads against each other for the same traffic. Google automatically rotates the ads, so given enough traffic, you'll be able to see a clear winner, and then write new ads to beat that one. (See Chapter 14 for a full treatment of AdWords split testing.)

In the next section on campaign settings, we show you how to set up testing for maximum benefit. And in Chapter 8, we go into ad writing in depth. For now, write a couple of ads that each highlight one element of your hypothetical phone response to your visitor's keyword. In the preceding example, we saw the following messages:

- ✔ **Variety:** *Many models and all sizes*
- ✔ **Suitability:** *Perfect fit or refund*
- ✔ **Price competitiveness:** *Guaranteed lowest prices*

So, our three initial ads might look like this:

> **Golf Glove Superstore**
> 1000s of models in all sizes.
> Your one-stop golf glove shop.
> joesgolfshack.com/golf-gloves

> **Perfect Fit Golf Gloves**
> Helpful sizing chart guarantees
> Perfect fit or your money back.
> joesgolfshack.com/golf-gloves

> **Cheapest Golf Gloves**
> Get the best prices on golf gloves.
> Low price guarantee. Free shipping.
> joesgolfshack.com/golf-gloves

After you generate your initial keyword list and first set of ads, place them into an ad group within a campaign. The campaign settings that you choose have the power to make or break your efforts; Google's default settings all but guarantee expensive and rapid failure. In the next section, we show you how to tweak those settings for maximum control and safety.

Recommended Campaign Settings

The easiest way to explain how to set up your campaigns is to show you with screen shots. Because AdWords is constantly evolving, though, the images you see here may very well not match your screen perfectly. If you find yourself getting lost for that reason, visit www.gafd3.com/book for updated screenshots, video tutorials, and other AdWords resources.

Google AdWords is a wonderful tool, but its default settings give you a lot of power that you most likely don't need when just getting started. And not changing those default settings would be like drinking water from a fire hydrant. Sure, it can be done, but you're more likely to get hurt than just quench your thirst.

Creating Your First Active Campaign

Google's campaign settings all default to getting you the maximum traffic to your website. We love traffic as much as the next PPC agency (we finally get to play in it), but too much of the wrong traffic is a recipe for not making money. Because you pay per click, showing your ads to millions of the wrong visitors is a costly proposition. We'd rather you throttled the fire hose down to a drinking-fountain level.

Or, to use another water metaphor, have you ever showered in a strange bathroom where you weren't used to the hot and cold controls? And you stood in the shower, directly under the shower head, and turned the water on full blast? Maybe you were prudent enough to turn on the water first, observe for steam, and then timidly stick a finger under the stream checking for a temperature that would cause neither burns nor shrinkage? If the latter, then you'll prefer our AdWords strategy to Google's defaults.

Adjust campaign settings

If you already set up campaigns to assess search volume, you can either repurpose those campaigns or set up new ones. To keep things simple, we take you through the creation of a brand new campaign so you can tweak Google's default settings just as you'll do every time you create a new campaign.

In Chapter 13, we share an advanced AdWords tactic that we call "campaign cloning," in which you can quickly replicate campaign settings in new campaigns in a few seconds. In this chapter, however, we go over the fundamentals, so you understand why you're going to set things up this way.

In the AdWords interface, navigate to the Campaigns tab and click the New Campaign button just above the campaign data table. Google prompts you to select the settings for your new campaign. Ignore the Load Settings option at the top; we'll do everything manually for maximum control.

1. Name your campaign.

Your campaign name serves three functions:

✔ Tells you at a glance what it's about

✔ Contains keywords that make filtering simple in AdWords editor

✔ Guides you in setting individual keyword bids

We'll call the golf accessories campaign "Accessories SEARCH $20."

The first part of the name (Accessories) describes the content of the campaign. (If your store also sells tennis gear and wing suits, you would add "Golf" to the name to distinguish it.) The second part (SEARCH) tells you that this is a search network campaign. And the third part ($20) tells you how much you can afford to spend, on average, to make a sale.

When you clone campaigns, you'll expand on this naming protocol by adding fields signifying geography, scheduling, demographics, and other campaign-level settings.

2. Select locations and languages.

We recommend selecting one single country as the largest geographic area to select. Obviously, if you advertise in a local area only, drill down into that area. In Figure 7-1, the choices narrow the geographic reach of the campaign in descending order, beginning with Bundle: All Countries and Territories and ending with City: New York, NY, US. (Thanks, Peter, for lending Howie your office for his summer solstice writing marathon. Sorry about using up all the batteries in your wireless keyboard.) As a rule, don't choose higher than Country; using bundles eliminates the control and feedback you need to manage your bids effectively.

Choose the language that your customers use, and that your keywords and ads are in. Stick to a single language per campaign.

3. Select networks and devices.

Select the Let Me Choose radio button and then deselect the Search Partners and Display Network check boxes (see Figure 7-2). You should see a yellow warning box informing you that your ads won't show on these networks. Google may be sad, but you should be happy — for now. (Later in this chapter, we share an exception in which you select the Display network and avoid the Search network.)

Similarly, eliminate mobile devices like smartphones and tablets by selecting the Let Me Choose radio button and deselecting Mobile Devices with Full Internet Browsers. See Figure 7-3. Again, you should see a yellow warning box.

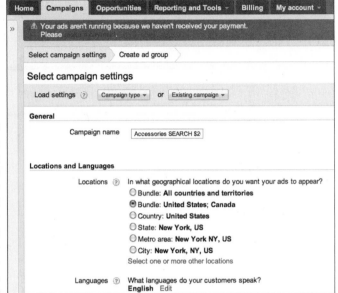

Figure 7-1:
Target at
the country
level or
smaller to
avoid poor
performance
and cross-
contamina-
tion of data.

Figure 7-2:
Keep away
from Search
Partners,
Display
Network,
and mobile
devices to
start.

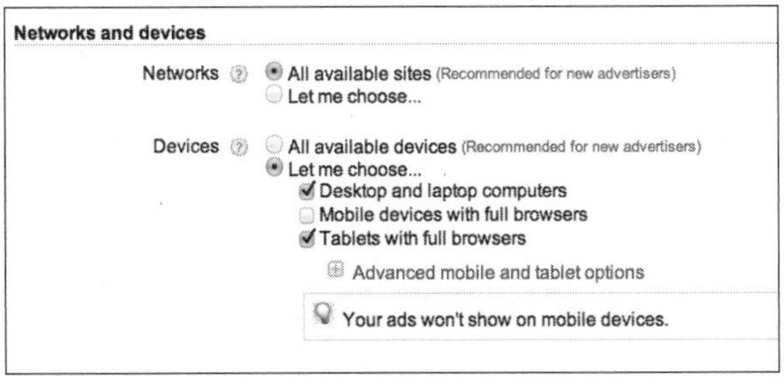

Figure 7-3:
You can
prevent
smartphones
from show-
ing your ads
in campaign
settings.

4. Set your bidding and budget.

Stick with manual bidding for clicks; automatic bidding removes you from the driver's seat entirely. Set your daily budget to a number that won't break your business. At this stage, although you're hoping to be profitable, your real goal is to reach the break-even point as quickly as possible so you can keep buying clicks and improving. Specify a budget that you can afford to lose each day. See Figure 7-4.

Next, click the link for Delivery Method (Advanced) and select the Standard delivery method: Show Ads Evenly over Time.

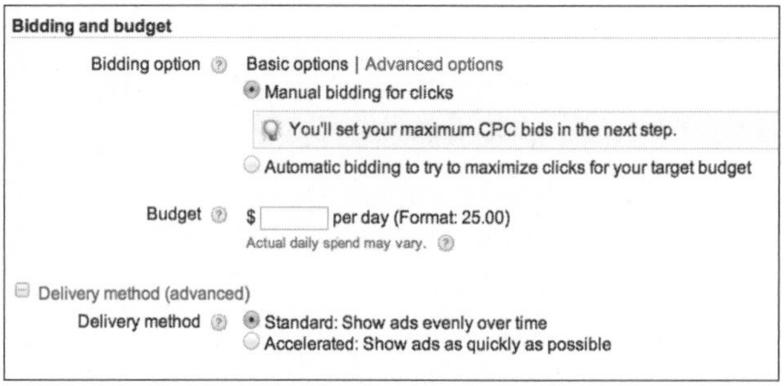

Figure 7-4:
Begin by showing your ads evenly throughout the day.

> **Bidding and budget**
>
> Bidding option ⑦   Basic options | Advanced options
>   ⦿ Manual bidding for clicks
>   💡 You'll set your maximum CPC bids in the next step.
>   ○ Automatic bidding to try to maximize clicks for your target budget
>
> Budget ⑦ $ [＿＿＿＿] per day (Format: 25.00)
>   Actual daily spend may vary. ⑦
>
> ⊟ Delivery method (advanced)
> Delivery method ⑦   ⦿ Standard: Show ads evenly over time
>   ○ Accelerated: Show ads as quickly as possible

Position preference is being retired by Google, so you might not have this option in your dashboard when you read this. (Ooh, that's so cool, writing to "future you." Could you e-mail Howie and remind him that he should exercise five times a week and lay off the sugar? Thanks.)

5. Skip the ad extensions for now.

6. Specify ad delivery options.

Under Advanced Settings, click the link for Ad Delivery: Ad Rotation, Frequency Capping and then select either Optimize for Conversions or Rotate: Show Ads More Evenly. If you set up and verified conversion tracking already, allow Google to optimize for conversions. It will save you time and money, and allow for much more aggressive testing and improvement. Otherwise, go with straight ad rotation. We almost never recommend enabling Optimize for Clicks, which is another way of saying, "Give more money to Google."

7. Click the Save and Continue button at the bottom of the page.

Congratulations! You just set up a container equipped to hold profitable ad groups. Now it's time to add the ads and keywords that you created in the outline earlier in this chapter.

Create the first ad group

After you save your campaign, name your first ad group and enter your first text ad. We'll call our hypothetical group "Golf Gloves" and enter the first of three ads that we created in the outlining/brainstorming phase.

1. **In the Ad Group Name field, name your ad group. See Figure 7-5.**

2. **Enter the ad text in the Create an Ad fields.**

3. **Enter your keywords in exact match in the Keywords text box.**

   You can enter your keywords directly, or copy and paste them from a spreadsheet or text file. See Chapter 2 for instructions on the mechanics of entering ad and keyword text.

4. **Enter Max. CPC (maximum cost per click) in the text box for Default Bid. See Figure 7-6.**

   If you already assessed your market as described in Chapter 4, then use the Max. CPC already proven to get you onto the first page of search results. If you aren't sure, enter any number you're comfortable with — you can always recalibrate later.

   Your default bid applies to each keyword in the ad group. You can later go in and adjust keyword bids individually, but you should do this only based on the data that shows you're over- or under-bidding. Chapter 10 covers this in detail.

Name this ad group

An ad group contains one or more ads and a set of related keywords. For best results, try to focus all the ads and keywords in this ad group on one product or service. Learn more about how to structure your account.

Ad group name: Golf Gloves

Create an ad

⦿ Text ad   ○ Image ad   ○ Display ad builder   ○ WAP mobile ad

To get started, just write your first ad below. Remember, you can always create more ads later. Help me write a great text ad.

Headline	Golf Glove Superstar
Description line 1	Helpful sizing chart guarantees
Description line 2	perfect fit or your money back.
Display URL ⍰	joesgolfshack.com/golf-gloves
Destination URL ⍰	http:// ⬍ joesgolfshack.com/golf-gloves

Ad preview: The following ad previews may be formatted slightly differently from what is shown to users. Learn more

Side ad
> Golf Glove Superstar
> Helpful sizing chart guarantees
> perfect fit or your money back.
> joesgolfshack.com/golf-gloves

Top ad
> Golf Glove Superstar
> Helpful sizing chart guarantees perfect fit or your money back.
> joesgolfshack.com/golf-gloves

Figure 7-5: Enter one of the ads you already brainstormed.

Keywords

⊟ Select keywords
Your ad can show on Google when people search for the keywords you choose here.

When creating your keyword list, think like your customers: how would they describe your products or services? Specific keywords (often containing 2-3 words) will help you show your ads to the most interested users. Try starting with 10-20 keywords. You can always expand or refine later. Help me choose effective keywords.

Enter one keyword per line. Add keywords by spreadsheet   No sample keywords available.

```
[gloves golf]
[golf gloves]
[gloves for golf]
[glove golf]
[lady golf gloves]
[footjoy golf gloves]
[champion golf gloves]
```

Estimate search traffic

⊞ Advanced option: match types

Important note: We cannot guarantee that these keywords will improve your campaign performance. We reserve the right to disapprove any keywords you add. You are responsible for the keywords you select and for ensuring that your use of the keywords does not violate any applicable laws.

Ad group default bids

Maximum cost per click (Max. CPC)
You can influence your ad's position by setting its maximum cost-per-click (CPC) bid. This bid is the highest price you're willing to pay when someone clicks on your ad. You'll input an initial bid below, but you can change your bid as often as you like. Try a bid now to get started, then revise it later based on how your ads perform.

Default bid ⑦ $ [1.25]

Figure 7-6:
Enter exact match keywords and your first Max. CPC bid to start showing your ads.

5. **Save the ad group.**

   You'll be taken to the Keywords tab of the ad group page.

Depending on your default bid, some of your keywords may be deemed "below first page bid," meaning that Google wants to you raise your bid in order to show your ad on the first page of search results. Don't do it yet, though, unless you're comfortable with the new bid amount. As long as some of your keywords are generating traffic, it's better to wait and see what you can afford to spend per click before turning into an AdWords high roller. And besides, sometimes Google gets it wrong, and your ads turn out to be so appealing that Google has no choice but to show ads for your *el cheapo* keywords on the first page, anyway.

Now, create additional ads.

1. **Click the Ads tab (just above the table of keywords) and then click the New Ad button just above the table of ads.**

2. **Select Text Ad from the drop-down list and change the auto-filled text to that of your second ad.**

3. **When the preview on the right is what you want, click the Save Ad button at the bottom left of the ad writing section of the page.**

4. **Repeat for each ad you want to test.**

Use only as many ads as your traffic will support. The more ads you run, the longer it will take to establish a winner. If you're in a low-traffic market, stick to a single split test (two very different ads) at a time.

Why can't I just deliver visitors to my home page?

Think of it this way: If you went to a grocery store and asked a clerk where the salt was, he could give you two potential answers. Which of the following would you find more helpful?

1. "It's right here in the store. Just look for the word 'salt' in one of the aisles. Duh!"

2. "Oh, it's on aisle 11 about half way down on your right, shoulder height. Would you like me to get that for you while you wait in line?"

The first answer is the equivalent of taking your visitors to your home page and making them poke around your site for what they're looking for. And although a few grocery shoppers might put up with that kind of customer disservice if you're the only store in town, your online competitors are always just a couple of clicks away.

Don't set the Destination URL as your home page if you have an internal page that is more relevant to your prospects' searches. Sending prospects straight to the most relevant internal page often improves conversion by 300–500% over sending them to the home page.

Creating multiple ad groups per campaign

How many ad groups should you have per campaign? Unfortunately, that's more of an "art" than a "science" question, and your answer relies on balancing the dynamic tension of both. The "science" has to do with the amount of traffic each ad group can generate. The more granular you make the ad groups — that is, the smaller you chop them up — the less traffic will flow into each group, and the longer you'll have to wait for conclusive test results and keyword ROI metrics. The scientist in you wants as few ad groups as possible.

The artist in you, on the other hand, prefers many different ad groups, each one containing a few very tightly related keywords. Your inner Picasso looks at the golf glove ad group and thinks, "I really need to separate these keywords into different groups so my ads can be highly relevant to each different market desire."

For example, someone searching for `ladies golf gloves` should see an ad specifically targeted to women. Each ad group keyword list needs to reflect a common desire. "Golf gloves for ladies" is a more specific desire than just "golf gloves," and a smart marketer would respond differently to the two requests. (Think again of the metaphor of the keyword as the phone call to your shop.)

Additionally, someone searching for a `lovejoy glove` is more likely to click an ad that mentions that brand name. Because a brand name search suggests a more advanced stage in the buying process, the content of the ad and the landing page need to cater to their current need for information.

Ben Hunt's excellent book *Convert!* includes a useful model he calls the Ladder of Awareness (see Figure 7-7). Every keyword in an ad group should ideally represent a searcher at the same level of awareness.

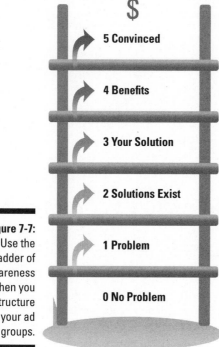

Figure 7-7:
Use the Ladder of Awareness when you structure your ad groups.

$

5 Convinced

4 Benefits

3 Your Solution

2 Solutions Exist

1 Problem

0 No Problem

Also, pay attention to differences of language as you create ad groups. Resist the temptation to translate synonyms in your mind and ignore the nuances. For example, `dallas real estate` and `dallas MLS search` might seem to be two different ways of articulating the same desire ("I'm looking for a house in Dallas"), but experiences shows that echoing search language in ads gets a much higher CTR. The ad on the bottom right of Figure 7-8 (Dallas, TX MLS Search) fades into the background against the two ads above it that both use Dallas Real Estate in the headline. (As an added bonus, keywords used in ads get bolded.)

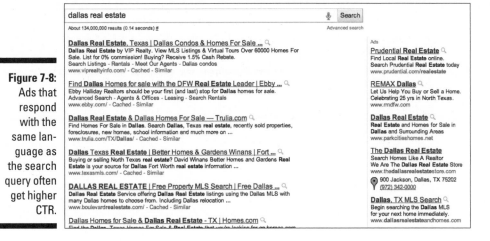

Figure 7-8:
Ads that respond with the same language as the search query often get higher CTR.

Picking a Network Based on Your Goals

We began this chapter by recommending a particular group of settings for your first campaign. These settings assume that your goal is to test a bunch of keywords to see if you can write ads and deploy web pages that can profitably turn those visitors into customers. We refer to this kind of campaign as the "Opposite of New York, New York." You know that line from the song, "If I can make it there, I'll make it anywhere"? This campaign is the inverse of that concept: If you can't make money selling to prospects who are actively searching for what you sell, and are using the exact keywords you specify, then you're definitely not going to succeed under less-ideal conditions.

However, your goals may require a different strategy and a different group of settings. Here are some variations that may fit your needs better.

Variation 1: Your site generates leads, not sales

If your website generates leads — not sales — and does so by means of an opt-in form where visitors leave some contact details in exchange for a report, white paper, or some other valuable information, then using the Display network will probably be more profitable than the Search network.

We still recommend starting with the Search campaign as we describe earlier, though. Because people are searching, you want to test different keywords and discover the profitable and unprofitable ones before spending a lot of money or muscle on search engine optimization (SEO). The Search network is also the most efficient place to test and improve the effectiveness of your website.

After you use this first Search campaign, with exact-match-only keywords to find the most promising keywords and to increase the conversion rate of your website, then you can set up a Display network campaign that may generate a lot more traffic at a lower cost. See Chapter 13 for the lowdown on setting and strategies for the Display network.

Never combine Search and Display networks in a single campaign. The goals of these campaigns are very different, and combining them into one is like yoking two donkeys together and asking them to pull in opposite directions. (No actual donkeys were harmed in the making of this metaphor.)

Variation 2: Nobody is searching for what you've got

Some businesses can't make a living off of Search because not enough people are searching. For example, a client of ours, Tantrum Kitesurf, runs what appears to be the most fun business in the world: Teaching people to kitesurf (look it up on Youtube if you've never heard of it before) on the beaches of Tarifa, Spain. Only two problems with their AdWords strategy: Most people have never heard of kitesurfing, and most people who have heard of kitesurfing don't know about Tarifa.

This means that Tantrum Kitesurf could run the world's greatest AdWords campaign but still receive only about a dozen clicks per month. Not only is that not enough to make a living on; it's not even enough to test and improve within AdWords.

To make AdWords pay, Tantrum Kitesurf needs to use the Display network to reach out to prospects who would be interested in a kitesurfing holiday in Tarifa — if they only knew what that was.

If the search volume for your products or services is very low, you don't have a choice: The Display network is the only place where you can run your ads and have prospects see them. But you need to appeal to a different mindset in Display. After all, you're engaged in interruption advertising, trying to draw people's attention away from what they're already doing on that page. You need to stoke their curiosity, promise a big benefit, and trigger strong emotions to get them to leave the page and visit your website.

You'll have a hard time getting your Display network visitors to pull their wallets out on a first visit. Because they weren't explicitly searching for you, you need to give them some time and cultivate a relationship before the vast majority of them will buy. So even if your website runs on a "wallet out" model (more on that in Chapter 1), you need to find a way to capture leads first.

So while Tantrum Kitesurf can offer online bookings to its visitors from Search, it needs to create a lead generation model for Display customers. This could include a request for a free DVD on Kitesurfing, a report on the best way to prepare for a kitesurfing vacation, or even a comparison of kitesurfing with the better known sports of windsurfing and lying on the beach.

Chapter 13 covers Display network strategies in detail.

Variation 3: Your business caters to a local market

If you run a local business, you generally have to give up the control that exact match keywords afford you because local markets don't provide enough search volume to accomplish effective keyword research and ad and landing page testing. In Chapter 13, we'll show you how to deploy some AdWords "worst practices" to succeed in local markets.

The Campaign Buildout Prime Directive

To repeat, the safest way to start using AdWords is to use Search network only and all-exact-match keywords. These settings remove all ambiguity, so you know exactly what you're getting and how much each element is contributing to your profit or loss.

Figure 7-9 shows a hypothetical (but very common) scenario in which the exact match keyword [supplements for women over 40] generates a sale at an average of $4.25 in click costs, whereas the phrase match of the same keyword generates a single sale after an average of $12.32, or almost four times the cost. Broad match requires $22.48 per sale, whereas the Display network cost jumps to $73.32 for a text ad and $125.54 for an image ad. Mobile ads generate sales at an average of $31.22, or more than seven times the cost of exact match.

Figure 7-9:
Starting
with the
Search
network and
exact match
only gives
you the best
chance of
initial
success.

Keyword	Type	Clicks	Avg CPC	Avg Position	Conv	Cost/Conv (CPA)
Supplements for Women over 40	Exact	194	$.35	3.4	16	$4.25
Supplements for Women over 40	Phrase	158	$.39	3.8	5	$12.32
Supplements for Women over 40	Broad	562	$.52	4.1	27	$22.48
Supplements for Women over 40	Display Text	326	$.45	4.5	2	$73.32
Supplements for Women over 40	Display Image	330	$.38	1.5	1	$125.54
Supplements for Women over 40	Mobile	69	$.45	1.3	1	$31.22
Total	All	1640	$.44	3.8	38	$19.09

The moral of this story can be found in the last line that totals clicks and conversion, while averaging the cost/conversion. If you had set up your first campaign the way Google recommends for new users, all you would see is a total cost per conversion of $19.09, or four and a half times more expensive than exact match. That's a major reason most advertisers give up on AdWords — they think the traffic is too expensive. Some of it is — but if this advertiser had followed our advice, he would be generating sales at $4.25 in click costs, giving him enough profit to start testing and improving his sales process to the point where he could begin to afford the more expensive networks.

After you master this basic campaign, your job is to expand ever outward into larger and less-controllable environments. Each expansion can provide additional traffic, but at higher and higher cost per conversion. In most cases, the expansion should proceed something like this:

 1. **Add the Search Partners network to your existing campaign.**

    Google doesn't allow you to show ads in the Search Partners network without also showing in Google search, and the effort involved in separating them out generally isn't worth it.

 2. **Clone (copy) your first campaign and change all the keywords to phrase match.**

    In Chapter 10, we show you how to clone entire campaigns in seconds using AdWords Editor.

 3. **Clone your first campaign and change all the keywords to Broad Match.**

 4. **Clone your first campaign and change the network from Search to Display.**

5. **Clone your Display Network campaign and replace text ads with image ads.**

   You can hire a graphic artist to create image ads, using the text that has proven most effective in your split tests (see Chapter 15), or you can use the free Image Ad Wizard (see Chapter 8).

6. **Clone your first campaign and change the network from computers to mobile devices.**

Chapter 8

Writing Magnetic Ads

. . . .

. . . .

*T*his sentence you're reading now contains the same number of characters — 130, including spaces — that Google allows in a text ad.

You get four lines of 25, 35, 35, and 35 characters to tell enough of your story to compel the right people to choose your ad over all the other ads and organic listings on the Google search page. If you're advertising on the content network, your ad is competing with articles, videos, games, and more. We've heard professional copywriters say that the Google ad is the most challenging form of salesmanship-in-print they've ever attempted.

Depressed? Don't be. Writing effective ads is hard for everyone, not just you. Spend some time preparing, practicing, and (especially) testing your ads, and you'll quickly rise to the top of your industry. As business philosopher Jim Rohn says, "Don't wish it were easier — wish you were better."

This chapter helps you stop wishing and start improving. First, we look at the two very different types of ads you'll be writing, depending on which network you target. Next, we reveal the three-pronged goal of your ad. Most advertisers focus on one prong only, to their detriment. You discover how to balance the first two goals for maximum profits by bringing in the right kind of traffic (not just the maximum possible traffic), and how to reach the third goal of setting visitor expectations so your prospects are primed for your website. Next, you discover how to tune your ad to your prospect's radio station, WII-FM (What's In It For Me?), based on the keyword. We share with you the missing link between your ad and your website — the call to action. We cover some basic strategies for effective ad writing, as well as a few top-secret (until now!)

"black belt" techniques that you'll need if you're playing in a hyper-competitive market. Finally, we introduce you to some alternatives to the standard text ad: image, mobile text, local business, and video ads.

Writing the Two Types of Ads

Here's a fun thought experiment: Imagine that it's a lazy Sunday morning in 1988, and you're at home when a water pipe bursts in your kitchen. Water is pouring out onto the floor so fast you fear for your collection of vintage Danelectro guitars and Marshall amps. You rush to the Yellow Pages (remember those?) and frantically thumb to the P section, briefly consider ordering pizza, and then remember what you're doing and find the listings for plumbers. The first listing you see includes a phone number, service area, weekend hours, license number, and a 30-minute emergency arrival guarantee. What do you do? Dial the number as fast as you can.

Now for a completely different scenario: It's a lazy Sunday morning in 1988, and you're at home browsing the sports section of the newspaper (remember those?). As you scan an article about the LA Dodgers playoff chances, you notice an ad for a local plumber. The ad looks like a Yellow Pages listing, including a phone number, service area, weekend hours, and so on. Do you jump off the couch, run to the phone, and dial that number? Of course not. You totally ignore the ad and return to the fascinating world of Major League Baseball.

How is it possible, then, that the same ad could perform so well in the first scenario and so poorly in the second? Easy; the burst pipe put the prospect in the mindset of searcher, who was actively looking for what the business provided. The second scenario involved an interruption of someone who had no prior interest in the offer.

In AdWords, the Search network corresponds to the burst pipe scenario, while the Display network parallels the sports section episode. That's one of the main reasons for separating Search and Display into separate campaigns: so you can write ads that are effective in each channel.

Permission advertising in the Search network

The Search network basically consists of people who want things right now, and ask questions about how to get those things. Every element on the search results page is there because Google thinks it will help a searcher quickly find exactly what they want. If your ad appears on that page, your job is to let the searcher know that you can help them. They're rooting for you; you have their permission to make an offer.

Offline analogs of the Search network include the Yellow Pages and classified ads.

Interruption advertising in the Display network

Within the Display network, your prospect is reading or watching video or looking at images or somehow interacting with material on somebody else's website, and your ad appears somewhere on the page. The Display network consists of what we call "interruption advertising" because you're attempting to interrupt that activity to compel prospects to visit your website. The offline equivalent is mass media advertising, such as television, radio, magazines, newspapers, and billboards.

Most of this chapter focuses on writing for the Search network. In most cases, the Search network is the best place to start, and it's the easiest to test and improve. The Checkmate Method (more on that later) of competitive positioning works best for Search, and after you master Search ads, the Display ads will be easy to write — as long as you understand the different requirements.

Understanding the Three Goals of Your Ad

A good ad attracts the right people — your best prospects — to your website. Your ad has three goals:

- ✔ Generate clicks from qualified visitors.
- ✔ Discourage the people who are unlikely to become your customers from clicking your ad.
- ✔ Set your prospects' expectations so that your website satisfies (and possibly even delights) them.

The following sections discuss these three goals in detail.

Attracting the right prospects

The AdWords medium encourages a stepladder approach. The job of the ad is to deliver drooling prospects to your website. Prospects don't even have to be drooling over what you want to sell them — just over what you're offering them in the ad. Sometimes the ad offer and the first sale are identical — selling a product they're searching for by name and model. Other times, you're dangling a magnet that will attract the quarters and ignore the wooden nickel.

Your four-line ad can't make a sale, any more than a door-to-door salesperson can ring the doorbell, utter one sentence, and sell a $1,000 vacuum cleaner. The first sentence is meant to make the prospect listen to the second sentence. Likewise, the Google ad isn't long enough to capture the prospects' attention, pique their interest, stoke their desire, and make them pull out their credit card. Let your website, e-mails, and phone calls accomplish the heavy lifting. Craft your ad to make or imply a promise that your landing page can keep.

Discouraging the wrong people

The rest of this chapter shows you how to write an attractive ad. Right now, though, we're going to tell you how to make your ad unattractive. After all, a click means you just paid Google. Clicks from the wrong people can cost you a lot of money without putting any of it back in your pocket.

You may remember magazine ads that featured a huge red headline of the word *sex*, with the subhead, "Now that I've got your attention . . ." The ad would go on to sell some product totally unrelated to the headline. Don't try that with AdWords. In cyberspace, folks are serious about their searches. If they feel misled by your ad, they'll cost you a click and never visit you again. For example

> Free Lindsay Lohan Pics
> Hundreds of exclusive photos
> and videos — all completely free!
> www.bootzrus.com/lindsaygoeswild

If your site actually sells custom inserts for cowboy boots, this ad will almost certainly achieve a higher click-through rate (CTR) than the more traditional ad that follows:

> Custom Cowboy Boot Inserts
> Instant relief of bunions and corns
> Cures athlete's foot — free shipping.
> www.bootzrus.com/cowboybootinserts

But how qualified is the traffic from the first ad? Aside from their anger at being duped when they arrive at a site featuring cowboys with corns and not the celebrity gossip or racy pictures they expected, how likely would they have been to *want* boot inserts in the first place?

The Lindsay mistake doesn't usually look that stark and ridiculous, but we see it all the time in our consulting practice. Big promises are great, but when they're too vague, they attract the wrong people. For example, NovaMind.com sells mind-mapping software to help writers and others brainstorm creatively and efficiently. Here's an ad that would probably beat all their other ads' CTRs, but wouldn't lead to many sales:

> Be More Creative
> Amazing Technique Helps You
> Brainstorm Brilliant Ideas
> www.novamind.com

This ad promises a big benefit — one that the software theoretically can deliver on — but doesn't qualify the benefit with any information that would allow someone to say, "Oh, that's not for me."

Here's a real ad:

> Mind Map Software
> Organize your Creative Thoughts and
> Mind. Download a Free Trial now!
> www.novamind.com

The headline states what the product is and by implication disqualifies people who don't own, like, or use computers. The free trial offer is appealing, but suggests that the product itself isn't free. *Free* is a powerful word and must be used cautiously in AdWords. People who have no desire to pay for something will still take something if it's free. If the ad had promised a free download without qualifying it as a *trial,* NovaMind would have increased CTR at the expense of the traffic quality.

Writing a personals ad

Think of your ad like a personals ad. If you're putting personals ads in local papers or Match.com, your goal isn't to attract every bozo in the county. Instead, you want to weed out the incompatibles and make every date a potential winner. Personals ads achieve this qualification by stating who should not apply:

> Divorced White Male, 53, in good health, seeks Single White Female, non-smoker, under 45; no cats or whistling cockroaches; must not be allergic to peanuts or mangos; must like Berlioz, Bartok, and organic kohlrabi.

Negative qualifiers not only weed out the wrong folks, but they also attract the right folks: "He's right — I could never live with a whistling cockroach. We're a lot alike. I wonder what he looks like. . . ."

Qualifying your visitor

Your ad can qualify based on location (Roslindale IT Consultant), price (Downloadable Book — $17.77), limited options (Red and Gold Only), platform (Not Mac-Compatible), profession (For Teachers), personality (No Whiners!), and many other characteristics.

For example, if you offer high-end, custom-designed jewelry, you don't want to pay for visitors looking for a $20 pair of earrings. You might use language like "designer," "high quality," or other terms that imply "expensive." Here's an interesting thing about disqualification: Do it right, and it actually attracts the people who are not disqualified. In the earlier personals ad example, the phrase "non-smoker" doesn't just tell smokers not to apply. It also tells non-smokers, "Gee, I think we might be a good fit based on our mutual dislike of second-hand smoke."

Disqualification is particularly important for business to business advertisers. Often, you can't separate the traffic by keyword. For example, a kitchen cabinet supplier that distributes its goods through contracting companies or architects might have to use the keyword [kitchen cabinets] even though 90 percent of the searchers might be consumers. In order to advertise profitably, the cabinet supplier needs to discourage the homeowner from clicking its ad because it doesn't have a business model equipped to profit from that inquiry. Using ad language like "Cabinetry for Builders" or "Supplying Quality Cabinets to Top Builders for 20 Years" would provide the appropriate slant.

Brainstorm a list of qualifiers by answering the question, "Who shouldn't buy from me?" If you sell a standalone version, and a prospect is searching for an enterprise edition, don't even waste a nickel of your cash or a minute of their time. If your keyword choices can't keep out your nonprospects, let your ad do it before they cost you money.

Which side do you want to err on?

Every ad has to choose between Mistake #1 and Mistake #2. Mistake #1 is the false-positive: Someone clicks who isn't your customer, meaning that you just wasted the click price. Mistake #2 is the false-negative: You send away someone who would have bought from you.

Which mistake is worse depends on how much each mistake costs you and how often it occurs. If your clicks cost 5 cents and your average sale is $800, you can afford a lot of false-positives (16,000 clicks at 5 cents each, to be exact) for each sale. On the other hand, if clicks cost $32 each, your campaign will hemorrhage cash if you aren't very particular about whom, exactly, you invite to your site.

Ultimately, the decision to widen or narrow the ad comes down to the value of a visitor from that ad to your website. One ad will simply make you more money (after subtracting your advertising funds spent) than all the others. Your mission is to keep writing ads until you find that one.

Telling your visitors what to expect

The third goal of your ad is to manage expectations. If your ad conveys playfulness, don't send your visitor to a dry and hyper-professional–looking landing page. If you advertise a free download, make it easy to find that download. If you highlight a benefit, focus the landing page on that benefit.

Show your prospect that you keep your promises, even the little ones that you make in your ads. Think of the ad as the headline of your landing page and make sure that it signals the precise benefit someone will get when she clicks through to your site.

What are visitors going to find? Free information? Training? Products to purchase? Professional services? Line them up so that the conversation in their head continues smoothly when they reach your site.

Using Permission (Search) Ads

As we show in the plumber example at the beginning of this chapter, permission and interruption ads have different approaches. Ads in the Search network need to understand and respond to the searcher's intent.

Tuning your ad to the Search intent

Imagine that your goal is to sell a photocopier to Al Schmendrick, a local business owner. Which ad headline has the best chance of success?

✔ Big Sale on Business Machines This Week

✔ Are You Tired of Clearing Paper Jams from Your Old Copier?

✔ Hey, Al Schmendrick: Are You Tired of Clearing Paper Jams from Your Old Copier?

If your kids' college tuition depended on the sale, you'd choose headline C in a heartbeat. Why? It's all about the prospect, and it's very likely to get his attention. In fact, if Al Schmendrick doesn't read the paper that day or skips the page that contains this ad, we'd bet that one of Al's friends will tell him about it.

The meta-message of your ad to your best prospect is, *"This ad is all about you."* Marketing consultant Dan Kennedy talks about the message-to-market match. The keyword defines the market — who they are and what they want. Your ad is the message that must address their self-identity and desires. As we talk about in Chapter 7, the tighter your ad groups, the more precisely your tone, message, and offer can match what each market will respond to.

Cutting through the cluttered search results page

The most important rule when trying to stand out in a crowd is, "When they zig, you zag." As you compose your ad, keep your prospect's big question in mind: "Why should I click your ad instead of all the other ads and organic listings on this page, instead of typing a different search term — and instead of blowing off this search entirely and logging on to Facebook for three hours?"

Using the Checkmate Matrix to study your competition

Vitruvian uses Howie's Checkmate Method of competitive analysis to find the "sweet spots" in the advertising landscape: you know, the niches that no competitor is targeting, the offer or emotional appeal that no competitor is making (see Figure 8-1). Search for your top 5 to 10 keywords and print the results pages. Then, for each page, complete the Checkmate Matrix to identify holes in the market. You can download the matrix and see examples of completed Checkmate analyses at www.gafd3.com/checkmate.

The main purpose of the Checkmate Matrix is two-fold. First, it gives you a vocabulary for analyzing the otherwise overwhelming search results page. Instead of staring at a sea of ads until your head spins, you have a tool for parsing the ads and nailing down their elements.

Second, the Matrix cleanses your mental palate by forcing you to focus on What Is for a while. Most of us approach ad writing with an agenda, like, "I really hope I write a good ad so I can pay the mortgage this month." Although that's natural, the goal-orientation can actually get in the way of our simply noticing the competitive landscape. The Matrix encourages you to put aside your anxieties and judgments, so you can clearly see the landscape in which you will place our own offer.

URL	Offer	Features	Benefits	Call to Action	Reason to Believe	Big Difference	"Voice"	Keyword

Figure 8-1:
The Checkmate Matrix offers a quick way to find strategic positioning in your search market.

Howie has taught the Checkmate Method in depth to hundreds of students, and one of the most powerful moments occurs after they complete the Matrix for the first time, before the next exercise. In most cases, ideas for powerful new ads spring up spontaneously as the workshop participants scan the completed Matrix. They suddenly "see" opportunities that their competitors are missing.

Complete the Checkmate Matrix as follows:

- **URL:** Write the domain of the ad URL to serve as a unique identifier for each ad. For an ad sending visitors to a page at g-form.com, you'd write **g-form.com**.

- **Offer:** What will the searcher get for clicking the ad? A product? A service? A free consultation? An online demo? The offer is the tangible thing or experience that the advertiser is promising. Not all ads contain explicit offers, so if you can't find one, no worries.

- **Features:** What are the stated facts about the offer? Most ads consist mostly of features, such as price, selection, free shipping, product specs, years in business, brand names, and so on.

- **Benefits:** What does the searcher achieve as a result of the features? Most ads are quite light on benefits. Sometimes this is appropriate if the market understands the benefits and is looking for a price differentiator. Other times, you can gain a huge advantage by stating benefits when all your competitors are going on about the features.

- **Call to Action:** What does the ad ask the searcher to do? Calls to action include imperative (command) verbs like "shop," "see," "order," "try," and "find," as well as urgency elements such as "today only" and "limited supply." Many ads lack a call to action; again, this is neither good nor bad in general, but something to notice as you strive for unique positioning.

- **Reason to Believe:** What are the elements of the ad that lend credibility to the offer or the benefits? Years in business; words like "authentic," "proven," and "original"; endorsements and testimonials; and strong brand URLs like Jenny Craig (`http://jennycraig.com`) are all designed to help the skeptical searcher suspend disbelief long enough to click the ad.

- **Big Difference:** How is this ad different from all the other ads? If you were to divide all the ads into two groups, with this ad in one group and all the other ads in the second group, how would you justify the split? Often, this is a hard exercise — not because you're not good at it, but because so many ads swim in a sea of sameness, completely undifferentiated from each other.

- **Voice:** If you were to hear the ad spoken, whose voice would you hear? An over-caffeinated used car salesman? A caring grandmother? An impartial news anchor? A giddy talk show host? A laid-back surfer dude? Most people hear words in their heads as they read. If the words of your ad can trigger the voice of someone they instinctively respect and trust, you have a huge advantage over the vast majority of "voiceless" ads that lack all passion and personality.

✔ **Keyword:** Just note whether the keyword appears in the ad. Leave it blank if the keyword does not appear, enter **1** if it appears once, and **++** if it appears more than once.

Don't get hung up on doing the Matrix "correctly." However you do it is perfectly fine. If you can't decide whether something is a feature or benefit based on our definition, just choose one. It truly doesn't matter. If you discover that the same element of the ad is a feature, a benefit, a reason to believe, and a big difference — no worries. That happens.

We recommend completing a Checkmate Matrix for at least five competitors per keyword. If you have thousands of keywords, don't despair. Choose one main keyword per ad group, and start with the ad groups likely to bring in the most traffic or the highest profits.

Positioning your offer

After you complete the Matrix, examine it for holes. First, look for visual holes in the table. Are any columns empty? If so, you can differentiate your ad by including that element. Second, look for what isn't being said. Are there market segments who are being ignored? Features that aren't being turned into benefits? Not a single ad with a personality? Does every ad include the keyword in the headline? If so, you have a big opportunity to stand out with a benefit-driven headline.

Different isn't enough, of course — your ad must be better. Your goal is to write an ad that sets you apart from the other ads in a way that connects you with your market. For example, say you sell industrial fans. You check out the AdWords competition and discover that the keyword [industrial fan] brings up ads that focus on models, features, and price. You can differentiate your company by writing an ad citing benefits and return on investment (ROI).

You can position your offer as unique in many ways. Your market research (detailed in Chapter 4) can give you ideas about what your market wants and what the competition is currently providing and talking about. Now you can write ads that address unmet needs.

When most businesspeople think of competition, they think first of price. If you can produce your goods and services more efficiently than others, you can compete on price. After all, Wal-Mart does it. But being the cheapest isn't usually the most compelling sales argument. Do you want the cheapest flooring in your living room? Do you want to drive the cheapest car? Do you want the cheapest heart surgeon operating on you? Besides, price wars often end up as a damaging race to the bottom for all involved, including the customer who finds that the business can't deliver quality at the price quoted.

If a segment of your market is searching for a particular model, like the Lifeline USA Power Wheel or the Canon PowerShot SX10IS, they may have decided on that particular model already and are now comparison-shopping for the best deal. In that case, an ad that mentions price can be effective.

Here are three fundamental ways to position your ad:

✓ **Slice the niche differently.** For example, if you sell martial arts training videos, books, and equipment, you might assume that the entire world of martial arts students and enthusiasts is your market. If you claim a slice of that market and speak to them specifically — for example, college-age women, senior citizens, bouncers — you can position yourself as their supplier of choice. Each of those niches might be small, but you can own them all if they self-identify with their keywords.

✓ **Make a better first offer.** Even though the goal of the ad is to make a first sale, you can offer other things that your prospects may want or need before they buy. Reviews, free samples (physical, informational, or software), advice, video demonstration, discussion, and so on can be dangled in front of prospects who haven't yet made up their minds. As long as the "magnet" attracts your prospects and leaves nonprospects cold, you can generate the right clicks by offering an intermediate step of value.

No matter what you sell, you can always position yourself as an expert in the field. Search, by definition, implies some gap between your customers' desires and the information they have about how to fulfill those desires. If your ad offers to guide and educate, rather than simply to sell, your offer can stand out.

✓ **Empathize more powerfully with your prospect.** The more you understand about how your prospect feels about their problem and their desired outcome, the better you can tune the ad to those feelings. For example, a search for gibson guitar returns several nearly identical, completely lackluster ads (see Figure 8-2 if you don't believe us). Four of the six ads focus on price, including language like "free shipping" and "low prices" in the ad copy. If you put yourself into the mind and heart of someone searching for a Gibson guitar, do you think price is really the most important thing they care about? What about choosing the right guitar? Getting help from a salesperson? Being allowed to return it?

And why does this person want a Gibson in the first place? Is he returning to electric guitar after many years, maybe to connect with and impress his kids? Is he a retired Baby Boomer who finally has the money to afford a $14,000 Eric Clapton Les Paul that he's been pining over ever since he heard "Hideaway" in 1966?

Even if you're not sure of the answer, don't be afraid to visualize your prospects and get inside their head. After all, AdWords is the world's easiest testing engine, and you'll discover soon enough if a description line of "Bite and Snarl like Clapton" is more appealing and profitable than "Free shipping — lowest prices guaranteed."

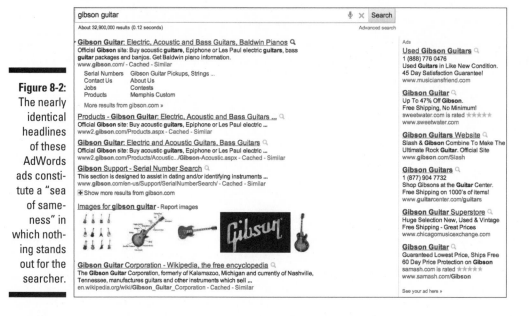

At Camp Checkmate, we create empathy with prospects by creating "avatars" — imaginary prospects with names, histories, occupations, homes, desires, fears, hobbies, families, and opinions. One participant described the experience this way: "I've been selling in this market for 15 years, but I feel like I just met my customer for the first time." If you don't mind a little New Age music, you can grab an "Avatar creation" mp3 and complete instructions at www.gafd3.com/avatar.

Motivating action in four lines

Everyone makes decisions rationally, right? People weigh the pros and cons, consider their values and priorities, and maximize benefits while minimizing costs. People balance risks and rewards, and get better over time as they learn from their experiences.

That doesn't sound like anybody we know.

The truth is that all people make decisions emotionally, in their guts. They justify those decisions using logic, but the part of the brain that can handle matrices and cost-benefit analyses is just slower than the part that acts out of fear and greed. Before they consciously ponder, that old reptile brain decides instantly whether someone is friend or foe, prey or predator.

Appealing to emotion

The AdWords ad heightens the emotional aspect of decision making because the rational brain has very little to go on: three lines of text and a web address. Marketing consultant David Bullock, of `www.davidbullock.com`, puts it this way:

How do you connect to the "right" click?

One second is all that you have to get the attention of your online visitor. That's it.

The fastest way to meet your revenue goal is to figure out what to say, write, or display in this little 1-inch space to get, hold, and motivate the viewer to click your AdWords ad.

Simply, the idea is to develop a stunning emotional appeal that gets the "right" click.

By definition, emotional appeal is the mental state that arises spontaneously rather than through conscious effort and is often accompanied by physiological changes; a feeling: the emotions of joy, sorrow, reverence, hate, and love.

As you boil it down, most of the decisions people make are based on fear and desire. All emotional states arise from one of these two states. We are either moving toward something or away from some situation.

Your ad has to hit the visitor/searcher right between the eyes, make an instantaneous connection and move the visitor to spontaneously gravitate towards your offer. It is not a matter of logic. Your visitor has no time to think about not clicking your AdWords ad. Your goal is to get them to your landing page and move forward in your customer-acquisition process.

Either you hit the mark or you are off. You either get the click or you don't. Period. End of story.

If your ad resonates with your visitors' the search intent — the conversation in their head — they will click to find out more.

Understanding their story

Your four lines must focus on emotions first and logic second. Your prospect will use logic to construct a search strategy (choosing keywords, searching for information, refining the search to longer and most specific keywords, and so on), but moves toward and away from search results and websites based on a subconscious emotional response.

To write effective ads, you have to understand the conversation that just took place inside the head of your prospect as he typed the keyword that brought his ad to them. What is his story? What is he telling himself about his situation and how to improve it?

And we mean *story* quite literally. Go check out a book of fairy tales, or rent a couple of Disney movies to remind yourself what a story contains: a hero (that's them), a problem, a trigger to action, obstacles and villains, and a happy ending. If your ad can connect to the right place in their story, you can grab their attention and lead them the rest of the way.

Guiding them through their "selling cycle" states

An old marketing acronym, AIDA, names the four states that have to occur, in order, in your prospect before you can make a sale:

- **Attention:** Attention is compelled by a headline that names the prospects or their pain, or connects with one of the big three motivators: greed, fear, or curiosity.

- **Interest:** Interest is raised by naming features and benefits (price, free shipping, options, works in zero gravity — you know the drill).

- **Desire:** The desire is the happy ending, or a promised step in that direction. (They can't slay the dragon until they find the enchanted sword.)

- **Action:** The action is the click, to go from the Google results page to your landing page.

All this highfalutin' theory is great, but time to get down to business. You have four lines to accomplish these marketing tasks. The following sections break down the task of each line so you can begin to create magnetic ads.

Grabbing their attention with the headline

The goal of the headline is to get your prospects' attention while leaving everyone else unimpressed. Classic headline gambits include the following:

- **Name Them**
    - Considering a Unicycle
    - Mind Maps for Teachers
    - Actor's Disability Insur.

- **Mirror Their Itch**
    - Suffering from Gout?
    - Rotten-Egg Water Odors?
    - Disorganized?

- **Pick Their Scab with a Provocative Question**
    - Suffering from IBS for Years?
    - Do You Hate Filing?
    - Got a Jerk for a Boss?

✔ **Make a Big Promise**

- Write and Publish a Book

- The "Beat Gout" Diet

- Jump Higher in 14 Days

✔ **Offer Unbiased Information**

- 8 Shower Filters Tested

- Flat-Panel TV Reviews

- Compare Dopamine Supplements

Developing their interest and desire with the description lines

No one formula for effective ad writing exists, and you have to make sure that the elements you combine make sense together and all pull in the same direction to match the visitors' search intent. In general, though, you won't go wrong by putting the big benefit on the first line and the differentiating feature on the second line. The second line will also contain the other crucial element of your ad: the call to action.

Develop a swipe file

A *swipe file* is a collection of successful advertising pieces from which you can draw inspiration. Professional copywriters rarely invent headlines and bullets from thin air; instead, they modify old standards. For example, John Caples famously (among direct marketing geeks, anyway) sold a piano home study course with the headline, "They laughed when I sat down at the piano but when I started to play . . . !" Today, copywriters model this formula in selling everything from baking magazines ("They laughed when I got up to bake") to dog training ("They laughed when I issued my $10,000 dog-trainer challenge . . .").

Perry Marshall recommends building your own AdWords swipe file quickly and inexpensively by visiting your local library or supermarket and copying the text on the covers of popular magazines. If you prefer to stay at home, go to www. magazines.com to view covers of current issues. Here are some headline formulas from *Cosmo, O, Woman's Day,* and *Vogue,* followed in parentheses by possible AdWords adaptations:

✔ 19 dresses that show who's boss (7 skateboards that show who's boss)

✔ The season's hottest styles (The season's hottest cameras)

✔ Weird male behavior decoded (Weird dog behavior decoded)

✔ Break your bad food habits (Break your bad skiing habits)

Reeling them in with a call to action

You usually want your prospects to click your ad. (In some cases, you may prefer a phone call; if so, include your phone number in the ad. See the section on ad extensions for more info.) Going back to the bursting pipes example from the beginning of the chapter, many ads for local plumbers include their phone number on the assumption that someone typing in **plumber** or **busted pipes** is in a state of near-hysteria and wants to contact a real person ASAP. Here are two tactics to compel the click: Offer something in exchange for action, and create a sense of urgency.

Making an offer with action words

When you offer something, use action words. Your prospect is searching with a "gatherer" mentality. Offer something bright and shiny to shift them into "hunter" mode. Active action words include

- Get, buy, purchase
- Order, call, sign up
- Try, download

More passive action words help the prospect make a decision:

- See, learn, compare, discover
- View, listen, watch

The following examples are from ads that appeared when searching for the keyword [data recovery]. Note how they all begin with action words.

- Get a Quote Today
- Call 1-800-555-1212 for Free Analysis
- Discover reliable data recovery.
- View demo — whitepaper

Fanning desire with urgency qualifiers

Nothing stokes desire as much as unattainability. If you can't have it, you want it all the more. Use urgency words to compel immediate action:

- Now
- Today
- By (date)
- While it lasts (in conjunction with a sale price)

Mastering the Medium and Voice at Haiku U.

After you choose your approach and selected elements that will compel action from the right prospects, you have to fit that content elegantly into 135 characters. Stop thinking *sales pitch* and start thinking *haiku* — the Japanese poetic art that paints a compelling mental picture in 17 syllables.

First, forget everything your high-school English teachers taught you about grammar. Your ad must read like a conversation, not an essay. Write like you talk — or better yet, write like your *market* talks.

Apple Computer has a very effective ad campaign featuring two actors portraying a Mac and a PC. The Mac actor is a hip young dude, whereas the PC actor is a pocket protector–wearing nerd who awkwardly stumbles and bumbles through life. If huge multinational companies develop personalities in the minds of consumers, your business, too, needs a voice. Your ads are the first words in this voice that your prospects will hear.

The best ads work both to attract a certain type of person and to strongly repel everyone else. In some markets (like Internet marketing, for example), your tone can be brash. In others, you must come across as professional and no-nonsense. You can be caring, efficient, funny, angry, matter-of-fact, exasperated, excited, clinical, or poetic. Test different voices to find out which one connects best with your market. But your best voice will most often be your genuine voice — just smoothed and amped a bit to cut through the clutter of Timid Timmies and Me-Too Mollies. Your prospects are looking for authenticity in a world full of fakeness. *Connect to them as your unique self and you're already cutting through the clutter.*

Almost everything about your business can be copied — except for you. No one else has your thoughts, your experiences, your unique point of view. Most businesspeople hide this aspect of themselves to appear professional. It's possible to do both — be real *and* be professional. Take advantage of your only true differentiator and be yourself whenever possible.

Vitruvian's Optimization Expert Garrett Todd cautions against rampant creativity. Extensive testing has shown him that classic direct-marketing approaches outperform offbeat, creative ads. His top two ad formulas are

> ✔ **Who Else Wants to . . . ?**
>
> Music On Hold
> Who Else Wants to Reduce Hang-Ups
> and Impress On-Hold Callers?
> www.impress-callers.com

> ✔ **If . . . , Then . . .**
>
> Music On Hold
> If You Want to Reduce Hang-Ups
> Then Try Custom Music On Hold.
> www.impress-callers.com

Garrett reports that the first ad generates an impressive 11.02 percent CTR. Note that his display URL includes a hyphen; he found that separating the two words increased CTR. This is especially helpful since Google has been displaying the domain in all lowercase letters since the beginning of 2011. The www prefix also improved CTR.

Standing Out Visually

It's crucial to stand out with your messaging, your offer, and your Unique Selling Proposition. You can also make your ad look different from other ads to attract attention through contrast.

Include the keyword

If you include the keyword in your headline, you can almost always increase your ad CTR. For example, an ad with the headline "Homebrew for Beginners" achieved a 3.88 percent CTR for the keyword [homebrew], but pulled only 1.01 percent for [home brew].

Matching the ad to the exact keyword tells your prospects that you understand them (even if you don't). Neurolinguistic programming (NLP) experts tell us that people build rapport by using the exact same words as others rather than paraphrasing. For additional visual benefit, Google bolds keywords on its results page.

Google also deems ads that include keywords as relevant to positively affect your quality score, which affects how much you pay for each click compared with other advertisers with higher or lower quality scores.

If your competitors are all using the keywords in their headlines (or, in the case of keywords of 20–25 characters, as their headlines), you'll want to choose a different strategy to stand out. In Figure 8-2, every ad includes the headline, the result of which is the "wallpaper effect": The searcher filters out the identical elements of the ads and doesn't even consciously register them. The only headline words that stand out are Used, Website, and Superstore.

That said, most ads benefit from inclusion of keywords somewhere in the headline, description, or URL.

Adding subdomains and subdirectories

We have improved many clients' CTRs by changing the display URL from
`www.OurClient.com` to `www.OurClient.com/keyword`.

Similarly, we have also used the subdomain area to include words to stand
out. This is especially useful for clients that sell products from various manu-
facturers and their ad can almost appear to be related to that manufacturer.
For example:

```
apple-ipad-cases.g-form.com
```

or

```
excel-training.elerttraining.com
```

Dynamic keyword insertion

Do you ever wonder how eBay and Amazon manage to bid on practically every
keyword in existence and show those keywords in their ads? They don't have
thousands of employees creating millions of different ads. Instead, they use a special format to stick the keyword right into a generic ad, as shown in Figure 8-3.

Figure 8-3:
These ads
dynamically
insert the
keyword.

> Ads
>
> **Howie Jacobson** at Amazon
> Millions of titles, new & used.
> Qualified orders over $25 ship free
> amazon.com is rated ★★★★★
> amazon.com/books
>
> **EBay Howie Jacobson**
> Great deals on new and used items.
> Bid or buy on eBay with confidence!
> ebay.com is rated ★★★★★
> www.ebay.com
>
> See your ad here »

We hardly ever use or recommend dynamic keyword insertion. In most cases,
it's unnecessary, dangerous (because you lose control of your ad text if you're
not exceedingly careful with your keyword selection), and sloppy. If you have
a business where keyword insertion would be useful (if you sell ringtones,
for example, and have thousands of different song title ringtones), visit `www.
gafd3.com/dki` for instructions and examples.

Extended headline

Google sometimes extends the headline in ads that appear above the organic results, in the premium position. You can't directly control whether your ads appear here, but you can write them so they're eligible for the longer headline. Your first description line needs to be a complete sentence (not continuing on into the second line). Google currently uses punctuation to determine this, so craft each description line as a full sentence with proper punctuation.

Ad extensions

Google provides several "extras" that you can use to make your ads stand out. These include

- **Sitelinks:** Extra links to additional web pages appear as part of your ad (see Figure 8-4)

- **Call extensions with Call Metrics**: An additional line with a Google-provided phone number (see Figure 8-5)

- **Call extensions for mobile**: An additional line with your phone number, which can be enabled for Click to Call to automate the visitor's dialing from a mobile device

- **Local extensions**: Your address, phone number, map location, and link to directions (see Figure 8-6; for local campaigns only)

- **Product extensions:** Listings, photos, and prices of products that you upload to Google Merchant Center (see Figure 8-7)

Figure 8-4:
Sitelinks come in three formats at the moment: two lines, one line, and embedded.

Norwood Portable **Sawmills** - Full & Mid-Sized Bandsaw **Sawmills**
portablesawmill.norwoodsawmills.com
Also Chainsaw **Mills** From $995 US.
Request Free Catalog & DVD - Spring Sale: Save Up to $500

Figure 8-5:
When searchers call the Google-provided phone number, you pay a flat fee (currently $1 per call).

Music 123 - Official Site
1 (855) 409 9347
Shop Top Rated Drums & More.
Free Shipping + Low Price Guarantee
www.music123.com

Figure 8-6:
If you have a physical location and your campaign is set up for a city, state, or metropolitan region, the ad can include information about your physical location.

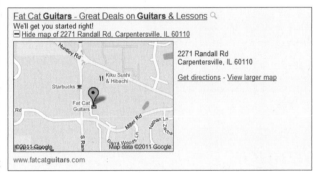

Figure 8-7:
The easiest way to show images of your products is to hook your product feed to Google's merchant center and connect it to your AdWords account.

These extensions change frequently. New ones are added, old ones retired, and requirements and instructions change. To get the most up-to-date information and video tutorials on how to add them, visit `www.gafd3.com/ad-extensions`.

Following Google's Ad Rules

We warn you about some commonly broken rules in the following sections, but you should still take ten minutes to read Google's editorial guidelines at `https://adwords.google.com/select/guidelines.html`.

Punctuation

Google's rules for punctuation in your AdWords ads are pretty simple:

- ✔ No more than one exclamation point in your text, and not in the headline.
- ✔ No repeated punctuation (Tired??!!).
- ✔ No unnecessary punctuation ($$ instead of *money* or $#!! standing in for an expletive).

Capitalization

The capitalization rules for AdWords ads are that you can't use excess capitalization, such as *FREE* or *SIDE EFFECTS*.

However, you can capitalize acronyms (SCUBA) and abbreviations (MPH).

Since early 2011, Google has been showing the subdomain and domain portions of the display URL in all-lowercase letters. It doesn't break Google rules to use capitalization in your display URL, but that won't show up in the search results as capitals.

As a best practice in our agency, we still use capital letters in our display URLs on the chance that Google will someday bring back display URL capitalization.

Spelling and grammar

Google doesn't like ads that look like they were written by toddlers. Make sure that all words are spelled correctly. If you don't have an eye and ear for grammar, get someone who does to review your ad. Spell checkers can't pick up mistakes like using *than* for *then* or *weather* for *whether*.

Copyright and trademark usage

You can't use copyrighted and trademarked terms in your ads without the permission of the rights holder.

This is a thorny and complicated issue for Google. If you sell one brand of mobile phone, can you compare it with a competing brand in your ad? Can you use copyrighted terms in your URL? The law is still being written on this topic — and lawsuits are mounting between companies claiming copyright infringement and "initial interest confusion." (Howie can throw these terms around thanks to his work as an expert witness at trial; obviously he's not a lawyer, and you should get competent legal advice before doing anything that may get you in trouble.)

A trademark by itself does not prevent advertisers from using the term in their ads. The trademark owner must specifically register the term(s) with Google before they are disallowed.

Competitive claims

If you say your business is the best, fastest, cheapest, most successful, and such, you need to prove it to Google (and the world) on your landing page.

Offers

If you offer it in your ad, your visitor must be able to get it easily from your landing page. Giving away a free trial download? Put the link in an obvious place on the landing page. If Google's editors visit your site and decide that your offer is fraudulent, your ad will be disallowed.

No offensive language

Unlike the late George Carlin, we *can't* tell you the seven words you're not allowed to use on Google. But if they get bleeped out of movies on TV, that's a pretty good clue to omit them from your ads.

Links

The domain of your display URL must be the same as that of your website. That is, if someone types your display URL into his browser instead of clicking your ad (thoughtfully saving you money!), he should still get to the same website, if not the exact same landing page.

Your destination URL must work properly and must resolve to a working web page, as opposed to an e-mail address or document or multimedia file.

Exploring the Other Ad Formats

Google is constantly exploring new places and media for its ads. You can now create graphical ads for websites, text ads for mobile phones, local business listings that appear on search results pages and next to Google Maps, and video ads.

Getting the picture with image ads

Image ads are graphical files that display on content sites, but not on Google's or its search partners' results pages. Publishers can choose to display image ads instead of text ads. Image ads typically generate higher CTRs than text ads, but convert to leads and sales at a lower level. If you're a website publisher who gets paid for clicks on the Google ads on your site, image ads can be very profitable because of their high CTRs. For you, the AdWords advertiser, the high CTR can be a double-edged sword. Keep image ads in their own campaigns so you can monitor ROI and delete any ads that threaten to break your budget without bringing you paying customers.

If you decide to try display ads, Google provides a Display Ad Builder that allows even those who failed 7th grade art to create decent graphics. From within the ad group where you want to create the image ad, click the Ads tab and then click the New Ad button. Choose Display Ad Builder from the drop-down list. Go to `www.gafd3.com/adwizard` for an online tutorial on using the tool.

Making the phone and the doorbell ring with mobile text ads

Google is going mobile, creating content that can be accessed and acted upon seamlessly from your smart mobile phone (and even from your mobile phone of average intelligence but with a nice smile). If your ad includes a link to a website, you have to make sure the site is created in a phone-compatible way. If you just want prospects to pick up the phone and call, or drive over and pay you a visit, create your ad and include an offer and call to action.

To create a mobile text ad, click the Ads tab and then click the New Ad button. Choose WAP Mobile Ad from the drop-down list. View your mobile text ad from your SMS-enabled phone by pointing your phone's browser to `http://google.com/mobile`. You can conduct searches and view maps, as well as access several other Google services, such as Gmail and Google News.

Click to Call

Within mobile ads, the Click to Call feature allows searchers to call you directly by clicking the number in your ad.

Going Hollywood with video ads

To create a video ad that shows on pages in the Display network, use the Display Ad Builder described in the previous section on image ads. On the next page, choose an image (Google is very picky about the size of this image, so make sure your graphic designer knows the dimensions Google accepts), enter display and destination URLs, name your ad, and upload your video. If your video is already uploaded to YouTube, this process becomes much easier. For an online tutorial about video ads, visit www.gafd3.com/video-ads.

Because Google runs a *blind* advertising network based on keyword search (meaning that you, as an advertiser, can't tell in advance where your ads will show; and the publishers can't predict accurately which ads will display on their pages), we recommend using Google video — if you must — but only in placement-targeted campaigns (more on this approach in Chapter 13).

Chapter 9

Giving Your Customer a Soft Landing on Your Website

- -

In This Chapter

▶ Creating relevant landing pages

▶ Establishing the credibility of your online store

▶ Moving your visitor from interest to action

▶ Generating leads and sales

- -

*W*hen (potential) customers click your ad and reach your website, they will decide to stay and shop or to return to Google within seven seconds. Everything about your landing page will either persuade your visitor to stay and play, or to hit the Back button and never darken your door again.

Don't just send customers to your site's home page. You have the ability to send your visitors to the page of their dreams, the one that quickly grants them their fondest wish, that scratches the itch they've never quite been able to reach before, that dreams the impossible dream — sorry, we were channeling Richard Kiley there for a minute. Deep breath. Orchestra fades. Where were we?

The text, the pictures, the design, the loading speed, the contact information, the logos, the multimedia, and the opportunities for interaction all combine to create a gestalt, an instant impression of Perfect Fit, Run Away Screaming, or something in between.

This chapter shows you how to make landing pages that are highly relevant to the keywords and ads that point to them. You discover the most important purpose of a landing page, along with several strategies for achieving that purpose. You find out a few sneaky tricks for building multiple landing pages by doing the work just once. We show you the elements of a landing page that you can tweak to improve performance, and discuss briefly ways to increase the quality scores of the keywords pointing to your landing pages.

Knowing Your Three Landing Page Audiences

Your AdWords landing page must impress three suitors: your visitor, the Google *spider* (the software program that evaluates your website), and the human reviewer at Google who subjectively decides the quality of your site.

Your visitor is the most important audience to consider. Only visitors can turn into customers and revenue. The rub is, though, that unless the Google spider and human reviewers approve of your landing page, you'll never get to show it to your visitor. So, you have to treat these gatekeepers with as much respect as you treat your VIP visitor.

Not every site gets reviewed by a human. If the spider finds something its algorithm that it deems fishy, or if you're in a highly scrutinized industry (such as weight loss or home business), a human reviewer will be deployed to peruse your site to be sure that it meets Google's policies, stated and unstated.

Pleasing the Visitor

Perry Marshall of `www.perrymarshall.com` shares a wallet-walloping calculation that should convince you to spend a lot of quality time working on your landing pages:

> Let's say you pay 50 cents for a click, and Barbara in Oregon goes to your website and spends eight seconds seeing what you're selling . . . then leaves.
>
> 50 cents divided by 8 seconds is $225 per hour.
>
> Barbara in Oregon's attention is pretty expensive, wouldn't you say?

Now, maybe Barbara was never your customer. She clicked because your ad aroused her curiosity, or was cute, or implied or promised something for nothing. Oh, well, can't win them all. And, most website owners are told to be satisfied with conversion percentages that are pathetically low: one-half of a percent, one percent. The web is a numbers game, they're told. Get enough traffic, and even a mediocre site can pay the rent.

Well, true, the web is a numbers game, but who says you have to be satisfied with the numbers? The entire premise of AdWords — in fact, the feature that rocketed AdWords into the top spot for search advertising within months of its birth — was the ease with which campaigns could be tested and improved. This improvement doesn't have to stop at the AdWords border with your website. You can deploy the market intelligence you gain by testing keywords and ad copy to create compelling landing pages that continue to attract and guide your best prospects.

In fact, pay per click (PPC) can and should be leveraged into powerful data to drive all your other marketing campaigns. To be sure, that topic is a book by itself (subtle upsell to our acquisitions editor), but the main point is to remind you that AdWords is a cost-effective tool with which you can test and measure everything about your marketing.

The goal of each landing page is to build an instant emotional bond with your prospects: to show them you understand their needs and can take away their pains. From that platform, you present your offer and guide them to take action. Your home page — the one that says, "Welcome to Acme Online Sock Emporium" — is hardly ever the right place to take AdWords traffic. If someone walked into your retail Sock Emporium and told you, "I'm looking for red-and-white-striped, over-the-calf dress socks," you wouldn't take them back to the front door and say, "Welcome to Acme Sock Emporium, for the finest in men's and ladies' dress and casual socks; sporting socks; and never-washed, vintage baseball stirrup socks worn by members of the 1958 Championship New York Yankees." Instead, you'd lead them directly to the wall displaying the red-and-white-striped, over-the-calf dress socks and ask them, "What size?" That level of specificity is the purpose of your landing page.

Your retail sock store is probably not located next to other sock stores. However, your *online* store's landing page is precisely two clicks away from just about every other online sock store in existence. If your landing page doesn't look like the next point on the shortest distance between your prospect's A and B, whoosh! Barbara from Oregon is here one second, Oregon the next.

Achieving relevance based on keywords

Keywords are the keys to your search visitors' desires. You bundle similar desires into ad groups, and send the traffic from each ad group to a landing page focused on that desire. Everything true about ad copy is also true about website copy; the message, the tone, the balance of features and benefits, and the next call to action all must connect with the conversation already going on in your prospect's mind. The only difference is that on the website, you are free from the space constraints and some of the editorial shackles imposed by Google. With great power comes great responsibility, as Peter Parker (another famous webmaster) learned the hard way in the *Spider-Man* comics. Use the power of your website to focus not on your business, but on your customer's desires as suggested by their keywords and the ad that triggered their visit.

If your traffic is derived from AdSense, you don't have a specific keyword to build on. Instead, you know which ad interrupted them like a talking white rabbit and caused them to detour into the rabbit hole of your site. In that case, your landing page should continue the conversation begun by the ad.

For example, if you sell computer training videos on DVD, part of your AdWords account and landing pages might look like the example shown in Table 9-1.

Table 9-1		Linking Keywords and Landing Pages	
Ad Group	**Subject**	**Sample Keywords**	**Landing Page Headline**
Ad Group A1	Microsoft Access Tutorial Keywords	`[Microsoft access tutorial]` `[access tutorial]` `[ms access tutorial]` `[access database tutorial]`	"Master Microsoft Access at Your Own Pace with This Award-Winning DVD-based Course"
Ad Group A2	Microsoft Access Training Keywords	`[access training]` `[access database training]` `[Microsoft access computer training]`	"Microsoft Access Training at Your Own Pace with this Award-Winning DVD-based Course"
Ad Group A3	Microsoft Access Best Performing Keyword	`[ms Access]`	"Become Certified in MS Access in Just 6 Weeks with this Award-Winning DVD-based Course"
Ad Group A4	Microsoft Excel General Keywords	`[excel xp training]` `[excel training]` `[excel 2007 training]` `[excel 2010 training]`	"Receive Professional Excel Training from the Comfort of Your Home with this Award-Winning DVD-based Course"

Product-focused landing pages

If you sell physical products, like clergy robes or protective padding or runners' watches with GPS, your landing page presents the most specific product you can offer, based on keyword and ad. In our www.g-form. com campaigns, the keyword [knee pads] produces a page showing knee pads, with text and images and videos that demonstrate their effectiveness for mountain biking, roller blading, field hockey, and Ultimate Frisbee. [Mountain bike pads] takes visitors to its entire display of protective gear for mountain bikers. And [knee pads for mountain biking] leads to a page featuring the knee pads, with the text and images focused entirely on mountain biking to the exclusion of other sports.

Concept-focused landing pages

Few online stores sell a wide variety of merchandise. Instead, most stores sell one or two items that solve a certain range of problems. For example, maybe you invented a clever filing system that automatically purges old files, or reminds people when to pay the energy bill, or sends flowers and chocolate to key people on Valentine's Day. You probably will generate most of your traffic not from searches for the solution (because people don't yet know it exists) but from descriptions of the problem:

```
paper clutter
messy filing system
messy office
```

Or they search for the one aspect of a potential solution that resonates with them at that moment:

```
bill pay reminder system
self-purging files
holiday and birthday reminders
```

Each of these six keywords should go to a specific landing page that addresses that problem or need. The final destination will be the same for all buyers, but the paths they take from problem to solution depends on where they're starting.

Scratching your customer's itch

Showing a "That's for Me" page keeps your visitor on your site for 30 seconds rather than 8. Your next task is to scratch their itch by fulfilling the promise of your ad.

Giving them what they want

If your prospects know exactly what they want, then give it to them. Are they ready to buy a G-Form Extreme 13" Macbook Sleeve? Put a photo, a price, a shipping policy, and a Buy Now button right on the landing page. Are they looking for more information to help them decide what to do next? Give them the information. Do they need to talk to a real human being? Put a phone number on your site and hire someone to answer it 24/7, or during business hours, or whenever your customers call.

Ben Hunt's Ladder of Awareness (see Chapter 7) from his book *Convert!* comes in very handy here. Don't create a landing page until you're clear what rung of the ladder your prospects are on when they arrive, and how far up the ladder your landing page can take them. The best guide to a prospect's awareness level, in the Search network, is their choice of keyword.

For example, use the Ladder of Awareness for G-Form's Extreme Sleeve for the 13" MacBook Pro.

Level 0: No Problem

No Search network traffic, and no visitors arrive at Level 0.

> Keywords: none

By definition, Search network traffic starts at Level 1, awareness of a problem. If someone is at Level 0 — No Problem — they aren't searching. You may encounter some Level 0 prospects in the Display network, but your ad must make them aware of the problem before they come to your landing page.

Level 1: Problem

Your prospects realize that this expensive piece of electronics is vulnerable. Perhaps they just replaced another laptop that they dropped and broke, or they heard a story about someone whose laptop was destroyed in their carry-on bag.

> Keywords: [prevent broken macbook], [laptop protection]

Level 2: Solutions Exist

Maybe your prospects walked out of the Apple store past the display of protective cases, but they'd already overspent their budget and figured that they'd get a sleeve later. Or they saw someone else stick a MacBook into a case or sleeve after use.

> Keywords: [macbook sleeve], [macbook case], [hard macbook case], [protective macbook sleeve]

Level 3: Your Solution

Your prospects have heard about G-Form, possibly from a friend, or a brief mention on an Apple-related blog, or they noticed an in-store display and took note of the name of the product. They don't know much more than that, though, and they don't understand the benefits or the differences between the Extreme Sleeve and other options.

> Keywords: [g-form macbook sleeve], [extreme sleeve], [g-form macbook protection]

Level 4: Benefits

Your prospects come already impressed, perhaps because a friend is an Extreme Sleeve owner and fan, or they've read a glowing review, or they've seen a YouTube video of a MacBook being thrown out of a second-story window and surviving, thanks to the Extreme Sleeve.

Keywords: same as Level 3

Level 5: Convinced

Your prospects are ready to buy. They've got their credit card out, they know which color they want, and they're just looking for the shopping cart.

Keywords: same as Level 3

The Ladder of Awareness shows the need for three different landing pages:

- ✔ **Level 1:** Awareness of a problem but not a solution.
- ✔ **Level 2:** Awareness of generic solutions, but no knowledge of the Extreme Sleeve.
- ✔ **Levels 3–5:** You can't easily separate those levels based on keyword choice.

This last landing page must, therefore, accommodate all three levels. For those who are already convinced, the Buy button must appear big and obvious, and appear *above the fold* (high enough on the page so that the searcher doesn't need to scroll down to see it).

For those who understand the benefits and need some convincing, G-Form must identify key objections and address them. Too expensive? Too bulky? Is the zipper well made? By communicating with prospects online and offline, you can glean very good idea of the most common objections.

And for those who know of the Extreme Sleeve but aren't clear on the benefits, benefit-laden bullets, testimonials, and endorsements as well as video demonstrations must paint a clear picture of why the Extreme Sleeve is the best choice they could make.

Agitating the problem

We don't want to get too disgusting here (actually, we don't mind, but our editor does), but we have to point out something important about this itch metaphor. Scratching an itch feels good for a while, but can actually make the itch worse. Sometimes you can scratch so hard that the irritation turns red and swollen and bleeds. Sometimes in the sales process, you have to agitate the problem and make your prospect feel even worse before they will take action.

So, if you sell a product that prevents rather than cures, you must be willing to paint the awful picture of what happens when the preventable event — hard drive crash, flood, heart disease, death without a will, yellow teeth, whatever — occurs. Scratching the itch in a case like that means taking advantage of your visitors' momentary spasm of responsibility and making them quake with fear at the prospect of not addressing the issue this very minute, and trembling with relief at having found you.

Guiding them with a headline

Each page on your website is about something. The headline — a prominent phrase or sentence near the top of the page — helps your visitor decide whether to spend time on a page by summarizing the content, promising a benefit, or tickling curiosity. Imagine a newspaper without headlines — just articles. How would you decide what to read and what to skip? The headline is a relevance shortcut that also primes the reader for the message to follow.

Establishing credibility

In his popular book *Blink: The Power of Thinking without Thinking* (Little, Brown and Company), Malcolm Gladwell shows how we make snap judgments about most things before we've even thought about them. The neural pathways that establish an emotional reaction are pre-thought. Before your prospects have read a word, identified the subject of a photograph, or listened to a word of audio, they've already decided whether they like you and trust you. They'll never be able to tell you why they feel the way they do because those decisions are outside of consciousness. They'll come up with justifications for their gut reactions, but are usually clueless as to the real causes.

Overall look and feel

Visitors will react instinctively to the design of your landing page. They will assume things about you based on logos, colors, shapes, border styles, text fonts and sizes, and movement. Different markets respond to different gestalts. If you're selling a "secret" of some sort, don't put up a standard corporate website. If you want to appear like an established company, spend some money on elegant design elements rather than putting up an ugly sales letter. If you offer bereavement counseling, use a subdued color palette. If you sell violent video games, consider light text on a black background. And so on.

Photographs can enhance credibility, especially in a medium comprising only electrons. Show visitors your face, your store, your warehouse, your products. Asepco, a firm that manufactures valves for the pharmaceutical industry, put a photo slide show on its site that documented the odyssey of one of its valves from the mountain where the ore was mined to the finished product. Go to `www.gafd3.com/valve` to get redirected to this page.

Basically, you want to subliminally get across the message that this trustworthy business will be around tomorrow.

Specific visual cues

In addition to the overall look and feel, you can add specific graphical elements that lend credibility by association, as shown in Figure 9-1. These include logos for credit cards, PayPal, credit card processors (like VeriSign), shippers (UPS, FedEx, and the U.S. Postal Service), and website certifications (the Better Business Bureau's BBB Online Reliability Program, Hacker Safe, and TRUSTe).

Another type of visual reassurance is the presence of subliminal "I Am Not a Crook" links, including privacy policy, website terms and conditions, shipping and refund policies, disclaimers, and so on. We're not sure anyone actually *reads* these documents, but their very presence can be reassuring.

Finally, the more contact options you include, the less you look like a fly-by-night with something to hide. Post office boxes don't cut it; instead, get a real mailing (street) address that gives the impression of an office. Give a phone number. Put your e-mail address where people can find it.

When you display your e-mail address on your website, put it in an image file rather than a live link. This will prevent spambots from harvesting it and sending you hundreds of unwanted e-mails every day.

Pleasing the Spider

Glenn Livingston of PayPerClickSearchMarketing.com experiments vigorously and shares generously what he discovers about ways to get Google to love your landing pages. Much of what follows is at least partially attributable to Glenn.

Demonstrate relevance

If Google got a tattoo, it would read, "Relevance." As applied to landing pages, it means that what you say about your page must match the keyword as closely as possible. Ideally, the biggest keyword in the ad group is included in the title tag, the description tag, the first paragraph, and some of the header tags. Even a few years ago, this sort of keyword matching was needed only for search engine optimization (SEO), but AdWords now includes a significant SEO component.

The title tag

At the very top of your web browser, above the URL even, you can read the "title" of the page you're visiting. For example, the title for `www.watercolour secrets.com` is "Watercoloursecrets.com — Watercolour Painting Made Easy." The title tells Google what your page is about. (Most human visitors to your site never even notice the title, so use it to show Google the connection between your keyword and your landing page.)

You or your webmaster can edit the title tag in any HTML-authoring program. You can find it in the source code for your page, near the top:

```
<title>Watercoloursecrets.com — Watercolour Painting Made Easy</title>
```

If your landing page has a nondescriptive title, like "Page 3" or "Welcome to VintageDirtySocks.com," Google will charge you more for clicks to punish you for sending traffic to a nonrelevant page.

Visit `www.gafd3.com/lp-seo` for a complete tutorial on how to add relevance to your landing page to please the Google spider.

The rest of the website

Google evaluates landing pages not in a vacuum, but in the context of the entire website with the same URL. Google is looking for *authority sites* — ones where visitors will land and immediately feel, "This is exactly what I was hoping to find. Thanks, Google, for another search well done."

Authority sites tend to be large, with lots of pages of unique content. They are frequently updated, so the information stays fresh. And the older they are, the more comfortable Google feels about giving them a great quality score. Obviously, you can't make a site older than it is, but you can make sure to add lots of relevant, unique content and include links from your landing pages to that content. Adding a blog is the easiest way to start building an authority site.

Pleasing the Google Reviewer

The Google reviewer gets involved when something on your landing page raises a red (or at least a yellow) flag. These might include the coding of your site, or your participation in a high-scrutiny industry, or less-than-kosher elements of your AdWords account. After the reviewer steps in, you have to demonstrate that he should feel comfortable sending his grandmother to your site.

Most of what works for reviewers also works for prospects. The reviewer sees her- or himself as the searcher's protector. If you're as fond of dating metaphors as we are, you might think of yourself as a high school boy, your prospect as a high school girl, and Google as her father. You want to be kind and trustworthy in front of both of them, but you'd probably behave differently depending on whether Dad was watching.

Squeeze or No-Squeeze

Online marketing strategist Sean D'Souza has crafted a website — www.psycho tactics.com—that still gets visitors' names and e-mails without forcing anything. Here are his (and our) opinions about opt-in strategy:

Imagine you went for a date with a person you hadn't met before. And your date wore a paper bag on his/her head. He/she refused to show you his/her face. That date refused to tell you anything about his/her past. Or let you into any information at all. Yet you had to give them information. Like your first name, last name, blah, blah, blah.

How do you feel?

Well that's exactly how the customers feel. They feel irritated, frustrated, and to choose a mild word: trapped. They know they want the information, but they can't seem to get any information from you without filling in that stupid form.

Squeeze pages are contrary to human nature. They force you into a corner. They force you to part with information based on some random headline and bullet points.

So why do we have so many squeeze pages on the Internet? Why do people catch colds and coughs? Yes, one person has it and then it spreads. One person put in a squeeze page; then everyone else decided to follow suit. Don't get me wrong. Squeeze pages work. They work wonderfully.

Well, so does Bruno, who's 6 foot 9 inches and weighs 400 pounds. Just because it

works doesn't mean you have to follow suit. Because there are other things that work. Like nonthreatening, non-Bruno, no-squeeze pages. Pages that get you to sign up not through intimidation and fear. But pages that get you to sign up because you want to do so. Because persuasion is stupid. Persuasion implies that you acted against your nature. And why get customers to act against their nature when they will gladly give you information?

A good opt-in page should entice. It should give you lots of details. It should answer your every question or objection. It should not make you feel icky, like being on a blind date.

At Psychotactics, we've collected names, addresses, home numbers, postal addresses, mobile numbers, city, country on our opt-in pages. All without twisting anyone's arms. We've done it to entice customers to subscribe to the newsletter. Or to opt-in to a workshop. Or to buy a product or service. Our customers give us bucket loads of information because they trust us. They believe in us. They know they're not on a yucky blind date.

I'd rather have that kind of customer, wouldn't you? Sure beats being squeezed!

Go to www.psychotactics.com and have a look around. And if you do subscribe (which we highly recommend), you'll experience Sean's noncoercive, warm and fuzzy opt-in process for yourself.

Here are some do and don't suggestions from Glenn:

- **Nothing hype-y, even if it's true:** Avoid using giant screaming headlines, lots of exclamation points, and too much yellow highlighted text. Keep things as dignified as possible.

- **Proof and trust elements:** Include these, as well as any reason why someone should trust your company or believe your advice. Some examples are logos from media outlets that featured stories about you or your products, client lists, and well-reasoned discussions that support the things you sell.

- **Good design:** Google appears to prefer landing pages that are well designed (that is, somebody spent money). A professional photo, good color and font scheme, and good-looking logo go a long way toward comforting the reviewer.

- **Upfront value:** Offer this right off the bat without asking for anything in return. In the olden days (2006 and before), Google didn't mind if you sent traffic to "squeeze pages," which were designed to force the visitor to give you their e-mail address before you gave them anything of value. Squeeze pages are no longer allowed by Google. You can still make getting the opt-in your top priority, but you must do it in a less-aggressive way.

Defining the Most Desirable Action (MDA) for the Landing Page

Before delving into the strategies for improving your conversion, you need to clearly define what a conversion means to you and your business. Start by asking yourself the big question: "What's the one thing I want my visitor to do as a result of visiting this page?" The possible actions include reading, watching, and listening; clicking a link; completing a form; making or requesting a phone call; or engaging in live chat.

Most clients we work with can identify a "point of no return" for their customers: a place in the sales cycle that, once reached, typically leads to a sale. For example:

- "After they request the free DVD, 90 percent of them become customers."

- "When I get them to call, I sell 75 percent of them right there on the phone."

- "After they request a quote, almost all of them sign up for the service."

If you have a step in your sales process that converts lookers to buyers, everything about your landing page should be engineered to get as many visitors to that step as possible. And in most cases, the first step on the way to the point of no return is getting your visitor's e-mail address.

E-commerce

If your online business model is *wallet-out* — meaning you want your visitor to buy something on your first visit — the MDA for your landing page is to have them click the Buy button. Use the Ladder of Awareness to design a sales process that begins at their current level and moves them up to Level 5 (Convinced) with clarity and appropriate persuasion.

Lead generation

If the purpose of your website is to generate leads to follow up with and sell to later, your goal is to get visitors to provide their contact information, known as "opting-in" to your marketing list. The mechanics of the opt-in are straightforward: Place a form on your site, tell people to fill it out, send them to a thank-you page, and start e-mailing. The only thing missing is the answer to your prospect's question, "Why on earth should I give you my name and contact information?" People protect their inboxes like geese protecting their nests. The last thing they want is a bunch of annoying e-mails trying to sell them something. The keys to achieving a high opt-in rate are to

- Give away something of value.
- Make the opt-in a logical next step in the relationship rather than a form of online extortion.
- Offer your visitors something they really want.
- Reassure them that you won't misuse their information.

Even if your online business model is e-commerce, you should still consider adding an "opt-in first" funnel if you plan on advertising in the Display network. First, Display network visitors weren't searching for you directly, so they're less likely to buy immediately. Second, the most successful Display network ads offer free things to entice browsers to click. Your ad can promise only what your landing page can deliver.

Moving Visitors through ASIDA

Attention, Interest, Desire, and Action (AIDA) is a time-tested sales formula. We add a new second step — Safety — to AdWords-driven sales because the process puts a gap between the safe and familiar world of Google and the alien landscape of your site. Apply ASIDA to the search-driven landing page to map out an effective conversion strategy.

Attention

The attention stage occurs when the prospect clicks your ad, homing in on your promise and ignoring — for the time being — everyone else's. After a prospect clicks, your job is to turn that momentary hit of attention into genuine interest in what you have to say. And the precursor of interest is safety. As soon as visitors' internal "danger meter" spikes, they think of nothing but finding the Back button and returning to the comforting arms of Google.

Safety

You make your landing page safe mostly through design choices. On a well-designed page, your visitor doesn't consciously think, "Oh, I feel safe here," any more than you walk into a building and think, "Oh, the air is okay to breathe here." Only when the safety or the oxygen is missing does it rise to consciousness.

You can also make your visitors feel safe by spending some time thinking about their expectations. Daniel Gilbert points out in *Stumbling on Happiness* that human beings are always "nexting": constructing assumptions about what is going to happen next. We can frustrate your assumptions, for example, by ending this sentence with an avocado. (Weren't expecting that, were you?)

And don't forget to practice anticipating assumptions: What should a page look like from an ad for mountain bike protective gear? What about the landing page from an ad for a therapist who helps patients with depression? How about an online payroll company? A quick and easy way to start checking assumptions is to preview your competitors' and organic listings' landing pages for your main keywords. On the Google search results page, simply click the magnifying glass next to any listing's headline to see a pop-up preview of that page (see Figure 9-1).

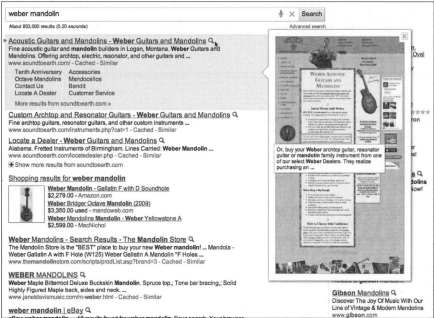

Figure 9-1:
Click the
magnify-
ing glass
next to any
listing on
the Google
search
engine
results page
(SERP)
to see a
preview of
that page.

Interest

"Interest" means getting your visitors to think, "Yes, I'm in the right place" as soon as they land on your page. The page has a prominent headline that validates the promise of the ad. The top navigation clearly shows everything that visitors can do on the site that will lead them to their goal. Some bulleted text quickly lays out the value proposition in an easy-on-the-eye style. The first paragraph engages the visitor by talking about their desires and goals, not the details of the product or service. Any images or videos tell a compelling story, and are not just "stock photo" fillers of multicultural people in business attire shaking hands, or attractive women wearing telephone headsets inviting a phone call.

Desire

In traditional direct marketing, the salesperson has to build desire. In search marketing, it's desire that fuels the search in the first place. It's already there. Spending too much time convincing someone that she needs protection for her MacBook Pro just bores people who already know that.

For search-driven landing pages, the goal at this point is to remove all obstacles to the fulfillment of that desire. In other words, answer the visitors' questions and identify and respond to their objections.

Action

The late Gary Halbert noted, "A sale is a fragile thing." At the point of taking action, many online shoppers and potential leads get spooked into abandoning their shopping carts or their opt-in forms. The big question we all ask ourselves when we're about to commit to something, no matter how large or small, is, "Am I doing something stupid here?"

Even giving someone your e-mail could be considered a mistake if that person misuses the e-mail by spamming you or selling it to other spammers. Behavioral economists tell us that humans do much more to prevent loss than to achieve gain. So your prospect's default action, given even the slightest doubt or hesitation, is inaction.

Most of the time we're just acting in damage control mode, asking ourselves, "What's the worst that can happen here and how can I prevent it?" At the threshold of opting in, prospects want to be reassured that you won't spam them; that they can stop the flow of e-mails easily at any time; and that you'll respect their privacy and not sell, rent, barter, or give away their contact information to anyone else.

And when prospects' mouses are hovering over the Buy button, they're mentally thinking about the Undo button. What if they're making a mistake? What if the product doesn't work or their spouse hates it? Smart online merchants deploy risk reversal strategies at the point of sale to reassure skittish shoppers and push them over the edge into conversion. Better-than-money-back guarantees, promises of ease of return, and pledges about customer service can all make clicking that Buy button an easier step to take.

Some top online retailers, like www.ebags.com and www.zappos.com, have made free shipping and free returns a key pillar of their value proposition. Online shoppers who visit and trust those sites are practically making impulse buys because they know it's so easy and risk-free to undo a bad buying decision.

Video

In the last few years, the World Wide Web has morphed from a text-based medium to a video-based medium. Putting a video front and center on your landing page can solve several landing page problems at once.

After all, video focuses the eye. Even if the video doesn't start playing automatically (generally a good idea), the Play button in the center of the video screen is just begging to be pressed. And because video moves in time, not space, you can put a complete sales presentation above the fold of the page, meaning the visitor doesn't have to scroll down to see the whole thing.

Video engages more senses than static text and images. We are moved by movies. The motion, the narrative, and the music all combine to create an emotional experience, not just a rational argument. When your prospects can see and hear you as you speak, they develop a level of trust and comfort that's much harder to achieve via the written word.

Video demonstrations constitute proof. G-Form has skyrocketed sales of its Extreme Sleeves using short, amateur video demonstrations. One video shows the Extreme Sleeve protecting an iPad from a bowling ball, while another shows an iPad thrown from an ultralight airplane. These videos convey the protective power of the product in a way that no amount of words could. (You can see them at `www.gafd3.com/sleeve-videos`.)

Entertaining and/or inspiring videos can go viral. G-Form's videos have been seen by more than one-quarter million viewers, most of whom weren't specifically searching for electronics protection. Their videos have inspired some customers to make their own Extreme Sleeve videos (some of which have also gone viral).

Video is much less expensive than you might think. And although professional video equipment and editing can be costly, sometimes the "iPhone video" look actually increases credibility by making the demonstration seem more real and less staged. And with free hosting at YouTube, inexpensive DIY hosting with amazon S3 (`www.aws.amazon.com/s3`) or inexpensive ad-free business hosting with companies like Viddler.com, you don't need a megafast web server to handle the added bandwidth.

Selling the Most Desired Action

After you define your sales process, your next big question is, "What stands between customers and the next step?" If you want them to download your free report, what do they need to be feeling and thinking in order to go ahead and do it? If you want them to call, what might cause them to hesitate and then bail? If you're asking for the sale, what action-freezing second thoughts might they be entertaining?

A cliché in the sales world is that you have to work as hard to sell a $10 item as a $10 million item. On the Internet, you have to work just about as hard to give something away free. Your landing pages must answer your prospects' questions, reassure their doubts, assuage their fears, and guide them clearly to what they should do next.

The masters of persuasive copy know a lot of tricks and techniques, but the basis for their effectiveness is a deep knowledge of what their prospects want to have and want to avoid. As you can read in Chapter 4, marketing tricks without having your finger on the pulse of a substantial market is like doing a technically perfect triple gainer into an empty swimming pool. So the following copywriting tasks can be accomplished effectively only against the backdrop of market insight.

Using bullets

Sales bullets are the foundation for all effective sales copy, whether they appear in actual bullet form on the page or not. Ken McCarthy, one of the top copywriting teachers online, gives you a very useful phrase to focus on whenever you sit down to write sales copy: Bullets Wound. (*Wound* here rhymes with *swooned.*) In other words, the purpose of the bullet is to highlight and stretch the gap in your visitor's mind between their current and ideal situations. The cure for the bullet is the next action you want them to take: read, click, download, call, chat, buy, whatever.

Translating features into benefits

As sellers, we become intimately acquainted with the facts of our products and services. It glows in the dark; it comes in yellow or black; it has a self-cleaning button; it's made from shea butter; and so on. After a while, we are in danger of operating under the illusion that our prospects understand why these features are important and beneficial. They don't have a clue, and if we fail to *translate* features into benefits, then we are asking our prospects to do interpretive work they have no interest in doing.

Here's a quick formula for figuring whether a particular statement is a feature or a benefit. Write down the statement. Look at it. Ask yourself whether your most impolite and brash customer could conceivably read it and snarl, "So what?" If so, you've got yourself a feature, not a benefit.

To turn a feature into a benefit, write down the feature, add the words ". . . and what this means to you is . . ." and then complete the sentence. Ken McCarthy thinks of this as "bringing the facts to life." For example, one of our clients, ITSM Solutions (www.itsmsolutions.com), provides service management training to IT professionals. Isn't that exciting?

Actually, the service *is* exciting, if you're an IT manager or CEO of a company with an IT department that could be more effective or efficient. Here's how to turn some features of ITSM Blended Learning Solution into benefits so that the ideal prospect sits up and says, "Wow, I need that."

✔ **Online self-paced training videos:** IT managers and workers can fit the training into their busy schedules whenever they want. They can pause, fast-forward, and rewatch at their convenience, with total control over their learning experience. Unlike a live classroom, where they might feel self-conscious about asking the instructor to repeat something or slow down, the learners get to set the pace to accommodate their own learning style and schedule.

✔ **Access to instructor/mentors plus LinkedIn–based mentoring community:** A big problem with online education is that it's too often lonely and isolating. Without other students to meet and an instructor to hold oneself accountable to, other priorities can easily overwhelm the commitment to study. The ITSM Solutions incorporation of a social network into the self-paced online course instantly creates a community of support, while access to instructors helps students from getting bogged down in unfamiliar material. (Get up to speed with *LinkedIn For Dummies,* 2nd edition, by Joel Elad.)

✔ **Instructor-led review sessions:** When confusion or questions arise, the learners aren't stuck with the canned material. They can ask professional instructors to clarify and give examples to clear up all questions. This is done online, so no travel is required. It's like being able to call the authors of a how-to book and ask them specific questions about situations that may not have been covered in the book. Instead of the normal setup, where the instructor spends most of his time lecturing, the ITSM model maximizes instructor value by focusing on important interactions, plus personalized advice on how to ace the exam and perform successfully on the job.

✔ **Methodology based on Kotter's 8-step change leadership model:** John Kotter is a well-respected change management theorist. Unlike most training, which fails to translate new knowledge into new behaviors, ITSM training is engineered to lead to better IT management.

✔ **Classes conducted by certified experts:** Unlike some IT service management training, ITSM Solutions hires expert practitioners with years of real-world experience managing IT projects. Their experience translates into stronger content, leading to higher exam pass rates and better practitioners.

✔ **Customizable training programs:** Stop wasting your employee's time by putting them through standardized training that they either won't use or have already mastered.

The high-level benefits that flow from these features include

✔ **Cost savings:** The ITMS Solutions Blended Learning Solution is 50–75 percent less expensive than traditional in-person training.

✔ **Efficiency:** Learners go through the program much faster, so they can get certified quicker and start performing better sooner.

> ✓ **Effectiveness:** Learners improve their IT management skills and add tangible value to their organizations through better project management, quality control, and communication.
>
> ✓ **Completion:** Because it's less expensive and faster, your IT department will actually get it done.

Make sure that your benefits relate directly to what you know or believe your prospects want. The benefits in the preceding two lists are meaningful to a corporate leader who fully understands the value proposition of IT service management training and the value of ITIL certification. If ITSM Solutions markets to a less savvy prospect, they must begin by describing the benefits of service management in terms of the operational problems it solves:

> *Is your IT department a constant series of annoyances and nightmares? Is it so siloed that the hardware and software engineers never talk except to blame each other for infrastructure failures? Do your IT services go down on a regular basis, and take ages to get back up again? Does your organization suffer from security breaches, or are you concerned that you aren't sufficiently protected against hackers? Are there persistent quality control issues around the IT services provided to end users? Do you mandate ongoing career training for your IT personnel, but lack any way to determine what they need to learn, whether they know it, or if they are in compliance with professional standards and certifications?*
>
> *ITSM Solutions provides top-quality, easily accessible, convenient, inexpensive training and certification to turn your IT department into a well-run team instead of a group of talented but mis-utilized individuals.*

Your goal is to help your prospects visualize the movie of their future, a future made rosy by the action they're about to take.

Provoking curiosity

If the next action involves education of your prospects, you have to whet their appetites for the information you have and they don't. Bullets that provoke curiosity include teasers ("The most dangerous seat on an airplane — page 5"), hidden information ("Best-kept secret in the travel industry"), promise of valuable knowledge ("How to spot slot machines that pay off most often"), warnings ("Surprise! Choosing the wrong private school for your child can cost you a bundle in tax breaks"), and questions ("Would you know how to keep your ticket safe if you won the lottery?").

Including third-party testimonials

For several reasons, third-party testimonials can sell more powerfully than you can. They can pull off this bit of magic because they are

✔ **Believable:** Your visitors have (unfortunately) been taught many times that salespeople will lie through their teeth to make a sale. Until you prove otherwise, you're presumed to be in that category. Your customers who say nice things about you don't have anything to gain by lying. On the contrary, they're risking their own "credibility capital" by going out on a limb and endorsing you.

✔ **Polite:** Grandma said that it's impolite to brag. If you can get your satisfied customers to do it for you, you can look bashfully pleased instead of boastful — while still getting your message across.

✔ **Benefit-based:** Testimonials are already formulated to highlight benefits because customers create them rather than you.

You can deploy four testimonial media on your landing page: video, audio, written text, and contact for more information. Video can be extremely effective if done well, but tends to be expensive, time-consuming, and a pain for your customers to give you. If your product margins are high enough and your customers thrilled enough, you could benefit from splurging on a videographer to capture those testimonials and edit them professionally.

Audio testimonials can be almost as powerful, and are much less expensive and time-consuming to produce. You can collect audio testimonials just by asking your customers to pick up a telephone and talk. Try it now: Call (214) 615-6505, extension 6900 and say something nice about this book. We may post your comment at `www.gafd3.com/readercomments`. You have to pay long-distance charges (because we're that cheap), but you can set up a toll-free audio line for just a few dollars a month. Visit `www.gafd.com/audio` for recommended services and advanced testimonial-gathering strategies.

Written testimonials by themselves are the least powerful, simply because you might have written them yourself. Including a photo of the customer next to the testimonial, along with their full name, title, URL, and physical location, can help a lot. Adding the written text below an audio or video, you can have the best of both worlds: believability and multiple modes of message delivery.

Finally, you can let your visitors know you have "references available upon request." This can work for big purchases later in the sales cycle; on the landing page, focus on delivering needed information immediately.

Giving clear instructions in the call to action

Somebody once said, "A confused mind always says 'no.'" In fact, if you're reading this book out loud, you just said it. Make sure your instructions for the action you want visitors to take are so clear and free of ambiguity that a reasonably intelligent hamster could follow them.

Not only will you explain exactly how to fill out the form, where the form is located, and what to click, but you will also tell them what happens next. What page will be served after they click "Send me the two free chapters!"? What will appear in their inboxes and in what time frame? Do they need to add you to their spam filters' white lists? If they phone you, who will answer? What extension should they ask for?

Tony Robbins likes to say that humans have a simultaneous need for certainty and excitement — a balance between what is known and what is unknown. At the point where someone is considering entering into a relationship with your website, your job is to reduce the already considerable uncertainty.

We highly recommend Ben Hunt's book *Convert!* to everyone who wants to make more money online next month than they made last month. Also, for a series of tutorials from Vitruvian's optimization team on landing page optimization using Google's free Website Optimizer tool, visit `www.gafd3.com/wso`. The combination of applying best practices and testing everything is the key to winning with AdWords.

Part IV
Managing Your AdWords Campaigns

The 5th Wave   By Rich Tennant

"Oh, we're doing just great. Philip and I are selling decorative jelly jars on the Web. I run the Web site and Philip sort of controls the inventory."

In this part . . .

After you create your campaigns, you'll probably lose money if you let them run just as you set up them originally. This part shows you how to manage bids, promote and demote keywords and placements, and perform some advanced keyword moves.

Chapter 10 introduces your new best friend, the free desktop program AdWords Editor. If you've gotten used to managing AdWords online, Editor requires a short learning curve and then turbo-charges your efficiency and ability to spot opportunities you'd miss otherwise.

Chapter 11 covers advanced keyword techniques to consider if your initial conservative strategy justifies expansion to less restrictive keyword match types.

Chapter 12 covers a special campaign type, for a local business seeking walk-in traffic to a store or phone calls to a service business.

And in Chapter 13, we give away the store by revealing some of the proprietary processes we use to continually optimize complex accounts as efficiently as possible.

Chapter 10

Saving Time with AdWords Editor

dWords Editor is a free desktop tool provided by Google that enables you to manage your account even when you are offline. If you've ever suffered from a slow Internet connection, you can appreciate how much time that feature alone can save. And about 99 percent of what you can see and do in the online AdWords interface can also be viewed and accomplished within AdWords Editor. (Let's just call it *Editor* for the rest of this chapter, shall we?) But rather than show you how to use Editor to do everything, this chapter shares just two AdWords tasks: cloning campaigns and managing bids. The former takes seconds in Editor and potentially hours online; the latter can be done elegantly in Editor with just some basic preparation and a few minutes per month. For the strategic use of campaign cloning, see Chapter 13.

This chapter needs an extra-whiny disclaimer about how quickly Google changes, and that what you see in Editor may be different from what we're showing here. These screen shots were taken on a Mac using Editor 9.0.1, which gives you an idea of how many updates Google has already made. But fear not: We're preparing an entire Editor section of this book's companion website that we'll keep updating. Besides, using Editor is really quick simple once you see it in action; much easier than any textual set of instructions might make it seem. View the online tutorials at www.gafd3.com/editor.

Downloading and Installing Editor

You can install Editor on your computer if you run Windows or Mac. Go to www.google.com/intl/en/adwordseditor/ (or simply search Google for AdWords editor and click the first organic listing that comes up), select your operating system, and click the Download AdWords Editor button. Save it somewhere you can navigate to easily, like your desktop or a Downloads folder, and then open and install the program. If you run Windows Vista and encounter error messages, look for troubleshooting instructions on that page.

Getting Your Campaigns into Editor

When you open Editor for the first time, don't panic when you don't see any data. You have to connect your account(s) to Editor, using your login e-mail and password.

1. **From the File menu at the top left, select Open Account and then click the Add Account button in the pop-up window.**

2. **Enter your account e-mail and password in the next pop-up window and then click Next.**

   The first time you do this, Google asks you to specify which part of the account you want to download.

3. **Select All Campaigns and then click OK.**

   A progress window (see Figure 10-1) shows you how many campaigns, ad groups, keywords, and ads are being downloaded into Editor.

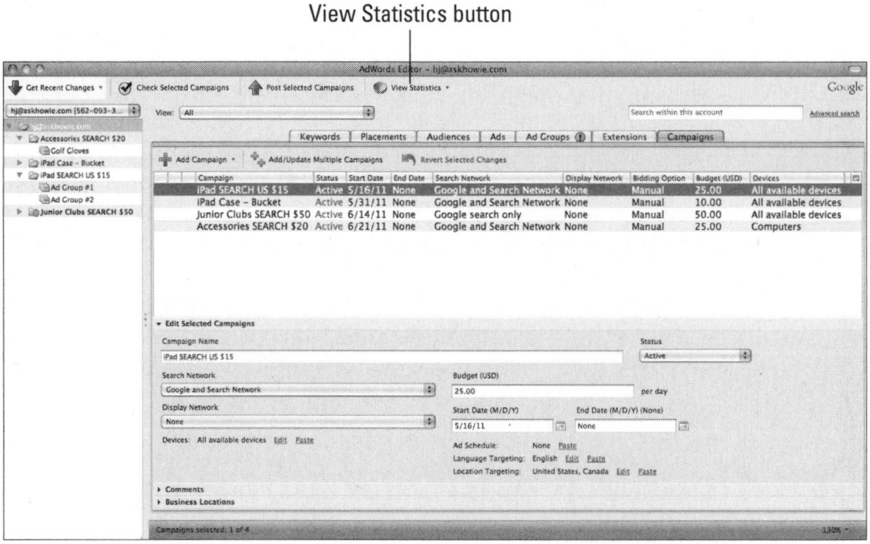

View Statistics button

Figure 10-1: Editor displays all your campaigns and ad groups as nesting folders in the left column and table rows in the main body.

Adding statistics

To this point, you've downloaded only your inputs: keywords, ads, ad groups, campaigns, settings, and bid and budget amounts. To manage bids using Editor, you need to download account statistics. To manage bids based on the last 30 days (a best practice we'll share in detail in a bit), follow these easy steps:

1. **Click the View Statistics button at the top center of the Editor Window (below the top menu; refer to Figure 10-1).**

2. **Select Whole Account (Slower) from the drop-down list.**

3. **Select Last 30 Days from the drop-down list of date ranges.**

4. **If you're asked to enter your login information again, do so in the pop-up window and then click Next.**

   A progress window shows you which statistics are being downloaded into Editor, and the View Statistics button now reads `Showing Statistics for: [The date range you specified]`.

Now you'll see data on clicks, impressions, click-through rate (CTR), and many other columns. You can recorder columns by clicking and dragging the column header to the left or right. You can show additional columns and hide existing ones by right-clicking any column name and selecting and deselecting column names. The columns appear and disappear instantly, so you can mold the interface to your liking without worrying about messing something up permanently.

Depending on the width of your computer monitor and your capacity to comprehend large volumes of numbers, you may want to hide columns that aren't immediately useful in managing the aspect of the account you're working on. For example, we often hide Status, Start Date, and End Date to open up the screen for more important data.

Adding conversion data

You'll be managing bids using conversion data (without it, you really have no rational basis for raising or lowering bids on specific keywords). Make sure that you add the following three columns: Conv. (1-per-click), Conv. Rate (1-per-click), and Cost/Conv. (1-per-click). In Figure 10-2, you can see AdWords Editor data that includes these three columns.

To add columns, simply right-click on any column header to bring up the Columns menu. Click next to any column name to add or remove it from the data table.

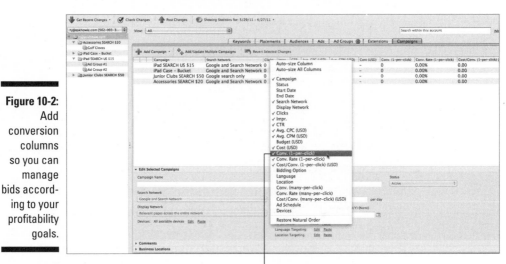

Figure 10-2:
Add conversion columns so you can manage bids according to your profitability goals.

Add these three columns.

In a bit, we'll explore a system for managing your bids in minutes per month. First, though, take a look at a more straightforward use for Editor: cloning campaigns.

Cloning Campaigns

In the old days, copying a campaign could take dozens of hours. Say that our client Bob Davies of WaterColour Secrets began with a UK-targeted campaign and wanted to expand into the U.S. market. Aside from the fact that the two markets would probably have very different economics and should be separated on that basis alone, there's a more immediate and practical issue: The British can't spell "color." (Kidding, kidding!)

To clone the UK campaign using the online AdWords interface, Bob would have to create a new campaign, input the new settings, add the ad groups one at a time (including all keywords and ads and perhaps even landing page URLs), and then manually change every instance of the word "colour" to "color" so the Yanks could find and relate to his business. In 2005, this would have been so time-consuming that Bob could easily have convinced himself that the effort just wasn't worth it (especially if he had a mature account with dozens of different campaigns, hundreds of ad groups, and tens of thousands of keywords).

Now, Editor can do the entire job in minutes.

Copying an existing campaign

Start by duplicating an existing campaign:

1. **Navigate to the Campaigns tab above the data table.**

2. **Select the campaign you wish to clone by clicking anywhere in its row so that the text changes to white on a blue background.**

3. **From the Edit menu at the top left, choose Copy from the drop-down list.**

4. **From the Edit menu, choose Paste from the drop-down list.**

   You will see a new row in the data table with the newly created campaign. It will have the same name as the old campaign, and an error icon (red circle with exclamation point) alerting you that your new campaign has the same name as an existing campaign. At the bottom of the Editor window is an area to edit the campaign.

5. **Start by changing the campaign name to one that signifies its new settings.**

   For example, Bob would change "Beginning Watercolour SEARCH ₤20 UK" to "Beginning Watercolor SEARCH ₤20 US."

Changing settings

Bob's next task is the change the geographic targeting of the new campaign because it inherited all the settings of its "parent" campaign.

To change campaign settings, make sure that the campaign you want to alter is selected in the campaign list. Go to the Edit Selected Campaigns section at the bottom of Editor. You can change anything you see in this section: name, status, networks, budget, devices, start and end dates, ad scheduling, and language and location targeting.

1. **To change location, click the Edit link next to Location Targeting at the bottom right.**

2. **From the pop-up window, you can select countries, regions, metropolitan areas, and cities.**

   As long as you aren't doing any fancy geo-targeting, like drawing lines on maps to define customized areas, you can use Editor. Otherwise, clone the campaign in Editor and then put the finishing touches on the campaign in the main online interface.

3. **Click OK when you're done.**

You can change multiple campaigns if their new settings will be identical. Simply hold down the Ctrl (Windows) or ⌘ (Mac) keys as you select campaigns to edit them together.

Making bulk changes to your account

Shifting gears a bit, we'll demonstrate how to make bulk changes in wording with a dummy account for the G-Form Extreme Sleeve for iPad. Pretend that in New Zealand, they spell the word "case" as "kase."

After we clone the iPad case campaign and adjust the settings to target New Zealand, we can use the powerful advanced search feature to quickly change "case" to "kase" everywhere in the new campaign, including keywords, ads, and URLs.

Changing keywords in bulk

1. **Select the new campaign from the nested list of campaigns and ad groups on the left.**

2. **Select the Keywords tab above the data table.**

3. **Click anywhere in the keyword list to select a row.**

4. **From the Edit menu at the top left, choose Select All from the drop-down list.**

5. **Click the small Replace Text link at the bottom left of the Editor window.**

6. **In the Replace Text dialog box that appears, enter the word you want to change (in this case, case) in the Find Text field. See Figure 10-3.**

7. **(Optional) Depending on the change, you may need to remove the check mark for Match Whole Words Only.**

8. **Enter the new word (kase) in the Replace With field.**

   You can preserve capitalization for your own benefit, but Google doesn't notice whether keywords are capitalized or not.

9. **Click the Find Matches button to make the replacements.**

10. **Confirm your desire to replace the text by clicking the Replace All button in the warning window that appears.**

Making bulk changes to ads

You can also change ad text in bulk in very much the same way as keywords. The only difference is instead of working from the Keywords tab, you now select the Ads tab.

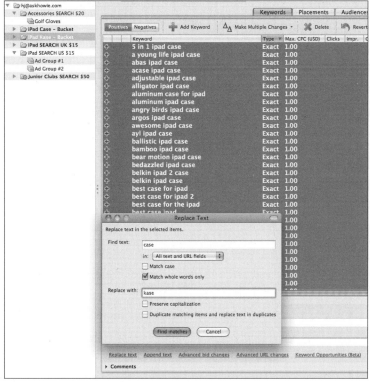

Figure 10-3:
Find and
replace
keywords in
bulk using
the Replace
Text feature.

1. **Select the new campaign from the nested list of campaigns and ad groups on the left.**

2. **Select the Ads tab above the data table.**

3. **Click anywhere in the ad list to select a row.**

4. **From the Edit menu at the top left, choose Select All from the drop-down list.**

5. **Click the small Replace Text link at the bottom left of the Editor window.**

6. **Enter the word you want to change (in this case, case) in the Find Text field of the Replace Text dialog box.**

7. **(Optional) Depending on the change, you may need to remove the check mark for Match Whole Words Only.**

8. **Enter the new word (kase) in the Replace With field.**

9. **Mark the Preserve Capitalization check box to retain the same capitalization scheme as the existing ads.**

10. **Click the Find Matches button to make the replacements.**

11. **Confirm your desire to replace the text by clicking Replace All in the warning window.**

If you want to change the ad group names, you have to do those individually. However, the important elements of the account — keywords, ad text, and display and destination URLs — now contain the changes.

Uploading the new campaign

When you're satisfied with your new campaign, upload it into your account. Look for the + sign to the left of the element row to identify campaigns, ad groups, and ad keywords that you have added via Editor but haven't yet uploaded to your account. Also, these elements are bolded. Changed elements show a triangle (delta sign) at the far left. See Figure 10-4.

Upload the changes by clicking the Post Changes button with the blue up-arrow at the top of the Editor window. Editor shows you the details of the proposed upload, so you can make sure you're not making a big mistake. If those details look right, click the Post button at the bottom of the window to "make it so."

In case you're worried about overwriting your entire account by mistake, you can proactively use Editor to create backups of your account. Visit `www.gafd3.com/editor-backup` for a quick tutorial.

Figure 10-4:
Editor indicates new and changed account elements that have not been made live with bold text and icons.

	Keyword	Type ▼	Max. CPC (USD)	Clicks	Impr.	CTR	Avg.
Δ	**monogrammed ipad2 case**	**Broad**	1.00	0	0	–	–
+	**yellow ipad2 case**	**Broad**	1.00				
	5 in 1 ipad case	Exact	1.00	0	0	–	–
	a young life ipad case	Exact	1.00	0	0	–	–
	abas ipad case	Exact	1.00	0	0	–	–
	acase ipad case	Exact	1.00	0	0	–	–

Tabs above table: Keywords | Placements | Audiences | Ads

Toolbar: Positives | Negatives | Add Keyword | Δ Make Multiple Changes ▾ | Delete | Revert Selected Chang

Managing Bids with Editor

The promise of Editor to save you time and make you money reaches its fulfillment when it comes to bid management. Now, "bid management" may not seem like a very exciting concept, so allow us to phrase it differently:

✔ Quickly lower bids on all keywords that are losing money.

✔ Quickly raise bids on all keywords where you can make more money by bidding higher.

Every keyword has a *sweet spot bid,* an amount that maximizes the amount of profit it will produce. Bids that are too high won't generate enough conversions to pay for the cost of the clicks. Conversely, bids that are too low won't generate enough traffic in the AdWords auction to produce profits. And if you have thousands or tens of thousands of keywords, you need an efficient way to find those keywords and change bids *en masse* — and Editor is your tool.

Campaign naming conventions

In Chapter 7, we share some best practices for naming your campaigns. Now you'll see exactly how to exploit these conventions to make bid management a snap in Editor.

The main campaign distinctions that AdWords beginners need to deal with include

✔ **Network:** Search or Display

✔ **Match Type:** Exact, Phrase, or Broad (for Search network campaigns only)

✔ **Location:** Country/Region

✔ **Value of a Conversion:** In dollars, or whatever currency you use

Of these characteristics, the value of a conversion is the most important for bid management. The other distinctions aren't strictly necessary for the nitty-gritty of bid management, although they will help you see the overall picture of the relative performance of the different campaign types.

Display campaigns typically convert less robustly than Search campaigns, and broad-match keywords generally convert far less effectively than exact match. For AdWords beginners especially, separating these campaign types can mean the difference between achieving profitability or giving up entirely after a month or two.

Return to the imaginary online golf equipment store that we use in Chapter 7 to see how this might work. Our store, www.joesgolfshack.com, sells items in the following price categories:

✔ Accessories (less than $20)

✔ Clothing ($50 to $200)

✔ Equipment ($200 to $500)

✔ Premium Products/Services (more than $1,000)

Each category becomes a single campaign. Because we're starting smart, each campaign is in the Google Search network only, US-only, and exact-match keywords only. In about five minutes, we'll use Editor to identify and throttle down keyword bids that are too high.

Start with the accessories campaign, which we named "Accessories SEARCH $20."

Monthly bid management

Unless your traffic volume is so huge and the market so variable that you need to stay on top of things much more frequently, we recommend managing bids on a monthly basis. For most beginners, once per month is perfect because your account will take that long to accrue actionable data.

And because raising and lowering bids are so different from a psychological perspective, we've found that separating them into different days makes each task a bit easier.

Day 1: Lower bids that are too high

Any keyword that costs more than it returns in profit should have its bid lowered. By comparing the cost per conversion for each keyword to the maximum cost per conversion in the campaign name, it's easy to find these keywords and lower their bids in bulk.

1. **Within Editor, download the account statistics for the previous 30 days. (See the section, "Adding Statistics" earlier in this chapter.)**

2. **Select the first campaign to manage by selecting its folder in the left column.**

   If you can't see the three 1-per-click conversion columns (Conv., Conv. Rate, and Cost/Conv.), right-click any of the column headers and select those three columns.

3. **To avoid making rash decisions based on too little activity, filter to eliminate all keywords that have generated fewer than two conversions in the 30-day period under scrutiny.**

   a. *Click the Advanced Search link at the top right of Editor.*

   b. *In the Advanced Search dialog box that opens, go to Performance Statistics and select Conv. (1-per-click) from the drop-down list.*

   c. *To the right, select Is Greater Than from the drop-down list.*

   d. *In the far right text box, enter the number **1** (see Figure 10-5).*

   e. *You'll be using this filter a lot, so select the Save This Search for Reuse check box and give it a name like Conv > 1.*

   f. *Click the Search button at the bottom left of the window.*

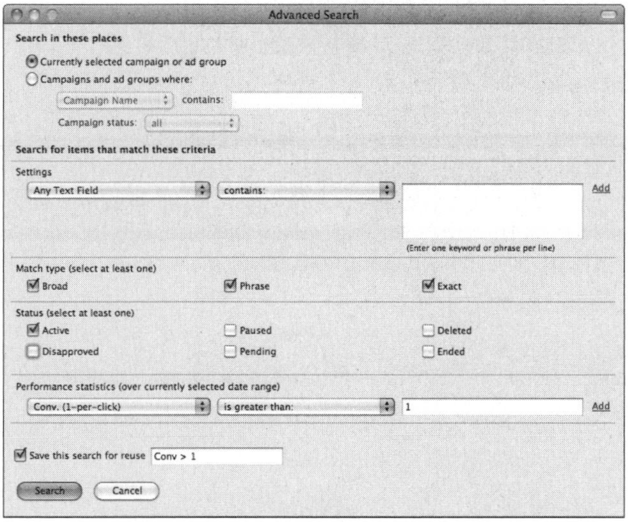

Figure 10-5: Filter out keywords that have generated fewer than two conversions to avoid overreacting to a fluke conversion.

Now you have a table consisting of all the keywords in that campaign that have generated at least two conversions in the past 30 days.

4. **Sort by Cost/Conv., descending, by clicking that column header so that it turns blue and a down arrow appears to the right of the text (see Figure 10-6).**

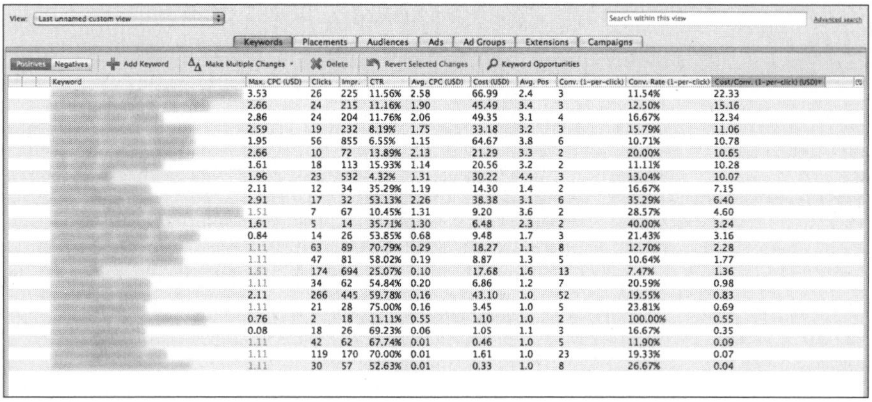

Keyword	Max. CPC (USD)	Clicks	Impr.	CTR	Avg. CPC (USD)	Cost (USD)	Avg. Pos	Conv. (1-per-click)	Conv. Rate (1-per-click)	Cost/Conv. (1-per-click) (USD)
	3.53	26	225	11.56%	2.58	66.99	2.4	3	11.54%	22.33
	2.66	24	215	11.16%	1.90	45.49	3.4	3	12.50%	15.16
	2.86	24	204	11.76%	2.06	49.35	3.1	4	16.67%	12.34
	2.59	19	232	8.19%	1.75	33.18	3.2	3	15.79%	11.06
	1.95	56	855	6.55%	1.15	64.67	3.8	6	10.71%	10.78
	2.66	10	72	13.89%	2.13	21.29	3.3	2	20.00%	10.65
	1.61	18	113	15.93%	1.14	20.56	3.2	2	11.11%	10.28
	1.96	23	532	4.32%	1.31	30.22	4.4	3	13.04%	10.07
	2.11	12	34	35.29%	1.19	14.30	1.4	2	16.67%	7.15
	2.91	17	32	53.13%	2.26	38.38	3.1	6	35.29%	6.40
	1.51	7	67	10.45%	1.31	9.20	3.6	2	28.57%	4.60
	1.61	5	14	35.71%	1.30	6.48	2.3	2	40.00%	3.24
	0.84	14	26	53.85%	0.68	9.48	1.7	3	21.43%	3.16
	1.11	63	89	70.79%	0.29	18.27	1.1	8	12.70%	2.28
	1.11	47	81	58.02%	0.19	8.87	1.3	5	10.64%	1.77
	1.51	174	694	25.07%	0.10	17.68	1.6	13	7.47%	1.36
	1.11	34	62	54.84%	0.20	6.86	1.2	7	20.59%	0.98
	2.11	266	445	59.78%	0.16	43.10	1.0	52	19.55%	0.83
	1.11	21	28	75.00%	0.16	3.45	1.0	5	23.81%	0.69
	0.76	2	18	11.11%	0.55	1.10	1.0	2	100.00%	0.55
	0.08	18	26	69.23%	0.06	1.05	1.1	3	16.67%	0.35
	1.11	42	62	67.74%	0.01	0.46	1.0	5	11.90%	0.09
	1.11	119	170	70.00%	0.01	1.61	1.0	23	19.33%	0.07
	1.11	30	57	52.63%	0.01	0.33	1.0	8	26.67%	0.04

Figure 10-6: All keywords that have generated two or more conversions in the past 30 days.

Pretending this campaign is our golf accessories campaign, where the average profit per order is $20, we see just one keyword in the red, the very top one with a Cost/Conv. of $22.33. That's about 10 percent over break-even, so a conservative course of action would be to lower its bid by 10 percent. Here's how.

1. **Select the offending keyword by clicking anywhere in its column, so that the column changes to white text on a blue background.**

   Note the Max. CPC of this keyword (currently $3.53).

2. **Click the small Advanced Bid Changes link at the bottom left of the Editor window.**

3. **In the Advanced Bid Changes dialog box that appears, select the Decrease Bids By radio button, enter the number** 10 **there, and leave the drop-down menu next to it set for Percent (see Figure 10-7).**

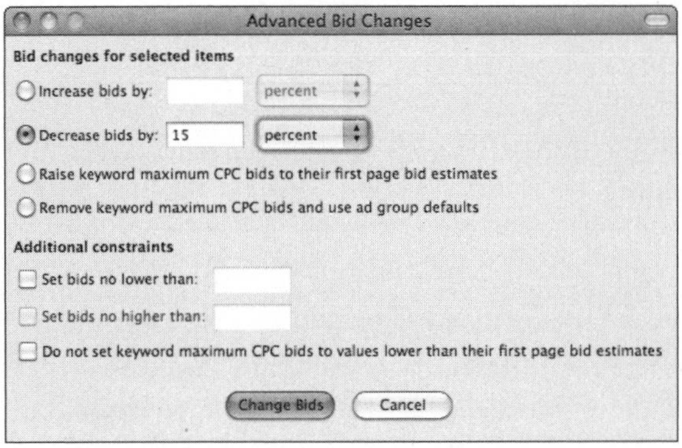

Figure 10-7: Editor will automatically lower the bid by the percentage you specify.

4. **Click the Change Bids button to save your changes and close the window.**

5. **Click Apply Changes to confirm your bid change.**

6. **Double-check that the keyword you selected now has a lower Max CPC bid than before.**

   Figure 10-8 shows that it does, at $3.18.

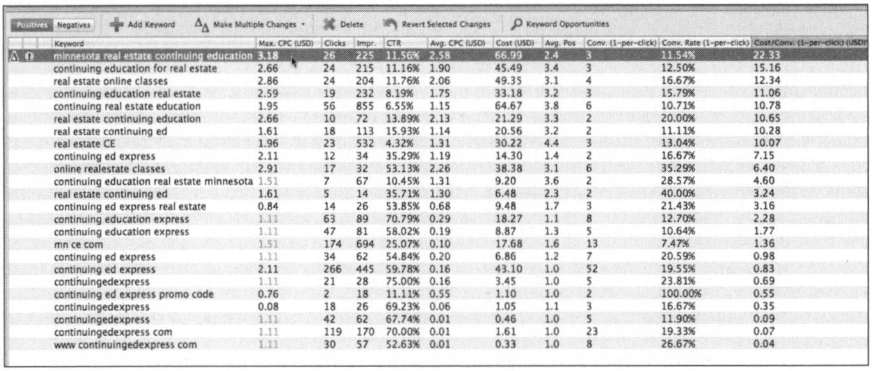

Positives | Negatives | Add Keyword | Make Multiple Changes | Delete | Revert Selected Changes | Keyword Opportunities

Keyword	Max. CPC (USD)	Clicks	Impr.	CTR	Avg. CPC (USD)	Cost (USD)	Avg. Pos	Conv. (1-per-click)	Conv. Rate (1-per-click)	Cost/Conv. (1-per-click) (USD)
minnesota real estate continuing education	3.18	26	225	11.56%	2.58	66.99	2.4	3	11.54%	22.33
continuing education for real estate	2.66	24	215	11.16%	1.90	45.49	3.4	3	12.50%	15.16
real estate online classes	2.86	24	204	11.76%	2.06	49.35	3.1	4	16.67%	12.34
continuing education real estate	2.59	19	232	8.19%	1.75	33.18	3.2	3	15.79%	11.06
continuing real estate education	1.95	56	855	6.55%	1.15	64.67	3.8	6	10.71%	10.78
real estate continuing education	2.66	10	72	13.89%	2.13	21.29	3.3	2	20.00%	10.65
real estate continuing ed	1.61	18	113	15.93%	1.14	20.56	3.2	2	11.11%	10.28
real estate CE	1.96	23	532	4.32%	1.31	30.22	4.4	3	13.04%	10.07
continuing ed express	2.11	12	34	35.29%	1.19	14.30	1.4	2	16.67%	7.15
online realestate classes	2.91	17	32	53.13%	2.26	38.38	3.1	6	35.29%	6.40
continuing education real estate minnesota	1.51	7	67	10.45%	1.31	9.20	3.6	2	28.57%	4.60
real estate continuing ed	1.61	5	14	35.71%	1.30	6.48	2.3	2	40.00%	3.24
continuing ed express real estate	0.84	14	26	53.85%	0.68	9.48	1.7	3	21.43%	3.16
continuing education express	1.11	63	89	70.79%	0.29	18.27	1.1	8	12.70%	2.28
continuing education express	1.11	47	81	58.02%	0.19	8.87	1.3	5	10.64%	1.77
mn ce com	1.51	174	694	25.07%	0.10	17.68	1.6	13	7.47%	1.36
continuing ed express	1.11	34	62	54.84%	0.20	6.86	1.2	7	20.59%	0.98
continuing ed express	2.11	266	445	59.78%	0.16	43.10	1.0	52	19.55%	0.83
continuingedexpress	1.11	21	28	75.00%	0.16	3.45	1.0	5	23.81%	0.69
continuing ed express promo code	0.76	2	18	11.11%	0.55	1.10	1.0	2	100.00%	0.55
continuingedexpress	0.08	18	26	69.23%	0.06	1.05	1.1	3	16.67%	0.35
continuingedexpress	1.11	42	62	67.74%	0.01	0.46	1.0	5	11.90%	0.09
continuingedexpress com	1.11	119	170	70.00%	0.01	1.61	1.0	23	19.33%	0.07
www continuingedexpress com	1.11	30	57	52.63%	0.01	0.33	1.0	8	26.67%	0.04

Figure 10-8: The new bid is 15% lower than the old bid.

The preceding example changes a single keyword bid. Most of the time, you'll discover that multiple bids need to be adjusted. You accomplish this in exactly the same way: Select all the keywords whose bids are too high and follow the same steps.

You have one more task to accomplish before moving on to the next campaign: managing keywords that aren't converting at all.

Day 1: Managing non-converting keywords

In this running example, when we filter for two or more conversions, we eliminate from view all the keywords that haven't generated a single conversion. If a keyword has generated thousands of expensive clicks but no sales, we certainly want to do something about it.

1. **From with the Keywords tab of your chosen campaign, click the Advanced Search link at the top right.**

2. **In the Advanced Search dialog box that opens, keep Conv. (1-per-click) as the measure but change the performance statistics filter to "equals" and "0" (see Figure 10-9).**

   Again, save this search for reuse — call it Conv = 0 — and select the Save This Search for Reuse check box.

3. **Click the Search button to filter for keywords that have generating zero conversions in the past 30 days.**

4. **Sort descending by cost by clicking the Cost column header so that it turns blue and displays a down arrow.**

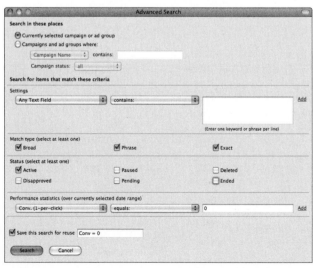

Figure 10-9:
Filter
for non-
converting
keywords
to eliminate
wasteful
spending
in your
account.

5. **Select all keywords whose cost is at least five times the average value of a conversion.**

   In other words, if the value of a conversion for your campaign is $20, you're looking for keywords with a cost of $100 or greater.

6. **Pause these keywords by changing their status in the bottom-right drop-down list from Active to Paused.**

7. **Make a note of any keywords that generate enough traffic to warrant an attempt at rehabilitation.**

   See Chapter 11 for keyword management strategies.

   For keywords whose cost ranges from two to five times the value of a conversion, you're not ready to pause them, but you do want to slow down the bleeding.

8. **Select these keywords and lower their bids by 25%.**

   In the biannual review (upcoming), you'll re-evaluate these keywords using six months of data.

After you do this for your first campaign, select another campaign and repeat, this time basing your decisions on the average value of a conversion in the next campaign. (For the imaginary golf store, that would be the $50 clothing campaign.)

Continue until you lower bids on all keywords that are producing conversions that don't fully offset the cost of clicks. When you're done lowering bids, don't forget to post your changes by clicking the Post Changes button at the top of the Editor window.

Then take a couple of weeks off and let the data accumulate. You're not being lazy; just patient and wise!

Having (95%) confidence in statistical significance

Why wait until a keyword has spent five times the value of a conversion before turning it off? Basically, you want to be at least 95% confident that we're making the right decision. For example, if you flip a coin twice and it comes up heads both times, would you jump to the assumption that it would always come up heads? Of course not — two flips don't give you enough data to reach that conclusion. What about four flips, all heads? Still not enough data. Ten flips, all heads? Are you getting a tad suspicious now? It could still be due to random chance — after all, every single flip of a fair coin has an equal chance of landing heads or tails — or, possibly, this is no fair coin.

The mathematics are beyond the scope of this book, but waiting for a cost of five times the average value of a conversion gives you close to that 95% confidence — meaning that you'll willing to make a mistake 1 time of every 20.

Day 15: Raise bids that are too low

Two weeks after lowering bids on too-expensive keywords, come back to Editor and look for keywords on which you want to bid more. If you have keywords whose Cost/Conv. is far below your value/conversion, you may find that by increasing their bids you can generate more conversions at a cost that is still below your account average.

The only way to increase impressions for those keywords is to bid more for a higher position on the page. If these keywords are already showing at Avg. Pos 1, you can't get them any higher than that. Ignore them for now by filtering out keywords in positions greater than 2.5.

1. **Filter for keywords with at least two conversions whose average position is 2.5 or greater.**

   a. *With a single campaign selected, navigate to the Keywords tab and click Advanced Search at the top right of the Editor window.*

   b. *In the Advanced Search dialog box, create a filter of Conv. (1-per-click) is greater than 1, and then click the Add link to create a second filter of Avg. Pos is greater than 2.5.*

   c. *Save the search with a name like Conv > 1, Pos > 2.5 and then click the Search button at the bottom of the window (see Figure 10-10).*

2. **Sort the table of keywords by Cost/Conv. ascending (the lowest values appear at the top of the table) by clicking the column header twice so that it turns blue and displays an up arrow.**

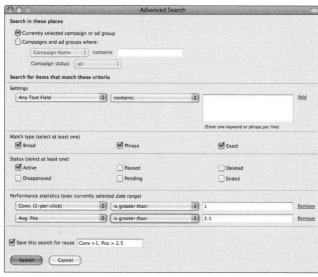

Figure 10-10: Filter for keywords with at least two conversions in position 2.5 or greater to find opportunities to raise bids.

3. **Find keywords whose Cost/Conv. is significantly below the value of a conversion.**

   In Figure 10-11, the first two keywords provide considerably more margin than the rest, with Cost/Conv. of $4.60 and $6.40, respectively. Given a cost per conversion of $20, you can raise these bids by 100% and still have plenty of margin left.

4. **Note the average position for these keywords.**

   In Figure 10-11, they are in position 3.6 and 3.1, respectively. Bumping up the bid prices will move the ads into a higher position, which should increase both impressions and CTR.

5. **Note the current Max. CPC of these keywords (in Figure 10-11, $1.51 and $2.91, respectively).**

6. **Select the keywords to bid up by clicking the top one, holding down the Shift key, and then clicking the bottom one whose bid you wish to raise.**

   All the keywords up to and including the last one you clicked should be highlighted.

7. **Click the Advanced Bid Changes link at the bottom left of the Editor window.**

8. **In the Advanced Bid Changes window, increase bids by 100% (doubling them) and then click Change Bids and Apply Changes to confirm your changes.**

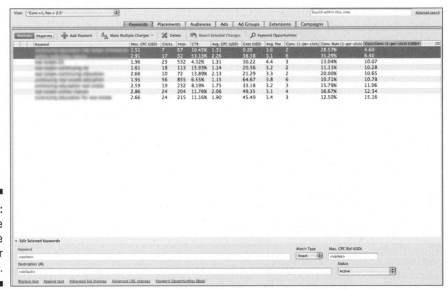

Figure 10-11:
Note the
average
position for
keywords.

9. **Check the Max. CPC of the keywords to make sure you did what you meant to do.**

   In Figure 10-12, the bids are now $3.02 and $5.82.

10. **In a month, come back and reevaluate.**

Please understand that you should not always raise bids by 100 percent. You might raise the bids by just 15 percent on the keywords in the $10 Cost/Conv. range because the $20 ceiling represents break-even. Also, if your account overall is not doing well, you can raise bids more conservatively by filtering for keywords with average position greater than 4, rather than 2.5. When in doubt, go slow and be conservative until you get the hang of bid management.

When you're done raising bids, don't forget to post your changes by clicking the Post Changes button at the top of the Editor Window.

Changing bids for Display network campaigns

If and when you expand into the Display network, you can no longer manage bids on the keyword level because keywords don't apply to Display campaigns. Instead, you have to change bids on the ad group level.

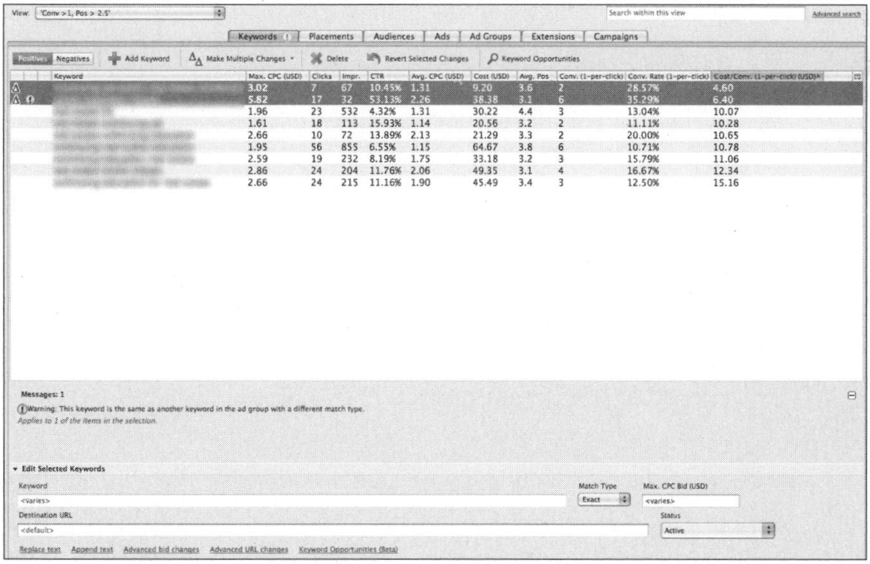

Figure 10-12: Raising bids on two very high-margin keywords can generate more traffic and still decrease the average customer acquisition cost of the entire account.

In Figure 10-13, you can see a table of six ad groups from a Display campaign. You can likely spot the one ad group that's not like the others — the top one has a Cost/Conv. of $63.07, compared with less than $2.50 for the other five. Assuming a conversion value of $50, you would lower the bid by about 25 percent on that top ad group.

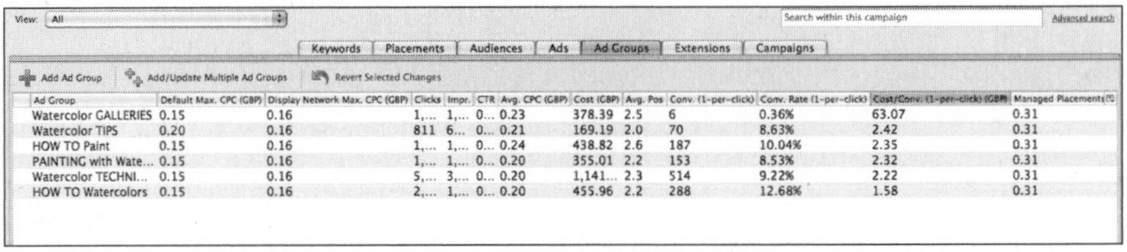
View: All
Search within this campaign
Advanced search
Keywords
Placements
Audiences
Ads
Ad Groups
Extensions
Campaigns
Add Ad Group
Add/Update Multiple Ad Groups
Revert Selected Changes
Ad Group | Default Max. CPC (GBP) | Display Network Max. CPC (GBP) | Clicks | Impr. | CTR | Avg. CPC (GBP) | Cost (GBP) | Avg. Pos | Conv. (1-per-click) | Conv. Rate (1-per-click) | Cost/Conv. (1-per-click) (GBP) | Managed Placements
Watercolor GALLERIES 0.15 0.16 1,... 1,... 0... 0.23 378.39 2.5 6 0.36% 63.07 0.31
Watercolor TIPS 0.20 0.16 811 6... 0... 0.21 169.19 2.0 70 8.63% 2.42 0.31
HOW TO Paint 0.15 0.16 1,... 1,... 0... 0.24 438.82 2.6 187 10.04% 2.35 0.31
PAINTING with Wate... 0.15 0.16 1,... 1,... 0... 0.20 355.01 2.2 153 8.53% 2.32 0.31
Watercolor TECHNI... 0.15 0.16 5,... 3,... 0... 0.20 1,141... 2.3 514 9.22% 2.22 0.31
HOW TO Watercolors 0.15 0.16 2,... 1,... 0... 0.20 455.96 2.2 288 12.68% 1.58 0.31

Figure 10-13: Change bids on the ad group level for Display network campaigns.

Biannual schedule

The monthly maintenance catches keywords whose bids are too high or too low — as long as they have enough traffic to establish some degree of statistical confidence. But what about all the keywords that lope along, gathering relatively few clicks and impressions month to month, but collectively comprising up to 30-50% of the account? Every six months, it's time to repeat all the processes we describe earlier, but using six months of data rather than 30 days.

Generate this data by clicking the Showing Statistics For: [date range] button at the top of the Editor window and then choosing selecting Whole Account and Create Customer Date Range from the nested drop-down lists. Then input your start and end dates and click OK.

After you get the hang of these steps and see first-hand the value of this kind of granular and ROI–based keyword bid management, you'll find yourself looking forward to the pruning and watering that keeps the garden of your business healthy and productive. And you'll be amazed at how little time you really need to devote to it.

Chapter 11

Improving Your Campaigns through Keyword Management

In This Chapter

▶ Finding new keywords

▶ Resuscitating keyword by tightening ad groups

▶ Segmenting keywords to control exposure and cost

▶ Deploying negative keywords

Time to go fishing, metaphorically speaking. The fish are your prospects, swimming around in that great big ocean called "the market." How do you get them into your bucket as paying clients and customers? You need a well-baited hook, of course — your ads. You also need a rod and reel, and maybe a net — your landing page and conversion process. Finally, you need a bucket — the goods and services you provide in exchange for their money.

All set? Ready to fish? Almost. You need a place to drop anchor. Sure, you can cast a line into a bathtub or city fountain, but chances aren't good that you'll come home with dinner.

In the Search network, keywords represent those locations and times. Each keyword represents its own medium and will respond differently to your offers and value proposition. The more "good fishin' hole" keywords you find, nurture, and bait appropriately, the more leads and sales you can make.

In this chapter, we cover ways of finding new keywords that may not be obvious choices, resuscitating poorly performing keywords by changing the bait, and exploring three different methods of keyword fishing: exact match (using a fishing pole), phrase match (using a net), and broad match (using dynamite). After you master exact match and start deploying phrase and broad matches, we also show you how to deploy negative keywords to avoid snaring old boots, tires, and dolphins.

Nurturing, Relocating, and Firing Keywords

The keywords in your account are either making money or losing money. They can be optimized or sub-optimized for performance. And they can be restricted by budget or unrestricted. Your job is threefold:

- ✔ Get all your keywords to make money.
- ✔ Optimize your keywords' performance.
- ✔ Get as much traffic for your ROI-positive keywords as you can handle.

Keyword performance in AdWords is a linear process. Each keyword must jump through four hoops, and in order, to be successful. Before you start trying to improve keyword performance, use the following four metrics to diagnose the problem:

- ✔ Impressions
- ✔ Clicks (CTR)
- ✔ Conversions (Conversion Rate)
- ✔ Return on Investment (ROI)

If your keyword generates no impressions, for example, don't focus on writing better ads. Similarly, if you're getting lots of clicks and not enough conversions, don't increase the bid price to appear higher on the search results page.

Tailor your response to the weakest link in the keyword chain.

The next few sections discuss these four metrics in detail.

Impressions

How often does the keyword deliver an ad to a searcher? A keyword that doesn't cause ads to be viewed can't generate clicks for those ads.

Think of impressions as the wind in your sails. Skillful sailors can harness winds of different strengths and directions, but they can't make the wind blow harder. If you have a keyword that people aren't searching for, there's not much you can do about that except find other keywords or interrupt folks on the Display network.

Don't judge too quickly, however. Sometimes a low impression count is an arti-fact of your account rather than a reflection of an anemic market. Before you give up, check for three things that might be suppressing your impression count:

✔ A daily budget that throttles your traffic

✔ A low Quality Score (1–2) that tells you Google doesn't want to risk its good name sending traffic to your website

✔ An average position that puts your ads on the second page of search results (or worse)

You can display three impression share (IS) columns that will help you figure out whether you're losing impressions because of over-stingy budgeting or low ad rank (getting muscled off the first page by your competitors' better ads).

You can see these metrics only at the campaign level; you can't drill down into ad groups or keywords.

1. **From the All Online Campaigns page, click the Columns button and select Customize Columns.**

2. **Under the Competitive Metrics header, select the Impr. Share, Lost IS (Budget), and Lost IS (Rank) check boxes. See Figure 11-1.**

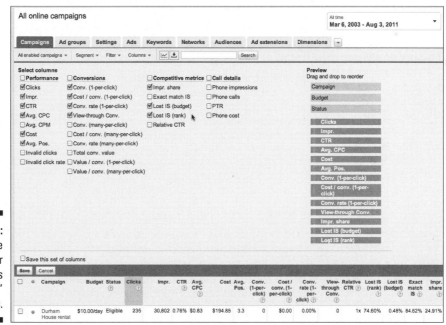

Figure 11-1: See where your campaigns are "leaking" impressions.

The impression share metrics shows you where your campaigns are "leaking" impressions because of inadequate budget or low ad rank. By "leaking," we mean that your ads didn't receive as many impressions as Google could have given them because something about your campaign wasn't fully in the "on" position. If your daily budget is too low, your ads will stop showing each day when you use up that budget. And if your ad rank is too low, Google preferentially shows your competitors' ads instead of yours.

3. Click Save.

Impression Mistake: Bidding high, budgeting low

A common Adwords mistake is to bid high with a low daily budget. For example, a $2 Max. CPC keyword in a $10/day campaign generates 5 clicks per day. As soon as click #5 comes in, Google shuts down the campaign for the day, even if it's only 4 a.m. Your ads won't benefit from any other search traffic until the following midnight. The solution there is to do one of the following:

✔ **Raise the daily budget.**

✔ **Stretch it.**

   • *Bid less aggressively.*

   • *Bid on less-expensive keywords (those with a lower Max CPC requirement).*

Imagine Joel taking a road trip from Denver to visit Howie in Durham, and refusing to use a credit card to charge his gas purchases. Instead, he relies on the ATMs at the service stations, whose daily maximum withdrawal equals $100. With a daily gas budget of $100 (his daily budget) and assuming a cost per gallon of $4, he can buy 25 gallons of gas per day. This amount of gas could fuel a 2010 Prius for 1,250 miles (representing a low CPC) but get him only 150 miles in a Class A motor home (symbolizing a high CPC). If he chose the motor home, it would take him 11 days to make the trip, while the Prius would get him there in less than 2.

If this analogy confuses you, blame Joel, who's probably sitting in a Papa John's off I-40 near Columbia, Missouri right about now.

Low Quality Score

Another reason you might not be getting as many eyeballs on your ads as possible is a low Quality Score. Google throttles those keywords with Quality Scores of 1 or 2. As a result, you're probably getting 10–20 percent as many impressions as are theoretically available to you. If your keywords earn a low Quality Score, you need to improve your landing pages and website. (See the discussion later in this chapter on "Resuscitating poor quality keywords.")

Here's one way to look at Quality Score. Joel decides on a different vehicular option for his road trip: a 1968 Chevy Valiant that hasn't been tuned up or washed since the Nixon administration. It may get Joel to Durham eventually, but not before being stopped every 30 miles by a state trooper determined to remove hazards like that from the highway.

Low Average Rank

If your ads aren't showing on the first page of Search (positions 1–8, typically), you need to raise your bids and/or CTR to qualify for the coveted first page. An average position of 37 indicates, for example, that your ad is languishing somewhere at the bottom of page 4 of the search results. When was the last time you clicked through to page 4 on Google? Your prospects aren't doing that, either.

If Joel's road trip to North Carolina suffered from Low Average Rank, he's probably walking old Interstate 24 instead of driving on I-40. His gas mileage (ROI) will be astronomical, but it will take him so long to get to Durham that Howie will have moved to South Africa by then.

Clicks (CTR)

After your ads are showing in response to a keyword, the next step is to compel searchers to click through to your website. Keywords generate clicks when the searcher looks at your ad and thinks, "This is for me, right now!" Your keyword won't generate clicks if the ad is irrelevant, undifferentiated, or too low on the page to be noticed.

Only when your keyword generates clicks does it have a chance of generating conversions.

When your keywords deliver lots of impressions but few clicks, the problem is the connection between the keyword and the ad. Move your keyword to an ad group that addresses the desire represented by that keyword or increase your bid to move the ad to a more desirable position.

You must show ad copy that's relevant to the intent of the search. Ask yourself: "What is this searcher trying to accomplish when they type this keyword? What are they looking for? What promise do they want to see?"

Consider also whether multiple meanings exist for the keyword. For example, "apple" can refer to a fruit, a technology company, a music studio, and a lane in Lawrence, Kansas. If your keyword is phrase or broad, adding negatives can improve CTR (and more importantly, ROI) by eliminating irrelevant searches. (See more about negatives later in this chapter.)

Also, if your ad position is at the bottom of the search results page, you can increase your bid to make your ad more visible.

If you've tried everything and can't generate clicks, you can pause or delete the keyword to avoid lowering your account's quality score.

Conversions (Conversion Rate)

Most AdWords users are satisfied with high CTRs and lots of visitors to their websites. Not you, oh wise *For Dummies* reader! You realize that getting lots of clicks means nothing more than paying Google lots of money. What you're looking for is conversions, or that money coming back to you with friends.

If your keyword generates lots of clicks but few conversions, there's a gap between the promise of the ad and the fulfillment of that promise on your website. You have to connect the two, either by altering the ad to reflect your site, or by changing your site to follow through on the ad's promise.

Return on Investment (ROI)

In simple terms, are you making money? You can have keywords that get lots of impressions, clicks, and conversions, but whose economics still put you in the red. For example, if your cost per click is $5, your conversion rate is 2%, and your average profit on a sale is $200, then you're losing $50, on average, on each sale. (A 2% conversion rate means that 1 of every 50 clicks turns into a sale, so you spend $250 in clicks for each $200 sale.)

After you set up conversion tracking (described in Chapter 6), you discover that some keywords appear to be doing well within the AdWords account — lots of traffic, good CTR — but don't convert to sales well enough to justify the cost of their clicks. (If you set up conversion tracking to track order value, you can determine the ROI of each keyword.) This type of underperformance is especially insidious because it's hard to identify. In Chapter 13, we show you how to spot Expense Account Gluttons that cost you more than they make for you.

You deal with negative-ROI keywords by first trying the tactic just described for low-CTR keywords: Point them to better ads. If the increased CTR doesn't make them profitable, write ads with negative qualifiers such as price and other disincentives to click (see Chapter 8).

Other ways to improve your keyword ROI include

- Bidding lower
- Increasing the conversion rate on your website by creating landing pages more relevant to the searcher's intent
- Increasing your prices and/or margins
- Building a back end of additional products and services

You can also separate different traffic streams and bid differently on each stream based on its unique metrics. (See Chapter 16 to discover the magic of campaign cloning.)

If nothing you do brings a particular keyword into profitability, you have to let that keyword go. Delete or pause it, and don't worry about it beyond that — someone else will blissfully (and cluelessly) continue losing money on that keyword. Just don't let it be you.

Before deleting or pausing keywords, try lowering the bid to see whether the keyword performs better at a lower cost.

Resuscitating poor-quality keywords

Since July 2006, Google has been rolling out regular changes to its bid price algorithm. These changes are designed to improve the search experience (and boost Google's profits). The most important factor in determining your bid price, aside from what your competitors are willing to pay, is your Keyword Quality Score. Quality Score takes into account your CTR (the higher, the more clicks and the more money Google makes) and a determination of the relevance and quality of your landing page to that search.

The Quality Score algorithm continues to evolve (and no one outside the hallowed halls of Google knows exactly what it is), but the trend is clear: Google wants to make money today (high CTR) and tomorrow (your customers can find what they want quickly and easily, with no hassle, so they continue to regard Google as the search engine of choice).

Keywords are ranked for quality on a scale of 1–10, with 10 being the highest. Google penalizes low Quality Score keywords by raising the minimum bid needed to appear on the first page. This makes sense from Google's perspective. After all, if your ad generates fewer clicks for a keyword than your competitor's ad, Google needs you to pay more per click to make the same amount of money for "renting" you the space on their search results page.

If you can't see the Quality Score column in the Keywords tabs of your statistics table, here's how to reveal it:

1. **From the Campaigns tab, click the Keywords tab.**

2. **Click the Columns button located just below the highlighted Keywords tab and select Customize Columns from the drop-down list.**

3. **In the leftmost column, select the Qual. Score check box and then click the Save button at the bottom of the Customize Columns section. See Figure 11-2.**

If a keyword's Quality Score is 1 or 2, the problem is your website. You're running afoul of a Google policy, or your site is loading too slowly, or some human Google reviewer has given your site the thumbs-down. In that case, fix the website before you do anything else in your AdWords account. (See Chapter 9 for landing page guidelines.)

Quality score check box

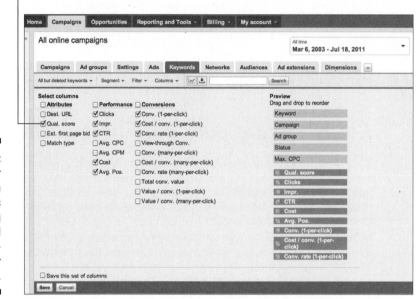

Figure 11-2:
Discover which keywords are being penalized for poor performance or relevance.

Google is extremely serious about landing page and website violations of its policies and standards. Act quickly, and go the extra mile in changing anything Google finds objectionable. Many AdWords advertisers have had their accounts suspended and even permanently banned for dragging their feet or making what Google considered a half-hearted effort at improvement.

If the keyword Quality Score is 3 or higher, the single largest factor (and we would argue, the only one worth paying attention to) is CTR.

To resuscitate a keyword, follow these steps:

1. **Move it to a new ad group.**

2. **Write a new ad with a message targeted specifically for that keyword.**

3. **Link the ad to a new landing page written with that searcher in mind.**

You don't need to do this for all your keywords. In fact, you may find keywords with low Quality Scores that generate lots of clicks, conversions, and profits. If so, leave them alone. We're sure you can find plenty of other aspects of your business to work on instead.

Finding New Keywords

According to Google, approximately one-half of all searches are brand new — that is, no one has ever typed them before in the history of Google. So when you're building your campaign, how can you determine all the possible keywords? You can't, from the start. Rather, you continually mine your campaign data and other sources, looking for new keywords to include.

Google gives you two internal tools to find new ideas based on your existing campaigns: the actual search terms your visitors use prior to clicking your ad and lists of keyword suggestions that Google terms "opportunities."

Actual search terms

For every phrase-match and broad-match keyword in your account, your ad is shown for many different search term combinations based on your keyword. You can see the actual search terms within your Google account if you know where to look (and yes, we're about to tell you).

Use this list to find new keywords and exclude irrelevant terms by adding them as negatives. To review your search terms:

1. **Navigate to the Keywords tab.**

2. **Select a desired date range.**

   a. *Click the down-arrow next to the current date range.*

   b. *Choose an option from the drop-down list, or select Custom Date Range and then use the calendar function to select start and end dates manually.*

If you're doing this for the first time, you can start with All Time, as shown in Figure 11-3. When you get into the habit of mining for keywords on a regular basis, you can do it on the first of the month and select Last Month.

3. **Click the See Search Terms button and select All from the drop-down list.**

4. **Review the list.**

   • *To add a keyword from the list:* Select the check box next to the keyword (or keywords) and select Add as Keyword.

   • *To exclude a keyword from showing:* Select the check box next to the keyword (or keywords) and select Add as Negative Keyword.

Figure 11-3:
Select a
date range.

By default, Google adds positive keywords in broad match and negative keywords in exact match. You can change the match type of any keyword by adding quotes or brackets at the start and finish of the phrase.

Opportunities

Google provides you with a list of ideas to try based on the contents and performance of your existing campaign.

1. **Select the Opportunities tab from the top row of tabs.**

2. **Scroll down to the Keyword Ideas section.**

3. **Select any link under the Idea column to review keywords.**

4. **To add a keyword, select the check box next to the keyword, as shown in Figure 11-4.**

    By default, the keyword will be added to the campaign and ad group that triggered the suggestion.

    You can select a different campaign and ad group:

    a. *Click the campaign/ad group in the right column.*

    b. *Select a different campaign and ad group.*

Google also gives you the option to specify the match type of the keyword you're adding. Click the keyword to bring up a drop-down list from which you can select broad, phrase, or exact match. We strongly recommend separating different match types into their own campaigns, or at the very least, their own ad groups.

After you review all the keywords, click the Apply Now button to add the suggestions to your campaign.

Figure 11-4:
Select
Keyword
Ideas to add
them to your
campaign.

After you apply the changes from a set of ideas, that list is removed from the Keyword Ideas list.

Other new keyword sources

You should spend a decent percentage of your AdWords time brainstorming and testing new keywords. Keep reading to discover additional sources, including the following:

  ✔ **Your website and your competitors':** You may be using keywords in your site copy that you just haven't thought to add to your keyword list. Google's keyword tool allows you to get keyword ideas from websites. At the top of the tool, enter a web URL to generate a list of keywords related to that site.

  When you add new keywords, start with exact match to give you total control over the traffic. To get Google's traffic estimates for exact match keywords, clear the check mark for the Broad Match type but check the [Exact] Match type in the left column, as shown in Figure 11-5.

Figure 11-5:
Google
analyzes
websites
and returns
relevant
keywords.

✔ **Content about your industry:** Trade journals, magazines, blog posts, and newspaper articles are often great sources of new keywords. Develop the habit of seeking out keywords whenever you read or listen to content about your product or industry. You'll be surprised how many new keywords pop up after you train your brain to filter for them.

✔ **Your Google Analytics account:** *Google Analytics* is a free service that measures the performance of your website, including the search queries that brought visitors to your site. If people are finding you via organic search, Analytics will show you the exact terms they typed, and you can add those to your AdWords account if they make sense (and add them as negatives if they don't).

If you don't have an Analytics account already, you can begin the setup process directly in AdWords. From the Reporting and Tools tab, choose Google Analytics from the drop-down list. From there, follow the onscreen instructions to set up your account.

We share a couple of important AdWords metrics found in Google Analytics in Chapter 13, but if you want more information on this powerful tool, many books are devoted entirely to increasing your online profits through Analytics.

Segmenting Keywords by Match Type

In Chapter 7, we show you how to create your first campaign. If you begin in the Search network, our advice is to use exact match keywords only. The great thing about exact match is the amount of control you exert over the traffic; you're getting just those searchers whose search terms clearly represent desires that you can fill. You can expect your CTR and ROI for exact match traffic to be higher than for any other type of traffic. That makes it a logical place to start advertising. Only after you achieve comfortably profitable margins with exact match campaigns does it make sense to venture into less restrictive match types.

The downside about exact match is that it limits the amount of search traffic Google will send you. So after you have exact match working, it makes sense to expand into the two other match types: phrase and broad. These match types give up some control and transparency (you can't always know what search queries are triggering your ads anymore) but in exchange gets more traffic. Google is now bird-dogging searchers for you, based on its algorithms.

Phrase match

After your exact match campaign is working well, clone it and change the match type for each keyword to phrase match. Because phrase match keywords include less qualified traffic, you're going to lower your maximum cost per click (Max. CPC) to aim for the same cost/conversion. We recommend bidding 80 percent of what you're bidding for the same keywords in exact match. If this sounds like a lot of work, don't worry. Using the free desktop program AdWords Editor and the techniques we share in Chapter 16, you can clone a complex campaign, change the keyword match type, discount all the bids, and upload the new campaign in about 45 seconds.

Take a look at part of our running example — G-Form — keyword set to see what this accomplishes. The exact match campaign for iPad sleeve includes the following keywords.

✔ [iPad sleeve]

✔ [iPad protective sleeve]

✔ [sleeve for iPad]

When we add those keywords to a phrase match campaign, we now can show ads for the following additional search queries, among many others.

Phrase Match Keyword	Possible Search Queries
[iPad sleeve]	yellow iPad sleeve iPad sleeve for iPad 2 what is an iPad sleeve cheap iPad sleeve Apple iPad sleeve under $20
[iPad protective sleeve]	yellow Ipad protective sleeve iPad protective sleeve reviews 2011 iPad protective sleeve reviews
[sleeve for iPad]	what's the best sleeve for iPad 2 does any sleeve for Ipad protect against water damage

Some of these search queries look promising, like `yellow iPad sleeve` and `iPad protective sleeve reviews`. But the ones that reference `cheap` and `under $20` won't deliver qualified prospects to G-Form's offer of a $60–70 high performance sleeve. In the upcoming section, "Deploying Negative Keywords," we show you how to eliminate those poorly matched search queries.

Run the phrase match campaign for a while to see whether you can achieve profitability. Deploy negative keywords, adjust bids using the AdWords Editor techniques discussed in Chapter 10, pause or delete keywords that can't deliver ROI-positive results, and test new ad copy until you either make money or give up on phrase match.

Sometimes, phrase-match campaigns don't get a lot of traffic. If that's the case, just watch your new campaign carefully for a couple of days and then venture into broad match.

Broad match

After your phrase-match campaign is profitable (or at least not bleeding cash), it's time to expand once again, this time into the most permissive keyword format: broad match. Again, use AdWords Editor to clone your profitable phrase match campaign. Change the match type from phrase to broad, and again adjust bids down to accommodate the lower quality of traffic.

We recommend shaving phrase-match bids by 25 percent for broad-match keywords; that gives you a broad-match bid of 60 percent of exact match.

This is just your starting bid; you'll adjust individual keyword bids to come in at or below your cost/conversion targets. And you'll keep doing all the campaign management best practices listed in the earlier section, "Phrase match," in search of higher relevance and bigger margins.

The G-Form broad match campaign keywords now include the following:

Broad-Match Keyword	Possible Search Queries
[iPad sleeve]	yellow iPad sleeve iPad sleeve for iPad 2 iPad cover where can I get a used iPad
[iPad case]	the case of the missing iPad should I bring an iPad just in case
[sleeve for iPad]	Cleaning iPad using your sleeve

As you can see, broad match is the hardest search traffic to convert because Google is so permissive in what it deems relevant. In fact, Google may actually punish you for having a great ad because the higher your CTR, the less relevant the search queries Google will deliver to you. If you use broad match, you want to add negative keywords to keep the worst search queries from triggering your ads. Or more advanced users can explore a hybrid match type: modified broad match.

Advanced match type: Modified broad match

Modified broad match is a recent Google innovation that's designed to bridge the gap between phrase match and broad match. It's complicated and typically unnecessary if you use broad match and negative keywords the way we recommend. If you're curious about modified broad match, we prepared a video demonstration at http://gafd3.com/mbm.

Deploying Negative Keywords

As we'll repeat long after you're sick of hearing it, the big problem with phrase- and broad-match types is unwanted traffic. Think of Google as a very enthusiastic puppy playing fetch. You throw the exact match ball, and Google returns with that same ball — or nothing at all. Throw the phrase match ball, and Google might return with that ball, a foam football, a hacky sack — pretty much anything round and smaller than the puppy's mouth. But chuck the broad match ball, and there's no telling what Google's coming back with: a ball, a stick, your neighbor's yoga pants from the washing line. Could be pretty much anything. Negative keywords tell the Google puppy, "Everything you think is relevant, except this. And this. And this."

Let's go to the movies again for a different negative keyword metaphor. In *The Verdict,* Paul Newman plays Frank Galvin, an outgunned lawyer representing an injured client in a medical malpractice lawsuit. When Galvin realizes that the defendant is hiding incriminating evidence, he requests delivery of the damning documents. The defendant delivers the evidence in a way that ensures (he hopes) it won't be found before trial — buried somewhere in truckloads of meaningless paper. Your AdWords traffic is the same — there are a few gems (your future customers and referrers) buried in a giant stream of nonbuyers. Negative keywords are your first line of defense: a filtration system that keeps the wrong folks away while letting the right folks see your ad.

Use negatives to improve phrase and broad match keywords

As you research keywords using Google's keyword tool, you'll certainly find keywords that Google identifies as relevant that you don't want to trigger your ads. If you stick to our recommended starting strategy of exact match keywords only, you're fine. Exact match keywords are simple: Don't add keywords you don't want, and Google won't bother you with that traffic. But after you achieve profitability with exact match and dare to venture into phrase and broad match, things aren't nearly as straightforward. You'll have far less control over which keywords trigger your ads, and you'll have to put a lot more work into making sure you don't get (and pay for) unprofitable traffic you don't want.

Say you sell wooden kits for building bat houses. You bid on the broad match keywords [bat] and [bats] and discover that for some reason, you're getting large numbers of impressions but very low CTRs. What's going on? Are your ads ineffective? Maybe. But the first problem you have to solve is related to keywords, not ads.

Check out the Google Keyword Tool to see keywords that Google thinks are highly relevant to your keyword. Make sure you select Broad Match type; then enter a keyword and click Search. In Figure 11-6, you can see lots of keywords that don't represent e-commerce traffic searching for bat houses. For example, baseball, cricket, and squash fans are also typing **bat** into Google, without the remotest interest in attracting mosquito-eating flying mammals by building houses for them.

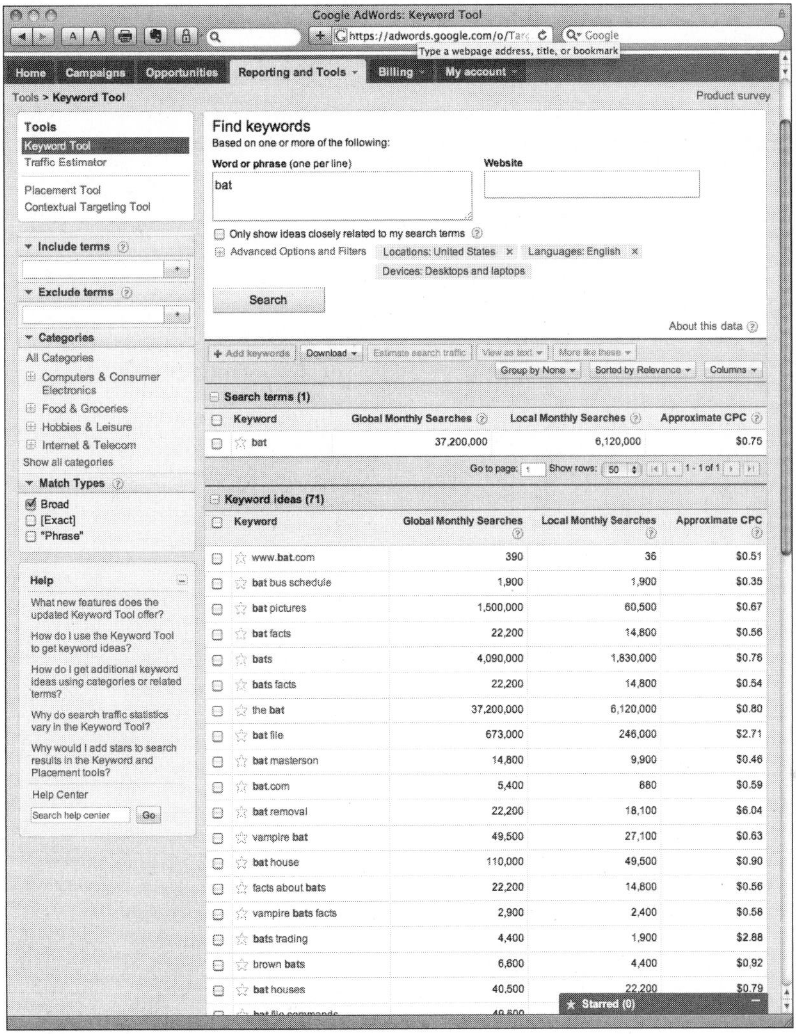

Figure 11-6:
The
keyword
[bat]
occurs in
many
contexts.

So, if you're bidding on [bat] as a broad match, you're going to show your ad to a lot of the wrong people. Any of them who click your ad are just costing you money unnecessarily. Fortunately, Google provides a solution to help you filter traffic you don't want: *negative keywords*.

Negative keywords are words and phrases that automatically disqualify your ad from showing should they appear in a search. In the [bat house] example, you'd designate the following negative keywords:

✔ [baseball]

✔ [softball]

 ✔ [ball]

 ✔ [easton]

 ✔ [milken]

Easton and Milken are brands of baseball/softball bats, so any search including those names as keywords are automatically disqualified. You don't need to include [base ball] or [soft ball] because [ball] already takes care of all variations in which [ball] is a separate word.

Brainstorming negative keywords

After you feel you've gotten all the profitable traffic you can get from exact match keywords, you're ready to venture into the wild and crazy world of broad and phrase match. To keep from losing your shirt with these more permissive match types, spend some serious time finding negative keywords.

One of the most common and costly AdWords mistakes is focusing all your attention on positive keywords. Positive keywords *bring* you traffic, whereas negative keywords *filter* it for you so that only the quality searchers ever get to your ad. A comprehensive list of negative keywords increases the quality of your traffic and improves your CTR significantly.

In the following sections, we offer some sources of negative keyword strategies.

Thinking about who isn't your customer

No database or tool can replace your own insight and common sense. For example, [bath house] may be a reasonable typo of [bat house], so you may well want to include the negative keyword [bath]. Consider other searches that may be triggered by your broad-match keywords. Do you want to show your ad to people concerned about bat bites, for example? They may be searching for an exterminator or a medical website, but perhaps you can entice them with an ad like this:

```
Bat Problems?
Don't kill them — Help them move!
Bat House Kits — vs. Yard Pests.
www.BatHouseKits.com
```

If your best efforts at selling to [bite] keywords fail, turn [bite] into a negative keyword and move on.

Looking at actual search terms to build your negative keyword list

The See Search Terms button (discussed in the earlier section on finding new keywords from actual searches) shows you the exact keyword phrases that got searchers to your website. If you're bidding on [bat problems] as broad match, this list will show you that one of the visitors to your site triggered that keyword match by typing **bat problems in the dugout**. Ah-ha! You just found another negative keyword — [dugout] — to add to your list.

Searching Google for negative keywords

For our running example, a Google search on bat brings up the following concepts, all unrelated to flying mammals:

✔ British American Tobacco (BAT) company

✔ Balanced Audio Technology

✔ British American Transfer

✔ Brockton Area Transit (BAT) Authority

Adding negative keywords

Add negative keywords quickly to your keyword list by clicking the Keywords tab from within an ad group, and then Add Keywords, just below the performance graph. See Figure 11-7.

You add negatives to your keyword list by typing a hyphen before the word or phrase: [-tobacco], [-baseball], and so on.

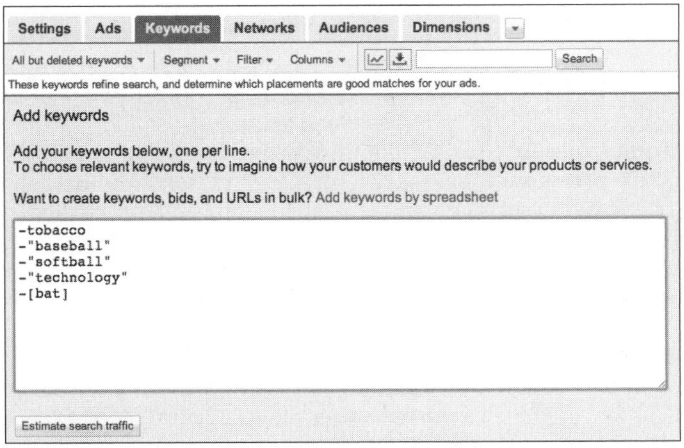

Figure 11-7:
Add negative keywords by typing a hyphen before broad, phrase, and exact match keywords.

Advanced negative keywords

Sometimes a single word is enough to disqualify an entire search phrase. If you sell bat houses, the word baseball anywhere in the search tells you immediately that you shouldn't show your ad to that searcher. Sometimes you have to gather enough data to show you that `[bat sleeping habits]` is bringing you negative-ROI traffic. And sometimes `[bat sleeping]` is fine, but adding the word `habits` is the problem. What's an advertiser to do?

Fortunately, just as you can use exact, phrase, and broad match keywords, you can do the same with negative keywords. Negative exact keywords look like this — `-[free bat house plans]` — and will exclude that search term only. So your ad would still show for `bat house plans` and `bat house plans for sale`.

More exclusive is the phrase match negative: `-"bat house plans"`

This negative keyword will exclude `[free bat house plans]` and `[best bat house plans]`, but not `[bat house pole plans]`.

And broad match negatives will knock out any search query containing the negated word:

`-baseball`

eliminates every keyword containing the word `baseball`.

These advanced negative keywords are known as an *embedded match*. For some clever ways to use embedded match keywords, visit `http://gafd3.com/embedded`.

Managing Using the 80/20 Principle

As you build your AdWords account, you'll keep adding keywords in various match types: exact, phrase, broad, negative, modified broad. You may be worried about your account growing to a level of complexity (think of the Sorcerer's Apprentice scene from Disney's *Fantasia*), but the campaign management techniques we share in Chapter 10 allow you to handle tens or even hundreds of thousands of keywords in your account.

The key to making this work is the 80/20 Principle, which roughly states that 20 percent of your keywords lead to 80 percent of your positive results. In other words, you need to nurture a very few keywords individually, with special love and attention. The vast majority of your keywords can be managed *en masse* using AdWords Editor.

Three types of keywords you'll want to pay extra attention to are

✔ **Scoundrels:** *Scoundrels* (high cost, low, or no conversions) eat up your budget by generating lots of clicks but few conversions. Pause them while you improve your website to better serve that traffic, or exclude them if you can't achieve break-even.

Zero-conversion keywords may seem like ordinary scoundrels, but they pose a hidden problem. When you sort keywords by cost per conversion, lower numbers are better than higher ones (in general). In other words, you'd rather pay $2 for a lead than $200. But keywords that generate no conversions at all are shown to have the lowest possible cost per conversion: $0.

We've seen lots of clever people manage the overpriced scoundrels while totally ignoring the zero-conversion keywords because they don't pop up where they expect them. Deal with the zero-conversion keywords by first filtering for keywords with zero conversions and sorting by spend. After you've spent five times the value of a conversion on any keyword without getting a single conversion, delete it and let your competitors bid on it.

✔ **Stars:** *Star* (high cost, high conversions) keywords often belong in their very own ad group, nurtured like milk-fed pumpkins or prize-winning pigs (or insert your own 4-H metaphor here). By putting them in their own ad groups, you can write ads that are optimized for these star keywords and make them most of them.

✔ **Slumberers:** *Slumberers* (low position) are keywords whose bids place them off the first page of search results (generally, position 11 or greater). If the Google Keyword Tool predicts lots of traffic for a keyword, but a low bid and/or low CTR are preventing it from triggering impressions, you don't know what you might be missing.

You can sort and filter for all these keyword types using AdWords Editor. See `http://gafd3.com/priority` for a tutorial on creating these filters and sorting to bring the most important and actionable keywords to the top of the screen and the top of your attention.

Chapter 12

Cornering the Local Market

· ·

· ·

*G*oogle functions as two completely different search engines, depending on whether its algorithm thinks the searcher is conducting a local or a national/global search. To see what we mean, compare the following searches: `barefoot running` and `fitness`. The `barefoot running` search triggers content like articles, footwear for sale (ironic, huh?), and debate in a podiatry forum. The `fitness` search is dominated by a large colorful map of your local area, decorated with red pins corresponding to the bulk of the organic listings. As you scroll down the page, the map moves with you so that you can locate the business establishments' physical addresses.

Consider this for a moment. "Fitness," as a concept, could have triggered articles, ads for gym equipment, debates in professional forums, and the like. Why did Google choose to show us the equivalent of the local Yellow Pages for `fitness` and not `barefoot running`?

Google has determined that searchers looking for `fitness` are most often looking for a *local* gym, yoga studio, or personal training business. When people want to find a local business, Google goes into "local mode," with maps, reviews, easy-to-find phone numbers and addresses, tap-to-call buttons for mobile phones, and a set of simple tools to allow local merchants to tap into the vast power of Google and AdWords without having to buy, say, *Google AdWords For Dummies*.

Local businesses can use AdWords to great effect, especially when they combine AdWords with other Google tools and programs designed specifically for local search. And the fact that you're reading this book will give you a huge advantage over your competitors who are just using the "out of the box" Google solutions for local advertisers.

Understanding the Local Marketing Mindset

Before we look at the specific tools, programs, and methods that will turn your business into a local hero, go back to basics: search intent. When searchers look for topics like barefoot running, they're looking for information: "Should I run barefoot? How should I get started? Is there a good book or video on the subject? Do I really need to buy a $110 pair of sneakers to run barefoot?"

Product search, in contrast, is transactional. Someone searching for `barefoot running shoes` is interested in brands, sizes, prices, shipping, and guarantees. Local search, on the other hand (um, foot), tends to be much more about location, convenience, and trust: "Where can I get it right now? What's the closest place that's open on Sunday? Which store has the best reviews?"

Mobile expert Dan Hollings of StepByStepMobile.com advises local advertisers to picture their prospect searching from a smartphone in their car (pulled over, with engine off for safety, of course) or at an airport lounge. You want to structure your ads and landing pages to appeal to the person on the go, who doesn't have much time. Keep the landing page short and to the point, and include a clear and compelling call to action.

In some ways, local search represents a breakdown in community. Ideally, you wouldn't need to rely on Google for the best bakery or gym or auto body shop or pediatric dentist. You'd just ask your trustworthy neighbors and take their advice. With less "over the fence" contact, we turn to search as a surrogate local guide — still looking to answer the same question, though: "Who's good that I can trust?"

In addition to the emphasis on instant gratification as opposed to patient research, local search differs from national search in a number of technical aspects:

- **Much less traffic:** First, local advertisers can expect much less traffic than if they were advertising nationally. If you're in a large local market like Los Angeles or New York, the numbers may be robust. But a ukulele teacher in Durham, NC may get only a couple of searches per week in her account. Obviously, the more common the search, the more traffic — after all, realtors, lawyers, and chiropractors are still more in demand than ukulele teachers (which says something about our society, no doubt).

  The Google Keyword Tool shows traffic volume on the national level (see Chapter 4). To find out how much traffic you can expect for a local keyword, simply multiply the national numbers by the local percentage of the national population. In other words, if the U.S. population is roughly 312 million (thanks, Wikipedia!), and the population of the

Durham region (including Raleigh and Durham) is approximately 1.7 million, you can expect local Durham keyword volume to be roughly 0.54% (1.7 divided by 312) of the national U.S. volume.

The keyword `[ukulele lessons]` receives 2,400 exact match impressions and 9,900 broad match impressions per month across the entire United States. A Durham ukulele teacher can therefore expect a whopping 13 impressions per month for the term "ukulele lessons" and a grand total of 54 impressions per month for all keywords combined. That, of course, assumes that local trends mirror national ones. That's a little less than a search every two days for "ukulele lessons" and two searches per day for all keywords combined. As you can see later in this chapter, these low numbers require a very different keyword strategy than we use in national campaigns.

✔ **Take a longer view:** In most of this book, we really hammer home the importance of paying close attention to your metrics as a way of constantly improving your results. With such low numbers, metrics take a long time to accumulate — especially conversion metrics. That's a good thing, actually, because few of your competitors will be tracking results and optimizing their accounts at all, let alone at the ninja level we'll show you later in this chapter.

✔ **Less risk:** Because your market exposure is so much smaller than with national campaigns, your risk is much less as well. It's often hard to spend a lot of money on local campaigns, even if you want to. You can take more chances with local search and relax some of the rules we've shared that are designed to keep you safe as you start advertising.

✔ **More and more local searches are mobile:** With smartphones and faster connectivity, the long-touted "mobile revolution" appears to be actually happening in 2011. Google reported in 2010 that fully one-third of all mobile searches had "local intent" — and in many developing countries, mobile searches outnumber those done at a computer.

✔ **Click to Call:** The AdWords Call extension makes it easy for local searchers to call you right from your ad if your campaign is mobile-enabled. If your market is in the United States or Canada, you can enable Call metrics and accept calls directly from regular computer searches. (Keep reading for set-up instructions.)

Call metrics solves the problem of nontrackable offline conversions. An *offline conversion* is one that doesn't occur on your website, so Google's standard conversion tracking won't catch it. Examples include phone calls and walk-in traffic. When you enable Call metrics, Google now reports data not just on clicks and conversions, but how many phone calls to your business were generated not only by each campaign, but even at the ad group level.

Google charges $1 per call when you use its Call metrics option, which may seem expensive if you're comparing it against 45-cent clicks. But if you've been in business long enough to remember the heyday of the Yellow Pages, you might know someone who paid $500 a month for a listing but never received 500 calls in any given month, or was never sure whether the listing generating any calls at all. If you want to know whether your keywords are worth bidding on, a buck per call is a bargain.

Phone calls aren't counted as conversions. If you track conversions as well as calls, you can simply add the two numbers to get a sense of your campaign performance. If you do get a lot of phone calls but few leads or sales or walk-ins, it's time to improve your staff's telephone skills.

Maximizing Google Places

Google Places is the latest incarnation of the Google local business center, where you can create a local listing for your business, including an interactive map, hours, updates, coupons, phone listings, customer reviews, and photos and videos. If you want to take advantage of the Local ad extension mentioned in Chapter 8, you need to create a Google Places listing.

If your business is entirely local, you can use your Places page as your ads' destination URL, meaning that your website isn't strictly necessary. Transactional business like dry cleaners, pizza restaurants, and carpet cleaners may be able to do fine with nothing but a Places page. If your business is significantly different from the competition, or requires proof of expertise (such as for an accountant, a guitar teacher, or a fashion boutique), the Places page may not be sufficient, though.

As mobile and local become more integrated, your Places page may be one of the best marketing venues you can create. In addition to connecting it to AdWords, you can also engage in search engine optimization (SEO) to drive your page to the top of the organic listings for your local market. We're not going to get into those strategies here. Instead, we'll focus on connecting Google Places to your AdWords account.

To get started, visit `http://google.com/places` and click the Get Started button under the Get Your Business Found on Google section. On the next page, enter your country and phone number to see whether Google already recognizes your business from its database. If it does, you can start editing that listing or you can create a new one. It's easiest to use the same Google account for Places as you already use for AdWords.

Dan Hollings recommends filling out all the fields as thoroughly as you can. By being a form-filling overachiever, you give Google enough information to rank your Places page highly on the search results page and your prospects enough information and confidence to start engaging with you. Don't leave any fields empty, even if they aren't required.

To take maximum advantage of Google Places, make sure the data fields are filled out exactly the same (including street abbreviations and suite numbers) as all your other local listings, such as foursquare, Yelp, Citysearch, and any online phone book advertising. Not exactly an AdWords trick, but we heard this advice from a local SEO expert and felt like passing it on.

Use keywords liberally in the description field. Make sure it reads well for humans, and also include the top phrases prospects use when they're searching for you. If you need ideas, you can search for your competitors directly on places and view their descriptions. You get only 200 characters, so think of it as a slightly more talkative Google ad.

For the Category field, you can invent your own, but we recommend using the Google defaults if possible so Google knows exactly where and when to display your listing. Start typing into that field to bring up a list of Google-recognized categories. As you can see in Figure 12-1, the list is reasonably exhaustive. You can add up to five categories.

Figure 12-1: Try to find a Google-recognized category for your business.

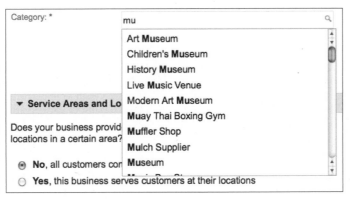

Most of the questions and fields are straightforward (service areas, hours of operation, payment options, and the like). Don't be tempted to skimp on photos and videos. Yes, those take time and effort and imagination, but Dan Hollings exhorts you to expend the extra effort to upload good ones. You can show as many as ten photos, uploading them from your computer or specifying their URLs on the Web. You get up to five videos, all of which need to be uploaded to YouTube in advance.

Later in this chapter, we'll show you how to connect your Places listing with your AdWords account.

Deploying photos and videos

What makes an effective photo? Ideally, you want to show happy customers interacting with your business. A smiling high school student getting fitted for winter boots. Enraptured diners savoring a hearty meal and mojitos. A well-heeled couple sitting at a conference table going over their growing investment portfolio with you.

Likewise, effective videos include you demonstrating caring and professionalism by interacting with customers, talking directly to the camera about your business, offering free advice and guidance, and sharing your passions and interests. If you can add video testimonials, either individual or edited into a montage, your Places page can be very compelling and persuasive.

Remember: People want to find places that other people like. The less you tell people how great you are, and the more you simply demonstrate it and let others blow your horn for you, the more powerful the message.

Using AdWords Express

If you have a local business and you want to tap the power of AdWords without having to work or think too hard, AdWords Express may be just the ticket. Google has been trying for years to balance two completely opposite goals:

- Make AdWords the most robust and results–accountable advertising medium ever.
- Make it simple enough for anybody to use.

In our opinion, Google has done a great job with the first goal, but at the expense of the second.

AdWords Express is Google's latest attempt to create an AdWords program for small business owners who don't want to deal with all the nitty-gritty details of keywords, CTRs, bidding strategies, or even ad writing. Again drawing on the example of Yellow Pages listings, in the old days, a Yellow Book rep would visit your store about three months before the new book was to come out and ask whether you wanted to put in a listing. You said, "Sure," and the rep basically did the rest. All you had to do was make sure the phone number was right and approve the design, and you had a professionally designed Yellow Pages listing.

Like the Yellow Pages, AdWords Express functions by taking the advertiser through a simple wizard and then creating the entire campaign automatically. Unlike the Yellow Pages, though, AdWords Express charges you only when it sends you a click. The only things you have to do are name your categories, write an ad with a headline and two description lines, and choose a maximum monthly budget (see Figure 12-2).

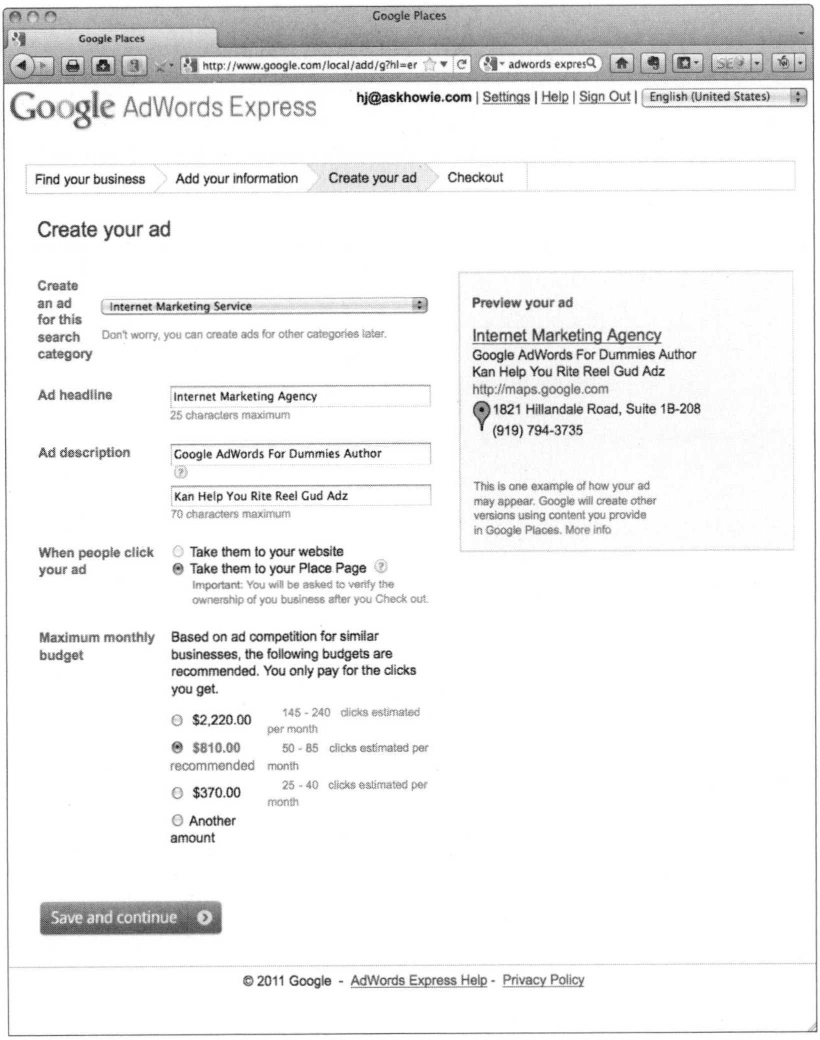

Figure 12-2:
AdWords
Express
takes about
a minute to
set up and
gives you a
bare bones
campaign
with few
options.

After you complete the page shown in Figure 12-2, you'll be asked to verify ownership of the business and possibly enter billing information. On the Dashboard, where you can set your Places e-mail preferences, make sure to select the check box for Performance Updates so that Google will let you know the level of customer engagement with your listing.

If you've read more than ten pages of this book without falling asleep or getting a splitting headache, AdWords Express is probably not for you. You give up a tremendous amount of control, and you still have to come up with ad copy, which is arguably one of the hardest parts of AdWords.

And because you don't get to choose keywords, or delete poorly perform-ing ones, or raise bids on effective ones, or even have any idea what kind of ROI they're getting, there's no systematic way to improve your Express cam-paign. Let your competitors rely on Express while you constantly improve your results using AdWords the way we teach it here.

Setting Up Local Campaigns

Yes, campaigns, plural. Even though the traffic from each local campaign may be paltry in comparison with the numbers you might see from national campaigns, you're still going to manage bids based on the value of a click. And different key-word match types, networks, and devices will attract visitors of varied interest in your offer. The best way to make local AdWords marketing profitable is to sepa-rate traffic sources into separate campaigns based on value. In Chapter 10, you discover how to clone campaigns quickly and easily using AdWords Editor. You'll use that technique here to create campaigns of ever-expanding reach and risk.

To create a local campaign from scratch, log in to AdWords and navigate to the Campaigns tab. Click the New Campaign button just above the data table, on the left. Name the campaign, including the words SEARCH, EXACT, and LOCAL in the name, along with a description of the contents of the campaign.

Location settings

Time to make location settings. Click the Edit link next to Locations. You'll see a list of locations to choose from, starting with the entire planet (minus the moon and presumably, the space station) and targeting tighter and tighter through country, region, metro area, and finally city.

Most local campaigns target at the city or metro area level. You can simply select one of the radio buttons to select that level, or you can click the Select One or More Other Locations button to bring up a tool that allows you to include and exclude multiple locations at different levels. For example, to include some cities in the Raleigh-Durham (Fayetteville), NC metro area, for example, here's what you do:

1. **Click the Browse tab.**

2. **Click the plus sign next United States (Country).**

3. **Scroll down and click the plus sign next to North Carolina (State).**

4. **Scroll down again and click the plus sign next to Raleigh-Durham (Fayetteville) NC (Metro Area).**

5. **Scroll down one more time and select the check boxes of each city you want to include (see Figure 12-3).**

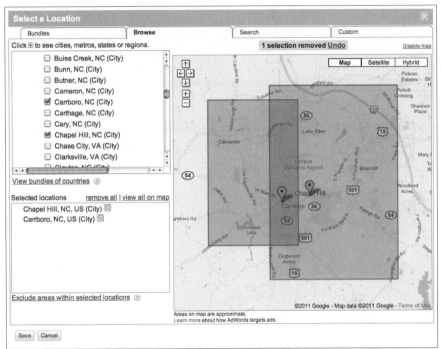

Figure 12-3:
Create your
location.

The Select a Location tool has a lot of sophisticated features: not necessarily hard to use, but devilishly detailed to explain. On the theory that a video is worth a million words, we've thoughtfully provided a short video at `http://gafd3.com/maptool` that takes the tool for a spin to see what it can do.

Networks settings

After setting your campaign locations, click the Edit link next to Networks and remove the check mark next to Display Network (as in Figure 12-4). You never want to combine Search and Display traffic in the same campaign because the two networks require different ad and landing page strategies.

Devices settings

Next, click the Edit link next to Devices to clear the Mobile Devices with Full Browsers check box. You can leave the Tablets with Full Browsers check box selected for now (see Figure 12-4).

Figure 12-4:
Configure
the settings
to limit
traffic to
search
not on
mobile
devices.

Networks ⑦	☑ Google search
	☑ Search partners (requires Google search)
	☐ Display Network ⑦
	⦿ Show ads on pages that match the broadest targeting method ⑦
	Example: Show ads if keywords match
	○ Show ads only on pages that match all selected targeting methods ⑦
	Example: Show ads only if both keywords and placements match
	🔍 Your ads won't show on Google's Display Network. Learn more
Devices ⑦	☑ Desktop and laptop computers
	☐ Mobile devices with full browsers
	☑ Tablets with full browsers
	⊞ Advanced mobile and tablet options
	🔍 Your ads won't show on mobile devices.

Ad extensions settings

After specifying your bidding options and budget, it's time to set up ad extensions for your local campaign.

Location extensions

Select the Extend My Ads with Location Information check box and then select the Use Addresses from a Google Places Account check box. If the Google Places account isn't the one you want to link, click on the Use a Different Account link and open a different Places account to use as your location setting.

Next, select the icon that will appear in your ad. The default is No Category Specified, which isn't all that exciting, in our opinion. Click the Choose Another link (see Figure 12-5) to get a list of icons to choose from, including a coffee mug for café, a pair of scissors for hairdresser, and a plate and utensils for restaurant. Then click the icon you want.

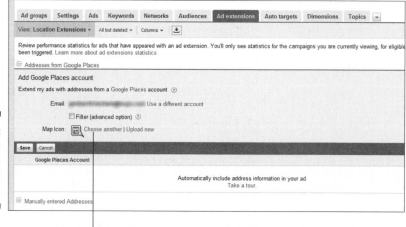

Figure 12-5:
Click here
to choose a
more helpful
icon.

Choose Another

Phone number extensions (optional)

As you see in Figure 12-6, the location extension already adds a phone number field to your ad if you're using data from your Google Places account. In that case, you can just use your regular local business number, which doesn't cost you anything. If you want to let Google help you track how many people are using that phone number, you can add call metrics instead of using the local phone number from your Places account and find out exactly how many phone calls are generated by this campaign. When using call metrics, Google provides you with a toll-free number, and charges you $1.00 (or the local equivalent) for each call.

The disadvantage of using call metrics is clear: It costs money. However, the advantage of being able to measure results often outweighs the cost. We recommend enabling call metrics at first so you can tell whether the campaign is succeeding. You can always turn off call metrics later.

Here's how to get started:

1. **Select the Extent My Ads with a Phone Number check box.**

2. **Select your country and then enter your business phone number.**

3. **Select the Call Metrics: Use Google Forwarding Number to Track Calls from My Ads check box.**

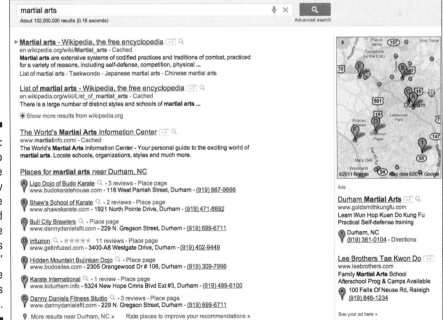

Figure 12-6:
The two ads on the right below the map are connected to the martial arts schools' Google Places pages.

Now searchers will see a toll-free number as part of your ad. If they click the ad through to your landing page, you pay the cost of the click. If they call the phone number, Google forwards the call to your phone and charges you one dollar.

TIP

Depending on your business, you may want to encourage calls at all hours, or you may want to schedule this campaign to show only when someone at your business is available to answer the phone.

Configuring your first local ad group

Now you must decide on a keyword strategy for this first campaign. If you want to find out the exact search volume for your main keywords, start conservatively with the exact match strategy that we show you in Chapter 4. A Durham, NC martial arts academy might include the following keywords in exact match:

✔ [martial arts]

✔ [martial arts school]

✔ [karate classes]

✔ [kung fu instruction]

✔ [brazilian jiu jitsu academy]

Because the campaign is locally geo-targeted, you don't need to add the place names to the keywords to get Google to show your ads. In Figure 12-7, Google returned a local search even though the keyword — [martial arts] — didn't mention a location.

Figure 12-7:
In a local campaign, even a short-tail keyword can be highly profitable.

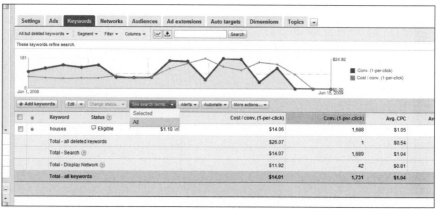

If, on the other hand, you want to get as much traffic as possible right away, don't mind a little risk, and want to collect as much data and drive as many leads as possible, you can use the Super Sloppy keyword strategy that would be a huge mistake in any campaign other than a local one.

The Super Sloppy ad group strategy

Because local campaigns tend to receive so little traffic, you can lengthen Google's leash and allow all sorts of search queries to show your ads, without risking a huge bill. As long as you have your campaign geo-targeted only to the local area this can be a fantastic strategy, and because you have conversion tracking installed (you do, don't you?), you can still exclude keywords that end up costing you more than they're worth. The Super Sloppy ad group strategy consists of bidding on the highest-volume keywords you can find in your market, in broad match, and then tracking performance of these keywords and the search queries that match them over time.

Joel pioneered this strategy for his Colorado real estate business, Automated HomeFinder.com. He noticed that his AdWords-savvy competitors were following the best practice of tightly targeted, highly relevant, long-tail keywords, such as [Castle Pines CO real estate], while avoiding high-volume, general, short-tail keywords, such as homes (Broad Match). Because bid prices are set by auction, the less desirable high-volume keywords usually cost much less than the highly competitive long-tail ones.

The question was, though, would an otherwise untargeted keyword like homes produce clicks and conversions? Or would it simply deliver lots of useless impressions — or worse, worthless clicks? Joel had conversion tracking set up and used the tactics we teach in Chapter 13, so he was willing to take the risk.

He discovered several unexpected keywords that proved to be incredibly profitable. In Figure 12-7, you can see the metrics for houses, broad match. (Notice that Google has found extra houses keywords he wasn't bidding on, as well as additional homes and even real estate keywords. This is because broad match gives Google permission to substitute keywords they think might be relevant. That can be good or bad, depending on your risk tolerance and how well those additional keywords perform.

In a market where a lead was worth $20.00 to $100, this keyword generated 1689 conversions (Leads) at an average cost of $14.07. The actual cost per click, $1.04, might have seemed high for such a nontargeted keyword, but ended up being a huge bargain. Many of his competitors weren't bidding on those terms, which made them even more lucrative.

Why does this work in local campaigns but not national ones? Basically, it's about the intent of the searcher. If your real estate agency is located in Guelph, Ontario, what are the chances that someone looking for houses in Edmonton or Cape Breton Island will be interested in a house on Dublin Street, Guelph? Slim to none. But someone in Guelph searching for houses might very well be looking to move out of an apartment into a home in the downtown area. Better yet, they might need to sell their existing home and move up or down to another home, meaning twice the commission to the fortunate realtor who understands local search.

Letting Google choose your Super Sloppy keywords

Another beautiful thing about the Super Sloppy strategy is that Google typically does your initial keyword selection work for you. Simply write an ad, including the URL of your website, and Google scans your site and suggests as many keywords as it can think of. If you were advertising nationally, you would need to include the local modifiers like city, postal code, or neighborhood to avoid getting eaten alive by irrelevant searches. In the locally targeted campaign, on the other hand, these keywords can be fantastic.

After you create and define settings for the campaign, Google asks you to create an ad group. So, you name the ad group and write a text ad. See Chapter 8 for details on ad creation.

Google scans the URL you entered in the Destination URL field for keywords. When it's finished, you'll see a list of keyword suggestions, listed by category. Then you add your keywords.

Go through the keyword list and either add entire categories by clicking the Add All From This Category link, or manually add keywords by clicking the Add link next to each one. You can collapse categories by clicking the down arrow next to the category name, and you can expand collapsed categories by clicking the right-pointing arrow next to the category name. See Figure 12-8 for an example of suggested keywords for a Russian Martial Arts school near Howie's home town of Durham.

Finally, set your default bid and save the ad group.

Now you sit back and let the traffic accumulate. Check in daily for the first few days to make sure your bid is high enough to get you sufficient exposure, but not so high that you're spending money you can't afford to lose.

If you can track conversions, follow the procedures outlined in Chapter 13 to manage and optimize this campaign. If you can't track conversions, you can use call metrics to measure how many additional phone calls you get from this traffic. (Read how to set up call metrics earlier in this chapter.) Or if you're trying to generate walk-in traffic, you can create a printable coupon either on your website or your Google Places page and manually count the number of brick-and-mortar visits you can attribute to this AdWords campaign.

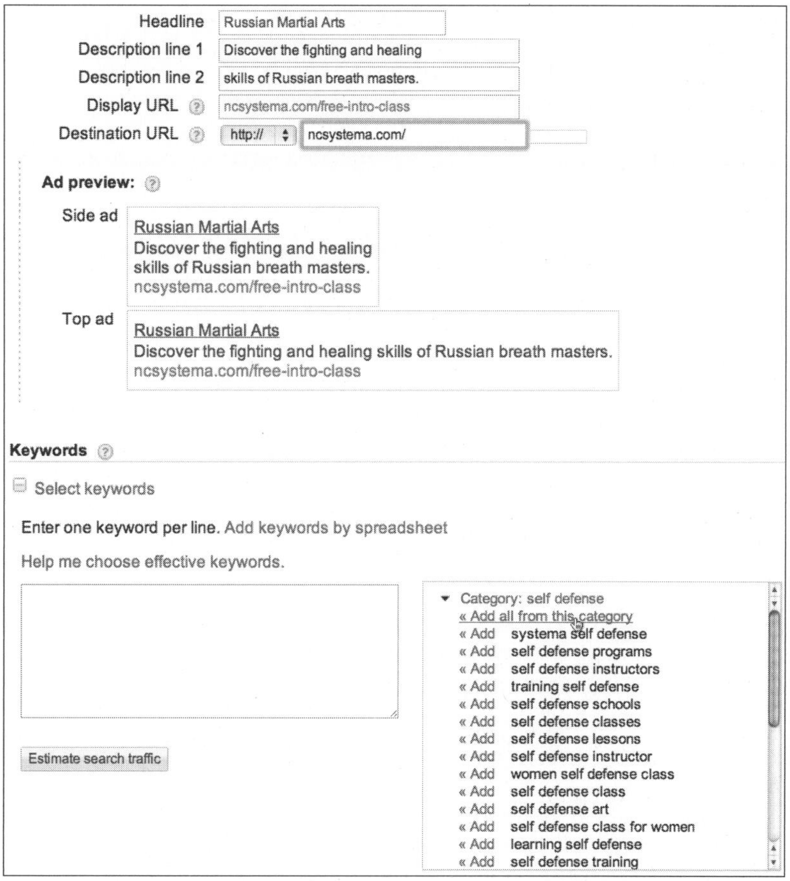
Headline
Russian Martial Arts
Description line 1
Discover the fighting and healing
Description line 2
skills of Russian breath masters.
Display URL
ncsystema.com/free-intro-class
Destination URL
http://
ncsystema.com/
Ad preview:
Side ad
Russian Martial Arts
Discover the fighting and healing
skills of Russian breath masters.
ncsystema.com/free-intro-class
Top ad
Russian Martial Arts
Discover the fighting and healing skills of Russian breath masters.
ncsystema.com/free-intro-class
Keywords
Select keywords
Enter one keyword per line. Add keywords by spreadsheet
Help me choose effective keywords.
Estimate search traffic
Category: self defense
« Add all from this category
« Add systema self defense
« Add self defense programs
« Add self defense instructors
« Add training self defense
« Add self defense schools
« Add self defense classes
« Add self defense lessons
« Add self defense instructor
« Add women self defense class
« Add self defense class
« Add self defense art
« Add self defense class for women
« Add learning self defense
« Add self defense training

Figure 12-8: Google suggests lots of broad-match keywords that you can use in your Super Sloppy strategy.

WARNING!

Don't make the same expensive mistake Joel made about eight years ago. He bid on the broad-match term `real estate` and forgot to limit the traffic to the Denver metro area. He set up the campaign before going to dinner with his wife, and came home a couple hours later to a big surprise: a Google bill for $2,500 for worthless clicks from all across the United States. The damage was limited only by his $2,500 daily budget for that campaign, but rest assured that Google would have happily sent him tens of thousands of dollars of bad traffic had he given his permission.

Creating additional local campaigns

Whether you start with an exact match or a Super Sloppy ad group, after you achieve profitability, your next step is to create additional campaigns to get more traffic and to target that traffic more precisely.

If you start with exact match, you can clone that campaign (see Chapter 10) for phrase and broad match, and adjust bids accordingly to maximize traffic at or below your target cost per conversion. Then you can get wild and crazy with the Super Sloppy strategy that we outline earlier.

Adding keywords to an exact match local campaign

If you start with Super Sloppy, you can create an exact match campaign based on the search queries that are bringing you profitable traffic.

Keywords and search queries aren't the same thing. Keywords are the words and phrases you bid on, and search queries are the words and phrases searchers enter into the search field.

When you bid on a broad-match keyword, Google shows your ad for a variety of search queries. You can see performance metrics for many of these search queries by using the See Search Terms feature:

1. **Navigate to the Super Sloppy ad group.**

2. **Click the Keywords tab.**

3. **Click the See Search Terms button just above the data table and select All from the drop-down list (see Figure 12-9).**

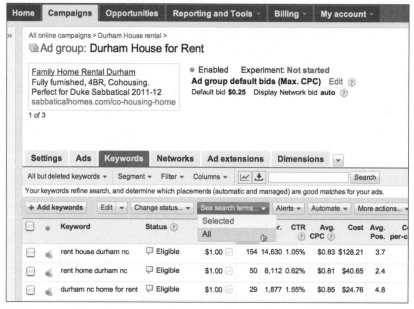

Figure 12-9:
See actual search queries triggered by your Super Sloppy keywords.

Adding keywords

You'll see all the search queries that generated at least one click. See Figure 12-10 for an example of Joel's AutomatedHomeFinder.com account. After you have big enough numbers, you'll start seeing keywords that you should add to your exact match campaign because they're doing well. Google allows you to add keywords, *but to this same ad group only,* which doesn't do you any good. Instead, you need to download the entire report into a spreadsheet that you can open in Excel (MS Office) or Numbers (Apple iWork). Sort the keyword list by cost per conversion, descending, and select the most profitable keywords to add to your exact match campaign.

Visit `http://gafd3.com/searchreport` for a video tutorial on saving, opening, manipulating, and re-uploading the promising keywords.

Excluding keywords

You'll also see keywords that make you go, "What was Google thinking? I've got to exclude this keyword — it makes no sense for my business!"

You can exclude a keyword by selecting its check box to its left and then clicking the Add as Negative Keyword button above the data table.

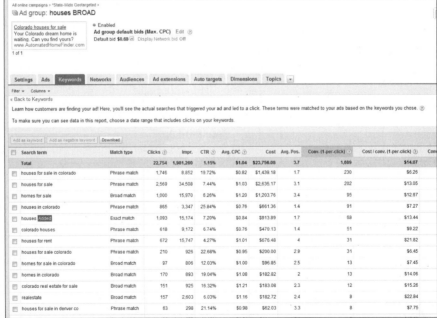

Figure 12-10: You can see your visitors' long-tail search queries even when you bid only on Super Sloppy keywords.

Creating phrase and broad match campaigns

After your exact match campaign has run for a while and you've had a chance to adjust bids, you'll find keywords that are profitable enough to add in phrase match type. (See Chapter 11 for a description of match types and how they play together within your account.) Simply clone your local exact match campaign, using AdWords Editor, and change all the keyword match types from Exact to Phrase. (See Chapter 10 for an introduction to AdWords Editor, and Chapter 16 for details on campaign cloning strategy.)

Run the phrase-match campaign and adjust bids to achieve maximum profits, and then clone the campaign again, this time in broad match. Now you have got four local campaigns: exact, phrase, broad, and Super Sloppy broad.

Profitable detour: Local SEO

Most local businesses can generate a lot more traffic with organic SEO than they can with AdWords. And unlike national SEO, which is extremely competitive, it's often quite easy and quick to rank for very important keywords in your local market.

The big problem in doing local SEO has always been knowing which keywords to optimize for. Not a single keyword tool, paid or free, has accurate data on search volume for local markets. Although you can do the "multiply by the population percentage" trick we showed you earlier in this chapter, that's still a poor substitute for actual data.

Running a local exact match AdWords campaign gives you actual search volume data, along with information about CTR and conversions. After you know which keywords are the best ones for your business, you can then engage in SEO activities for those keywords. Without this knowledge, you could spend a lot of time and money optimizing for keywords that bring you little traffic, or the wrong traffic, or the right traffic to the wrong design and content on your website.

Creating a local Display network campaign

If your search campaigns are running well, you can next expand into Display. Alternatively, if your business generates leads rather than sales initially, you may want to get into the Display network from the start. See Chapter 7 for instructions on Display network campaigns, and just adapt the national settings to local ones.

Make sure that your local Display network campaigns don't include traffic from mobile devices. If you've ever tried reading a website on an iPhone, you know how easy it is to tap the wrong link by accident. The quality of mobile Display traffic is likely to be quite poor.

Exploiting Mobile Search

You have every reason to expect local mobile search to explode within the next couple of years. If it's big for your local business now, it's certain to get bigger. According to Google, fully one-third of all mobile searches were local in intent: finding a restaurant, a shop, an event, and so on.

As of this writing, Google announced a bid to purchase Motorola Mobility. This kind of investment shows how serious Google is about competing in the mobile search space.

Creating a local mobile campaign

We separate mobile from other forms of search for two main reasons. First, you need to be much more aggressive in your bidding in a mobile campaign. Unlike desktop search, where as many as 11 advertisers share a single page, mobile search requires that your listing be one of the first two or three on the page — after all, mobile screens are so small. Ideally, you want the number one position for mobile search.

Second, because you want to send mobile traffic to a mobile–friendly web page, it's crucial to separate visitors with mobile devices so you can show them different destination URLs.

If you enabled the Click to Call and Call metrics ad extensions in your local search campaign (see Chapter 8), you can simply clone that campaign as the basis for your mobile campaign. If these extensions weren't activated, skip the following Steps 1 and 2 and create the mobile campaign from scratch.

In a mobile campaign, Click to Call means that your prospect can simply tap your phone number within the ad to call you.

1. **Clone your local search campaign using AdWords Editor, and add MOBILE to the campaign name.**

2. **Post the new campaign to upload it to your account.**

3. **Navigate to the new campaign's settings and scroll to the Networks and Devices section.**

4. **Under Devices, clear the check boxes for Desktop and Laptop Computers and also Tablets with Full Browsers, but select the Mobile Devices with Full Browsers check box (see Figure 12-11).**

5. **Save the new settings.**

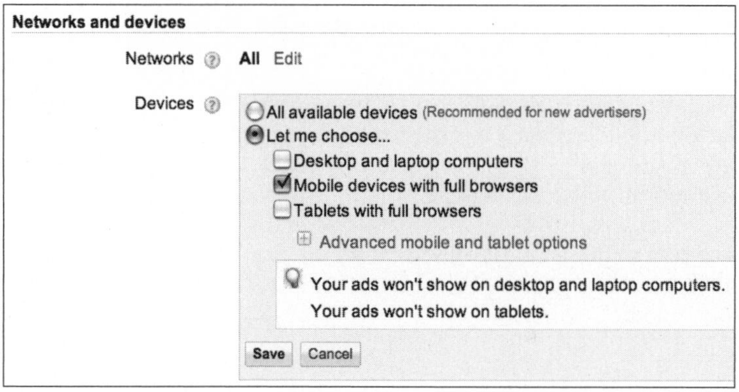

Networks and devices

Networks ⍰ **All** Edit

Devices ⍰ ○ All available devices (Recommended for new advertisers)
● Let me choose...
☐ Desktop and laptop computers
☑ Mobile devices with full browsers
☐ Tablets with full browsers
⊞ Advanced mobile and tablet options

💡 Your ads won't show on desktop and laptop computers.
Your ads won't show on tablets.

Save   Cancel

Figure 12-11:
Adjusting campaign settings for a mobile campaign.

If you just created this campaign from scratch, you need to navigate to the Ad Extensions tab and create a new Local extension linked to your Google Places page, as well as a new Call extension with your phone number. See earlier in this chapter for detailed instructions.

Building mobile landing pages

Google makes it simple to create mobile landing pages and entire mobile-friendly websites with its free mobile site builder, available via redirect at http://gafd3.com/mobilebuilder.

If your site is built on the WordPress platform, you can install a free mobile plug-in that shows mobile-friendly pages to any visitor viewing your site on a mobile phone. The one we currently recommend is WPtouch, found at http://gafd3.com/wptouch.

We wanted to write a lot more about mobile strategy and how to create great mobile landing pages, but our editor gave us that "What part of 'scope creep' don't you understand?" look. If you're excited about mobile, Vitruvian ally Dan Hollings has put together a great tutorial on mobile marketing that he's making available to our readers for free. You can register for the tutorial at http://gafd3.com/mobiledan.

Chapter 13

Analyzing the Numbers for Maximum Performance

*A*fter an AdWords account is humming along and doing okay, it's natural to want to just forget about it and spend your time on other things. Generally, this is a bad idea. Because AdWords is so competitive, standing still is the same as going backward. Bid prices increase, margins erode, positions slip, ads get stale; it's not a pretty story.

Try to keep working on AdWords from both the right- and left-brain perspectives. Right-brain (creative) activities focus on getting in the minds of your prospects and developing ever-more-effective messages and offers and sales processes. Left-brain (analytical) activities involve filtering, sorting, and parsing the huge amounts of data generated by your AdWords account to find and expand the profitable parts and shrink or eliminate the bits that are costing you money. This chapter shows you how to streamline the left-brain activities.

Most advertisers approach AdWords optimization like a San Francisco gold prospector in 1848: with pick, axe, pan, and sieve; and no idea of where to look or what to look for. In AdWords, that approach consists of always looking for new keywords that might generate the profits you're hoping for. Leave the pick and axe method to your competitors. In this chapter, we show you how to use a high-tech metal detector to discover valuable nuggets resting right under your nose in your existing data. Ready to start prospecting?

Mining for Gold on the Campaign and Ad Groups Tabs

AdWords is such a powerful and complex program that Google has to hide many of its features behind innocuously named buttons to keep us from getting overwhelmed by an ocean of options and data. In this section, we show you some of the most useful features hiding in the AdWords interface.

Impression Share

In Chapter 11, we show you how to view the impression share data. Impression share shows what percentage of available impressions your keywords have generated. An impression share of 100% indicates that every time folks in your geo-target search for your keywords, your ad appeared on a page of search results that was served to them. An impression share less than 100% means that you aren't getting all the traffic available to you. And because you get a precise number, you can tell exactly how many more impressions could be yours if you do the right things.

Say that your current impression share for a campaign is 25%, and the loss is due to a combination of budget and ad rank limitations (see Chapter 11). This tells you that you could get four times as much traffic by raising your bids and your budget. Should you go out and do this immediately? That depends. If the traffic you're getting is profitable, you can open the spigot much wider by increasing your daily budget. You can also open the traffic spigot by increasing your bids, but you don't want to increase them past the point of profitability.

Here are two reasons you wouldn't be receiving 100 percent of the traffic available to you:

- ✔ **Your daily budget is too low.** If your impression share is less than 100% because of a daily budget limitation, simply raise your daily budget to get more traffic. Don't raise your daily budget until you're profitable. As soon as your revenues from AdWords traffic exceed your expenses, getting more profits is as simple as turning up the dial.

- ✔ **Some of the keywords you're bidding on aren't ranking high enough to be on the first page of Google.** If you're losing impression share because of rank, you have a different problem entirely. Turning up the volume won't help you unless your goal is to run out of money faster. Your keywords are ranking too low is because you aren't bidding high enough. If you have healthy margins, raise your bids. If your margins can't support higher bids, you need to increase conversion rates so that you can raise your bids. Focus on three strategies to increase your conversion rates:

- *Increase the effectiveness of the landing page you're driving traffic to.* See Chapter 15 about using Website Optimizer.

- *Bid only on the most effective match types and keywords.* See Chapter 11.

- *Make sure you're bidding on the right networks based on your goals and objectives.* See Chapter 3.

Segments

Google gives you several ways to slice and dice your data to find meaningful and actionable nuggets. Find these by exploring the Segment button, located just above the data table in the campaign, ad group, and keyword tabs. See Figure 13-1.You can segment by network, click type, device, experiment, and Top versus Side. (That last one was added a week before this text was written, so we give it short shrift here and promise you a nice video demonstration of its rather awesome power.) You can ignore the network segment because you can get more useful data from the Networks tab.

Click type

If you're using ad extensions (see Chapter 8), click type will be an interesting slice-and-dice metric. An *ad extension* is an extra feature you can attach to a Search text ad, such as a phone number or links to additional pages on your website (sitelinks). The good thing about ad extensions is that they can boost click-through rate (CTR). The bad thing is that it's hard to tell what specifically caused the increase in CTR. Segmenting by click type shows you the relative impact of your headline, a sitelink, or mobile click-to-call link on your performance.

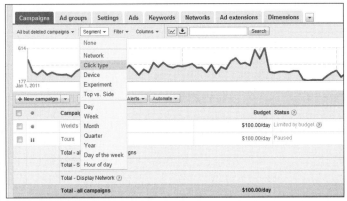

Figure 13-1: Explore the options from the Segment button.

Segmenting the campaign shown in Figure 13-2 by click type reveals that mobile clicks-to-call have received no clicks, but the conversion rate for sitelinks is more than twice as high as that for the headline of the ad (26.06% versus 11.80%). Most times, ad extensions will improve your results. Sometimes, however, they can hurt you, and segmenting by click type will quickly help you decide.

Figure 13-2:
Segmenting by click type can reveal underground pockets of profitability.

	Campaign	Budget	Status ⑦	Impr. ⑦	Clicks ⑦	CTR ⑦	Avg. CPC ⑦	Cost	Avg. Pos.	Conv. (1-per-click) ⑦	Conv. rate (1-per-click) ⑦	Cost / conv. (1-per-click) ⑦	Total conv. value
●	Minnesota - TPA	$60.00/day	Eligible	78,874	7,075	8.97%	$1.09	$7,729.58	2.8	862	12.18%	$8.97	55,296.2
	Headline ⑦			78,874	6,887	8.73%	$1.11	$7,655.56	2.8	813	11.80%	$9.42	52,587.6
	Sitelink			6,201	188	3.03%	$0.39	$74.02	1.7	49	26.06%	$1.51	2,708.6
	Mobile clicks-to-call ⑦			659	0	0.00%	$0.00	$0.00	1.9	0	0.00%	$0.00	0

Device

When you set up a new campaign, it defaults to Show on All Devices. "Devices," in Google parlance, include computers, tablets, and smartphones. If users of all these devices perform exactly the same when encountering your ads and website, you don't need to worry about separating them. However, this is rarely the case. More likely, these traffic streams will be drastically different, and if you're not watching them separately, you could be losing a lot of money (or leaving a lot of money on the table.)

A quick and easy way of looking at differences in performance is to use the segmentation feature in AdWords. At the campaign level of your account, all you need to do is click Segment and then select Device from the drop-down list. If you're tracking conversions, you'll be able to see the difference in performance between computers, mobile phones, and tablet devices. In Figure 13-3, computer users cost $8.99 per conversion, mobile users cost $10.35, and tablet users are the most profitable at only $2.05 per conversion.

Figure 13-3:
In this campaign, tablets outperform computers and mobile devices.

	●	Campaign	Budget	Status ⑦	Impr. ⑦	Clicks ⑦	CTR ⑦	Avg. CPC ⑦	Cost	Avg. Pos.	Conv. (1-per-click) ⑦	Conv. rate (1-per-click) ⑦	Cost / conv. (1-per-click) ⑦	Total conv. value
	●	Minnesota - TPA	$60.00/day	Eligible	78,874	7,075	8.97%	$1.09	$7,729.58	2.8	862	12.18%	$8.97	55,296.2
		Other ⑦			24	0	0.00%	$0.00	$0.00	1.7	0	0.00%	$0.00	0
		Computers ⑦			76,368	6,829	8.94%	$1.11	$7,572.36	2.9	842	12.33%	$8.99	54,313.1
		Mobile devices with full browsers ⑦			2,268	222	9.79%	$0.65	$144.93	1.8	14	6.31%	$10.35	598.8
		Tablets with full browsers ⑦			214	24	11.21%	$0.51	$12.29	2.2	6	25.00%	$2.05	384.2

If all devices perform at the same levels, you can leave them all in the same campaign. If any of those devices performs better or worse than the others, though, you're wasting money by keeping them together. The good news is that separating them into different campaigns takes only a few minutes through a process that Joel developed called "campaign cloning" (described in detail in Chapter 16).

Experiment

Wondering whether you should be bidding $0.50 per click or $0.75 per click? How about whether you should be bidding on broad match terms or exact match? The AdWords Campaign Experiments tool exists to answer those questions. After you set up an experiment (see Chapter 14 for full instructions), you can see the results by segmenting your data by experiment. Simply click the Segment button and then select Experiment from the drop-down list.

In some cases, you can discover more from experiments; sometimes, campaign cloning (covered in detail in Chapter 16) will prove more valuable. Use experiments for short-term questions like "Should I add this keyword?" and "What will happen if I raise my bids in this ad group?"

Two advantages of experiments over cloning are that

- ✔ They don't permanently increase the complexity of your account.
- ✔ They automatically perform randomized split tests.

Cloning, on the other hand, creates new campaigns that are more or less copies of existing ones, and requires some fancy footwork to split traffic more or less evenly among accounts.

Cloning is preferable when you want to separate traffic streams based on the

- ✔ Value of those clicks
- ✔ Need to optimize differently from each of those streams

Mining for Gold on the Dimensions Tab

Knowing what keywords bring in profits is great and will make you a lot of money. Having said that, how, when, and where you use those keywords is more important. The Dimensions tab can give you a lot of insights and a big boost to your account's bottom line. If you've been using AdWords for a couple of years, you might remember the Reporting tab. That's been discontinued, and all its functionality moved to Dimensions.

Time

You might have heard advice that the worst time of day to advertise is between midnight and 6 a.m. That might be the case (or not), but (assuming you're tracking conversions) one way to find out is to navigate to the dimensions tab and drill down to the Time of Day section.

1. **Select the Dimensions tab from the center row of tabs.**

2. **Select a date range from the upper right (choose 30–60 days of data to get a good idea of trends).**

3. **Click the View: Day button and then select Time and then Hour of Day from the drop-down list.**

4. **Click the Hour of Day header to sort by hour of the day, starting with 0 (midnight to 12:59 a.m.) and ending with 23 (11 to 11:59 p.m.).**

Say that the maximum acceptable cost per conversion is $20 (see Figure 13-4). It turns out that Hour 0 generates traffic that's too expensive ($36.88 per conversion), whereas Hour 1 brings in profitable traffic ($13.40 per conversion). This campaign should be shut down entirely between the hours of 2 a.m. and 4:59 a.m. (no conversions at all). Hours 0, 21, and 22 can have their bids dropped until the traffic comes in at or below the $20 threshold.

Hour of day	Cost / conv. (1-per-click) ⑦	Impr.	Clicks ⑦	CTR ⑦	Avg. CPC ⑦	Cost	Avg. Pos.	Conv. (1-per-click) ⑦	Conv. rate (1-per-click) ⑦
0	$36.88	12,237	306	2.50%	$1.55	$474.27	4.8	3	4.17%
1	$13.40	9,426	184	1.95%	$1.45	$267.54	4.8	3	10.71%
2	$0.00	6,920	119	1.72%	$1.57	$186.98	4.6	0	0.00%
3	$0.00	6,154	82	1.33%	$1.52	$124.60	4.4	0	0.00%
4	$0.00	5,832	72	1.23%	$1.39	$99.89	4.4	0	0.00%
5	$5.83	6,071	146	2.40%	$1.25	$181.93	4.4	3	12.00%
6	$12.80	9,804	328	3.35%	$1.38	$454.01	4.8	7	7.87%
7	$9.88	17,218	579	3.36%	$1.41	$817.91	4.7	15	10.95%
8	$10.12	27,405	920	3.36%	$1.42	$1,308.34	4.8	23	11.39%
9	$9.79	39,298	1,333	3.39%	$1.32	$1,759.99	5	30	10.34%
10	$7.58	42,763	1,438	3.36%	$1.36	$1,955.88	5	50	14.37%
11	$8.53	41,509	1,443	3.48%	$1.35	$1,948.56	4.9	47	13.13%
12	$10.82	43,893	1,444	3.29%	$1.34	$1,939.81	5	40	10.20%
13	$8.63	44,151	1,562	3.54%	$1.30	$2,035.58	4.9	43	12.32%
14	$8.05	43,728	1,553	3.55%	$1.28	$1,988.76	4.9	49	12.53%
15	$9.13	40,293	1,464	3.63%	$1.32	$1,937.01	4.8	46	12.20%
16	$15.54	35,832	1,214	3.39%	$1.34	$1,624.14	4.8	24	7.57%
17	$14.29	28,852	968	3.36%	$1.35	$1,302.64	4.9	20	8.44%
18	$18.16	28,212	984	3.49%	$1.35	$1,331.90	4.8	18	6.87%
19	$12.47	27,966	1,005	3.59%	$1.36	$1,371.16	4.8	25	9.82%
20	$12.89	29,381	922	3.14%	$1.30	$1,199.10	4.7	25	9.19%
21	$23.32	27,230	909	3.34%	$1.31	$1,191.61	4.7	13	5.08%
22	$25.30	22,478	694	3.09%	$1.36	$944.77	4.7	11	5.16%
23	$8.52	14,952	429	2.87%	$1.31	$560.48	4.9	17	15.18%

Figure 13-4: The Hour of Day view shows you when to bid higher and lower during the day.

You can use other items on the Time drop-down list to examine conversion costs by day of the week, day of the month, week, month, quarter, or year. With these insights, you can adjust what you're willing to bid based on performance differences. Rather than just bidding $1.55 per click at all times, you can change the campaign setting for scheduling and turn the campaign off at certain hours. You can also raise bids during low-cost per conversion hours. In Figure 13-3, Hour 5 has the most profitable cost per conversion: $5.83. But the CTR is low at 2.40%, due in part to the relatively low position of 4.4. During that hour, this advertiser can bid higher, and perhaps double or triple their traffic while staying under their profitability threshold.

Conversions

If you track different types of conversions, the Conversions dimension will be a very helpful tab. You can view conversions by the name you gave them when you set them up (eBook download, request for quote, purchase of seat on Virgin Galactic) or by the tracking purpose you assigned each conversion from Google's short list (lead, purchase, and so on).

On the regular campaign tabs, all conversions are aggregated, so the cost/conversion numbers are sometimes impossible to interpret. This segment shows how many of your conversions were leads, and how many were revenue-generating sales. If you track only one type of conversion, you don't need to analyze this metric.

Destination URL

Wondering whether your "Seven Secrets to Preventing Peanut Butter from Sticking to the Roof of Your Mouth" or "Seven Peanut Butter Eating Mistakes" landing page is converting better? A look at the Destination URL dimension will tell you.

This information doesn't replace the output of scientifically split-testing landing pages, which we discuss in most of its glory in Chapter 15. But if you haven't yet started testing landing pages via Website Optimizer, the Destination URL dimension can give you a head start in evaluating the performance of your landing pages.

Demographic

In the Display network, you can pick and choose demographic segments to target (see Chapter 12). But how can you know which are your best prospects?

If you track conversions and advertise in the Display network, you can figure that out using Demographic segmentation. After you know that, you can stop wasting money targeting the wrong audiences.

1. **Select Demographic from the View drop-down list.**

2. **Click the Columns button and select Customize Columns from the drop-down list.**

3. **In the Level of Detail column, check the boxes next to Age and Gender and click Save.**

4. **Sort the table by number of conversions and take a look at the age and gender breakdowns for the highest numbers of conversions.**

During the writing of this chapter, Google completed changed the look and functionality of the demographic segment — and, frankly, hobbled most of its useful features. We're describing what we're seeing now, with no idea whether the good old demographic segment will return, or in what form. Stay updated by checking `http://gafd3.com/demographic` for updates on how to best squeeze the sponge of this data.

Imagine that G-Form is contemplating a series of ads in *USA Today*. Wow, millions of people seeing iPad sleeves and portfolios and other protective coverings for consumer electronics. Assuming that G-Form has enough in the bank to cover the check, should G-Form do it?

On the one hand, lots of people with expensive portable electronics to protect likely read *USA Today*. G-Form can reach a significant segment of its target market through these ads. On the other hand, the vast majority of *USA Today* readers don't fit G-Form's target demographic. G-Form's gear has a distinctive "extreme" look that turns off as many people as it attracts. So an ad purchased in *USA Today* means spending a lot of money to show these ads to the wrong people.

Imagine if G-Form could magically target its ads for iPad sleeves and portfolios to appear only in publications sold to males aged 18–49, which is the group most likely to groove to their aesthetics. Although *USA Today* can't pull off that kind of magic, the AdWords Display Network can.

When G-Form bids on the keyword [iPad portfolio] in the Display network, it's paying for traffic from men, women, 15-year-olds, 65-year-olds, and just about any other demographic that's looking at those pages. But by using demographic bidding, G-Form can restrict the traffic to just those demographics most responsive to their offer. Or it can create separate campaigns for highly responsive traffic (for which it would bid higher) and less responsive traffic (for which it would lower its bids).

The Demographic dimension gives you data that allows you to exclude, include, and segment your Display Network traffic. We show you how to select traffic by demographics in Chapter 12, and explain campaign cloning in Chapter 16. "Cloning" is our name for creating multiple campaigns to optimize your account for different traffic streams. After the Dimension tab reveals opportunities for optimization, cloning allows you to exploit those opportunities.

You can also use demographic data from the Display network to write more compelling ads in the Search network. If you sell a product or service that theoretically could appeal to young and old prospects, suppose you discover that your conversion rate from Display network traffic is double for prospects age 65 and older. You can now write ads that call out your preferred demographic: "Skateboard protection for seniors," for example.

Geographic

One of the most common mistakes we fix when we take over management of a client's AdWords campaign is undifferentiated global bidding (which we don't think of by its acronym, UGB). When a client first sets up an account, giddy with possibility, he might have selected the entire world as his geographic region ("Who doesn't need light-up stress balls?", he reasoned) and bundled all that traffic into a single global campaign. So he's treating prospects in the United States, the UK, Canada, and Australia the same as prospects from the rest of the world, from Afghanistan to Zimbabwe.

Depending on your industry, certain countries may not be worth your effort. You may have a business model that doesn't fly culturally, or with regulators. For example, credit card use online varies widely around the world. Some countries are havens for online fraud, and exposure there can get you in trouble with your credit card processor. Still other countries could do well for you but would require different keywords, a different marketing message, and a different bidding strategy.

The geographic dimension can also drill down to states or provinces (by adding the column for Region), metropolitan areas, and cities. In Figure 13-5, you can see cost per conversion numbers ranging from $8.60 in Minnesota to $164.37 in Indiana. Separating states into their own campaigns could allow this advertiser to manipulate bids to increase profitability. They may decide to eliminate Indiana and Connecticut entirely, based on the steep price of each conversion in those states.

Figure 13-5:
Geographic
reports
show you
opportuni-
ties to raise
and lower
bids to
increase
profitability.

Campaigns	Ad groups	Settings	Ads	Keywords	Networks	Ad extensions	**Dimensions**								

View: Geographic ▾   Filter ▾   Columns ▾   📥

Country/Territory	Region	Cost / conv. (1-per-click) ⑦	Impr.	Clicks ⑦	CTR ⑦	Avg. CPC ⑦	Cost	Avg. Pos.	Conv. (1-per-click) ⑦	Conv. rate (1-per-click) ⑦	Total conv. value	Impr. share ⑦	Exact match IS ⑦	Lost IS IS (budget) ⑦	Lost IS IS (rank) ⑦
United States	Minnesota	$8.60	96,493	8,780	9.10%	$1.10	$9,692.24	--	1,095	12.88%	68,217.6	--	--	--	--
United States	Pennsylvania	$43.14	56,286	2,149	3.82%	$1.60	$3,441.43	--	75	3.72%	5,408.6	--	--	--	--
United States	Indiana	$164.37	23,208	1,540	6.64%	$1.50	$2,309.00	--	13	0.95%	303.5	--	--	--	--
United States	Georgia	$69.43	45,143	1,286	2.85%	$1.69	$2,178.54	--	28	2.46%	1,806.7	--	--	--	--
United States	Wisconsin	$21.66	14,109	979	6.94%	$1.33	$1,299.02	--	53	6.03%	5,713.9	--	--	--	--
United States	Rhode Island	$40.79	9,902	825	8.33%	$1.31	$1,080.48	--	26	3.19%	1,492.4	--	--	--	--
United States	Hawaii	$26.29	11,566	674	5.83%	$1.39	$939.00	--	36	5.32%	1,752.4	--	--	--	--
United States	Tennessee	$101.19	25,268	623	2.47%	$1.67	$1,040.30	--	9	1.70%	234.6	--	--	--	--
United States	Washington	$73.35	28,610	545	1.90%	$1.93	$1,054.22	--	13	2.72%	549	--	--	--	--
United States	Connecticut	$161.59	5,181	414	7.99%	$1.56	$646.37	--	4	0.97%	179.7	--	--	--	--
United States	Oregon	$39.25	6,618	374	5.65%	$1.62	$605.12	--	13	4.44%	822	--	--	--	--
United States	Virginia	$89.54	7,623	313	4.11%	$1.32	$414.07	--	2	1.27%	59.9	--	--	--	--

Use geographic reports from the Dimensions tab to evaluate different geographic traffic streams. You'll most likely see that conversions in one area are a lot more expensive than those from another, even though you're bidding on the exact same keywords and driving traffic to the exact same landing pages with the exact same ads. With that knowledge, you can separate geographically diverse traffic to give you more control over your bidding, messaging, and profitability.

Search Terms

Don't worry about this dimension. You can get this information more quickly via the ordinary AdWords Dashboard, and you can get much more in-depth and useful keyword data from Google Analytics.

Automatic Placements

We recommend viewing Automatic Placement data from the Networks tab rather than from the Dimensions tab. See the next section for details.

Mining for Gold on the Networks Tab

Use the Networks tab to peek under the hood of your Display network campaigns. You can find poorly performing placements and then either exclude them or manage them. You can also promote promising placements from Automatic to Managed status to get the most profit from them.

The Dimensions tab allows you to *observe* different segments of your account to gain insights that will make your efforts even more profitable. The

Networks tab combines this dashboard of observation with a workbench where you can make the changes suggested by the data.

The Networks tab shows what percentage of your traffic is coming from the Search network compared with traffic coming from the Display network, but the real value here is your ability to see which automatic placements have delivered conversions. Now you can easily graduate them into a Managed Placement position from which you can bid higher or lower on each site individually. The ability to manage the bids on each placement often means the difference between profiting or losing money in the Display network.

Finding placements that generate sales or leads

When advertising on the Display network, you have two choices: Managed and Automatic placements. *Managed placements* are specific sites that you specifically select to show your ads. Unfortunately, there are hundreds, if not thousands, of websites that will generate profitable clicks that you could never have predicted (or even known about). So, start your Display network advertising with Automatic placements, in which Google basically sprays your ad everywhere it can reach and leaves you to evaluate and refine that approach. Automatic placements allow you to reach 10 to 100 times more potential customers than Managed placements.

With all this extra traffic, though, comes the need for extra vigilance. And after you know where to look, you'll discover sites that deliver a lot of conversions at an affordable price, as well as sites that are leaking money and delivering worthless traffic.

Click the Show Automatic Placements link to view Automatic placements. You can see the data by website, or you can drill down to individual URLs by clicking the See URL List button above the data table, and then selecting All from the drop-down list. After you identify the good, the bad, and the unprofitable, you can exclude unprofitable placements and promote promising sites and pages to Managed Placements with a couple of clicks.

Managing automatic placements

We're about to share two techniques we use at Vitruvian to help our clients win big in the Display network. Joel has field-tested these techniques with dozens of multi-million dollar companies. Granted, a lot more can be done, but here is a suggested bare-minimum schedule, regardless of whether your advertising budget is seven figures per month or seven dollars per day.

The Expensive Zero-Conversion Placement Sweep

If your ads are showing on websites and pages that generate no conversions while racking up considerable costs, you can systematically catch these wasteful placements and sweep them up and exclude them. We recommend doing a massive sweep the first time, as described here (and then following up with monthly and biannual sweeps):

1. **At the top right, select All Time as the date range.**

2. **Click the Networks tab.**

3. **Click the Show Details link next to Automatic Placements (just above the bottom row that totals the data from all networks).**

4. **Filter for only sites that have had zero conversions:**

   a. *Click the Filter button on the line just below the Networks tab, and select Conversion (1-per-click) from the drop-down list.*

   b. *Select = from the drop-down list in the box of operators to the right.*

   c. *Type **0** (the number zero) into the box on the right and then click the Apply button to apply the filter to the data.*

   d. *Scroll down to the table for Display Network: Automatic Placements and sort by cost by clicking the Cost header for that column.*

   You'll see the placements listed in descending order of how much they've cost in clicks. Your mission now is to exclude all the placements where you've spent at least five times the value of a single conversion. In other words, if a lead is worth $30 to your business, you want to exclude every placement that has cost you at least $150 in clicks without delivering a single impression.

   e. *Select the check box next to any placements where you've spent the equivalent of conversions' worth of clicks.*

   f. *Click the Exclude Placements button above the data table and choose whether you want to exclude them at the ad group or campaign level.*

   g. *Click Save.*

   Exclude by the ad group level if the same placement is performing well in a different ad group. Choose campaign level exclusion to remove this placement from the entire campaign. By excluding those sites, you will improve the effectiveness of your campaign's performance overall.

The first time you do this, you'll want to show all data since the day you started tracking conversions. After that, you can redo this technique on a monthly basis by changing the date range to Last Month.

The High-Potential Placement Graduation

When a placement shows promise by generating at least one conversion, you want to graduate it from the masses of Automatic Placements into the more coddled and carefully monitored world of Managed Placements. Here's how:

1. **From the Networks tab, select All Time as the date range.**

2. **Change the filter from Step 4 in the preceding step list to show placements that have generated at least one conversion:**

   a. *Select the greater than or equal to operator ($\geq$).*

   b. *Type the number **1** in the text box.*

   c. *Click Apply.*

3. **Sort the list of Automatic Placements by cost per conversion by twice clicking the header of the Cost/Conv. (1-per-click) column.**

   You should see the lowest Cost/Conv. numbers at the top of the table.

4. **Select the check box next to every placement that has brought you at least one conversion at an acceptable price (less than the value of a conversion).**

5. **Click the Manage Placements and Bids button at the top left of the table.**

6. **When Google asks how much you want to bid for your managed placements, leave the Specific Bid fields empty so you continue to use your default bid.**

After you conduct your first Placement Graduation, repeat the procedure monthly. Instead of showing data for all time, simply show the previous month's data by selecting Last Month from the drop-down list of date ranges. Each month, you graduate converting placements from Automatic Placements into Managed Placements. With time, you'll notice that your Automatic Placements cost more per conversion than your Managed Placements, despite having lower bids. That's because you've cherry-picked the best placements from Automatic and placed them into Managed.

Eventually, you'll weed out automatic placements entirely, or cut the cost so low that their expense is insignificant. Either way, you'll have more control over the Display network, you'll decrease your cost per conversion, and you'll generate more conversions.

Sending negative-ROI placements to reform school

The Placement Sweep procedure just described deals with an extreme situation — expensive placements that generate zero conversions. What about placements that do bring you conversions, but cost too much? You can manage them the same way you manage the high potential placements.

Instead of raising bids of the placements that have delivered profitable traffic, simply lower bids of the placements that delivered traffic that was too expensive per conversion.

1. **At the top right, select All Time as the date range.**

2. **Click the Networks tab.**

3. **Click the Show Details link next to Automatic Placements (just above the bottom row that totals the data from all networks).**

4. **Click the Filter button.**

5. **Create a filter to show placements that have generated at least one conversion:**

   a. *Select the greater than or equal to operator (≥).*

   b. *Type the number **1** in the text box.*

   c. *Click Apply.*

6. **Sort the list of Automatic Placements by cost per conversion by clicking the header of the Cost/Conv. (1-per-click) column.**

   You should see the highest Cost/Conv. numbers at the top of the table.

7. **Select the check box next to every placement that has brought you at least one conversion at too high a price (greater than the value of a conversion).**

8. **Click the Manage Placements and Bids button at the top left of the table.**

9. **When Google asks how much you want to bid for your managed placements, enter a Specific Bid value 20–50% lower than the ad group bid.**

We suggest dropping bids on keywords that cost 25 percent more than you'd like to spend by 20–50 percent, depending on whether you care more about ROI or conversion volume. The important thing is not to over-adjust. If those placements are still misbehaving next month, you can adjust again until every placement in your account is performing exactly how you'd like it to perform.

Watch videos of the Sweep, Graduation, and Reform School Automatic Placement techniques at `http://gafd3.com/automatic`.

Building a Customized Maintenance Schedule

One of the biggest mistakes you can make when maintaining your AdWords account is to over-manage it. If you manage your account too often, not only do you run the risk of making changes that do you more harm than good because of making changes based on insignificant data, but you end up spending five or ten times as much time as necessary managing your account.

Unless you have an account with hundreds of conversions a day, daily maintenance (other than initially setting up an account) is likely doing nothing for you other than unnecessarily occupying your time. If you really feel like spending a lot of time improving your AdWords account, focus more on getting into the minds and hearts of your prospects, studying the competition, and sharpening your positioning in the marketplace.

Daily activities

When you first set up an account or a new campaign, check it daily for a few days to make sure that everything is working as expected. You'll catch any incorrect settings, and ensure that you're not bidding too much or too little on keywords and ad groups.

Another time to schedule daily check-ins is the first couple of days after making a major change to your account, such as adding campaigns, adjusting bids by a large amount, or adding or deleting a lot of keywords or ads.

Other than the preceding two suggestions, daily maintenance of an AdWords account bringing in fewer than 500 or 1,000 conversions per month is simply creating too much work for yourself.

Ongoing activities

After performance levels are established after the first month or so, many accounts will do fine with nothing more than ongoing maintenance and expansion work.

Whether these activities are done weekly, bi-weekly, or monthly really depends on the amount of data the account generates. When an account shows low "traffic velocity" (our fancy term for the amount of traffic you get for the keywords in your account), don't feel guilty about leaving it alone for a month. The actions you take based on insufficient data are almost always worse than just leaving things alone until you have real numbers to guide you.

Also after performance levels are established after the first month or so, most accounts generating fewer than a few hundred conversions per month require no more than monthly maintenance. In fact, there are only about five tasks per month that we recommend separating into weekly activities, for two reasons:

✔ The tasks are quick and not at all daunting when you do them one at a time.

✔ Different tasks require different mindsets, and you'll find it easier and more efficient to group certain tasks and separate others.

Here is a sample maintenance schedule for January 2013. To perform these tasks, you need a desktop copy of AdWords Editor hooked up to your account, as well as familiarity with the basic functions of this fine program. If you need to download AdWords Editor and skim Chapter 10 at this point, that's fine. We'll wait.

You're back? Great. Let's walk through a month of AdWords account maintenance. For the purposes of this demonstration, assume that the most you're willing to spend on a conversion is $10.

Monday, January 1, 2013

On the first day of the month, deal with all the keywords in your account that are converting too expensively. In AdWords Editor (hey, just call it Editor from now on; we're all friends here), download the past 30 days of data:

1. **Click the View Statistics button at the top.**

2. **Select Whole Account.**

3. **Select Last 30 Days as the date range.**

Don't worry about missing a day in December (or having two days of overlap in March). This data is robust enough to withstand a little messiness.

Then, follow these steps:

1. **Click the Keywords tab to view the data at the keyword level.**

2. **Click the Cost/Conversion column header to sort by Cost/Conversion with the highest numbers on top.**

You can click and drag that column to the left, next to the keyword, to make it easier to read. You can also right-click any of the header names to bring up a menu where you can show and hide columns.

3. **Reduce bids on all keywords that are converting too expensively (above $10/conversion in our example).**

Reduce bids in a two-step process. "Step 1" drops the bids of the more expensive keywords by a lot, while "Step 2" lowers the bids of the less-expensive (but still too-expensive) keywords by a lesser percent.

For example, suppose you have several keywords that cost $15–20 per conversion. Reduce those bids by 35%:

a. *Select the keywords with Cost/conv. between $15 and $20.*

b. *Click the Advanced Bid Changes link at the bottom left of the window.*

     c. *In the Advanced Bid Changes dialog box, select the Decrease Bids By radio button and enter **35** in the Percent data field. See Figure 13-6.*

     d. *Click the Change Bids button.*

     e. *Select keywords that cost $12–15 per conversion and drop their bids by 20%. (These are the "less expensive but still too expensive" keywords that get handled in Step 2.)*

Tuesday, January 2, 2013

Check your account to make sure it didn't experience a large decrease in traffic. Mark your calendar to repeat this process on February 1 and 2.

Monday, January 8, 2013

Now it's time to handle all the Display network ad groups that are converting too expensively. Download the last 30 days of data and filter for Display network campaigns. We recommend adding the word *DISPLAY* to the name of each of these campaigns precisely to make it easy to find them using Editor (see Figure 13-7).

1. **Click the tiny Advanced Search link at the top right.**

2. **Select the Campaigns and Ad Groups Where radio button and type** DISPLAY **in the text box next to Campaign Name.**

3. **Make sure the Active Status check box is selected, and remove any other performance statistics.**

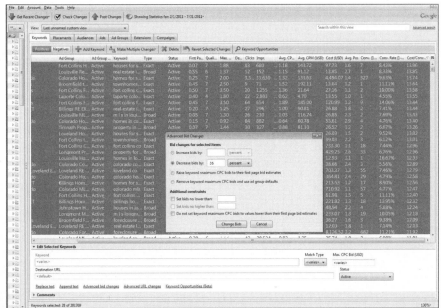

Figure 13-6:
Quickly reduce bids for all keywords that are too expensive.

4. **Select Save This Search for Reuse check box and type** DISPLAY **in the text box.**

5. **Click Search.**

You can modify display network bids both for ad groups and Managed placements. Automatic placements get adjusted only at the ad group level, while Managed placements can be altered individually. First, handle the Automatic placements:

1. **Click the Ad Groups tab.**

2. **Sort the table by Cost/Conversion, with the highest numbers on top.**

3. **Select all ad groups whose cost per conversion exceeds $15.**

4. **Click the Advanced Bid Changes link at the bottom left.**

5. **Select the Display Network Max. CPC radio button.**

6. **Select the Decrease Bids By radio button and enter** 25 **next to the Percent drop-down.**

7. **Click Change Bids.**

You can see this process in Figure 13-8, brought to you courtesy of Joel's AutomatedHomeFinder.com AdWords account. The rightmost column shows descending cost/conversion figures, and everything above $15 is highlighted.

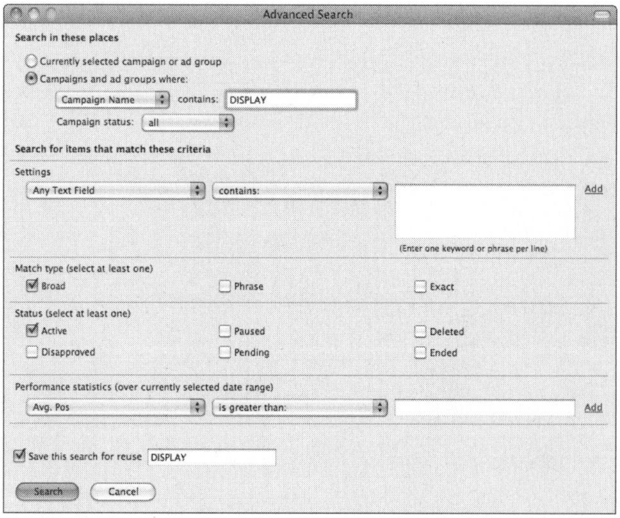

Figure 13-7:
Find all Display network campaigns by filtering for the word *DISPLAY* in the campaign name.

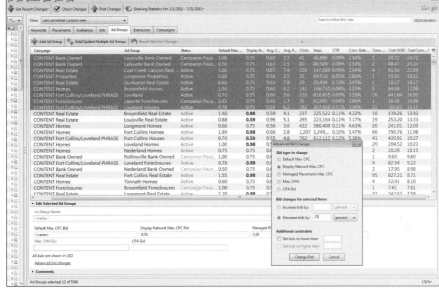

Figure 13-8:
In a couple
of clicks,
you can
decrease
bids for
all the ad
groups that
are bringing
in traffic too
expensively.

Just like on January 1, if the most you want to spend per conversion is $10, you'll want to reduce ad groups where the cost per conversion is above $20 or $25 by about 50 percent. Reduce ad group bids with cost per conversion between $15 and $20 by about 35 percent. Ad groups with an average cost per conversion between $12 and $15 should be reduced by about 20 percent.

If you're following the Expensive Conversion Placement Sweep procedure we outline earlier in this chapter, now is the time to reap the rewards of that effort. You can now adjust bids on individual Managed placements, giving you exquisite control over your spending and return.

1. **Click the Placements tab in Editor.**

2. **Sort by Cost/Conversion in descending order.**

3. **Select all placements whose cost per conversion exceeds $15.**

4. **Click the Advanced Bid Changes link at the bottom left.**

5. **Select the Decrease Bids By radio button and enter** 20 **next to the Percent drop-down.**

6. **Click Change Bids.**

In Figure 13-9, you can see eight placements that cost $12 per conversion or higher (two of them more than $60!). The first step is to reduce all those bids by 20 percent. That's fine for the six placements that are just a little over budget.

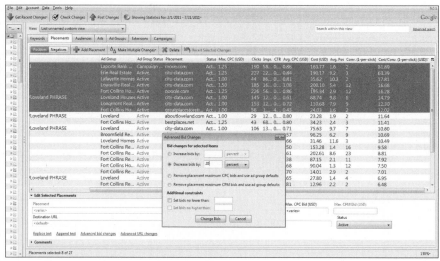

Figure 13-9:
In a couple
of clicks,
you can
decrease
bids for all
Managed
placements
that are
bringing in
traffic too
expensive.

To handle the two extreme big spenders, repeat the process:

1. **Select all placements whose cost exceeds $20 per conversion.**

2. **Reduce their bids by an additional 20 percent by repeating the process you just went through.**

Monday, January 15, 2013

So far, we've been in disciplinarian mode: finding keywords and placements that are too expensive, and contracting them by lowering bids. Now it's time to get generous and expansive by rewarding keywords that are bringing in inexpensive traffic. On the 15th of each month, you want to identify all keywords that are bringing in conversions that aren't being bid aggressively enough and raise their bids, thereby making them more competitive.

1. **In Editor, click the View Statistics button and download the last 30 days of data for your entire account.**

2. **Click the Keywords tab to view all keywords for the account.**

3. **Sort the table by cost per conversion, ascending.**

4. **Ignoring keywords with zero conversions, scroll down and select all keywords whose cost per conversion is less than $5.**

5. **Raise their bids by 35 percent.**

6. **Highlight all keywords converting between $5.01 and $8, and raise those bids by 20 percent.**

Download the most recent 30 days of data, view data at the keyword level, and sort by cost per conversion. If your acceptable cost per conversion is $10, scroll down to the keywords converting between $1 and $5, highlight them all, and raise bids by about 35 percent. Then highlight all keywords converting between $5.01 and $8 and raise those bids by about 20%.

Figure 13-10 shows Joel increasing bids on his $6–8 keywords by 25 percent. He's being a bit aggressive here, but the point is that it really doesn't matter if you go a bit over or under our suggestions. As long as you repeat this process monthly, you'll quickly hone in on the optimal bids for each element of your account.

Monday, January 22, 2013

Now you're going to spread the bid-raising love to the Display network. On the 22nd of each month, raise bids on all Display network ad groups and placements that deserve more exposure.

1. **Download the last 30 days of data by clicking the View Statistics button.**

2. **Filter for Display campaigns (refer to Figure 13-7 and the steps there).**

3. **Click the Ad Group tab.**

4. **Sort the ad groups by cost/conversion, ascending.**

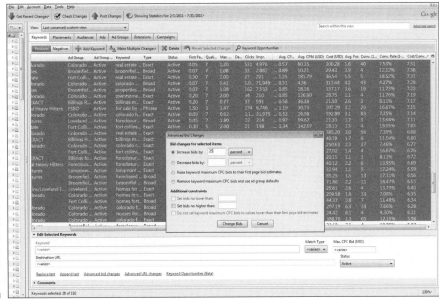

Figure 13-10: Raise bids on keywords that can give you more traffic and still be profitable.

5. **Ignoring ad groups with zero conversions, scroll down and select all ad groups whose cost per conversion is between $0.01 and $5.**

6. **Raise their bids by 35 percent.**

7. **Highlight all ad groups converting between $5.01 and $8.**

8. **Raise their bids by 20 percent.**

In Figure 13-11, Joel is rewarding seven Display network ad groups by raising their bids by 20 percent. (You may notice that his Display network campaigns are labeled CONTENT rather than Display. That just tells you that Joel's been at this for a while — the Display network used to be called the Content network.)

Next, start humming *Pomp and Circumstance* as you reap the rewards of your High Potential Placement Graduation (described earlier in this chapter, unless you're Benjamin Button, in which case it's described later in this chapter).

1. **Click the Placements tab.**

2. **Sort the Managed placements by cost/conversion, ascending.**

3. **Ignoring any placements with zero conversions, scroll down and highlight all placements with conversions costing less than $7.**

4. **Raise their bids by 20 percent (as shown in Figure 13-12).**

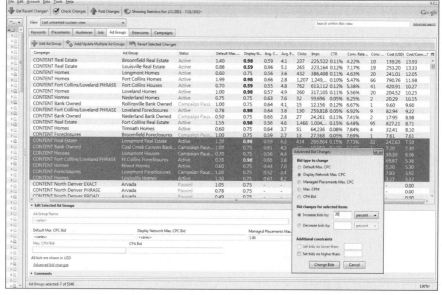

Figure 13-11: Reward cost-effective Display network ad groups by raising their bids.

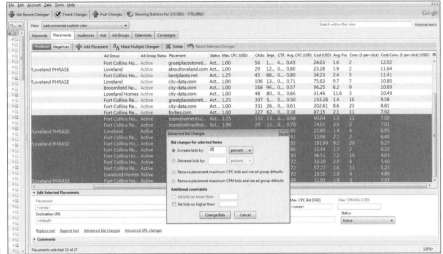

Figure 13-12:
Raise bids on Managed placements to get more profitable traffic.

Thursday, January 31, 2013

On the last day of each month, you're decluttering your account by shedding keywords and placements that haven't generated any conversions.

Decluttering keywords

1. **In Editor, click View Statistics and download the last 30 days of data.**

2. **Filter for campaigns bidding in the Search network only.**

   The easiest way to do this is to add the word SEARCH to the name of every campaign in the Search network. Then you can filter for SEARCH the same way you filtered for DISPLAY back on January 8 (refer to Figure 13-7).

3. **Click the Keywords tab.**

4. **Filter for keywords with zero conversions by clicking the Advanced Search link at the top right and going to the Performance Statistics section.**

5. **Select Conv. (1-per-click) from the first drop-down list, Equals from the second drop-down list, type 0 (the number zero) in the text field, and click Add. (See Figure 13-13.)**

6. **Remove any other performance statistics filters and click Search.**

   Your data table should show only keywords with zero conversions.

7. **Sort the keywords by Cost, descending.**

8. **Highlight all keywords whose cost is at least equal to five times the value of a conversion (in this example, 5 × \$10 = \$50).**

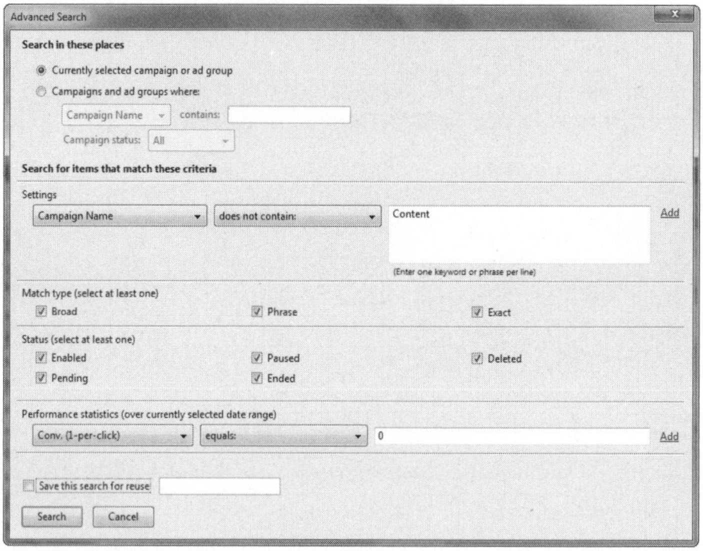

Figure 13-13:
Filter for zero-conversion keywords so you can deactivate them.

9. **At the bottom right of the Editor window, change the status of these keywords from Active to Paused.**

10. **Select all keywords that have cost between 2 and 5 times the value of a conversion (in this case, $20–49.99).**

11. **Reduce their bids by 50 percent.**

Decluttering Display ad groups

1. **Filter for Display network campaigns (refer to Figure 13-7).**

2. **Click the Ad Groups tab.**

   This step is very important because if you stay on the Keywords tab, you could end up deleting all your keywords because they don't accrue data in the Display network.

3. **Filter for ad groups with zero conversions by clicking the Advanced Search link at the top right and going to the Performance Statistics section.**

4. **Select Conv. (1-per-click) from the first drop-down list, Equals from the second drop-down list, type 0 (the number zero) in the text field, and click Add.**

5. **Remove any other performance statistics filters and click Search.**

   Your data table should show only ad groups with zero conversions.

6. **Sort the ad groups by Cost, descending.**

7. **Highlight all ad groups whose cost is at least equal to five times the value of a conversion (in this example, 5 × $10 = $50).**

8. **Right-click any of the highlighted ad groups and choose Delete from the contextual menu.**

9. **Next, select all ad groups that have cost between two and five times the value of a conversion (in this case, $20–49.99).**

10. **Reduce their bids by 50 percent.**

Throttling down poorly performing Managed placements

Finally, you want to make sure you don't have any managed placements that are costing you a lot of money without delivering conversions in exchange.

1. **Click the Placements tab.**

2. **Filter for placements with zero conversions (see Steps 3–5 of the earlier section, "Decluttering keywords").**

   Your data table should show only placements with zero conversions.

3. **Sort the placements by Cost, descending.**

4. **Highlight all placements whose cost is greater than five times the value of a conversion (in this example, $50).**

5. **At the bottom right, change their status from Active to Paused.**

6. **Highlight all placements that have cost between $10 and $49.99 by 25 percent.**

You don't want to pause or exclude these placements permanently because of one bad month. That would be like benching your star player because of a few bad games. You'll catch the fading stars in your twice-yearly Six Month Tuneup before they can do too much damage.

Although the preceding steps might seem like a lot of work, remember that you're doing each one only once per month, and none of them takes more than ten minutes after you master the steps. That's a small price to pay for an account that runs like a well-tuned Omega Seamaster.

If you'd like ongoing reminders of this schedule, you can subscribe to our Google Calendar for AdWords maintenance and updates at `http://gafd3.com/calendar`.

Semi-annual activities

Every six months, monitor for keywords and placements that are doing poorly but receive so little traffic on a monthly basis that they've managed to avoid the axe simply be keeping their heads down. If you don't aggregate the data over a six-month period, your account could be bleeding copiously from what Joel calls "death by paper cuts." Although each low-volume, ROI-negative keyword and placement isn't doing much damage individually, the cumulative effect can seriously erode your margins. In other words, in any given month, you didn't spend enough money on them to even notice how poorly they were performing, but over six months, you'll be able to more easily identify those nonprofitable ad groups, keywords, and placements.

The following sections describe what you need to do Monday, July 1, 2013 and Wednesday, January 1, 2014.

To heal ad group paper cuts:

1. **Download the last six months of data:**

    a. *Click the View Statistics button.*

    b. *Select Whole Account.*

    c. *Select Create Custom Date Range from the drop-down list.*

    d. *Manually enter the dates corresponding to the last six months.*

    e. *Click OK.*

2. **Click the Advanced Search link at the top right to filter for zero conversions.**

    Hopefully all your campaigns will disappear because each one will have generated conversions. You need to drill deeper to find zero-converting elements in your account.

3. **Click the Ad Groups tab to view all ad groups that haven't generated a single conversion in the past six months.**

    If the table is empty, skip to "healing keyword paper cuts" (next topic). If you can see ad groups with no conversions, continue with step 4.

4. **Sort the ad groups by Cost, descending.**

5. **Select all ad groups that have cost at least five times the value of a conversion (in this example, $50).**

6. **At the bottom right of the Editor window, change the status of these ad group from Active to Paused.**

    If there are ad groups in the table with zero conversions and a cost of between two to four times the value of a conversion ($20–49.99, in this example), continue to Step 8. If not, skip to the next topic on healing keyword paper cuts.

7. **Click the Advanced Search link to add a filter for Display network campaign only, keeping the zero conversions filter in place.**

8. **Select all ad groups with zero conversions that have cost between two to five times the value of a conversion ($20–49.99, in this example).**

9. **At the bottom right, change their status from Active to Paused.**

To heal keyword paper cuts:

1. **Click the Keywords tab to view all keywords that haven't generated a single conversion in the past six months.**

2. **Sort the keywords by Cost, descending.**

3. **Select all keywords that have cost at least five times the value of a conversion (in this example, $50).**

4. **At the bottom right of the Editor window, change the status of these keywords from Active to Paused.**

5. **Drop bids on all keywords that have cost between two to five times the value of a conversion ($20–49.99, in this example) by 25 percent.**

To heal placement paper cuts:

1. **Click the Advanced Search link at the top right and add a filter for Display network only.**

2. **Click the Placements tab to view all placements that haven't generated a single conversion in the past six month.**

3. **Sort the placements by Cost, descending.**

4. **Select all placements that have cost at least five times the value of a conversion (in this example, $50).**

5. **At the bottom right of the Editor window, change the status of these ad group from Active to Paused.**

6. **Select all placements that have cost between two and five times the value of a conversion by 25 percent.**

Setting Alerts

The steps in "Building a Customized Maintenance Schedule" most likely will take you more time to read than to actually do, so there really shouldn't be any excuse not to add it to your calendar. But sometimes you'll need to intervene in your account on an emergency basis, and you'd rather not wait until the next scheduled maintenance session to discover the problem.

Set up alerts to get notified about serious performance or account problems, such as significant changes in traffic (up or down) or in costs:

1. **Navigate to the Campaigns tab of your online AdWords Dashboard.**

2. **Click the Alerts button, just above the data table.**

3. Select Create a Custom Alert from the drop-down list and explore the options.

For example, you can ask Google to e-mail you when your spend reaches a certain percentage of your daily budget, when your number of clicks increases or decreases by a percentage you specify, or when your number of conversions plummets.

Don't rely on alerts for ordinary account maintenance; instead, set up a follow a schedule, and save alerts for situations when out-of-the-ordinary measures are called for.

Part V
Expanding and Leveraging Your Results

The 5th Wave   By Rich Tennant

"Hey-here's a company that develops short memorable domain names for new businesses. It's listed at www.CompanyThatDevelopsShort-MemorableDomainNamesForNewBusinesses.com".

In this part . . .

*O*ur absolute favorite thing about AdWords is how it can be used as an inexpensive and speedy test bed. As Frank Sinatra widely observed about AdWords, "If I can make it there, I'll make it anywhere." This part reveals how AdWords can and should be the foundation of every marketing initiative, product launch, and start-up venture.

Chapter 14 explains how to continually improve your ads by running multiple ads simultaneously and showing the different versions randomly to Google searchers. We also cover the very cool AdWords Campaign Experiments feature.

Chapter 15 continues the split-testing theme by introducing you to Google's free Web Site Optimizer tool, which allows you to perform simple and robust split tests (in English: "really cool and powerful stuff") to improve the performance of your website.

Chapter 16 covers a technique we pioneered: campaign cloning. It's an elegant and quick way to reward success with greater opportunity, and to divide markets into measurable segments so you can squeeze more profit from each segment.

Chapter 17 explores a feature so powerful that even if you never bid on a single keyword or placement, you could double or triple your website's effectiveness just with remarketing.

Chapter 14

How You Can't Help Becoming an Advertising Genius

*T*he mechanics of AdWords are complex, but not difficult to master. You'll soon become familiar with keywords, bids, networks, positions, CTRs, and all the rest of the strange lingo and concepts unique to AdWords. By following the advice in this book, you'll have a clear advantage over competitors who don't understand the mechanics and therefore don't optimize for them.

But mechanics are not where the big breakthroughs occur. The big money is made by powerfully connecting with your prospects through magnetic ads, compelling landing pages, clear and authentic websites, and sensitive follow-up. Most advertisers don't achieve this connection on the first try. Most, in fact, never achieve it at all, and end up struggling on the hamster wheel of minimal margins and marketing mediocrity. The one discipline that reliably separates successful AdWords advertisers from the rest is *split testing* — putting various messages into the market to discover which resonate and which fall flat.

Perry Marshall of http://perrymarshall.com gave a talk in which he demonstrated the need for split testing by challenging audience members — professional marketers all — to choose the more effective ad or headline from a series of ten split tests. The best of us got no more than 4 or 5 out of 10 correct. As we held our hands up high and proud for having achieved 50 percent on the test, Perry shot us down: "If I had flipped a coin, I would have done as well as you. Congratulations. You guys are as smart as a penny."

If you want to be smarter than a penny, you must apply the most powerful tool in the marketer's arsenal: split testing.

In this chapter, we show you how to set up split testing with AdWords and analyze the results. First we look at simple ad split testing, which is so powerful that it may be the only type you ever need. Next we introduce you to a beta AdWords feature, AdWords Campaign Experiments, which allows you to evaluate entire parallel universes to see which one you'd rather live (and advertise) in.

Capturing the Magic of Split Testing

Nothing leads to improvement faster than timely and clear feedback. Although a million monkeys typing would eventually produce the entire works of Shakespeare, they would get there much faster if they got a banana every time they typed an actual word and an entire banana split when they managed a rhymed couplet in iambic pentameter. (Can you tell we've been reading *Shakespeare For Dummies,* by John Doyle and Ray Lischner?) And for every nonword, someone would chuck a copy of *Typing Shakespeare For Monkeys* at them.

Now suppose the monkeys could keep and understand a written record of the characters that produced bananas, banana splits, and no reward. After a while, you would see more and more real words and Shakespearean phrasing, and fewer xlkjdfsdfsr. Ouch!

AdWords contains the world's simplest mechanism for getting timely and clear feedback on your ads. You can create multiple ads, which AdWords shows to your prospects in equal rotation, and you can receive automatic and ongoing feedback.

Split testing is not an AdWords innovation. Direct marketers have been testing customers' response rates since Moses got two tablets of commandments. *Reader's Digest* used to choose headlines for its articles by sending postcards to readers, asking which articles they would be interested in reading in an upcoming issue. The list of articles was actually a list of headlines for the same article.

Here's how split testing works in AdWords:

1. Run multiple ads simultaneously within a single ad group.

2. Let Google monitor all ads' effectiveness at eliciting the customer response you want.

   Depending on the campaign-level setting you select, Google can automatically promote winning ads and depress losing ones.

3. Keep adding new ad ideas and let Google test them automatically.

Until early 2011, we advocated manual split testing. But with the addition of a new ad rotation option — Optimize for Conversions — it's much easier and more effective to include lots of ads and let Google orchestrate the contest. You don't need to delete poorly performing ads because Google will stop showing them automatically. And the more data Google has to work with, the smarter it gets at matching the right ad with the right keyword, location, time of day, and more.

The beauty of this split-testing system is that you can't help but improve your results over time. If a new ad proves worse than existing ones, Google simply stops showing it. The added beauty is that you don't even have to know what you're doing to improve your ad's effectiveness. Although market intelligence, creativity, and writing skill help, mere trial and error — when funneled through split testing — can boost your results significantly.

One of Howie's early AdWords projects was an ad for a direct-marketing home-study course for small businesses (see the series of ads in Figure 14-1). An early ad, headlined "Cold calling — now illegal," achieved a 0.7% click-through rate (CTR). The final ad he used — "Cold calling not working?" — nearly quadrupled that with a 2.7% CTR. The big lesson from this long series of ads is this: He had no idea what he was doing at the time, yet he still succeeded. Take a few minutes and examine each of the ads carefully. Be honest — could you predict which of these ads would do better than the rest? Howie couldn't. (He still can't.) But the numbers don't lie, and he was able to turn a marginal product into a success thanks to split testing.

Ad	CTR	Ad	CTR
Cold calling not working? Discover a powerful alternative. Free report and 2 chapter download. www.LeadsIntoGold.com	2.60%	**End cold calling forever** Small business marketing system. Download 2 chapters for free. www.leadsintogold.com	1.35%
Cold calling not working? Discover an effective alternative. Free report and 2 chapter download. www.LeadsIntoGold.com	2.35%	**Stop cold prospecting.** Small business marketing system. Free report and 2 chapter download. www.leadsintogold.com	1.04%
End cold calling forever Lead generation system explained. Free report and 2 chapter download. www.LeadsIntoGold.com	2.28%	**End cold calling forever** and make more money. Free report and 2 chapter download. www.leadsintogold.com	1.00%
End cold calling forever Lead generation system explained. Free report and 2 chapter download. www.leadsintogold.com	2.26%	**End cold calling forever** Small business marketing system. Free report and 2 chapter download. www.leadsintogold.com	0.83%
Cold calling ineffective? Discover a powerful alternative. Free report and 2 chapter download. www.LeadsIntoGold.com	2.22%	**Stop cold calling forever** Small business marketing system. Free report and 2 chapter download. www.leadsintogold.com	0.82%
End cold calling forever Attract customers automatically. Free report and 2 chapter download. www.leadsintogold.com	2.18%	**Cold calling -now illegal** Effective alternative explained. Free report and 2 chapter download. www.LeadsIntoGold.com	0.76%
End cold calling forever Attract customers automatically. Free report and 2 chapter download. www.LeadsIntoGold.com	2.04%	**End cold calling forever** Free report and 2 chapter download. Attract customers automatically. www.leadsintogold.com	0.00%
End cold calling forever Free report and 2 chapter download. Lead generation system explained. www.leadsintogold.com	1.95%	**Stop wasteful advertising** Small business marketing system. Free report and 2 chapter download. www.leadsintogold.com	0.00%
End cold calling forever Small business marketing system. Free report and 2 chapter download. www.leadsintogold.com	1.76%		

Figure 14-1: One of the authors ignorantly split-tests his way to profitability.

Basic Method: Multiple Ads

Recall that an *ad group* is a collection of ads shown to a specific traffic source, whether keyword- or placement- or audience-based. In Chapter 2, we show you how to create your first ad within an ad group. Now you can create challenger ads within the same ad group and let your prospects tell you which ones are most effective.

Creating a challenger ad

Creating your second ad is even easier than creating your first:

1. **Navigate to the Ad Group you want to split-test.**

2. **Click the Ads sub-tab to display the ads in your ad group.**

3. **Click the New Ad button just below the statistics chart.**

4. **Choose Text Ad from the drop-down list.**

   An ad template with the copy from one of your existing ads appears onscreen, as shown in Figure 14-2.

5. **Type over the existing copy and URL with your challenger ad's copy and URL.**

6. **Click the Save Ad button.**

7. **Repeat for as many ads as you want to test.**

If your traffic volume is low, you may want to limit your tests to two or three ads at a time. If your ad group generates lots of impressions, you can run more ads simultaneously (up to ten variations).

Optimize for CTR or conversions

After you install conversion tracking (see Chapter 6), you can compare the profitability of your ads. Until then, the only thing you can compare is the CTR. If you can track conversions, you must select the appropriate campaign-level setting:

1. **From the Campaigns tab, click the Settings tab.**

2. **Click the name of the campaign whose settings you want to edit.**

3. **Scroll down to Advanced Settings, Ad Delivery: Ad Rotation, Frequency Capping.**

4. **Click the Edit link next to Ad Rotation.**

5. **Select the Optimize for Conversions radio button, as shown in Figure 14-3.**

6. **Click Save.**

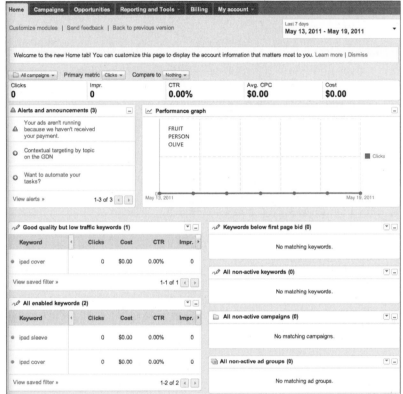

Figure 14-2:
Creating
a new ad
on the Ad
Variations
tab.

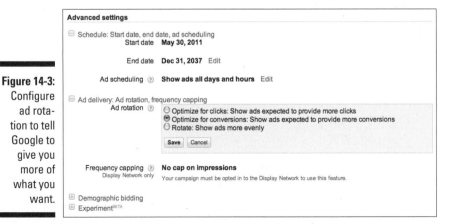

Figure 14-3:
Configure
ad rota-
tion to tell
Google to
give you
more of
what you
want.

If you can't track conversions, then your next best option is Optimize for Clicks.

Applying split-test intelligence

Google runs the tests automatically, selecting winners and losers based on ad performance. You don't need to turn anything on or off — that all happens without you. The only reason to watch the split-test results is to discover which messages are most effective with different audiences. You can then use that intelligence to craft successful campaigns in other media (see Chapter 18).

Advanced Method: AdWords Campaign Experiments

A key scene in the movie *Sliding Doors* shows Gwyneth Paltrow's character Helen Quilley catching a London Underground train — or not. From that point, the movie splits into two parallel universes, each of which plays out differently based on whether Helen makes it past the sliding doors. AdWords Experiments is a beta feature that allows split testing of elements other than ad copy by creating a parallel universe in which you get to change certain elements in a given campaign.

Setting up an experiment

You set up experiments on the campaign level, in a two-step process. First, you activate the experiment in campaign settings. Then you create experimental conditions.

Activate the experiment

Here's how to activate the experiment:

1. **Click the name of the campaign in which you want to experiment.**

2. **Click the Settings tab and scroll to Advanced Settings, at the bottom of the page.**

3. **Click the Experiment link.**

4. **Click the Specify Experimental Settings button.**

5. **Specify the experiment settings, as shown in Figure 14-4:**

a. *Name:* Name your experiment so you can identify it later.

b. *Control/Experiment Split:* What percentage of impressions do you want to be subject to the experimental conditions versus existing conditions? You'll get results the fastest at half control/half experiment. But if your control is working well, you may not want to risk half your traffic on an unknown condition. In that case, you may want to play it safe by keeping 80 percent of your impressions under existing conditions, and just send 20 percent to the untested conditions.

c. *Start:* When do you want the experiment to start? If you're ready to go, select the lower radio button and then click in the box next to that button. A calendar will appear, from which you can choose a start date. To start the experiment manually, leave the No Start Date radio button selected.

d. *End:* The default experiment length is 30 days. If you don't get much traffic to this campaign, you may want to extend it to 60 or 90 days. Conversely, if you get lots of traffic, you may want to cut the experiment to one or two weeks. You can always stop an experiment early if the results are conclusive one way or the other.

6. **Click Save.**

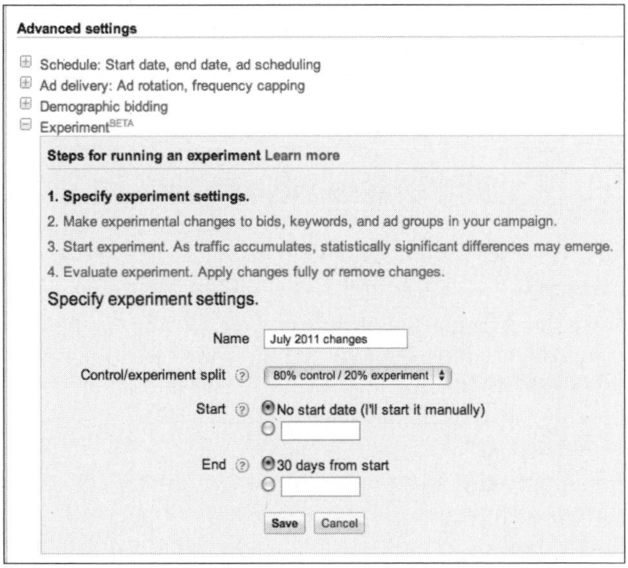

Figure 14-4:
Specify experimental settings on the campaign settings page.

Advanced settings

- Schedule: Start date, end date, ad scheduling
- Ad delivery: Ad rotation, frequency capping
- Demographic bidding
- Experiment BETA

  Steps for running an experiment Learn more

  1. Specify experiment settings.
  2. Make experimental changes to bids, keywords, and ad groups in your campaign.
  3. Start experiment. As traffic accumulates, statistically significant differences may emerge.
  4. Evaluate experiment. Apply changes fully or remove changes.

  Specify experiment settings.

Name	July 2011 changes
Control/experiment split ⑦	80% control / 20% experiment ▲▼
Start ⑦	⦿ No start date (I'll start it manually) ◯
End ⑦	⦿ 30 days from start ◯

  Save   Cancel

To this point, you've set up the experimental bucket, but you haven't yet filled it with changes. The next step is to create experimental conditions.

Make experimental changes

From the Campaign tab, start making changes. You can do any or all of the following:

- ✔ Create new ad groups that run only in the experimental condition.
- ✔ Add and remove keywords and placements.
- ✔ Change keyword and placement bids.
- ✔ Create or remove ads.

Experimental ad group

To create a whole new ad group that exists only in the "Helen caught the train" universe, create the ad group as you would normally. Like in any campaign, click the Ad Groups tab, click the Create New Ad Group button and then write an ad and select keywords. At the bottom of the page, though, select the Add as Experiment Only Ad Group check box before saving (see Figure 14-5). If you don't see that option, you haven't yet configured that campaign for experiments. See the preceding section for details on setting up your experiment.

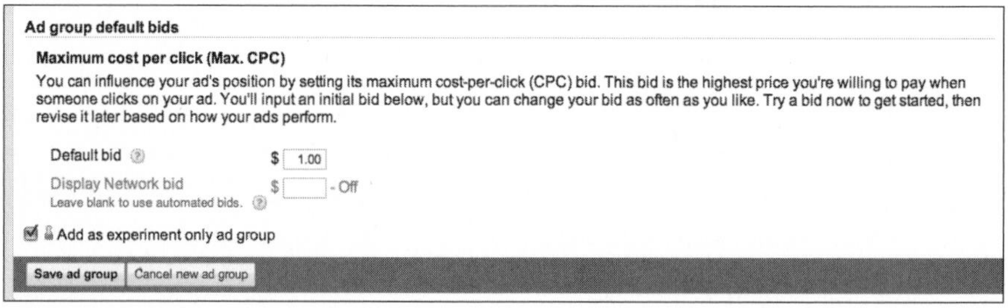

Figure 14-5:
Create an experimental ad group and play "what if" with reality.

Ad group default bids

Maximum cost per click (Max. CPC)

You can influence your ad's position by setting its maximum cost-per-click (CPC) bid. This bid is the highest price you're willing to pay when someone clicks on your ad. You'll input an initial bid below, but you can change your bid as often as you like. Try a bid now to get started, then revise it later based on how your ads perform.

Default bid ⑦ $ 1.00
Display Network bid $ [   ] - Off
Leave blank to use automated bids. ⑦

☑ 🔒 Add as experiment only ad group

Save ad group   Cancel new ad group

Experimental new ads

Similarly, you can add experiment-only ads on the Ads tab by clicking the New Ad button, creating the new ad, and then selecting the Add as Experiment Only Ad check box, just above the Save button.

Experimental new keyword

Add experiment-only keywords on the Keywords tab by clicking the New Keyword button, selecting one or more new keywords and then selecting the Add as Experiment Only Keywords check box, just above the Save button.

Experimental new placement

You can't add new experimental placements to an existing ad group; instead, create an experimental ad group and put the experiment-only placements in that ad group.

Experimental ad elimination

Wonder what would happen if you eliminated an ad from your account? You can try this fun experiment at home by navigating to the ad you're curious about. Just to the left of the ad text is a small icon with a green circle and a beaker. Click the icon and select Control Only from the drop-down list (see Figure 14-6). The icon will change to an empty beaker, signifying that ad will not show in the experimental condition.

Figure 14-6: Change an ad's status to Control Only to eliminate it from the experiment.

Experimental keyword elimination

On the Keywords tab, click the green-circle-in-front-of-beaker icon and select Control Only from the drop-down list. The icon will change to an empty beaker, meaning that this keyword will appear in the control condition only.

Experimental placement elimination

You can't directly delete placements from the experiment and run them only as controls. Instead, create an identical copy of your control ad group (and append **Experiment** to the new ad group name to avoid confusion) and then remove any placements you want to eliminate within that experimental ad group.

Experimental keyword bid adjustment

To adjust keyword bids up or down, navigate to the Keywords tab and click the Segment button just below the highlighted Keywords tab. Select Experiment from the drop-down list. Each keyword in the table will expand to include three new rows: Outside Experiment, Control, and Experiment.

To change the experiment-only bid, click the number in the Experiment Max. CPC Column. You can then either add or subtract a percentage from that bid. Either keep the plus sign or change it to a minus sign; then enter the percentage change. Google instantly shows you the actual new bid based on the percent you enter (see Figure 14-7). Click Save to retain the new experimental bid.

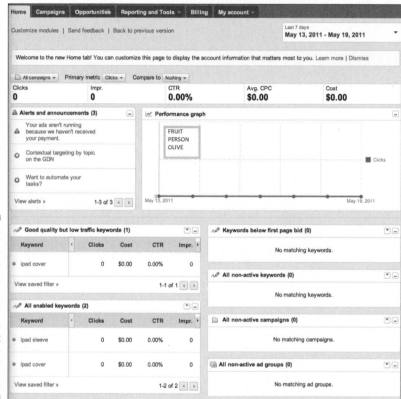

Figure 14-7:
You can experiment with modified keyword bids to see the effect on your traffic and conversions.

Experimental placement bid adjustment

As of this writing, Google doesn't allow you to adjust experimental bids for individual placements. Instead, you can create an experiment-only ad group that contains the placements you specify at your desired bids and run it against the control ad group with the original bids. Not the most elegant setup in the world, but better than nothing.

Knowing when the experiment is conclusive

This is the part of the book where in previous editions you got a complicated lesson on statistical significance. While this topic is still endlessly fascinating, Google has removed the need for you to understand it. Now the experiment just runs until the end date, while Google shows you the "horse race" in real time for each experimental change. Using a visual library of up and down arrows, you can quickly see which changes lead to different results, and how confident you can be that those results are real, rather than due to random chance.

As this feature is still in beta, we're willing to bet all the details we show you now will be semi-obsolete by the time you read this. Fortunately, we've discovered a really neat medium (the World Wide Web) that allows for easy updates and multimedia, too! For a full-color tutorial on monitoring AdWords Campaign Experiments, visit `http://gafd3.com/experiments`.

Applying or rejecting experimental changes

After your experiment has run its course, or when you've seen data indicating that the experimental changes have either improved or worsened your results, you can apply or reject the experimental changes.

Go to the Campaign Settings tab and scroll down to the Experiment settings. If the experiment has concluded automatically, by reaching your specified end date, you'll see two buttons: Apply: Launch Changes Fully and Delete: Remove Changes. If you're stopping the experiment manually because you know the answer already and don't want to waste any traffic by sending it to an inferior ad, keyword, placement, or bid, you'll see a third button: Stop Running Experiment. Stop the experiment first, and then either apply or delete the experimental changes with one of the other buttons.

To accept all experimental results and make them into the new control, click the Apply: Launch Changes Fully button. To reject the experimental changes and return to the way things were, click the Delete: Remove Changes button.

Limiting experimental changes

You'll notice that Google gives you only two choices: Accept everything or reject everything. That limitation may seem unduly restrictive, but it's actually based on sound statistical science. When you make a bunch of changes, you can't actually attribute a result to just a portion of those changes. The whole new environment contributed to the new results.

For example, look at Kristie's husband Tom's band, Chicago Plush. The three members play lively dance music from the 1970s and '80s, dress in jeans and t-shirts, and joke around a lot while performing. Suppose Chicago Plush gets an average of three new booking inquiries every time they perform in a local bar or restaurant. Then one day Tom has the bright idea, "Hey, let's add kazoo, harmonica, and banjo players, dress in tuxedos, play early 1990s UK trip hop, speak only in Klingon, and perform at nursing homes."

Suddenly their booking inquiries plummet; but what caused the drop? Tom introduced too many variables into the equation, so it looked like the entire experiment was a failure. If Chicago Plush had kept everything the same except for the tuxedos, perhaps they would have seen an increase. Maybe the tuxedo/Klingon combo would have been a big winner. Perhaps the change of venue to nursing homes was the big mistake.

Just because AdWords Experiments gives you the power to test everything at once doesn't mean it's a good idea. The best way to avoid confusion and overwhelm is to limit the variables you're testing per experiment. You can always conduct followup experiments on other elements you're curious about.

Strategies for Effective Split Testing

Many AdWords beginners understand the concept of split testing, but do it haphazardly and without strategy. They learn that split testing is too confusing and complicated, and give up on the most powerful weapon in their marketing arsenal. Here are two strategies to assure a streamlined and effective split-testing process:

- ✔ **Start wide, get narrow.** When you begin to split-test in an ad group, choose very different ads. You may want to focus on different markets (stay-at-home dads versus divorced/widowed dads with full custody), different emotional responses (greed versus fear), or different benefits (lose weight versus prevent heart disease). Get the big picture right before drilling down to the details. It does you no good to test *easy* versus *simple* in a headline if your prospects don't care about ease or simplicity, but just whether it can run on batteries.

  After you discover the right market, key benefits, and the emotional hot buttons of that market, you can start testing more-specific elements. See the upcoming section, "A Split-Testing Protocol: Generating Ideas for Ad Testing."

✔ **Ask intelligent questions.** Split testing can become so mechanical, it's easy to forget that the purpose is to make you smarter by learning what makes your customers tick — er, *click*.

Perry Marshall distinguishes between true market research and what he calls "opinion research." Opinion research is what people *say* they'll do. Market research is what they *actually* do. Split testing is a powerful form of market research that provides answers to whatever questions you ask. As computer programmers are fond of saying, "Garbage In, Garbage Out." If you ask intelligent questions, you'll get useful answers.

So before you run a split test, take a moment to write down (in your lab notebook, of course) the question you want your prospects to answer for you. Then design a split test that asks that question.

A Split-Testing Protocol: Generating Ideas and a Plan

You want to test broadly different ideas before getting into details. Don't worry about whether description line 2 should have a comma in it before you figure out the answers to your big questions. Imagine that you're searching for the most delicious plum in the world. First, you test the orchard to make sure that it has plum trees and not orange trees. When you find the plum orchard, start testing trees to find the tree with the best plums. When you find the best tree, see whether you prefer the plums near the top or closer to the ground. On the north or the south side. Then taste the fruit on different limbs, and after you find the most promising limb, see which branch yields the best fruit.

Do you know the answers to the following four questions? In a competitive market, the winner (practically by definition) is the merchant who can best answer these questions. If you're not sure, split testing is one of the quickest, most reliable, and least expensive ways of finding out.

✔ **Who is the prospect?** Among all the people searching for your keyword, who is your prospect? Can you identify them by sex, age, occupation, location, marital status, political views, cultural preferences, lifestyle, hobbies, or any of dozens of demographic and psychographic factors?

In addition to the preceding list, which reflects inherent qualities of the searcher, you might think of search-specific aspects of the searcher's identity. For example, the same woman might conduct four distinct searches within a given day, each in a completely different role — one as a realtor looking for a logo, another as a mother searching for a summer camp for her son, a third as a Tracy Grammer fan looking for concert tickets, and a fourth as a daughter helping her mother understand the her Medicare Part D benefits.

Take our running example company G-Form as an example. Who is searching for knee pads? Men or women? Obviously, some of both, but is one group predominant? They could test a headline featuring "Women's knee pads" against one for "Men's knee pads" against one for "Athletic knee pads" to see whether a gender-specific message increases or decreases the flow of converting traffic.

✔ **Why are they searching?** After you know who is searching, the next question probes their motivation. Say that G-Form discovers that its best prospects for knee pads are male mountain bikers. What's the motivation: to be as safe as possible, or to survive ever-more-dangerous trails? To have the very best protection, or to find knee pads light and comfortable enough that they'll actually put them on?

G-Form can test ads touting freedom to handle the gnarliest (is that still a cool word?) trails against ads promising ultimate protection against breaks, bumps, and bruises to determine the desires of their prospects.

✔ **What do they want?** If G-Form discovers that its male mountain bikers want to perform ever-more-dangerous stunts while avoiding bone-breaking injury, its job isn't over. Is the searcher ready to buy right now? Or is he looking for reviews, testimonials, and forums with other mountain bikers? Does he have a particular competitor's brand in mind? Does he even believe that a soft pad could possibly protect better than a hard-shelled one?

In other words, what promise do they want to see in the perfect ad? G-Form can test product offers, reviews, demos, and discussions to bring the ideal prospect into a sales conversation.

✔ **How do they want it?** Suppose our freedom-seeking male mountain biker has his wallet out and is looking to make a purchase. Does he have a color preference? Does he want to purchase elbow pads and shin guards separately, or would he prefer a full-body package? Would he prefer free shipping or a discount? Would he respond better to a promise of a large selection, or just one top-notch product?

Syntax and Format Testing

After you test the big ideas, turn your attention to the little things that can make a big difference:

✔ **Order of lines:** If you're highlighting the benefit on line 1 and explaining a feature on line 2, try switching the order of the two lines.

✔ **Synonyms:** Try variations of your benefits: simple/easy/quick/no sweat.

✔ **Capitalization:** Does capitalizing the first letter of every word increase clicks and conversions? Or perhaps no capitalization at all makes your ad stand out from the rest?

✔ **Punctuation:** Most people read by hearing the words spoken in their heads. You can use punctuation to make those words more melodic and persuasive. Figure 14-8 shows what happened when Howie used a comma to put the emphasis on *You* rather than *Instead*:

Figure 14-8:
In this
split test,
a comma
quadruples
the CTR.

Variations	CTR ▼
Cold Calls Don't Work Prospects Hanging Up on You? Get Them to Call You, Instead! LeadsintoGold.com	2.02%
Cold Calls Don't Work Prospects Hanging Up on You? Get Them to Call You Instead! LeadsintoGold.com	0.49%

The ad with the comma is four times as effective as the other one. There's no way to predict such a profound effect; without testing, you would never know. With testing, you can market like a genius by following the advice of the only person who's qualified to give it: your prospect.

Chapter 15

Making More Sales with Google Website Optimizer

*I*n the movie *Groundhog Day,* Bill Murray plays a surly, cynical weatherman fated to relive the same day — February 2 in Punxsutawney, Pennsylvania — over and over again. Along the way, he learns to sculpt ice, play piano, and dance. Eventually, he falls in love with his producer, played by Andie MacDowell. In his quest to win her heart, Murray's character fails repeatedly to impress and attract her. But he learns from every failure and adapts his behavior, until he has transformed himself into a suave, considerate, and heroic companion.

When you split-test pages on your website, you can accomplish the same sort of trial-and-error adaptation with your visitors and prospects, without having to spend quasi-eternity in Pennsylvania. Your tool of choice, compliments of Google, is the free, powerful, and elegant Google Website Optimizer (which we'll just call Optimizer from now on).

Optimizer allows you to test different variations of your web pages to see which ones give you more of the results you want. Will your visitors respond better to a product photo, video, or testimonial in a given region of the page? Will more people buy if you offer a 50 percent discount or a two-for-one sale? Should your headline read, "Natural Soaps for All Occasions" or "You Probably Stink"?

Testing has been practiced since Moses came down the mountain with two tablets. In the early days of direct marketing, advertisers would test direct mail campaigns at a cost of thousands or tens of thousands of today's dollars, and would get results months after initiating the test. On the World Wide

Web, you can generate the same quality of data with a few minutes of setup and a few days or weeks of data gathering. Most site owners never test, so they never discover that they're missing 50–100 percent increases in sales — and that range is conservative because you won't believe the real possibilities until you experience them for yourself.

In this chapter, we borrow heavily from the expertise of Garrett Todd, Optimization Specialist at Vitruvian. We guide you to identify the conversion events, set up an Optimizer benchmark test to establish your current reality, monitor tests for statistical and practical significance, and create a "quick wins" testing strategy. You'll discover how you can fail your way to great success, and win the AdWords game by achieving the highest value per click in your industry.

We can't share everything we know about Optimizer in a single chapter. Rather than getting into the details, we show you how to set up the most basic tests and interpret and act on the results. We recommend first testing simple elements (such as colors, fonts, and images) before moving on to more sophisticated tests of strategic positioning and emotional appeal. In our experience, conversion optimization is addictive, so if we start you with some quick and easy wins, you'll get to the more complex tests anyway. At that point, you can crack open any of a number of excellent books on website optimization (our favorite is Ben Hunt's *Convert!*).

Determining Whether Using Website Optimizer Is Worth the Effort

When someone asks us whether we can improve their website performance, we ask in return whether they've been testing page variations in a systematic and scientific manner. If their answer is No, ours is Yes. Smart testing improves performance. This attitude isn't boasting, or blind faith in our magical marketing abilities. Rather, it's based on probability theory and years of experience, plus a clever trick that Charlie Darwin discovered when he wasn't getting seasick on the *Beagle*.

Your website is the curtain you're sticking with

Begin with probability theory, specifically the infamous "Monty Hall problem." This mathematical riddle asks you to imagine yourself on the game show *Let's Make a Deal*. Monty Hall, the host, shows you three curtains and tells you that two of them conceal piles of elephant poo, while the third hides a million dollars. You choose one of the curtains, and Monty then pulls it back (actually, the lovely Carol Merrill pulls it back) to reveal a steaming pile. Monty then asks whether you want to stick with your curtain or switch to the other curtain that hasn't been opened.

The mathematically correct yet intuitively wrong answer is to switch. Most people either say it makes no difference or that it's better to keep your first choice. But probability theory states that switching is twice as good as sticking — at least if your current outlook values money more than dung.

You can see the correctness of switching through this thought experiment: What if instead of three curtains, you were facing a million of them? You choose one, and the lovely Carol Merrill pulls back 999,998 of them, leaving you with your choice and one other. At that point, do you really think that your one in a million guess is equal to Carol's knowledge about where the money is?

If you haven't tested multiple variations, your website is the first curtain you chose from an infinite number of possibilities. Yes, there is an infinitesimal but real chance that you *are* that smart, that you created the best possible site that could have been created — but logic and the laws of probability strongly indicate room for significant improvement.

On *Let's Make a Deal,* you do have to make a difficult decision. With website testing, you can say, "Let's open all of them, and then I'll choose." Your testing ability is limited only by your imagination and the volume of visitors that you can send to your site.

Charlie Darwin's trick

Charles Darwin's theory of natural selection explains why you don't need to be a genius to generate significant improvements through testing. Darwin found that evolution proceeded via trial and error, with successful genetic mutations thriving and unsuccessful ones dying out. In other words, individual failures are as important to the overall project as successes — which is a good thing because in any trial and error system, there are bound to be more errors than positive outcomes.

Say you test ten variations of your most important landing page against your control. You were having a bad day when you designed the variations, so nine of the ten fail miserably, while the tenth improves the conversion rate by only 3 percent. Does that sound like a waste of time? Well, guess what? You actually created a huge success. You learn from the nasty nine what *not* to do next time, and you have a new winner that will generate slightly more cash from the same inputs as your previous best. Repeat this seemingly dismal scenario just five times, and thanks to the miracle of compound interest, you have a new page that outconverts the original not just by 15 percent but by nearly 16 percent.

But wait — there's more! That 16 percent improvement is pure profit. After all, you already paid for the clicks. You just made those clicks 16 percent more valuable, which means you have a delicious choice:

- ✔ You can keep spending what you've been spending and make 16 percent more ongoing.
- ✔ You can increase your keyword or placement bids, which means you can get higher rankings, leading to more traffic, which means you can now test and fail and improve even faster than before.

The name of the game here isn't Let's Make a Deal, but Let's Improve Faster than Your Competitors. After your business gets the wheel turning on this virtual cycle, you become competition-proof under those market conditions.

Identifying the Single Conversion Event

Before you jump into optimization, you need a clear target. Your first step is to identify the one conversion event you want to measure and improve. The two most common options are conversion to lead and conversion to sale.

If you have multiple desired actions for your visitors on a single visit, you're just going to confuse people and reduce the overall number of conversions significantly. Say you want people to watch a video, watch an interactive demo, sign up for a free trial, call you for more information, and buy the product: You have to choose one visitor action as the primary conversion event for a single visit. Garrett likens a multitude of conversion options to a web page that tries to optimize for four different languages simultaneously. By trying to have it all, you end up with a mess that appeals to no one.

Establishing a baseline

After you decide what you're measuring, the next step is measuring current performance. You may already know that (or think you know — we find that unless website owners track metrics very carefully, they often overestimate the numbers and receive a bit of a shock when we show them the facts), or you may have only the vaguest notion.

If upon being woken from REM sleep at 2 a.m., you can't provide your current conversion data, including conversion rate, cost per conversion, and value per conversion, you're not as in touch as you need to be with one of most sensitive levers of online profitability. Don't feel bad, though. That's all about to change. If you discover that your numbers are worse than you thought, don't feel bad, either, because that's about to change, too. The good news is that the lower the baseline, the easier to improve and the bigger the improvements you can expect.

We *benchmark* — determine the initial performance metrics — before jumping to optimization so we can tell whether we're moving in the right direction or just running in place on a treadmill to nowhere.

Setting up Optimizer for benchmarking

You can run a benchmark test without Optimizer by digging through AdWords data or analytics, but we recommend using Optimizer for a couple of reasons:

- ✔ Optimizer is designed to give you these metrics — and, in many ways, is more valid and reliable than AdWords or Analytics.
- ✔ Establishing a baseline with Optimizer familiarizes you with the tool in "flight simulator mode" so you can get comfortable and proficient with the interface before you start actual testing.

Setting up an A/A split test

The simplest type of Optimizer test is an A/B split test. Optimizer randomly splits your traffic between original page (A, henceforth known as the *control*) and test page (B, which we now call the *challenger* to avoid confusion).

For benchmarking purposes, though, you're not testing two pages but instead getting data on a single page. So you need to make an identical copy of your control page, give it a slightly different URL (see Figure 15-2), and run it as the challenger against your control. That's why it's an A/A test: You aren't actually testing, just measuring current reality.

You also need a Thank You page (what Google calls a "conversion page"). In Google's words, "This is an existing page on your website that users reach after they've completed a successful conversion." In other words, a visitor can reach this page only by completing the conversion, be it lead or sale, and every visitor who converts must end up on this page. In the jargon of logical philosophy, the conversion is a necessary, sufficient, and exclusive cause of a visit to the conversion page. In the words of Irving Berlin, "If you don't want my peaches, you'd better stop shaking my tree."

Access Optimizer by clicking the Reporting and Tools tab and then choosing Website Optimizer from the drop-down list (see Figure 15-1). You may need to authorize your Optimizer account, which you can do by following the prompts and instructions on the signup page, or you may just see the Optimizer interface ready and waiting for your command.

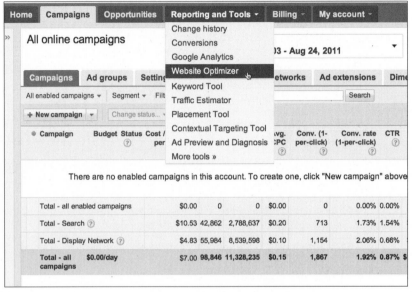

Figure 15-1:
Access
Optimizer
directly
from the
AdWords
Dashboard.

When you first visit Optimizer, you see an empty data table and a couple of links inviting you to create a new experiment.

1. **Click one of those links to get to a page that asks you what kind of experiment you want to set up: A/B or Multivariate.**

2. **Choose A/B.**

   Multivariate experiments, which explore the relationships between several different variables at once, are quite powerful, and work better with some dynamic content management systems such as WordPress, but are beyond the scope of this chapter. Visit `http://gafd3.com/multivariate` when you're ready for some advanced testing methods.

   You next see an A/B experiment checklist, which reviews the three steps:

   a. *Select a page to test.*

   b. *Create an alternate version.*

   c. *Identify a conversion page.*

3. **Check the I've Completed the Steps Above and I'm Ready to Start Setting Up My Experiment check box to signify your completion of these steps, and click the Create button to begin setup (as shown in Figure 15-2).**

4. **Name your experiment.**

   You can call this first test **Benchmark**, and also add any details about the specific conversion or landing page you're assessing.

5. **Enter the URL of the copy of the original page in the Original Page URL field, as shown in Figure 15-2, and name the variation** Copy of Original **or something equally informative.**

   When you click outside the text field, Google tries to find the page. If it does, you'll see a green check mark next to the URL and the words `Page Found` below it. If you mistyped or the page doesn't yet exist, be prepared for the yellow warning triangle and the words `Page Not Found`.

6. **Enter your conversion page URL and click the Continue button.**

   After you correctly enter data in all three URL fields, Google lets you continue. At any point, you can pause and save your work by clicking the Save Progress and Finish Later link at the bottom right.

Name experiment and identify pages > <u>Install and validate JavaScript tags</u> > Preview and start experiment

A/B experiment set-up: Name your experiment and identify pages

1. Name your experiment

The experiment name will help you to distinguish this experiment from others; your users won't see this name.

Experiment name:

Benchmark Consultation Request

Example: My homepage test #1

2. Identify the pages you want to test

Add as many variations as you like, naming them so you can easily distinguish them in your reports. At least two (including the original) are required. These URLs could be bookmarked by your users, so after your experiment finishes, you may want to keep these URLs valid. <u>Learn more</u>

Name:	Original page URL: ⓘ
Original	✔ http://vitruvianway.com/consultation-request
	Page found

Name:	Page variation URL: ⓘ
Copy of Original	✔ http://vitruvianway.com/consultation-request-2
	Page found

✛ <u>Add another page variation</u>

3. Identify your conversion page

This is an existing page that users reach after completing a successful conversion. For example, this might be the page displayed after a user completes a purchase, signs up for a newsletter, or fills out a contact form. <u>Learn more</u>

Conversion page URL:

✔ http://vitruvianway.com/thank-you-consultation/

Page found

(Continue »)   <u>Save progress and finish later</u>

Figure 15-2:
Set up your benchmarking test by entering the original, variation, and conversion page URLs.

Installing and validating JavaScript tags

After you specify the experiment pages, Google creates what we online professionals call "little bits of code" that you must place, just so, on the proper pages. If you aren't sure how to insert JavaScript *snippets* (as they're also known), Google gives you the option on the following page to send a link and instructions to your webmaster. If you'll be doing it yourself, select the You Will Install and Validate the JavaScript Tags radio button on that page to get the snippets and installation instructions.

Installing JavaScript snippets is a little like making a paper airplane: pretty simple to do, but pretty hard to explain in words and diagrams. Basically, you add three different snippets to your original, variation, and conversion pages, just after the opening <head> tag for each page. If you need more guidance than that, watch our short video tutorial that walks you through the process: http://gafd3.com/install-tags. On that page, we also include our current recommendation for an Optimizer plug-in that works with WordPress.

When you or your webmaster has installed the code on the pages, click the Validate Pages button near the bottom of the page. If you make a mistake installing the script, Google will let you know so you don't think you're running an experiment that doesn't exist. Then after Google congratulates you, click OK and then Continue to preview and launch the benchmarking experiment.

Previewing and launching the experiment

Click the Preview link on the following page to make sure that you tagged the right pages. Google opens a new browser tab and shows you the original and allows you to view the variation (which in this case is identical to the original) from the drop-down list at the top left of the page.

To launch the experiment, return to the Optimizer browser window and click the Start Experiment button at the bottom of the page. Just to be doubly sure, now visit the original page and complete a conversion yourself. First, make sure it still works. Second, check Optimizer in about three hours to see whether it's collecting data. At the very least, it should register one conversion.

Monitoring the experiment

Within three hours of starting the experiment, Optimizer begins displaying data. Click the Report link near the top of the experiment page to view the results as they accumulate. Figure 15-3 shows the report interface before data has come in. Optimizer shows conversion rates (and actual numbers of conversions, as well as observed improvement and the variation's chance to beat the original.

Because the two test pages are identical, you should expect the conversion rates to be very close as well. At first, they may not be close because random variation can be louder than real trends in the short term. But as you collect data, the "truth" about your conversion funnel will present itself. In general, you can call your benchmarketing test after you get at least 250 visitors to each page (500 total) and the two pages conversion rates are almost identical.

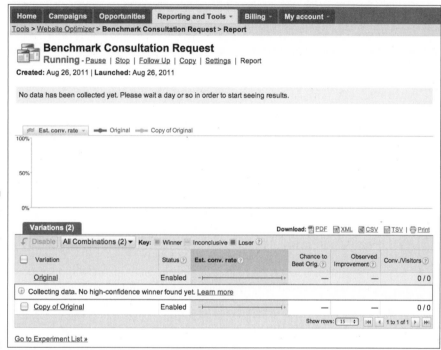

Figure 15-3:
See Optimizer comparative conversion rates and absolute conversion numbers.

At this writing, no automatic notification system exists to alert you by e-mail, SMS, or gentle electric shock that your test has achieved statistical significance. So, you must keep checking Optimizer until the test has run its course. The benchmarking experiment is the hardest to monitor because, by definition, you're looking for the opposite of a statistically significant difference between the two pages. In the experiments where you're trying to beat your control, Optimizer clearly indicates when you have a winner.

Deciding What to Test

While your benchmarketing experiment is running, you can return to your website and make a list of elements you want to test. After you know the conversion rate that you're trying to beat, you'll be able to evaluate and act on the results of all subsequent tests.

Here's the problem: Your landing page consists of dozens of different elements — headlines, subheads, body copy, navigation bars, images, fonts, color schemes, and on and on — and each can be changed in practically infinite ways. If you were to test each element randomly, you'd feel like a monkey at a keyboard aiming to produce *King Lear*. It would take forever, you'd have no guarantee of ever getting there, and you'd develop a nasty case of simian carpal tunnel syndrome.

And, you've already created the best site you could build. So where can you go for new ideas?

Testing Principle #1: Start big, get smaller

In Chapter 13, you see some examples of very tiny changes in ad copy that lead to very different results. We've seen the addition of a comma increased CTR four times! So you might think that similar small changes would work for site testing as well. Generally, though, they don't. Instead, go for giant differences. That way, you'll get clearer results faster.

For example, you may want to find out whether your visitors will respond better to a video or a still image at the top of the page. That's a big difference. Do they prefer a short page or a long page? A professional-looking site or one that could have been put together by your nephew in about 15 minutes?

After you answer the big questions, you can look at the nuances and details. If your first tests show no difference in results, the difference between options A and B aren't big enough to matter.

Testing Principle #2: Tests are just questions in action

Maybe you still have flashbacks to 11th grade chemistry class, where you had to write down hypotheses and experimental methods in your marble cover notebook, and then try to avoid setting your hair on fire with a Bunsen burner? If so, please relax when it comes to scientific website testing. Running a test is just asking a question and inviting your visitors to answer with their actions.

One of Howie's tests started with his question, "How much do the visitors to this page know about me already?" Does he need to spend time introducing himself and establishing credibility by telling them he's his mother's favorite AdWords author, or cut right to the chase and entice them to sign up for Camp Checkmate?

His test had to put that question into action, by creating an option that assumed familiarity and an option that didn't. He created two pages, cleverly named Long and Short. The long page introduced him in depth before getting down to business, and the short page started talking about their situation and why participating in a live event was exactly what they needed.

Testing Principle #3: Focus on the weakest link

Your sales funnel is a chain of events, from the keyword (or placement) to the ad to the landing page to additional web pages to the conversion event. Your overall success at any one moment is limited by only one part of this chain: the weakest link. You can set up goals in Google Analytics to identify the most broken parts of your sales funnel (the ones where the most visitors "leak" away from the desired path) and then run Optimizer tests to improve those pages.

You can identify the weakest part of a single page by watching how visitors interact with that page. For example, if Analytics tells you that the average AdWords visitor spends eight seconds on a particular landing page before returning to Google for another search, you need to improve whatever appears at the top of that page — whatever first thing the visitor sees. In that case, your page might be loading slowly, so most visitors don't have the patience to wait. Or the headline or the design of the page might contradict the expectations they took from your ad.

Testing Principle #4: Embrace testing "failures"

Testing isn't always about finding things that work better. Sometimes you learn more when your great idea falls flat. Instead of shaking your head and saying, "Well, that bombed," get an inquisitive look in your eyes and ask, "Now why didn't my visitors go for that?"

That question gets you out of your head and into the heads of your visitors — the people who are interacting with your site in an attempt to achieve a personal goal. When you understand what your visitors don't like and what gets in their way, you can apply that knowledge to the rest of your marketing — online and off.

When you test, you're developing your instincts for what works and what doesn't work. Over time, this is where testing really pays off. By experiencing success and failure, you gain insight into your market and become better at creating effective promotions for them.

Testing Principle #5: Start testing the simple stuff

As Jerry Garcia might have sung had he been a website owner, "Well, the first tests are the hardest tests." If you've never created split tests, the whole thing can seem daunting, and the rewards uncertain. In our experience, the best test is the one that gets conducted. After you start, your familiarity and enthusiasm and testing intelligence will increase naturally. That's why we had you start with an A/A test (read about those earlier in this chapter), despite many other methods you could have used to determine your starting conversion rate.

Before you get into the psychology of the visitor and the complexities of the relevance of your messaging to their desires and fears (which is awesome stuff to think about, except when it freezes you into inaction), do the simplest tests you can think of. Red versus blue top navigation. Two different photos. Black or gray text. These elements don't require a lot of thought, or a lot of coding, so they can be tested quickly, inexpensively, and often to great effect. Our website optimization clients are always amazed at the big differences in performance that are due to simple cosmetic changes.

Figure 15-4 shows the results of one of an ongoing series of Optimizer tests that we ran for a client, GiveBackTimeShare.com. As you can see, the original page converted visitors at 2.96%, while each of the variations generated conversions at higher rates. Variation 3, the winner (indicated by the starred message, "Combination 3 has a 99.8% chance of outperforming the original"), converted visitors at a whopping 4.34%, or almost 50% better than the original. (Simply adding a single line of text above an opt-in box increased conversions by 46.4 percent.)

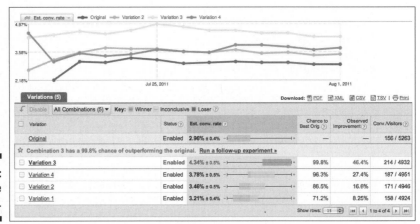

Figure 15-4:
Test the
simple stuff.

You might be wondering what sort of geniuses we are to have achieved such a tremendous increase (answer: cute and cuddly ones who deserve to be well paid and pampered with regular massages and gourmet chocolate), so you'll probably be a little let down when you see the test. Garrett looked at the landing page, which was designed to get a visitor to fill out a lead form to request a consultation, and noticed that there was no call to action above the form. No instructions or encouragement or rationale for completing the form. So Garrett simply created four different calls to action and tested them in the four variation pages. As the numbers show, a call to action outperformed the original with no call to action. And Variation 3 had the best one, as seen in Figure 15-4.

Variation 4, which also improved on the original, although only by 27.4 percent, was nearly identical. See whether you can spot the difference between Figures 15-5 and 15-6.

Spotted it? The difference between the wildly successful landing page and the less successful one was a single word: "YES!" instead of "HELP!"

Figure 15-5:
This less-successful variation was identical to the winner with one tiny yet meaningful exception.

Figure 15-6:
The winning
variation.

What you're *not* to do, of course, is take away from this example the idea that the word "YES!" is always better to lead a call to action than "HELP!" The Beatles, for example, might not have topped the 1965 pop charts with a song called "Yes!" with the chorus, "Won't you please, please, yes me?"

The point is to perform your own tests and pitting ideas and principles against one another in a fair fight. Garrett could easily have tried to convince our client that "HELP!" is a more powerful word, given the emotional state of the prospect when they reach the page. And the client might even have believed him. Luckily for everyone, Garrett simply asked the experts: the site visitors who complete the forms and ultimately pay all our salaries.

Testing Principle #6: Next, test to overcome objections

While you brainstorm questions to turn into tests, familiarize yourself to all the reasons your visitors aren't doing what you want. Is it too hard? That is, do you have a usability issue of complicated menus, cumbersome forms, and hidden buttons? Or are visitors not persuaded? If so, you need to work on the elements that create comfort, build credibility, and describe relevant and desirable benefits.

Karl Blanks and Ben Jesson of `www.conversion-rate-experts.com` make this simple with their objection/counter-objection approach:

1. Determine the likely objection.

2. Make changes that address that objection.

For example, if the objection is, "I don't trust you or your company enough to buy something or give you my contact information," then you add trust elements: endorsements; photos of your staff, office, or warehouse; years in business; Hacker Safe seals; and so on. If they can't differentiate your product from your competitors', then test elements that show the advantages of your product. If they're afraid of making a mistake, introduce and test risk-reduction strategies, such as a free trial or money-back guarantee.

Bottom line, don't focus your testing on the elements of your site ("Red or blue headline here?"). Focus on what the users need in order to feel good about doing what you want them to do.

Creating a Testing Plan

At each stage in the testing process, the answers you receive will likely generate further questions and additional, "I wonder whether? . . ." Richard Mouser of ScientificWebsiteTesting.com (`www.scientificwebsitetesting.com`), one of our testing mentors, taught us these simple steps:

1. Make a list of things you want to test.

2. Prioritize that list.

3. Start testing and keep adding to the list based on test results.

The next few sections discuss these steps in detail.

Making your list of things to test

You might not feel like you have any ideas worth testing at this point, but don't worry. You just need to start getting ideas down on paper regardless of whether the ideas are good.

If you follow this process, you'll end up with more ideas than you have time to test, and you'll never stop adding to your list. The most promising ideas will bubble to the top of your list, your website will get a little better with each test, and your marketing skills will get sharper in the process.

Think back to when you launched your website

Richard Mouser has a wonderful suggestion to help you come up with testing ideas. He notes that in the frenzy of getting a website built, there are always compromises. No one has the time to create the perfect website on the first try. And even if you had all the time and money in the world, how could you possibly know for sure what "perfect" would look like?

Take a deep breath, follow our mesmerizing pocket watch swinging back and forth, and feel your mind free-floating back, back, back to when you were creating your site and thought:

> "Okay, that's good enough for now."

> "Not exactly what I had in mind, but I guess it works."

> "We don't have time to do it over again."

Browse your site to jog your memory. Look for areas of compromise, of "Good enough for now," or "Gee, I hope that works." Make a list of every element that just maybe could improve.

Getting inspired by your competition

Next, take a good look at your competitors' sites. You can preview your competitors' landing pages without clicking their ads (it's bad karma to cost them money to spy on them) by clicking the magnifying glass next to the ad headline (see Figure 15-7). You can also do this for organic listings.

Compare their landing pages with yours. Ask yourself the following questions:

- ✔ What are they doing better than I am? Do they have better copy, headlines, pictures, design, or something else? Can I use their site as a template on which to improve?

- ✔ What's on their site, but missing from mine? Can I test adding that?

- ✔ What's on my site, but missing from theirs? Can I test removing that?

- ✔ Is their site more focused on the customer, the customer problem, or the solution?

- ✔ Does their site seem more credible or professional than mine?

- ✔ Do they have more elements or different elements above the fold (visible without scrolling) than my site? Could I test these changes?

- ✔ Does their site deliver on the promise made in their AdWords ad?

- ✔ Is their checkout or sign-up process more intuitive and easier to follow than mine?

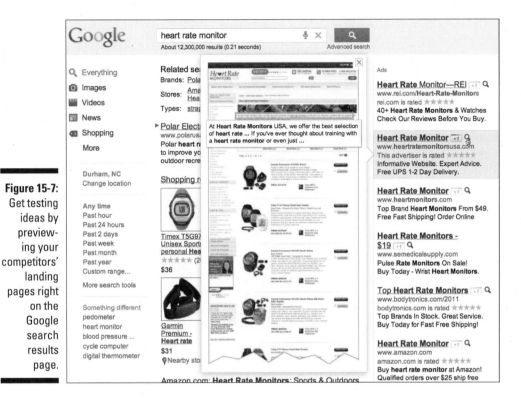

Figure 15-7:
Get testing
ideas by
preview-
ing your
competitors'
landing
pages right
on the
Google
search
results
page.

Your competition can give you lots of ideas on what to improve, add, and remove from your website. Sometimes you can find good ideas by study-ing and modeling your competitors. Don't assume, though that something is good just because someone else is doing it. After all, most online markets consist of the clueless copying the clueless. Until you test, be skeptically curious.

Prioritizing your list

After you set up tools to capture information about visitors and use that information to generate ideas to test, grade each idea so you can prioritize the tests based on expected ROI. You move the ideas with the highest grades to the top of the list and test them first.

Apply the following 11 criteria to each item you're thinking of testing. The items that receive the most checks rise to the top of your testing list. These represent your first tests. (In case of a tie, we recommend flipping a coin. We like the U.S. 2005 Oregon quarter with a picture of Crater Lake, but that's totally up to you.)

- The item is on a high traffic page.

- The test result, if positive, can be applied to other pages on the site.

- The item is *above the fold* (that is, most visitors can see it without having to scroll down or sideways).

- The item is the most prominent feature on the page.

- The item relates to a high-leverage conversion, such as an opt-in or a first sale.

  High-leverage items in most businesses are gateways to multiple purchases and customer loyalty.

- The item addresses a frequent customer question or problem.

- This item affects all customer sales (as part of the checkout process, for example).

- The item fills a competitive gap.

- The item enhances the credibility of your site.

- The item contributes to your site's uniqueness.

- The new version of the item is very different from what's shown on your site.

This exercise provides you with a prioritized list of what to test on your site. When you come up with new ideas, add them to the list, but be sure to re-prioritize before you select the next item to test.

Start testing (and never stop)

Are you ready to pull the top idea off the list and start testing? First, you need to create the resource to test. You already have your original — your A version. Now put together your B version. You might have to write some copy, create an image or video, and get some HTML code to tie it all into a working page. Upload that page to your site, and commence testing!

Here are three rules to help you achieve useful and valid test results:

- **Test one thing at a time:** If you test the headline font and header graphic simultaneously in an A/B split test, you won't know which element mattered and which element didn't.

- **Keep traffic streams separate:** Each ad group should send visitors to a unique landing page so when you're testing elements on that page, you're looking at how a specific market segment interacts with it. If you send all your traffic to a single page, you'll almost certainly miss chances to optimize the page for different groups of people.

✔ **Balance speed of results with limited exposure:** By default, every Optimizer test sends all your traffic to the original page through the test. If you're testing one variation against the control, this means that half your traffic is now going to see the variation page. Yes, that's the fastest way to get results, but it's also the fastest way to go out of business if your test page is much worse than your original. Think about it: If you had a salesperson of known ability and a totally untested rookie, would you give half the territory to the rookie on her first day?

You can limit the exposure of your traffic to your test conditions on the Experimental Settings page, after you set up your test.

1. **On the Experiment List page, find the experiment you want to throttle down and then click the Edit Settings link under the Status column.**

2. **Scroll down to the Settings and Design section.**

3. **Next to Total Traffic Sent through This Experiment, click 100% to activate the drop-down list (see Figure 15-8).**

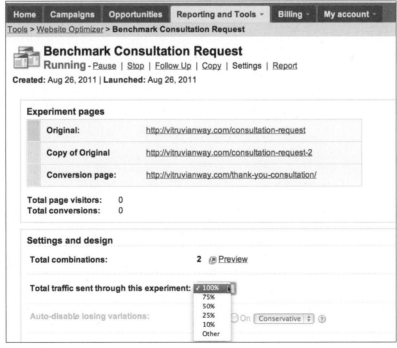

Figure 15-8: You can reduce the amount of traffic that flows to your untested pages to minimize risk.

4. **Choose a lower percentage.**

   If none of the defaults in the list appeals to you, click Other and then enter any number from 1 to 100.

5. **Click the Save Changes button at the bottom of the page.**

Now whatever percentage of visitors you specified will be parceled out equally to the original and the variation pages, and the remaining percentage will be excluded from the experiment and just see the original page. So if you select 50%, for example, and your test consists of an original and three variations, then 1,000 visitors to your original page would be divided as follows:

- ✔ 500 to original page (not counted in experiment)
- ✔ 125 to original page (counted in experiment
- ✔ 125 to Variation 1
- ✔ 125 to Variation 2
- ✔ 125 to Variation 3

The more traffic you have, the more variations you can include and the more traffic you can exclude from the experiment and still get statistically significant results in a reasonable time frame. If you don't have the luxury of lots of traffic, you may have to stick to A/B experiments with all the traffic entering the experiment to make it worthwhile.

If you're in a market that simply doesn't generate a lot of traffic, you can still test profitably. The slow pace of data collection will probably discourage your competitors, so even if it takes months to get a scientifically valid result that improves your website, it's worth it. And if your competitors are getting more traffic than you because they have more money to spend and a more profitable business model, then you must test to even the playing field.

Conducting Ongoing Experiments

If you've conducted the benchmarking experiment described early in this chapter, then you already know how to set up A/B split tests. The discussion of Figure 15-4 shows you how to read and interpret the results. We end this chapter by covering a few additional details to make sure you can run lots of successful Optimizer tests.

Setting up multiple variation pages

To add a second or third or fourth variation page (as A/B/C/n split test), simply click the Add Another Page Variation link on the Experiment Set-up page (bottom left of Figure 15-9). Name your new variation and enter the page URL. Repeat this process until you add all your variation pages. You can test as many variation pages as you like in a single A/B/C/n split test, where "n" represents the total number of variations (and gives us flashbacks to high school algebra).

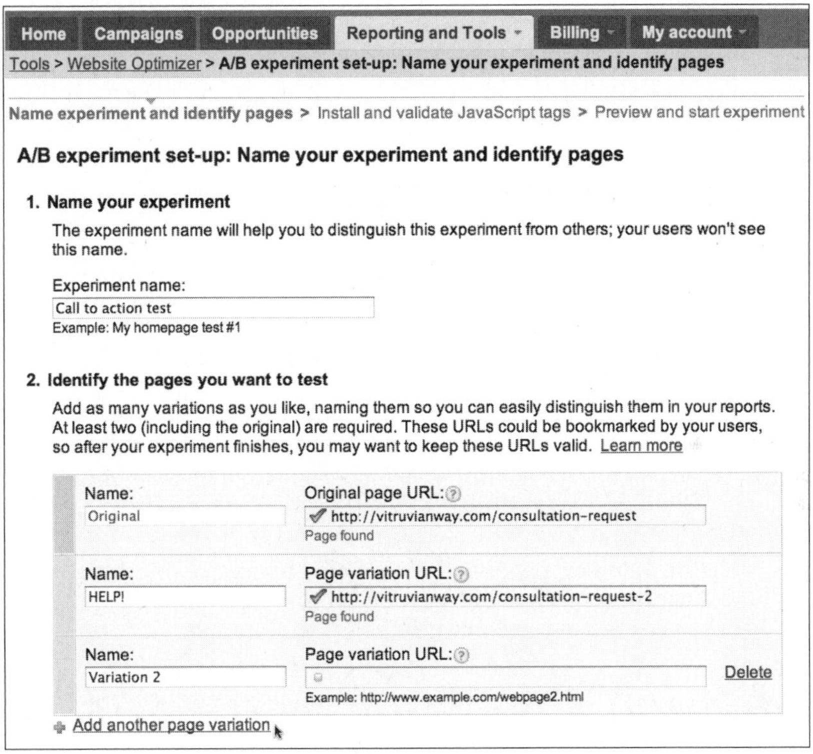

Figure 15-9: Test as many variation pages as you like.

Ending your experiments

After Google identifies a winning page, either your control or one of the variations, you want to end the experiment and reap the rewards of your curiosity and diligence. First, you have to stop the experiment. Then you tell Google what to do next. You have two choices.

✔ Rerun the experiment as a true A/B split test with the original going up against the single strongest variation.

✔ End the experiment entirely.

Running a follow-up experiment

In Figure 15-10, you can see the two options. If your experiment consists of many variation pages and the difference between the original and the top variation page was not huge, it may make sense to hold a "run-off election" that will send all traffic to the single contest. To do so, select the Help Me Create a Follow-up Experiment radio button and then click Continue.

Figure 15-10: End a statistically significant test by running a follow-up experiment or sending all traffic to the best performing page.

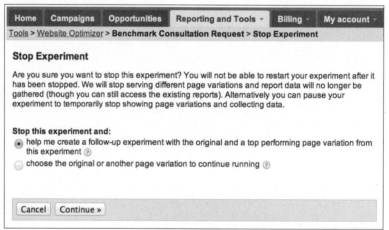

On the following page, Google asks you to choose one variation to test against the control. Make your selection using the radio button next to the best performing variation and then click Continue.

On the next page, as shown in Figure 15-11, you have to specify the amount of traffic you want to send to the variation. Google assumes that because the variation has beaten the original, you want to send at least half and as much as 99.9 percent of the traffic to that variation. The more imbalanced the split, the longer it will take the follow-up experiment to achieve significance. Again, you're balancing the need for speedy information against the need to send your traffic to presumed winning pages. If you truly aren't sure which page is better, choose 50%. The more certain you are that the variation is better, the higher the traffic percentage you can send to it.

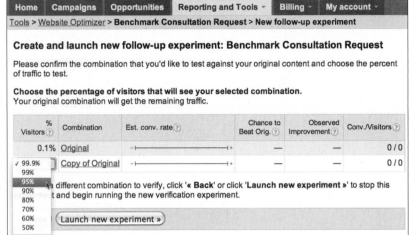

Figure 15-11:
You can
send almost
all the traffic
to the win-
ner variation
in a follow-
up test.

Ending the experiment

If you're satisfied with the results, as we were in the earlier GiveBackTime Share.com example, you just want to stop the experiment and send all traffic to the best page, whether original or variation. In that case, navigate to the experiment page and click the Stop link at the top. On the next page, select the Choose the Original or Another Page Variation to Continue Running radio button (refer to Figure 15-10) and then click Continue.

On the next page, select the radio button next to the page — original or variation — that you want to keep. Click the Save Changes button. Now Optimizer will automatically send all traffic that hits the original page to whichever page you specified. This buys you time to go back to all the pages you tagged and remove those tags. Now you can start over with a brand-new experiment.

Chapter 16

Cloning Your Campaigns for Greater Precision

In This Chapter

▶ The benefits of campaign cloning

▶ Push-button cloning with AdWords Editor

▶ Limitations to cloning

▶ Cloning examples

Conventional baseball wisdom holds that poor teams can only afford marginal players, so they just can't compete with the rich teams. In *Moneyball*, Michael Lewis profiles Billy Beane, a general manager for the Oakland Athletics baseball team, which won the most games in Major League Baseball in 2002 despite having the smallest payroll.

He did it by being an egghead about statistics, rather than just going with his gut or following conventional wisdom. He was able, for example, to predict which minor league players would succeed in the major leagues by using a couple of key statistics that no one else realized were significant.

He won games by fiercely playing the percentages: where to position the outfielders, when to bunt, when to replace the starting pitcher with a relief pitcher, and a thousand other situations. By having data at his fingertips and understanding how to interpret and act on it, he found an advantage in every encounter.

The result: The Oakland Athletics won 103 games, the same number as the New York Yankees. The Yankees paid $126 million in payroll, while the Athletics paid only $40 million. One of the most important sentences in the book applies directly to you and me: "In professional baseball it still matters less how much money you have than how well you spend it."

AdWords is also an unfair game. Some advertisers have brand names, deep pocketbooks, and lots of staff. Others are scrappy startups with just enough cash for payroll — sometimes — and one or two key people who perform every role from CEO to janitor. And like baseball, what determines AdWords success is not the amount of money you have, but how well you spend it.

Campaign cloning is the AdWords equivalent of *Moneyball.* By slicing and dicing the data as granularly as possible, you'll discover dozens of opportunities to optimize your bids and messaging that your less industrious competitors will overlook. You'll bid smarter, achieve greater margins, and snowball your advantage into better ad positions and more traffic. And after you set up cloning, finding and interpreting the most actionable data becomes quick and easy. Instead of searching for a needle in one gigantic haystack, you're now finding lots of needles in a pin cushion.

Campaign Cloning Explained

Campaign cloning is simply making a copy of an existing campaign and changing a single campaign-level parameter. For example, if you have a Search campaign that you want to expand into the Display network, you can copy the Search campaign, change it to Display, and upload it to AdWords in about 5 clicks and 45 seconds.

Have a campaign that's working great in the UK that you want to try it in Australia and New Zealand? That clone might take eight or nine clicks and a minute and a half. Want to target iPad users? Clone a computers campaign in Editor and then spend 30 seconds tweaking your settings online.

We cover the mechanics of campaign cloning in Chapter 10, our elegy to Editor. In this chapter, we go far beyond mechanics and tactics into the most advanced AdWords strategies we use to give our clients every advantage in the marketplace.

Later in this chapter, we cover specific situations where cloning is indicated, as well as cases where it isn't. Right now, though, we need to reiterate the reasons for cloning as opposed to just adding a network or a couple of countries or a device to an existing campaign.

Why Clone?

You clone campaigns for three reasons:

✔ **Account expansion:** You've optimized your "sweet spot" traffic to comfortable profitability, and now you want to expand your reach to less-targeted, but still potentially profitable, traffic.

✔ **More accurate bid management:** You know or suspect that a campaign is targeting two or more subgroups whose cost per conversions are significantly different and you have enough traffic volume to support the split.

✔ **More targeted messaging:** You know or suspect that a campaign is targeting two or more subgroups whose mindsets and buying criteria are significantly different and you have enough traffic volume to support the split.

Cloning for account expansion

Unless you just opened this book for the first time and reached this page at random (or, if you're reading this on a Kindle, they've added an "I feel lucky" button), chances are you've already heard us give the fire and brimstone sermon about separating traffic into different campaigns rather than accept the Google default of "All Networks, All Devices, All Countries, All Demographics, All the Time." And you've also been hit over the head, no doubt, on the importance of starting with your *"sweet spot"* traffic: the prospects most likely to resonate with your offer and thus convert into leads or sales at the lowest cost per conversion.

To illustrate graphically why this is so important, and why so many AdWords advertisers mistakenly think that AdWords traffic is too expensive and therefore give up, check out the following hypothetical statistics in Table 16-1 for a keyword in one of those Yes to All Traffic campaigns.

Table 16-1		**Aggregate Campaign Data**			
Keyword	*Clicks*	*Avg. Cost/ Click*	*Avg. Position*	*Conversions*	*Avg. Cost/ Conv.*
[Supplements for women over 40]	1,640	$0.44	3.8	38	$19.09

Some background: This e-commerce advertiser sells herbal supplements online, and the average value of a conversion (the average profit per order) for this keyword is $10.

The question is, how long does a smart advertiser keep spending $19.09 to make $10.00? The answer: not very long. If these were your metrics, you would probably have pulled the plug by now. But, as you probably guessed, that was a trick question! The smart advertiser doesn't build All Traffic campaigns. Just for fun, break out the traffic for that one keyword by match type, network, ad type, and device; see Table 16-2.

Table 16-2	Campaign Data by Source					
Keyword	*Type*	*Clicks*	*Avg. Cost/ Click*	*Avg. Position*	*Conversions*	*Avg. Cost/ Conv.*
[Supplements for women over 40]	Search network, Exact	194	$0.35	3.4	16	$4.25
[Supplements for women over 40]	Search network, Phrase	158	$0.39	3.8	5	$12.32
[Supplements for women over 40]	Search network, Broad	562	$0.52	4.1	27	$22.48
[Supplements for women over 40]	Display network, Text ad	326	$0.45	4.5	2	$73.32
[Supplements for women over 40]	Display network, Image ad	330	$0.38	1.5	1	$125.54
[Supplements for women over 40]	Mobile devices	69	$0.45	1.3	1	$31.22
[Supplements for women over 40]	Total	1,640	$0.44	3.8	38	$19.09

When all that traffic is merged into one campaign, the distinctions get lost, and with them your ability to bid intelligently. The first amazing thing about this data (which isn't from an actual account, but is typical) is that the exact match keyword in the Search network is quite profitable, with an average cost per conversion of $4.25. That represents a profit per order of $5.75 — hardly a reason to stop doing it.

It's the rest of the table that's the problem, with costs ranging from just over break-even ($12.32 for phrase match keywords in the Search network) to ridiculously high ($125.54 for image ads in the Display network).

Had this advertiser followed our advice from Chapter 7, their first campaign would have been exact match in the Search network only. They would have generated a healthy margin, albeit with low volume. (Remember, though, that we looked at just one keyword. If this campaign had dozens or hundreds of keywords, the volumes would be much higher.) So the natural next step would have been to clone that campaign and change match type to phrase match.

Cloning for bid management

Our smart advertiser would soon have discovered that the value of a phrase match click was not nearly as high as the exact match. In fact, phrase turned out to be almost three times less valuable than exact (costing $12.32 for a sale versus $4.25). During their first round of bid adjustments (see Chapter 13), they would have lowered their Max. CPC bid to reflect the decreased worth of that traffic.

Assuming that responsive bid management could bring the cost per conversion of the phrase campaign down to $8.50, our supplement seller is now profitable in exact and phrase match, and is itching to try out broad match with its much greater traffic potential. That traffic indeed generates more conversions, but at an unfortunate $22.48 cost per conversion, or more than double what they can afford to pay and still break even. Even lowering bids and adding lots of negative keywords to refine the traffic can't turn a profit here.

Cloning for targeted messaging

The broad match cost per conversion can get to $15 or so just via bid management and negative keywords, but we still have one more powerful tool on our optimization belt: split testing for optimized messaging. By testing ads and landing page copy, as well as the functionality of the shopping cart and design of the checkout process, for example, our smart advertiser can continually slash conversion costs so that the next tier of traffic becomes cost effective.

Especially when shifting from Search to Display, you need different kinds of ads. Searchers want the facts, the big promise, the quickest path to satisfaction. People surfing the Display network need to be interrupted, most often by curiosity and a zero-risk offer. If you can optimize response by giving different messages to different subgroups of your traffic, then cloning in order to target those messages appropriately can be your biggest source of improvement.

Exploiting Expansion Protocols

Where you start and how you expand depend mostly on your online business model. We recommend that e-commerce and lead generation sites begin with different traffic streams to start with the traffic "most likely to succeed."

In the following lists, each level represents a turn of the faucet in the "open" direction: more volume, less qualified traffic. That's why it's so important to achieve profitability at one level before setting your sights on a more permissive one. And of course, you can and should adjust your bids based on the data you collect in your account.

E-commerce expansion

For e-commerce advertisers, we recommend starting with exact match keywords in the Search network only, then expanding in order, as follows:

- Exact match, Search network (computers and tablet PCs only)
- Exact match, Search network (mobile phones)
- Phrase match, Search network (bid 80% of exact match to start)
- Broad match, Search network (bid 60% of exact match to start)
- Text ads, Display network (bid 50% of exact match to start)
- Image ads, Display network (bid 25% of exact match to start)

Lead generation expansion

For advertisers whose primary website goal is lead generation, we also recommend beginning with exact match keywords in the Search network for research purposes (see Chapter 4). Additional expansion steps depend on the results of this first campaign, as follows:

- Exact match, Search network

  If exact match campaign isn't profitable in the Search network, skip to Level 4. If it is profitable, continue with Level 2.

- Exact match, Search network (mobile phones)
- Phrase match, Search network (bid 80% of exact match to start)
- Broad match, Search network (bid 60% of exact match to start)
- Text ads, Display network (bid 50% of exact match to start)
- Image ads, Display network (bid 25% of exact match to start)

Here's a little pop quiz:

> **Question:** In which e-commerce scenario should you clone your exact match campaign to expand into phrase match keywords?

Scenario A

Exact match cost per conversion: $10

Acceptable cost per conversion: $6

Scenario B:

Exact match cost per conversion: $6

Acceptable cost per conversion: $10

Answer: Only in Scenario B should you bother cloning the campaign. In Scenario A, the exact match campaign is losing money on each click. Why would you want more traffic that would lose even more money? In Scenario B, you have enough of a margin with the exact match keywords that you have a reasonable chance of achieving profitability with a phrase match campaign using a combination of bid management, negative keywords, and split testing.

Campaign Cloning Examples

Now that you understand the why and how of campaign cloning, it's time to get specific with some of the most common scenarios in which you'll use this great technique. Not all will apply to every account, but unless your traffic is minimal and your cost per conversions prohibitive, you will find at least a couple of these examples directly applicable to your AdWords account.

Expanding into additional Networks

As we repeat endlessly, you shouldn't combine Search and Display traffic in the same campaign. When you're ready to expand from one Network into another, keep them separated by campaign. You can accomplish this entirely in Editor:

1. **After you make a copy of the original campaign and assign its new name, select the new campaign and find the Edit Selected Campaigns section at the bottom of the window.**

2. **To change from Search to Display, select None from the Search Network drop-down list and Relevant Pages across the Entire Network from the Display Network drop-down list.**

3. **Adjust the bids: in this case, by lowering them.**

    a. *Select the new campaign from the list of folders on the left.*

    b. *Click the Ad Groups tab to show all ad groups in that campaign.*

    c. *Select all the ad groups by clicking Edit from the top menu and selecting Select All from the drop-down list.*

     d. *Click the Advanced Bid Changes link at the bottom of the Editor window.*

     e. *Select the Decrease Bids By radio button and enter the percent by which the new campaign's ad groups bid amounts will be discounted.*

     To go from exact match to display, for example, we recommend that you decrease bids by at least 50 percent from your exact match keyword bids. (See Figure 16-1.)

     f. *Click the Change Bids button to confirm the change.*

4. **When you're done, click the Post Selected Campaigns button at the top of the window to send the cloned campaign to your AdWords account.**

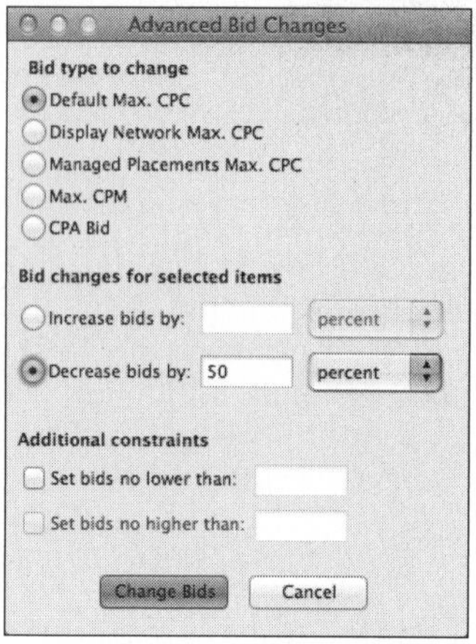

Figure 16-1:
When expanding from Search to Display, reduce all bids by 50% to start.

Special case: Cloning a campaign for search partners

You may recall that Google offers two different Search networks: Google.com and its global variations and browser toolbars, and the Search Partners network, consisting mostly of Internet service providers (ISPs) like Netscape and AOL. Sometimes Search Partner traffic performs much worse than straight Google search, and therefore requires its own campaign where you can lower bids to reflect the lower quality of traffic.

There's no campaign setting for "Search Partners Only," and the workaround is too complicated and convoluted to present in this chapter. If you find that your Cost/Conv. metrics vary greatly between Google and Search partner traffic, check out this tutorial at `http://gafd3.com/partners`.

Campaign cloning can be the solution when search partners perform worse than Google's search network, but not vice versa.

You can see your traffic segmented by network by clicking the Segment button just above the data table and selecting Network from the drop-down list. In Figure 16-2, the Search Partners traffic is more valuable than Google search ($4.97 versus $7.92 Cost/Conv., even though the traffic costs more per click ($0.15 versus $0.11). When Search Partners traffic performs *better* than Google search, as in Figure 16-2, it's currently impossible to separate Search Partners traffic.

Figure 16-2:
Sometimes the Search Partners network outperforms Google traffic.

Campaign	Budget	Status	Cost / conv. (1-per-click)	Clicks	Impr.	Avg. CPC	Conv. (1-per-click)	Conv. rate (1-per-click)	CTR	Cost	Avg. Pos.
Total - all campaigns	$20.00/day		$7.00	98,837	11,327,160	$0.15	1,867	1.92%	0.87%	$14,339.16	5
Howie's awesome campaign	$1.00/day	Paused	$5.35	82,469	10,443,116	$0.10	1,607	1.95%	0.79%	$8,604.95	5.2
Google search			$7.92	20,884	1,781,034	$0.11	278	1.33%	1.17%	$2,202.78	6.8
Search partners			$4.97	5,667	275,242	$0.15	175	3.09%	2.06%	$869.21	7.4

Match type

Some of our colleagues prefer to separate match types by ad group, rather than campaign. They point out that you can still manage bids separately in ad groups, and that creating too many campaigns can lead to unnecessary complexity in your account structure. They're right, and if you generate so few monthly conversions that it takes years for you to accrue enough data to make intelligent decisions, campaign cloning for match type might be overkill.

We think campaign-level separation is the "better best practice" for most advertisers because you can spot trends and differences quicker and more starkly than if you separate match types by ad group. But if you find yourself in a giant argument over this topic, rest assured that both methods are miles better than not separating at all.

Cloning campaigns for match type is just as simple as for Networks (see the earlier instructions). Simply select all the keywords in your new campaign and change the match type.

Ad type

In the Display network, you can show both text and image ads. Because image ads typically deliver lower-quality traffic, you want to clone Display network campaigns that use text ads when you're ready to expand into image advertising.

Don't start with image ads.

- ✔ Because they generally produce lower ROI than text ads, you want to make sure your text ad campaign is profitable before opening the faucet wider.

- ✔ Your winning text ads will show you what text to use in your image ads. Text ads are easier to build and test, giving you a head start in determining the best messaging for your image ads.

Before cloning a Display text ad campaign as a Display image ad campaign, create some image files and save them in a folder on your computer. Acceptable formats include JPG, GIF, PNG, and SWF. Each image must be less than 50K in size, and must conform to one of the following dimensions (numbers are in pixels):

- ✔ 300 x 50 (Mobile leaderboard)
- ✔ 468 x 60 (Banner)
- ✔ 728 x 90 (Leaderboard)
- ✔ 250 x 250 (Square)
- ✔ 200 x 200 (Small square)
- ✔ 336 x 280 (Large rectangle)
- ✔ 300 x 250 (Inline rectangle)
- ✔ 120 x 600 (Skyscraper)
- ✔ 160 x 600 (Wide skyscraper)

Here's the easiest way to clone a Display text ad campaign as a Display image ad campaign:

1. **Copy the campaign, rename it, and go to the Ads tab and delete all the text ads.**

2. **Click the Image Ads tab to the right of the Text Ads tab and then click the Add/Update Multiple Image Ads button at the top left.**

3. **From within the popup window, click the Browse for Image Files button and navigate to the folder where you saved your image files and select the ones you want to upload.**

4. **Click Next.**

5. **Clear the My Image Ad Information below Includes Columns for Campaign and Ad Group Names check box.**

6. **Select the check box next to the campaigns where you want to add the image ads.**

By default, the image will be added to all ad groups within each selected campaign.

7. **Click Next.**

8. **Preview the image files and ad names, and when you're satisfied that you sent the right ads to the right campaigns and ad groups, click Process at the bottom right.**

9. **Click Finish and Review Changes to return to the main Editor interface to keep or reject the changes.**

Device

After you establish profitable metrics by limited your exposure to computer users, you can explore smartphone and tablet users. Currently, Editor offers a limited set of options; for example, as of this writing, you can't select tablet computers. Here's the easiest way to create a cloned Device campaign:

1. **Copy, rename, and upload an existing campaign using Editor, log into your AdWords Dashboard, and navigate to the Settings page of the new campaign.**

2. **In the Networks and Devices section (scroll to get there), click the Edit button next to Devices.**

   - *Limit your audience to smart phone users.* Select the Mobile Devices with Full Browsers radio button.

   - *Select iPad, XOOM, and other tablet users.* Select the Tablets with Full Browsers radio button.

   These choices aren't mutually exclusive; Google's default is to display your ads in all these devices.

3. **Click the Advanced Mobile and Tablet Options link to further refine your selection based on operating system and mobile carrier.**

   In Figure 16-3, we targeted only Apple's iOS operating system, meaning that the ads will be shown to iPad users only. If you have some reason to exclude certain mobile carriers, you can do that as well.

Android, iOS, and webOS are operating systems for mobile devices. Android runs Google-powered devices, iOS powers Apple's mobile lineup, including iPhone, iPad, and iPod Touch; while webOS runs some Palm and HP mobile devices.

If you target mobile devices, you need a mobile-enabled landing page, if not an entire mobile website. Don't waste your money sending cell phone traffic to a full web page that can't be navigated without endless scrolling, pinching, and squinting. For resources on created mobile-friendly landing pages, see the end of Chapter 12.

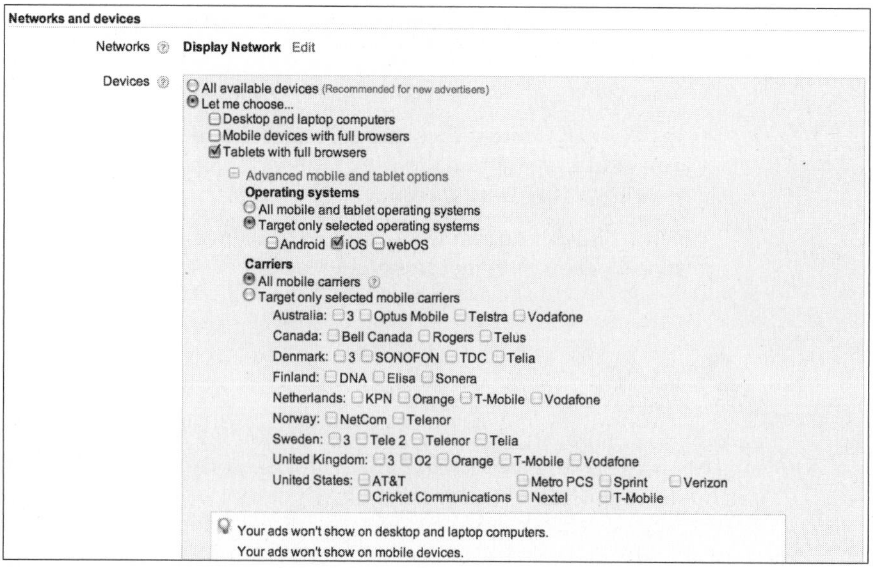

Figure 16-3:
This
campaign
targets
iPads only
(tablets
using iOS).

Global differences

If you do business globally, you will almost certainly find different degrees of responsiveness based on country. We recommend starting with one country (the one where you expect the highest ROI) and then expanding into other countries in cloned campaigns. If you're already running multi-country campaigns, you can see country-specific differences in the Geographic view of the Dimensions tab (see Chapter 13).

In Figure 16-4, you can see that despite the Avg. CPC being virtually identical across the US, the UK, Canada, and Australia ($0.12–$0.13), the Cost/Conv. varies from a low of $3.98 in the US to a high of $5.16 in Australia. That is, Australian conversions are 30 percent more expensive than those from the US. Time to move the Australian traffic into its own campaign and manage those bids separately from the rest of the world.

We could debate why Australian conversions are costlier than those from the U.S. (more competition, landing pages that use U.S. terms that confuse Aussies, other cultural differences, and so on are all possibilities), but we don't need to know the reason in order to optimize for that fact.

Changing countries in cloned campaigns is a snap with Editor. Simply select the campaign to clone, copy it, rename the copy, and then click the Edit link next to Location Targeting, at the very bottom of the page. In Figure 16-5, we selected Australia as the only specific location.

Figure 16-4:
Conversions from one country are often more expensive than those from another.

Country/Territory	Clicks	Impr.	CTR	Avg. CPC	Cost	Conv. (1-per-click)	Cost / conv. (1-per-click)	Conv. rate (1-per-click)
United States	24,299	3,519,938	0.69%	$0.13	$3,066.32	771	$3.98	3.17%
United Kingdom	7,301	761,114	0.96%	$0.12	$912.54	162	$5.63	2.22%
Canada	4,097	564,002	0.73%	$0.12	$472.03	108	$4.37	2.64%
Australia	5,596	540,247	1.04%	$0.13	$748.79	145	$5.16	2.59%

By keeping the Target One or More Countries and Territories radio button selected, we're not asked to select states or territories (regions) or individual cities. Because this is a country-based campaign, we're not interested in more granular geographic targeting. When you're done, click OK to save your changes. Then post your new campaign to activate it.

Figure 16-5:
You can specify individual countries using AdWords Editor.

Before uploading a new country campaign, consider any regional spelling or linguistic differences between your original and new countries. For example, a Vitruvian client, WatercolourSecrets.com, needed to change the spelling of "color" to "colour" for the UK market. Also, Howie is very sensitive to linguistic variation ever since going clothes shopping in London for his wedding outfit. He asked the clerk at Marks & Spencers for a fancy vest and suspenders. Imagine his surprise when the bemused clerk raised an eyebrow and brought out an undershirt and a garter belt.

Regional differences

If your national account generates sufficient traffic, you may create additional profit pockets by separating campaigns by regions within a country. If you started with a national campaign, visit the Geographic segment of the Dimensions tab for that campaign to see which states or provinces should be moved into their own campaigns.

You may find that the easiest division is by large region; for example, you may divide the United States into Northeast, Southeast, Midwest, Southwest, and Northwest regions. You may find that the coastal states perform similarly, so it makes sense to group New Jersey, Massachusetts, Connecticut, New York, Delaware, California, Oregon, and Washington state in a single campaign.

If you have some time on your hands and you're a high-volume AdWords user (generating at least 1,000 conversions per month), you may find it worthwhile to create 52 separate campaigns: 50 states, the District of Columbia, and Untrackable. You can create the 50 states and DC campaigns in Editor (tedious work, but simple). For the Untrackable campaign, which collects impressions from searchers whose locations are for some reason not trackable to a particular state, you need to accomplish that via campaign Settings online, as in Figure 16-6. For U.S. campaigns, just clone the national campaign and exclude all the states and DC, as follows:

1. **Navigate to the Settings tab for the campaign you want to set up as Untrackable.**

2. **Click the Edit button under the list of Locations.**

   You should see just United States in the list of Selected Locations.

3. **Click the link to Exclude Areas within Selected Locations.**

4. **Select the check boxes next to each state (including District of Columbia)**

5. **Click the Done Excluding button.**

6. **Click Save.**

If you find some states need to be managed separately but you don't have enough conversions to justify the 52-campaign setup, you can create campaigns for individual states and then simply exclude those states from the national campaign.

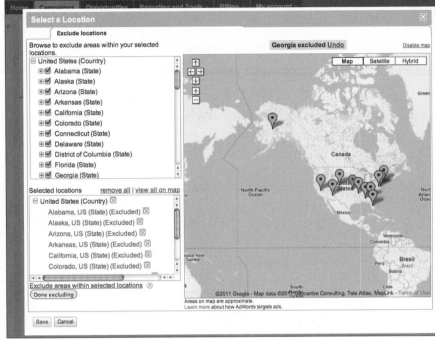

Figure 16-6:
You can capture Untrackable traffic by setting up a national campaign and exclude all regions.

Demographics (Display network only)

In the Display network, you can get surprisingly good data on who is viewing and responding to your ads based on gender and age. By using demographic targeting settings, you can clone campaigns to bid and market differently to different demographic segments of your prospect base.

Sometimes you can see the need to clone campaigns by demographic segments by exploring the Demographic view in the Dimensions tab. At the moment, Google's demographic reporting feature isn't particularly enlightening, so you may have to clone campaigns in order to discover the differences, let alone capitalize on them.

Demographic bidding works only in the Display network. Currently, Google doesn't share information on the demographic profiles of users in the Search network.

Gender

Sometimes men and women respond differently to the same offer, and sometimes you can market more effectively by changing your messaging and design to accommodate the buying preferences of each sex. Both are good reasons to consider separating traffic into men's and women's campaigns.

You can play with demographics only via the campaign settings in the online AdWords interface. We'll demonstrate with the example of a campaign that you'll split into men's and women's campaigns. Begin by cloning the campaign using Editor and then making the final adjustments online:

1. **Make two copies of an existing Display network campaign and add** MEN **to the name of one and** WOMEN **to the name of the other.**

2. **Upload the changes to AdWords.**

3. **Navigate to the campaign settings for the Men's campaign and scroll to the Advanced Settings section at the bottom of the page.**

4. **Click the Demographic Bidding link and then click the Edit link next to No Demographic Settings.**

   You see a summary of the last seven days of demographic data for that campaign. In Figure 16-7, you can see that women convert almost twice as inexpensively as men ($0.99 compared with £1.95).

Demographic bidding ☒

This summary shows how your ads have performed on sites that offer demographic data. Click any row to adjust your bid for that demographic group. You can also use the exclude checkboxes to hide your ad from that group.

0.00% of total impressions are from sites with demographic data. ⑦

Traffic Reports by Gender and Age (for last 7 days)

Gender	Exclude	Modify bid	Clicks	Impr.	CTR	Avg. CPC	Cost	Conv. (1-per-click)	Cost / conv. (1-per-click)	Conv. rate (1-per-click)	View-through Conv.
Male	☐	Bid + 0%	10	11,962	0.08%	UK£0.20	UK£1.95	1	UK£1.95	10.00%	
Female	☐	Bid + 0%	17	9,547	0.18%	UK£0.17	UK£2.96	3	UK£0.99	17.65%	
Unspecified			0	269	0.00%	UK£0.00	UK£0.00	0	UK£0.00	0.00%	
Total			27	21,778	0.12%	UK £0.18	UK £4.91	4	UK£1.23	14.81%	

Age	Exclude	Modify bid	Clicks	Impr.	CTR ⑦	Avg. CPC ⑦	Cost	Conv. (1-per-click) ⑦	Cost / conv. (1-per-click) ⑦	Conv. rate (1-per-click) ⑦	View-through Conv. ⑦
0-17	☐		2	3,533	0.06%	UK£0.20	UK£0.40	0	UK£0.00	0.00%	
18-24	☐	Bid + 0%	4	7,464	0.05%	UK£0.18	UK£0.73	0	UK£0.00	0.00%	
25-34	☐	Bid + 0%	0	4,950	0.00%	UK£0.00	UK£0.00	0	UK£0.00	0.00%	
35-44	☐	Bid + 0%	8	2,126	0.38%	UK£0.19	UK£1.52	0	UK£0.00	0.00%	
45-54	☐	Bid + 0%	4	1,568	0.26%	UK£0.16	UK£0.64	1	UK£0.64	25.00%	
55-64	☐	Bid + 0%	3	1,032	0.29%	UK£0.19	UK£0.58	0	UK£0.00	0.00%	
65+	☐	Bid + 0%	6	706	0.85%	UK£0.17	UK£1.04	3	UK£0.35	50.00%	
Unspecified			0	399	0.00%	UK£0.00	UK£0.00	0	UK£0.00	0.00%	
Total			27	21,778	0.12%	UK £0.18	UK £4.91	4	UK£1.23	14.81%	

Data from the past 48 hours may not be included here. For site-specific demographic data, visit the Report Center and run a Demographic Performance report.

Resulting combinations
When two demographics overlap, your increased bids for both are added together.

For example: If these are your settings   Then your resulting combination is
    Gender: Female   Bid + 10%   Female and 18-24 = Bid + 25%
    Age: 18-24   Bid + 15%

[Save] [Cancel]

Figure 16-7:
You can exclude or modify bids at the campaign level based on gender and age.

If this were your account and you were willing to pay $2.50 per lead, you could simply double the bid for the female demographic by clicking the Bid + 0% box in the Female row and entering **100** in the Percent field. You wouldn't necessarily need to separate the traffic. The downside of this is the fact that you're basing this adjustment on just seven days of data. If your campaign generates at least 100 conversions per month on average, it's better to split it so you can accrue data for longer periods.

5. **Select the Exclude check box in the Female row.**

6. **Click Save at the bottom of the window to save the change.**

7. **Repeat the whole process for the Women's campaign, excluding Male this time.**

8. **Repeat the same process for the original campaign, this time excluding Male and Female.**

Why include a campaign that excludes male and female? Because sometimes Google doesn't know, and you don't want to lose that traffic.

Now you can optimize the men's and women's campaigns independently. You'll often find significant savings and/or opportunities by getting this granular.

Age

One of Vitruvian's clients sells a service of great value to certain types of senior citizens. They generate leads on their website, but close the sales on the phone. Their sales staff reported to Joel that their closing rate was much higher for older prospects. Joel took this information to create an "Older" campaign in which he raised bids to reflect the higher value of the click.

First, decide how you want to segment your campaign by age. As you can see from Figure 16-7, the existing data tend to be rather sparse. The more conversions per month your campaign generates, the more segments you can support. For most advertisers, it's probably sufficient to create just two age segments: say, 18–54 and 55+, or 0–34 and 35–54 if your offer skews to a younger demographic. You can exclude age groups without watering down your conversion data.

The process of campaign cloning for age segmentation is identical to that for gender targeting. Just substitute the appropriate age group for the gender in the preceding instructions. And if you want maximum traffic across all age groups, make sure to create one campaign in which you exclude all age groups to catch the untrackables.

Day parting

Day parting involves turning your campaign off or adjusting its bids based on time of day. Many advertisers who are savvy enough to have discovered ad scheduling just assume that they should stop showing ads when their business is closed. The data in the Hour of Day view in the Dimensions tab may suggest otherwise. (See Chapter 13 for an example.)

Suppose you discover that clicks during business hours are worth two times as much, on average, as clicks during non-business hours. The easiest way to optimize bids within a single campaign is to discount all bids by one-half during those off hours. You don't need to clone the campaign; you can do this on the Campaign Settings page:

1. **Scroll down to Advanced Settings and click the Schedule: Start Date, End Date, Ad Scheduling link if that section isn't already expanded.**

2. **Click the Edit button next to Ad Scheduling.**

   You'll see a grid with days of the week down the left and times of day across the top.

3. **Click the bid adjustment link above the grid.**

   To cut bids by one-half from 5 p.m. until 9 a.m., make the changes for Monday and then copy Monday's settings for the other four weekdays.

4. **Select the Running All Day check box in the Monday row to make changes.**

5. **Create the first time period, 12AM to 9AM. Also change 100 to 50 in the Percent box.**

6. **Click the Add Another Time Period link.**

7. **Create the second time period, 9AM to 5PM. Keep the bid percentage at 100%.**

8. **Create the third time period, 5PM to 12AM. Change 100 to 50 in the Percent box.**

   See Figure 16-8.

9. **Click the Copy button and select To All Days from the drop-down list, as in Figure 16-8.**

   Assuming that your business is closed on the weekend, you need to make some adjustments to Saturday and Sunday.

10. **Click the time period box in the Saturday row and change the 100 to 50 in the 9 a.m. to 5 p.m. time period.**

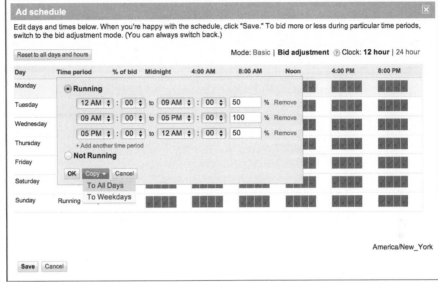

Figure 16-8:
Create three
time periods
per day
to reduce
bids during
off-hours.

11. **Click Copy and select To Weekend from the drop-down list.**

12. **Click Save.**

If you did it correctly, your Ad Schedule will look like Figure 16-9. (The weekend days are hiding, unfortunately, but they will look completely flat.)

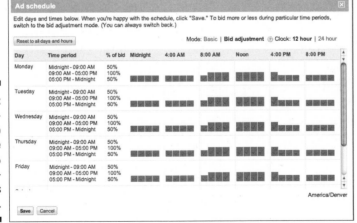

Figure 16-9:
Ad sched-
uling to
reduce
bids by 50%
during non-
business
hours.

After all that, let us explain why campaign cloning is a much more profitable way to handle day parting. Using the single-campaign bid adjustment method, you're forced to treat all keywords and placements the same, even if some of them are so profitable that you don't want to reduce their bids ever. By creating a 9 a.m.–5 p.m. campaign and a 5 p.m.–9 a.m. campaign, you can manage keyword and placement bids individually. If this sounds like a full-time job, check out Chapter 13 for the Minutes a Month method of account optimization.

To clone for day parting, use Editor to copy, rename, and upload a new campaign based on the one you want to divide. You can call one **ON HOURS** and the other **OFF HOURS**, or anything similarly clever. Next, go online to the ON HOURS campaign and navigate to the Campaign Settings page. You should see the Basic Mode by default (you won't see a column for bid adjustments).

1. **Click the Running All Day box next to Monday.**

2. **Enter the time period** 9AM to 5PM.

3. **Click Copy and select To All Days from the drop-down list.**

4. **Click the time period in the Saturday row and select the Not Running radio button.**

5. **Click Copy and select To Weekend from the drop-down list.**

6. **Click Save.**

   Your grid should look like Figure 16-10.

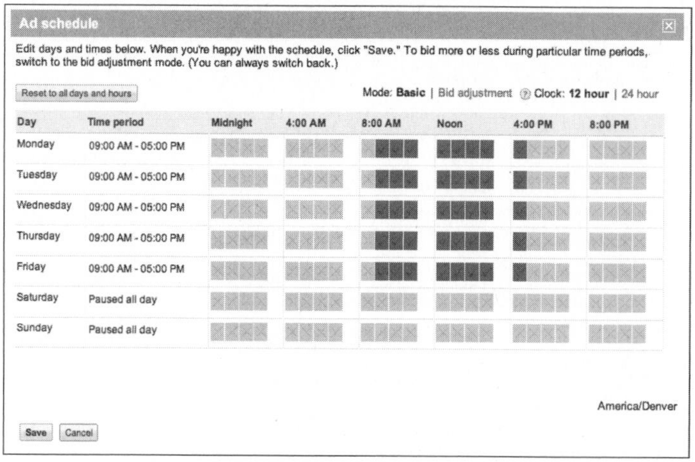

Figure 16-10: A cloned campaign that shows ads only between 9 a.m. and 5 p.m. on weekdays.

Ad schedule							
Day	Time period	Midnight	4:00 AM	8:00 AM	Noon	4:00 PM	8:00 PM
Monday	09:00 AM - 05:00 PM						
Tuesday	09:00 AM - 05:00 PM						
Wednesday	09:00 AM - 05:00 PM						
Thursday	09:00 AM - 05:00 PM						
Friday	09:00 AM - 05:00 PM						
Saturday	Paused all day						
Sunday	Paused all day						

Next, repeat the preceding procedure for the OFF HOURS campaign, reversing the instructions so the campaign runs on weekdays only between 12 a.m. and 9 a.m., and then again from 5 p.m. to 12 a.m., and all day Saturday and Sunday. See Figure 16-11.

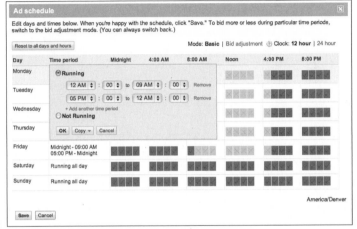

Figure 16-11:
This campaign runs during off-hours only.

Campaign cloning is the safest and surest way to expand into all the potentially profitable nooks and crannies of AdWords, and to maximize your results by spotting opportunities that remain hidden without this powerful tactic. In this chapter, we've given you the Standard Issue basics of campaign cloning. If you get to the point where you're interested in Advanced Campaign Cloning (such as 6x day parting and Operation Camouflage to befuddle your competitors), check out http://gafd3.com/cloning.

Chapter 17

Following Your Best Prospects around the Web

*I*n a 2005 *Doctor Who* episode, a conspiracy theory website about a mysterious man called "The Doctor" chronicles his uncanny appearance in photos and drawings related to pivotal moments in history. Thanks to his time machine, the TARDIS, we see The Doctor next to JFK's motorcade the day he was assassinated in 1963; next to a family who canceled their voyage on the Titanic the day it sailed in 1912; and on the island of Sumatra the day the Krakatoa volcano exploded in 1883.

You may not be a time-traveling humanoid alien, but you can get your AdWords ads to seem uncannily ubiquitous to your best prospects. This feature of AdWords is so powerful that it can backfire if you aren't careful. But done well, it can transform your business — even if you don't use AdWords for anything else.

Imagine Lila visits your site and for whatever reason isn't ready to buy or opt-in yet. She leaves your site after a few seconds (maybe the phone rings, the baby cries, she gets a Facebook chat notification, or she remembers that she promised to buy sauerkraut before the supermarket closed), and all your hard AdWords work has been wasted. Lila is gone forever, never to return, right? But now something strange happens.

Lila starts seeing your ad on her favorite blogs and on sites she's never visited before. On *The New York Times* and the *Huffington Post* and TechRadar and *Forbes.* She starts thinking, "Wow, these guys are everywhere. They must have a huge advertising budget. They must be the leaders in their field. You know, it's funny, I think I even visited their site once. I'd better go back and check it out again."

Lila isn't seeing your ads appear everywhere because you have a TARDIS, but because you're taking advantage of the magic of *remarketing:* instructing Google to show your ads all over the Display network to people who already visited your website. In this chapter, we'll show you how to set up remarketing in its most elementary form, discuss its strategic uses, and give you some intermediate and advanced strategies to consider.

The Advantages of Remarketing

The biggest advantage of remarketing is that it addresses the vast majority of your website visitors: those who don't opt in or buy. If the average e-commerce site converts 1 percent of its visitors into customers, remarketing goes after the 99 percent who leave without buying. Until remarketing, all you could do was kiss that traffic goodbye and hope they remembered your URL or searched for you again. With remarketing, you can now follow them around the Web with your best ads for up to 180 days.

A second advantage of remarketing pertains to your prospects' perception of your business. When your ads show up everywhere, your prospects can't help but think that you're a bigger player than you actually may be. Joel's brother Jason runs a tiny one-man tutoring agency in Portland, Maine and uses remarketing. He often receives calls from prospects who assume he's bigger than *Kaplan* and *Princeton Review* because they see his ads everywhere. And Howie, who should know better, was himself duped into complaining that his web host was neglecting his support tickets because they were growing too fast. His evidence? He kept seeing its ads and assumed they were blitzing the planet with them. The truth? Only he and others who had visited their site were seeing them at all.

Third, remarketing can be used to advance a relationship with existing customers by validating their initial decision to buy from you in the first place. You can offer upsells and generate word of mouth advertising by seeming like the "obvious choice" to people who may otherwise forget about you or even develop buyers' remorse.

Fourth, remarketing is often extremely cost effective because it's so highly targeted. You tend to get higher conversion rates when advertising in front of people who have already demonstrated an interest in your wares by visiting your site.

Setting Up Remarketing

Remarketing should be done in its own dedicated campaign. That way, you maintain maximum control, keep it simple, and avoid mixing traffic that should be kept separate.

We'll cover three flavors of remarketing: basic, product-based, and behavioral. We highly recommend starting with basic, even if you are a hyper-intelligent Time Lord from the planet Gallifrey (yes, another *Doctor Who* reference). The initial steps for all three types are the same, and you need a traffic threshold before remarketing kicks in at all. And for many businesses, basic remarketing is all you'll ever need. Even if you've read this far and haven't yet bid on a single keyword or sent a single AdWords visitor to your site, you can have remarketing set up and working within an hour without ever touching the rest of AdWords.

Basic Remarketing

In basic remarketing, you set up a single campaign and create a single remarketing audience: everyone who has visited your website. Your ads will follow those prospects around the web for a specified length of time, and you'll measure the effectiveness of those ads.

Set up a remarketing campaign

You can either create a new campaign from scratch, or clone an existing one using AdWords Editor (see Chapter 10). The advantage to cloning is that you don't have to retype your ads or change your geographic settings; the disadvantage is that you have to delete all keywords and any ad groups that aren't relevant to your remarketing efforts. For the sake of simplicity, say that you'll create a new campaign from scratch.

1. **Create your new campaign (see Chapter 2) and add the word** Remarketing **to the campaign name so you can find it easily during ongoing account management.**

2. **Under the Networks and Devices setting, select Display Network only, and select the Show Ads on Pages That Match the Broadest Targeting Method radio button.**

3. **Under Bidding and Budget settings, select Manual Bidding for Clicks and set a budget that you're comfortable with.**

4. **Under the Advanced Settings, find Ad Delivery. Under Ad Rotation, select the radio button for Optimize for Conversions: Show Ads Expected to Provide More Conversions.**

5. **For Frequency Capping, select the No Cap on Impressions radio button.**

   This means you set no limit on the number of times someone can see your ad in a given time period.

After you have remarketing running, you can experiment with caps to see whether you can increase conversion rate by not oversaturating your prospects with your advertising. Some experts advise the use of frequency capping to avoid *ad blindness* (your prospects seeing the same ad so many times that they stop noticing it). In our experiments, frequency capping has not decreased cost per conversion, but simply (and unfortunately) lowered lead volume. We prefer to deal with the issue of ad blindness by split-testing lots of different ads in each remarketing ad group, and have found that by doing so, conversion rates can actually go up.

To finish, click the Save and Continue button to finish setting up the campaign and start setting up the ad group.

Creating a single ad group

Here's how to create a single ad group:

1. **Name your ad group so you can recognize it later.**

2. **Enter the text for one of your best ads.**

    If you'll be using image ads, you can add those at a later step.

3. **Skip the Keywords and Placements sections and enter a default bid (the most you're willing to pay per click).**

    We recommend bidding roughly the same as what you're currently bidding in your other Display network campaigns for the same product or service. If you're using only the Search network, then start by bidding 50% of those bids.

4. **Ignore the yellow warning box telling you that the ad group isn't quite ready and then click the Save Ad Group button.**

5. **(Optional) If you want to add more ads, click the Ads tab and then click the New Ad button to the left of and just above the table of ads. Repeat this step until all your best ads are in this ad group.**

You'll often hear that you need to go to great lengths to make sure your remarketing ads are different from your other AdWords ads. As our childhood pal Oscar the Grouch puts it, "Baloney!" Ads on national TV ads get repeated hundreds or thousands of times, as long as they keep working. You'd be silly not to repeat your best performing ads in your remarketing campaigns (at least until your split-testing efforts find a better performing ad).

A quick and easy way to find your best performing ads is to look at the last three or four months of data in your AdWords account, drill down to the Ads tab, and sort all ads in your entire account by number of conversions. Add the top performing ads to your new remarketing campaign.

Creating an audience

Okay, so you have no keywords and no placements. How are you going to get people to see these ads? Instead of specifying keywords to trigger the ads, or particular web pages to display them, you're going to create an audience — a group of people who will see these ads by virtue of landing on your website. Before you can add audiences by clicking the Audiences tab, you have to create them first.

1. **If it's hidden, show the left navigation area by clicking the double arrows just below the Home button and then clicking the Control Panel and Library link (see Figure 17-1).**

Figure 17-1:
Start here
to get to the
Audiences
tab.

2. **Click the Audiences link in the left navigation area and then click the New Audience button in the center of the page.**

3. **Select Remarketing List from the drop-down list (see Figure 17-2).**

4. **Name and describe the remarketing list.**

   The name should concisely describe how people got onto this list. For example: "Visited G-Form site."

5. **Select a membership duration between 1 and 540 days. Here are some hints:**

   • *You can easily change it later.*

   • *The higher the number, the longer a prospect will remain on your remarketing list.*

The default is 30 days, meaning that your ads will follow a prospect for about one month after they first land on your site and trigger the remarketing cookie.

- *Choose a duration based on what you know or believe about the sales cycle for your particular product or service.*

Someone shopping for Vitamin D supplements will probably make their purchase within a couple of days of the start of the search. A higher-end purchase, like a $500 suitcase or a massage chair, may take weeks to be completed. Long-lead consulting can take months. Also take into account the likelihood of urgency; a vacuum cleaner repair shop might remarket for only a couple of days, while a tarot reader might go for a full year (or, if they draw the Devil card, possibly less).

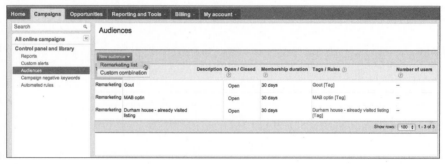

Figure 17-2:
Create a new audience from a remarketing list.

6. **Click Save to be taken to the list of audiences.**

You'll see your new audience and some details, including how many prospects ("users") are in that audience.

Google says . . .

Google requires you to display specific elements of your privacy policy on your site if you place remarketing cookies on your visitors' computers. Quoting the Big G:

"The privacy policies should include the following information:

Third party vendors, including Google, show your ads on sites on the internet.

Third party vendors, including Google, use cookies to serve ads based on a user's prior visits to your website.

Users may opt out of Google's use of cookies by visiting the Google advertising opt-out page."

You can read the whole policy at http://gafd3.com/google-privacy.

The link for Google's opt-out page is http://google.com/privacy/ads.

Generating the website tag for your audience

After you save an audience, Google generates a snippet of code (a "tag") that you need to place on every page on your website that you want to count toward remarketing. If you offer only one product or service, every page on your site can get the tag. If you offer multiple product lines, select only the pages relevant to your ads.

For example, if G-Form is remarketing with ads about its consumer electronics protection, the tag for that ad group might go on all the pages related to consumer electronics but not on pages for sports protection. (You could make the case that someone who searched for mountain biking protection probably has a laptop or tablet or smart phone to protect as well.)

1. **Click the link of the name of the tag you just created in the Tags/Rules column to bring up the code snippet to add to your web pages.**

   Generating this code works fine in the Safari browser for Mac, but didn't work in Google's own browser, Chrome. Hopefully this bug will be fixed by the time you read this, but be prepared to try a couple of different web browsers.

2. **Change the Page Security Level at the top from HTTP to HTTPS; see Figure 17-3.**

   This allows your code to work on any web page, regardless of its security setting. That way, your visitor won't see security warnings when they land on your site (never a confidence-boosting experience).

3. **Click anywhere in the code to highlight the entire snippet. Copy the code and paste it into a text file, and save the file on your computer.**

4. **Place that code snippet on all the web pages that will trigger the remarketing campaign.**

Figure 17-3: Generate more-versatile code by selecting the HTTPS option before copying the snippet.

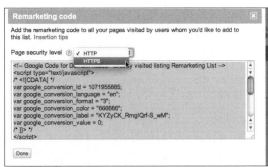

Multiple browsers

Speaking of browsers, if you're super-geeky like Joel and have multiple Google accounts that you constantly log in and out of, multiple browsers can be a very good friend. You could use Internet Explorer or Safari for your primary Gmail account, Google Chrome for your AdWords account, and Firefox for your secondary AdWords accounts. That way, you can have multiple Google accounts open at the same time without having to log in and out of each.

On most web pages, this code goes just above the `</body>` tag. If your site is built on WordPress, the easiest way to add the code is to place it in an untitled sidebar widget. If you have no idea what we're talking about, feel free to ignore this paragraph or just mark the check box that instructs Google to mail specific instructions straight to your webmaster. (Then send them a copy of this book. Or three.)

Adding the audience to your ad group

Nope, you're still not done. But you're so close to the finish line — don't give up now!

1. **Navigate back to the ad group within the remarketing campaign that you just created.**

   Remember how Google was a little worried about you because you hadn't chosen any keywords or placements for this poor ad group? Now you show Google how clever you are by adding your remarketing audience to the ad group.

2. **Click the Audiences tab and then click the Add Audiences button (see Figure 17-4).**

3. **Click the Remarketing Lists link to get to the list you just created (see Figure 17-5).**

4. **Click the Add link to the right of the list you want to add as an audience.**

5. **Click Save.**

   Now you'll see the Audience listed in the data table, in the same format as keywords and placements. You can manage bids based on the data you accrue, using the same steps we show you in Chapter 13. You can do this in AdWords Editor (see Chapter 10) and simply manage the ad group bid.

Figure 17-4:
After you
create your
remarketing
list, you can
add it to an
ad group.

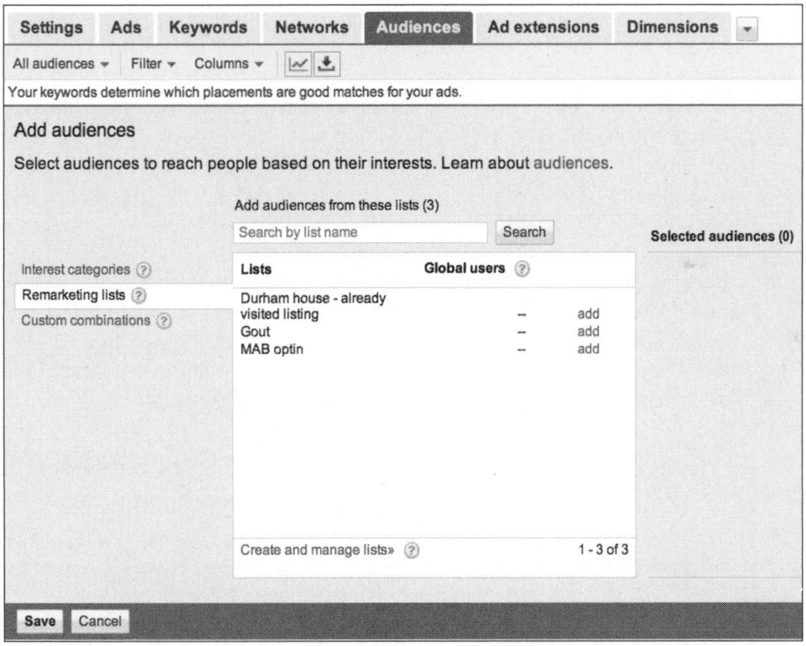

Figure 17-5:
Click the
Remarketing
Lists link to
find the list
you created.

You'll probably find that you can bid higher for remarketing clicks because they represent already-interested prospects who are more likely to take you up on your offer. If you track conversions, you'll probably be pleasantly surprised to find that your remarketing campaigns are converting into sales at a higher rate than your other website traffic.

TIP

You can start collecting audiences before you create remarketing campaigns and ad groups. Simply create an audience and place the code on your site. Whenever you're ready, you can start remarketing to that audience.

Product-Based Remarketing

Basic remarketing involves a simple yes/no distinction: Did someone visit your website? If yes, let my ads follow them around the web. You generate one audience and place the remarketing tag everywhere on your site. In product-based remarketing, you add a layer of complexity by segmenting your audience by product category. If you sell only one product or service, this level of remarketing isn't necessary. But if you sell multiple products at varied price points, you'll be able to create campaigns distinguished by different conversion values.

For example, www.joesgolfshack.com, an online golf store that sells accessories (average profit $10), clothing (average profit $70), clubs (average profit $150), and electric carts (average profit $800) could create four remarketing campaigns, one for each conversion value. Instead of placing one remarketing tag site-wide, Joe would create four different audiences, one for each of the product areas on the website (see Figure 17-6). In this case, Joe decides to follow his prospects for 90 days, except for those interested in electric golf carts, which experience has shown requires a longer sales cycle.

Joe places the remarketing tags on the relevant pages of his site: Golf clubs tags go on all the pages featuring golf clubs, and so on. Now Google will begin to populate the audiences with all the visitors to these pages, regardless of how they got to Joe's site — AdWords, organic SEO, a referral link on some other website, or typing **joesgolfshack** directly into the browser URL bar.

Next, Joe creates four new remarketing campaigns, each with its own target cost/conversion, as shown in Figure 17-7.

Figure 17-6:
Create multiple audiences to segment your remarketing traffic based on product interest.

Home	Campaigns	Opportunities	Reporting and Tools ˅	Billing ˅	My account ˅

Shared library >
Audiences

New audience ˅

Type	Name	Description	Open / Closed ⑦	Membership duration ⑦	Tags / Rules ⑦	Number of users ⑦
Remarketing	Electric golf carts		Open	180 days	Electric golf carts [Tag]	--
Remarketing	Golf clubs		Open	90 days	Golf clubs [Tag]	--
Remarketing	Golf clothing		Open	90 days	Golf clothing [Tag]	--
Remarketing	Golf accessories		Open	90 days	Golf accessories [Tag]	--

Show rows: 100 ⇕ 1 - 4 of 4

Figure 17-7:
Product-
based
remarketing
separates
audiences
into different
campaigns
based on the
value of the
conversion.

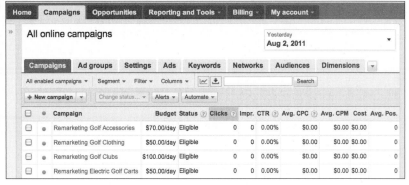

Finally, Joe adds the appropriate audience to each campaign. In Figure 17-8, the Golf Accessories list is being added to the Remarketing Golf Accessories ad group within the Remarketing Golf Accessories campaign.

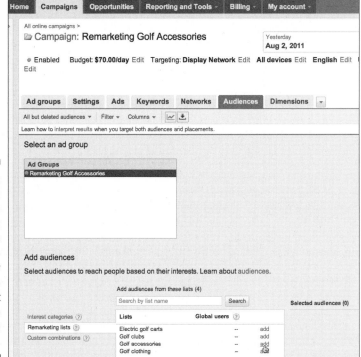

Figure 17-8:
With
multiple
remarketing
campaigns
and audi-
ences, simply
attach the
relevant
audience
to each
campaign.

If your traffic volume allows, you can further divide remarketing campaigns into multiple ad groups, each with its own audience. For example, the Golf Clubs campaign could include PING, TaylorMade, and Callaway ad groups, each with its own audience culled from that particular section of the website (see Figure 17-9). This strategy works only if you have enough visitors — Google doesn't show your remarketing ads unless your audience at any given time consists of at least 500 members. If your numbers can't sustain multiple ad groups, stick with the single ad group per campaign method until you generate enough traffic to get specific.

Figure 17-9:
If you have enough visitors, you can hyper-target your remarketing efforts based on specific brands or models.

| Home | Campaigns | Opportunities | Reporting and Tools ▾ | Billing ▾ | My account ▾ |

» All online campaigns >
📁 Campaign: **Remarketing Golf Clubs**

Yesterday
Sep 24, 2011

● Enabled   Budget: **$100.00/day** Edit   Targeting: **Display Network** Edit   **All devices** Edit   **English** Ed

| Ad groups | Settings | Ads | Keywords | Networks | Audiences | Dimensions | ▾ |

All but deleted ad groups ▾   Segment ▾   Filter ▾   Columns ▾   [~] [±]   [   ]   Search

[+ New ad group]   [Edit]   [Change status... ▾]   [Alerts ▾]   [Automate ▾]

		Ad group	Status ⑦	Default Max. CPC	Display Network Max. CPC ⑦
☐	●	Remarketing Clubs PING	Eligible	$1.25	auto
☐	●	Remarketing Clubs TaylorMade	Eligible	$1.25	auto
☐	●	Remarketing Clubs Callaway	Eligible	$1.25	auto

The tighter you can target your visitors, the less expensive your conversions tend to be. Expect micro-targeted remarketing campaigns to deliver conversions up to half as costly as your "regular" AdWords traffic.

Think none of this applies to you because you sell apples and the majority of your sales come from working the phones? If you can get your salespeople to walk potential apple vendors through a demo of your super-sleek apple ordering system, guess what? You now can add those prospects to your remarketing campaign by placing the remarketing code on the demo page! If your salespeople don't close the deal on the phone, your ads (that can include customer testimonials) will suddenly start appearing everywhere that prospect goes on the web. Your odds of getting the deal the next time your sales staff calls have just about doubled. In the words of *Good Will Hunting,* "How you like them apples?"

But suppose your sales staff lands the sale. Now you don't want to keep showing your prospect ads to customers. Read the next section to discover how to adapt your remarketing based on visitor behavior on your site.

Behavioral Remarketing

Behavior remarketing takes the practice to its most sophisticated — and potentially creepy — heights. Now you target your ads based on visitors' behaviors on your site. For example, what if you could identify everyone who visited your site, shopped, selected a product and added it to their cart, and then left without buying. You could remarket to them using a coupon code as an added incentive to return and complete the purchase. Your visitor might see your ad on their favorite blog and think, "Hey, what a nice coincidence! I almost bought something from them. Lemme grab this coupon code and complete the purchase."

On the other hand, suppose your ad said something like, "Hey, you forgot to check out. Come back and I'll give you 15% off." Now that feels like digital stalking, and is likely to give your prospect what we online marketing professionals refer to as the "heebie-jeebies."

Yes, remarketing is a bit sneaky, and no, most people have no clue that it's happening to them. The marketing they experience changes based on things they've done that they're not aware anybody else knows about. So you have to be very sensitive in your remarketing ad copy not to spook your prospects into thinking that you're somehow spying on them. (You're not; Google is.)

Setting up behavioral remarketing

Behavioral remarketing requires creating multiple audiences and then combining them to create the rule you want. In the case of cart abandoners, you need the following audiences:

- ✔ Visitors who placed an item in your shopping cart
- ✔ Visitors who arrived at the "Thank You" page after completing a purchase

1. Create those two audiences (see Figure 17-10).

Figure 17-10: Create multiple audiences based on where they go on your site.

Type	Name	Description	Open / Closed	Membership duration	Tags / Rules	Number of users
Remarketing	Purchasers	Visitors who made a purchase	Open	180 days	Purchasers [Tag]	--
Remarketing	Checkout page	Visitors who placed an item in their cart	Open	180 days	Checkout page [Tag]	--

Shared library >
Audiences

New audience ▾

2. Place the purchasers tag on your site's "Thank You" page.

3. Place the Checkout Page tag on the checkout page of your shopping cart.

4. Create a custom audience within the Audiences tab by clicking the New Audience button above the data table and selecting Custom Combination from the drop-down list. See Figure 17-11.

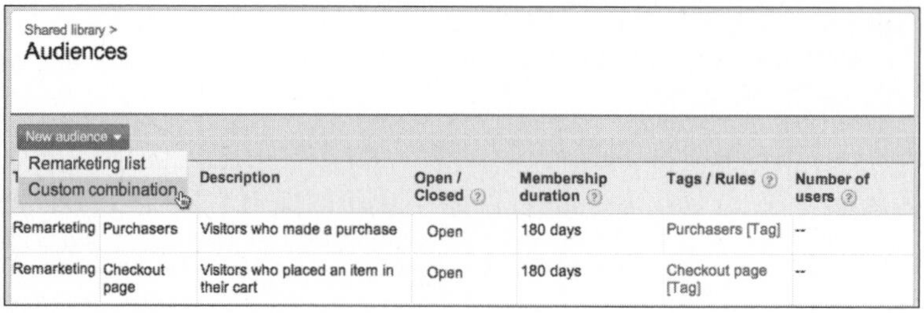

Figure 17-11:
Use custom combina-
tions to
set up
behavioral
retargeting.

5. Give the combination a descriptive name that you'll understand later (like "Cart Abandoners").

6. Click the Select Audiences button, click Interest Categories, and select Remarketing Lists from the drop-down list.

   You'll see the Topics list below replaced by the remarketing audiences you've created. Click the Add link next to the Checkout Page list and click OK to add that list (see Figure 17-12).

7. Click the Add Another link, click All These Audiences, and select None of These Audiences from the drop-down list.

8. Click the Select Audiences button, replace Interest Categories with Remarketing Lists, and click the Add link next to the Purchasers list.

9. Click OK to save.

10. Click Save.

    You'll see the combination list named Cart Abandoners in your list of audiences (see Figure 17-13). You don't need to specify a membership duration because that's already been determined by their membership in the two audiences that make up this one. You also don't need to add a tag for this audience to your website because it's generated by the two existing tags.

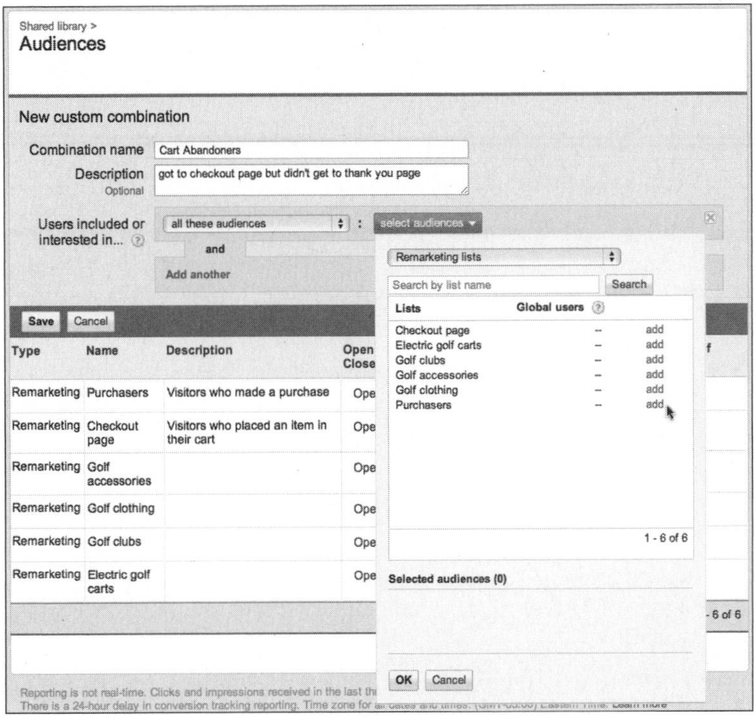

Figure 17-12: Create custom combinations by including and excluding remarketing lists.

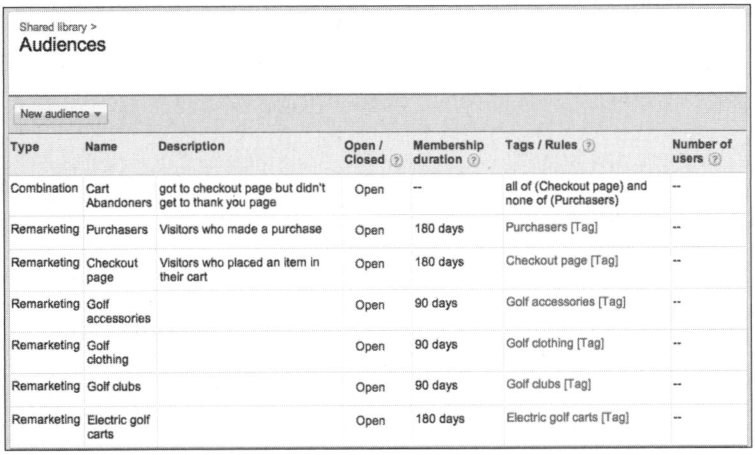

Figure 17-13: Combination remarketing audiences give you the ability to target cart abandoners with special offers and incentives.

Advanced remarketing

We could talk a lot more about the power and potential of remarketing (and we do in our remarketing webinars, which you can register for at `http://gafd3.com/remarketing`), but we don't want to confuse you until you've tried and succeeded at the basics.

On our webinars, we share advanced remarketing strategies, such as

- ✓ Remarketing to visitors who don't buy, but show heightened interest by visiting a particular kind of page (price lists, "About Us" pages, and so on)

- ✓ Remarketing to purchasers to reinforce their decision and prevent buyers' remorse

- ✓ Remarketing to purchasers of one product to get them to purchase a related product (the "Would you like fries with that?" principle)

- ✓ Mixing and matching remarketing lists and interest categories (imagine specifying visitors to an online golf store and adding the interest category of Travel to show ads and a landing page for an exotic golfing vacation)

- ✓ Partnering with complimentary websites to place your remarketing tag on their site

- ✓ Combining remarketing with geotargeting to create different ads and pages for locals versus out-of-towners

After you get the hang of remarketing, you're limited only by your imagination (or our imaginations, if you want to pick our brains).

These advanced behavioral types of remarketing can deliver astounding ROI; if you do it right, you can expect cost per conversions as low as 10 percent of your "normal" AdWords traffic.

Part VI
The Part of Tens

In this part . . .

This part covers important stuff that didn't quite fit in the rest of the book. We gathered these tidbits and assembled them into top-ten lists.

We gathered the worst mistakes we've encountered in our years as AdWords consultants in Chapter 18. Avoid these, and you shave two years off your learning curve.

Chapter 19 contains case studies that highlight the principles revealed in this book. You find a broad range of businesses, challenges, and solutions that are meant to bring the concepts to life and inspire you to make your own AdWords success stories.

Chapter 18

The Ten (or So) Most Serious AdWords Mistakes

In This Chapter

▶ Split-testing snafus

▶ Campaign calamities

▶ Ad agonies

▶ Keyword, er . . . problems

AdWords can have a steep learning curve, as well as an expensive one. In this chapter, we quickly run through the most common and expensive mistakes we've seen as an AdWords consultants and managers.

Neglecting to Split-test Your Ads

When you compare two very different ads head to head, one of them will almost always be better than the other — more compelling, more attractive, or more in tune with the innermost desires of your market. The problem is that you don't know which one is going to be better. Even the world's best marketers are wrong more often than they're right. In fact, the chances of them being right the first time without any testing are laughably small. If you run a single ad, the probability of that ad being the best of all the possible ads in the universe is laughably small.

When you've run the test long enough to have statistically significant data, you gracefully retire (or unceremoniously fire, whichever you prefer) the losing ad and put up another challenger. You continue the process, directing the survival of the fittest ad until you find the one unbeatable control that maximizes your business goals.

In the old pre-Internet days, split-testing was complicated and expensive, a high-level business process reserved for huge companies with giant mainframe computers and millions of dollars on the line. Now, Google AdWords makes split-testing as easy as sending e-mail; when we see advertisers neglecting this fundamental improvement strategy, we feel like the mom telling her kid to eat his peas because there are children starving somewhere else in the world. We want to shake them and shout, "Don't you realize how lucky you are to be able to split-test so easily and cheaply and achieve such quick and conclusive results?"

If you aren't split-testing at this point, contact our office. Joel will pack his WrestleMania Split Test Avenger outfit, fly (business class only, please) to your place of business, and shake some sense into you.

Practical advice:

- ✔ When you set up a new ad group, always have several different ads ready.

- ✔ Think of split tests as experiments you're conducting to satisfy your curiosity. Keep a journal of questions, prioritize them, and keep turning them into ads and adding them to your account.

- ✔ Split-test wide variations first and then narrow down to smaller details.

- ✔ With ad split-testing, experiments, and Website Optimizer, wait until Google declares a winner. Don't jump the gun and mistake a fluke for a reliable trend.

- ✔ Split-test landing pages and e-mail sequences as well as AdWords ads. With the right tools, these split tests are almost as easy as the AdWords split-testing interface.

See Chapters 14 and 15 for best practices in split-testing.

Split-testing for Improved CTR Only

Ads that generate a high click-through rate (CTR) can be wonderful. They attract more visitors to your site at lower cost, and rank higher than other ads bidding the same amount. They also teach you about your market's desires and fears.

But when you split-test two ads and choose the winner based solely on CTR, you are in danger of worshipping a false god. Understand that the AdWords game is based on one rule: Get more outputs for your inputs than anyone else. Okay, CTR is a key throughput — but leads, customers, and dollars are what you're after.

A mention of Paris Hilton in your ad text may generate a high CTR, but just like the old magazine ads with the four-inch red headline of the word "sex," she may be attracting eyeballs belonging to nonbuyers. Remember that lots of clicks translate into lots of money for Google — not for you. Getting the right clicks is more important than getting lots of clicks.

When you split-test your ads, make sure you run conversion reports and don't rely on CTR alone.

Creating Ad Groups with Unrelated Keywords

The easiest way to set up an ad group is to write an ad, dump every keyword you can think of into that group, and send it to your home page. Heck, that should take you about ten minutes of work if you're using some of the powerful keyword tools we talk about in Chapter 5. It's much more complicated and time-consuming to create tight ad groups, based on a narrow set of related keywords matched closely to the ads and the landing page, but your results will be well worth the extra time and effort.

Keywords unrelated to ads and landing pages produce poor CTR and conversion results — and cost a lot of money because of the poor Quality Score penalty. Each keyword represents a mindset, so take the time to group your keywords by similar mindsets, and write your ads and landing pages to address the desires and fears attached to those mindsets.

You can tell when your ad groups are too broad if the CTRs of different keywords in the same group vary wildly. You may discover that the successful keywords are found in the ad headline and repeated in the description or URL. Peel the underperforming keywords out of that ad group and stick them into their own group, with an ad written just for them.

Muddying Search and Display Results

Joel reports that when he's brought in to consult for a company that can't figure out why their AdWords account isn't working, nine times out of ten, one single check box is the culprit.

Many beginners rely on Google's default settings when creating campaigns. These defaults usually serve to simplify your account and to increase Google's revenue. Sometimes those two goals are compatible with your goals, but most times they aren't. Now, about that check box (which even advanced users sometimes forget to uncheck because it's hidden): One of the campaign settings you need to change right away is in the Networks section. For search campaigns, make sure you clear the check box next to the Display network (see Figure 18-1).

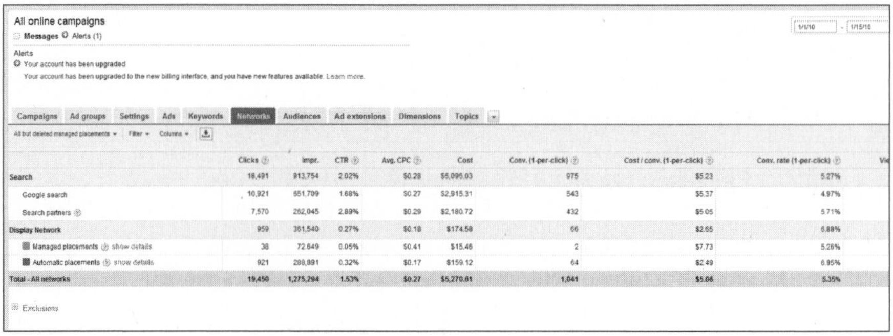

Figure 18-1:
Separate
Display
from Search
network
from Google
traffic on
the Edit
Campaign
Settings
page.

If you run both search and display traffic through the same ad group, you lose the ability to distinguish among the very different kinds of traffic. Display Network Traffic consists of people who were interrupted while they were reading or surfing or watching something else. Search Network Traffic consists of people who are actively looking for your keywords. Not only do they arrive at your site driven by different motivations and desires, but they respond differently to your ads and offers.

In many cases, Display Traffic overwhelms Search Traffic. When that's true, you lose the ability to split-test ads properly; your accurate CTR and conversion data from the search traffic is drowned by the flood of content traffic. Figuring out what your market is telling you is like trying to hear a cricket at a heavy metal concert.

When you choose winning ads and identify profitable keywords based on poorly converting search traffic — and try to apply those lessons to your search marketing — in essence, you're surveying penguins to try to sell to chimpanzees. The two market channels are very different, and should be studied and treated differently.

See Chapter 7 for detailed instructions on how to split Search and Display Network Traffic into different campaigns.

Always Starting with the Search Network

If you're advertising a "wallet-out" business, where you expect your prospect to purchase from your e-commerce store on their first visit, then you definitely want to start with the Search network. And only expand into Display network after you achieve profitability and comfortable margins with exact, phrase, and broad match keywords.

However, lead generation businesses generally should avoid the Search network until they achieve comfortable profitability in the Display network. Because of the longer sales cycle and need for more significant qualities of "conversion" — from skeptic to believer, from stranger to friend, from ignorant to savvy — Display traffic lends itself better to the structure and economics of patient lead generation.

Forgetting Keywords in Quotes (Phrase Matching) or Brackets (Exact Matching)

When you put a keyword in quotation marks, you tell Google that the quoted words or phrase must appear exactly as written somewhere in the keyword. Brackets are even more specific: They signify that the searcher must enter the keyword exactly as it appears within the brackets, with nothing added or removed.

When you use broad match keywords only (putting no quotes or brackets on the keyword), you don't really know what your visitors actually entered as search terms. You lump many different searches into a big vague basket and miss some valuable market intelligence.

Phrase and exact match keywords often achieve higher CTRs than broad matches achieve because you can create ads that speak directly to the exact words and phrases that your visitors type.

Because of the hierarchy among broad, phrase, and exact match keywords, be aware that phrase match keywords cannibalize their broad match counterparts, and exact match keywords steal impressions from both. If the CTRs differ among the three match types for high-traffic keywords, peel the underperformers and stick them into their own ad groups. (See more about keyword matching in Chapter 5.)

Ignoring Negative Keywords

Negative keywords keep certain searchers from seeing your ads. If you get significant traffic from broad- or phrase-match keywords, you may find that Google is matching your ad to some irrelevant searches. If you want to deter tire-kickers from costing you clicks, you may want to add negative keywords like -[free] and -[complimentary].

If you target upscale buyers, you can improve your ROI by eliminating [discount] and [cheap], as well as certain brand names that have low-end connotations. If some of your search terms are ambiguous (for example, [anthrax] refers to both a disease and a heavy metal band) or could refer to two different niches of the same market ([auto glass] and [plate glass] windows), save your click money by adding negative keywords to your keyword list.

Monitor your keyword-conversion performance over time to find new negative keywords. If you sell golf clubs and none of your [golf instruction] keywords converts, you can add [instruction] as a negative keyword.

Idolizing Quality Score

Quality Score (QS) tells you how much you must bid in order to show your ad at a certain position for a given keyword. A low QS theoretically puts you at a huge competitive disadvantage in your market. It makes sense, therefore, to spend vast amounts of time and psychic energy fretting about QS, right?

Not really, for two reasons. First, we've seen lots of cases where low QS keywords outperform keywords with much higher QS. Keywords seem to have an inherent QS, and because Google is grading on a curve, a QS of 5 for one keyword may actually be quite good compared with your competitors, who all have QS of 3 for the same keyword. So trying to raise the 5 to a 7 could be both pointless and impossible.

Second, although QS is determined based on a number of factors, experience strongly suggests that the overwhelmingly most important one is CTR. The best way to improve QS is to raise the CTR by writing better ads and matching keywords more closely to relevant ads. Focus on this, and QS will take care of itself.

We need to mention one exception: A QS of 0–2 is a different animal altogether from QS 3-10. When your QS is less than 3, Google is telling you about a serious problem with your website. A QS of 2 is putting you on notice that your AdWords account will be suspended if you don't quickly comply with

Google's rules. At this point, you're seeing only 10–20 percent of the traffic you would otherwise be getting. When QS drops to 0 or 1, you won't get any traffic at all. That's why we often see QS of 1 across the board in an entire campaign or account; the website is deemed unworthy of Google traffic. Not only will you not generate impressions, click, and conversions, but you also run the risk of being banned entirely from the AdWords program. So if you see QS 0–2 in your account, take those numbers seriously and do what it takes to fix the problems.

Adjusting Keyword Bids Too Often

Setting keyword bids can be one of the trickiest and most time-consuming parts of managing your AdWords account — but it doesn't have to be. The temptation to micromanage bids stems from the fact that just about every bid is either too high or too low. Every click generates a complicated auction that Google manages with startling speed and efficiency.

Have you ever completed a negotiation to your satisfaction but still ended up with a niggling feeling that you could have gotten a slightly better deal? If you pore over your AdWords data continually, you could conceivably feel that way several thousand times a day. And while making yourself miserable that often might have a certain appeal, the real danger lies in the possibility that you'll keep changing bids in an effort to close the perceived gap between the deal you're getting and the deal you could be getting.

Changing bids too often doesn't allow the data to accumulate to the point where you have solid evidence to guide you. It's like shooting free throws in the dark with no feedback; you can't expect improvement in that scenario.

Wait until you accumulate evidence in the form of a month's worth of data before shifting any bids. Follow the schedule detailed in the last part of Chapter 13 to adjust bids for maximum benefit in minimum time.

Spending Too Much in the Beginning

If you open your wallet too much by specifying too high a monthly budget or daily spend, you'll lose all your money before you have time to learn the ropes. When you figure out that something isn't working, turn it off right away while you make changes. Chances are — even with this book under your belt — you'll take some time to get the feel of AdWords and develop proficiency. If you rush, you'll blow through your budget several times and walk away going, "This stuff doesn't work."

If you ever took a driving lesson, you may remember that your instructor made you drive slowly for a long time, showing you how to steer and brake and stop fiddling with the satellite radio settings, before ever letting you open up on a highway. Your AdWords budget is your miles per hour — take it easy until you learn how to drive safely.

Remember the expansion protocol we discuss in Chapter 16, about campaign cloning. For "wallet-out" businesses, start with low-volume exact match keywords and expand into phrase and broad match keywords only when the exact match campaigns turn profitable. For lead generation businesses, start in the cheaper Display network and only add more expensive Search campaigns after you're profitable in Display.

Spending Too Little in the Beginning

Other advertisers are so hesitant that they set daily and monthly budgets far too low to generate enough traffic. They don't get enough impressions to split-test and improve their ads and keywords, and they give up in frustration. Without enough statistically significant data, they don't know how to improve their campaigns and quit in frustration. That's like learning to drive by never going faster than five miles per hour. The experience of going 55 mph (or 85, which Joel wouldn't know about, especially not on I-70 in Colorado just east of Glenwood Springs, he swears) is qualitatively and quantitatively different from inching along in an empty parking lot. The super-slow experience just doesn't transfer to the real thing.

The happy medium involves setting a "learning budget" and sticking with it. Do your homework (see Chapter 4) to estimate the amount of traffic you can expect. Your advertising spend (as well as the daily or weekly attention you'll need to give your account) depends on the velocity of that traffic. At first, don't expect to make money, or even come close to breaking even. You're not advertising to earn it back; instead, you're running market tests so you can come out swinging when you open up your wallet and your traffic. Your goal is to get your ROI into the black within a few months.

Automating Too Much

Some Google fans will be outraged at some of the omissions in this book, most notably Conversion Optimizer (CO). CO is an advanced AdWords feature that puts Google in charge of your bidding. It's designed to take advantage of Google's brilliant algorithm and unfathomable amounts of data to determine how much to bid in every single scenario to get you maximum return.

In theory, CO can do a much better job of bidding than you can because of its access to data you simply don't have (for example, it might determine that someone searching at 3 a.m. in Champagne Castle, South Africa is twice as likely to convert as someone else searching the very same keyword at noon in Guelph, Ontario).

Maybe someday CO will live up to its potential, and folks like us who insist on manual bid management will end up like John Henry in the folk song, busting our hearts out in futile competition with a superior technology. (If you don't know the reference, ask Watson, the current *Jeopardy!* champion — and a computer.)

We've seen too many cases of CO returning twice the traffic at five times the specified cost per action (CPA). And our friend and colleague Shelley Ellis was shocked when she was charged $88.01 for a single click on a keyword with only two competing ads because of CO's determination of the value of that click to her business. At this point, the control you give up by letting Google manage your bids isn't sufficiently offset by the likely improvement in performance.

Joel has experimented with CO, and although there are plenty of pros to it, there is one single con that in his experience outweighs everything else. Because you can't see the data CO uses to set bids, you can't learn from that data. As we show in Chapter 18, the real value of AdWords most often lies in the insights you can apply to the rest of your marketing.

Letting Google completely automate your AdWords account is like hiring Mario Andretti as your chauffeur for the pace car for the Indianapolis 500 while you hunker down in the back seat. You'll have a pretty good time and you get a great view, but you aren't learning anything that could help when you need to drive that car yourself. When Google takes over your account, you lose the opportunity to gain powerful insights about your business that you can leverage in much bigger settings.

Many other tools exist to automate other parts of AdWords. You can automatically generate keyword lists, ads, and Display network placements. The big problem with relying on these tools is that if other people have access to the same tools, you lose any competitive advantage that you might achieve by actually thinking. Automation is great when it saves you time, but can be profoundly disempowering when it starts doing your thinking for you.

And powerful automation tools in the wrong hands can deplete your advertising budget and give you nothing in return. When Howie uses a manual hacksaw to trim a bit of extra weather seal from his minivan door, he can do only so much damage. But put a Sawzall 11 amp reciprocating saw in his hands and watch him accidentally sculpt a convertible.

Chapter 19

Ten (or So) AdWords Case Studies

*T*he best way to see the strategies and concepts from this book in action is by viewing actual examples. We can't show you all the details because successful advertisers guard their keywords, strategies, and metrics as carefully as the recipe for Coca-Cola. We've compiled case studies from our own files (most on an anonymous basis, so you have to trust that we're not hallucinating these results) as well as from other consultants who hope you'll think they're clever enough to hire them. We looked for simple changes that lead to significant improvements, hoping you'll be inspired to take quick and simple actions to improve your own AdWords campaigns.

Giving Prospects the Time of Day

The challenge

One client came to us with a simple complaint: namely, that its lead acquisition costs were too high. This client was paying, on average, $403.40 per lead (a completed Request for Quote form). With an average CPC of $13.45 just to cling to position 4 on the first page of Google for its most important keywords, the client was clearly in with a highly competitive market. Lowering bid prices would reduce lead flow by moving Fast Money further from the top of the page.

And although landing page optimization to increase the site conversion rate was clearly in order, with a conversion rate of 3.33%, that would take time. This client was in a hurry. What could we do that would instantly reduce costs without sacrificing conversions?

The solution

We poked around the Dashboard for a while, not finding much, until we hit the Dimensions tab (see Chapter 13). When we ran a campaign performance report by hour of the day report for the past 60 days, we saw our opportunity. Some times of day delivered much more valuable traffic than other times.

So, we set up ad scheduling for this campaign, with the following parameters:

- ✔ Did not show ads for hours that had generated 0 conversions in the past 60 days

- ✔ Reduced bids to 75 percent of default CPCs during down hours (when clicks were less likely to convert to leads)

- ✔ Increased bids to 125 percent of default CPCs during best hours (when clicks were more likely to convert to leads)

The result

We compared two consecutive four-day periods, one just before and the other just after we implemented the scheduling changes. The results are summarized in Table 19-1.

Table 19-1	Before and After Scheduling Restrictions			
Time period	**Clicks**	**Impr.**	**CTR**	**Avg. CPC**
Fri–Mon before the change	90	9,251	0.97%	$13.45
Fri–Mon after the change	82	6,859	1.20%	$12.75
Time period	**Cost**	**Conversions**	**Cost/ Conv.**	**Conv. rate**
Fri–Mon before the change	$1,210.21	3	$403.40	3.33%
Fri–Mon after the change	$1,045.54	6	$174.26	7.32%

As you can see, both clicks and impressions are down following the changes. CTR is up by 24 percent, and the average cost of a click is 5% lower. The real story here is told by the three columns on the right. Conversions doubled, the site conversion rate more than doubled, and the cost of acquiring a lead fell by 57 percent, from $403.40 to $174.26.

This isn't enough data to be conclusive, so we're still monitoring carefully to make sure the trend continues (as of late August, 2011), but because the changes were based on solid analysis of campaign performance, we have every expectation that the improvements will last. And now we can focus on the longer-term task of testing and improving the website.

Squeezing More Leads from the Display Network

The challenge

One of our clients was getting millions of impressions each week in the Display network and had a very strong website that converted visitors into leads at 11.5%, at a cost per lead of $25.51. The client could afford to pay up to $29 per lead and still be profitable, so they were eager to find more good lead sources in the Display network.

The solution

One look at their account told us that the first big opportunity was to manage their placements with greater control. Their display campaign was run entirely on Automatic Placements, which had done a great job of finding lots of relevant sites. Now it was time to move the converting sites into Managed Placements so we could bid appropriately at the site level. See Chapter 13 for information on graduating placements from Automatic to Managed status.

Here's what we did:

1. Created a new "Managed Placement" campaign

2. Identified placements that had generated conversions and moved them into the new campaign

3. Excluded all those placements from the Automatic Placements campaign to force Google to send all traffic from those placements to the new campaign

4. Monitored the managed placements and raised or lowered bids to maximize the number of leads that cost $29 or less

The result

Table 19-2 tells the first part of the story. Impressions increased from 6.5 million to 8.4 million, and clicks went from 5,294 to 6,524 in one week, an increase of 23 percent. Although the conversion rate dipped slightly, from 11.50% to 11.24%, indicating a slight decrease in the quality of the traffic, the number of conversions rose by 20 percent, at an average cost per conversion of $25.99. That's still well less than the $29 cap required for profitability.

Table 19-2		Before and After Managing Placements			
Week	*Impr.*	*Clicks*	*CTR*	*Avg CPC*	*Cost*
7/25	6505620	5294	0.08%	$2.93	$15537.74
8/1	8424607	6524	0.08%	$2.92	$19048.43
Week	*Avg Pos.*	*Conv.*	*Conv. Rate*	*Cost/Conv.*	
7/25	1.5	609	11.50%	$25.51	
8/1	1.5	733	11.24%	$25.99	

The weird thing is that this case study is only half done (and our editor isn't willing to wait). We actually haven't even begun to adjust bids yet, which we usually assume will have the biggest positive impact on results. So the moral here is that simply putting converting placements under management delivered more traffic that was pretty much just as high quality as before. A 20 percent increase in sales in one week, with much more expected. That's the power of granular campaign management, which we describe in Chapter 13.

Paying More to Get More

The challenge

This same client was also showing ads in the Search network, where the bid prices were almost twice as high as in the Display network. Their leads were coming in at an average cost per conversion $29.57, which was slightly higher than ideal. Concerned about overspending, the client limited its daily budget. We examined the Impression Share metrics (then available at the campaign level only, and now viewable at the ad group level as well) to find that the budget limited the number of collectible impressions, clicks, and potential conversions on any given day.

The solution

We simply raised the daily budget. Because we kept the bid prices static, we expected that this change would result in more traffic of the same quality.

The results

As you can see in Table 19-3, this did happen. Impressions and clicks rose, and conversions jumped from 734 to 962. So far, so good.

Table 19-3	Before and After Increasing Daily Budget			
Week	**Impr.**	**Clicks**	**CTR**	**Avg. CPC**
8/1	169731	4135	2.44%	$5.26
8/8	187995	5508	2.93%	$5.03
Week	**Cost**	**Conv.**	**Conv. Rate**	**Cost/Conv.**
8/1	$21768.37	734	17.80%	$29.57
8/8	$27691.64	962	17.48%	$28.75

But what was really interesting (and delightful!) was that the cost of these clicks and leads decreased. Average position hardly changed, but the CTR skyrocketed from 2.44% to 2.93% — an increase of 20 percent. The average CPC dropped from $5.26 to $5.03. And despite the site conversion rate dipping a bit, the all-important average cost per conversion dropped to within the ideal range, from $29.57 to $28.75. Raising the daily budget delivered 228 more leads in a single week, and those leads were $0.82 less.

Milking the Display Network for Leads

The challenge

One of our clients, whom we'll call Rick (because that's his name), uses AdWords to drive online leads to his telephone sales staff to close. In the last months of 2009, he hired additional sales staff to be ready for what he assumed would be a huge spike in January, 2010. Unfortunately, end-of-year results suggested that January sales would be about the same traffic as the previous year, rather than the 30–50 percent increase he was counting on. When we came to us, he was paying as much as he could afford on the keywords he was targeting, and was at a loss about how he was going to be able to generate enough leads to keep his team busy.

The solution

Because Rick was generating leads for his sales staff, and lead generation marketing has a natural affinity for the Display network, that was the first place we looked for additional traffic. When we ran the numbers for the first half of January, 2010 (see Figure 19-1), we found that he was being far too conservative in the Display network, where he was picking up only a fraction of all the available traffic.

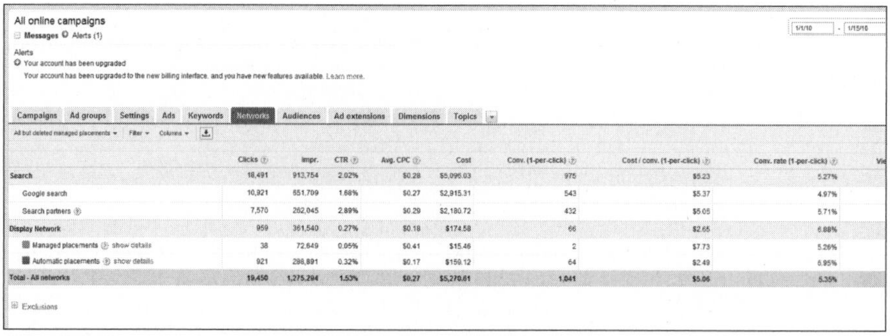

All online campaigns

Messages Alerts (1)

Alerts

Your account has been upgraded

Your account has been upgraded to the new billing interface, and you have new features available. Learn more.

Campaigns | Ad groups | Settings | Ads | Keywords | Networks | Audiences | Ad extensions | Dimensions | Topics

All but deleted managed placements | Filter | Columns

	Clicks	Impr.	CTR	Avg. CPC	Cost	Conv. (1-per-click)	Cost / conv. (1-per-click)	Conv. rate (1-per-click)
Search	18,491	913,754	2.02%	$0.28	$5,096.03	975	$5.23	5.27%
Google search	10,921	651,709	1.68%	$0.27	$2,915.31	543	$5.37	4.97%
Search partners	7,570	262,045	2.89%	$0.29	$2,180.72	432	$5.05	5.71%
Display Network	959	361,540	0.27%	$0.18	$174.58	66	$2.65	6.88%
Managed placements show details	38	72,649	0.05%	$0.41	$15.46	2	$7.73	5.26%
Automatic placements show details	921	288,891	0.32%	$0.17	$159.12	64	$2.49	6.95%
Total - All networks	19,450	1,275,294	1.53%	$0.27	$5,270.61	1,041	$5.06	5.35%

Exclusions

Figure 19-1: The Display network wasn't pulling its weight for the lead generation business.

As you can see in Figure 19-1, the Display network had generated only 66 conversions in the first half of January 2010, compared with the Search network's 975. We immediately changed his Display network campaign setting from Show Ads Only on Pages That Match All Selected Targeting Methods to Show Ads on Pages That Match the Broadest Targeting Method. The first option was drastically limiting his exposure by restricting advertising only to a handful of websites.

In addition, we raised bids and increased the budget for Display network campaigns, and moved converting sites from automatic into managed placements for greater control.

The result

Figure 19-2 shows the data for the first 15 days of January 2011, for comparison purposes. Overall search volume was about the same in 2011 and 2010, but the number of leads nearly doubled (from 1,041 to 2,001) with only a slight increase in cost per conversion (from $5.06 to $5.24) through robust use of the Display network. With attentive bidding strategies (the ones we share in Chapter 13), Display network leads ended up about 15 percent less expensive than Search network leads.)

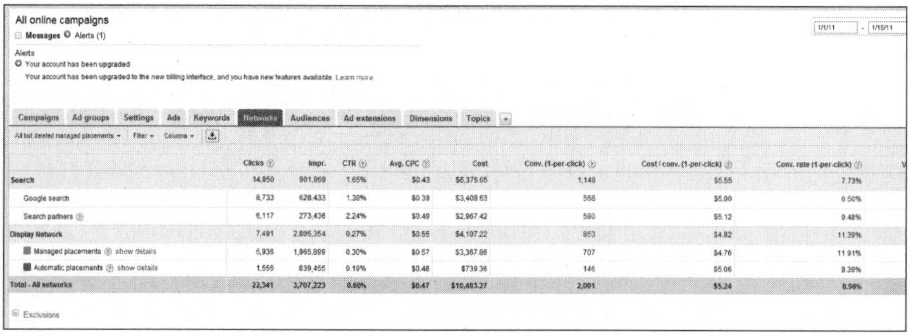

All online campaigns

Messages Alerts (1)

Alerts

Your account has been upgraded

Your account has been upgraded to the new billing interface, and you have new features available. Learn more

Campaigns | Ad groups | Settings | Ads | Keywords | Networks | Audiences | Ad extensions | Dimensions | Topics

All but deleted managed placements | Filter | Columns

	Clicks	Impr.	CTR	Avg. CPC	Cost	Conv. (1-per-click)	Cost / conv. (1-per-click)	Conv. rate (1-per-click)
Search	14,850	901,869	1.65%	$0.43	$6,376.05	1,148	$5.55	7.73%
Google search	8,733	628,433	1.39%	$0.39	$3,408.63	568	$6.00	6.50%
Search partners	6,117	273,436	2.24%	$0.49	$2,967.42	580	$5.12	9.48%
Display Network	7,491	2,805,354	0.27%	$0.55	$4,107.22	853	$4.82	11.39%
Managed placements show details	5,936	1,965,899	0.30%	$0.57	$3,367.86	707	$4.76	11.91%
Automatic placements show details	1,555	839,455	0.19%	$0.48	$739.36	146	$5.06	9.39%
Total - All networks	22,341	3,707,223	0.60%	$0.47	$10,483.27	2,001	$5.24	8.96%

Exclusions

Figure 19-2: The Display network brought in many cost-effective conversions after we gave it permission.

Getting Rid of Bad Apples and Polishing the Good Ones

The challenge

An e-commerce client came to us hoping to increase online sales. The client wasn't in a position to just raise its budget because the cost per conversion was already slightly too high for comfort. With five product categories spread among three sloppily set up campaigns, it was extremely tedious to find opportunities in the existing data.

Because there were too many kinds of products in each campaign, the client couldn't distinguish profitable from unprofitable keywords and product lines.

The solution

To identify the problem areas, we ran the data through AdWords filters looking for keyword and ad group names that shared similarly poor conversion numbers. We discovered that one product category was eating 35 percent of the entire AdWords budget, yet generating only 3 percent of online sales. We immediately eliminated that product line, freeing up around $15,000 per month to spend on better performing keywords and ad groups. We applied that $15,000 toward campaign elements that had already been profitable, and could now aggressively pursue and optimize for that traffic.

The result

We began working with this client on May 1, 2010, corresponding to the cross-hatch below the graph lines in Figure 19-3. As you can see, and to our surprise, conversions grew rapidly, and the cost per conversion immediately stabilized and then continued to steadily improve.

Figure 19-3: Simply finding and eliminating unprofitable product lines and keywords put this account on strong footing.

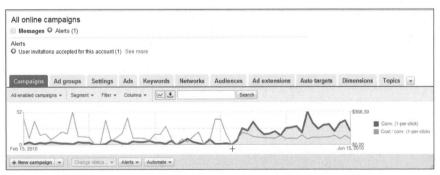

Using AdWords to Build Brand Awareness and Drive Conversions

The problem

Shelley Ellis of OnlineMarketingPerformance.com was approached by a startup company in the "daily deals" space (a fairly new industry that has only become popular in the last couple of years with the growth of Groupon and LivingSocial). The client needed to build brand awareness and share their marketing message, while at the same time driving sales to fund further growth.

Shelley realized that neither the Search nor Display network was sufficient by itself to generate both brand awareness and conversions. Additionally, the traditional Display network strategy of automatic placements would limit her client's exposure, so she needed to use a more aggressive form of Display network targeting. Finally, her client had a target cost per acquisition (CPA) of $15, so all leads had to come in at cost per conversion or lower.

The solution

The goal of the campaign was to provide immediate value to the client through customer signups, even as the client was building brand awareness. Those signups would allow the client to e-mail daily deals to the consumers. Online Performance Marketing approached this in three main areas: search, banner ads in Display, and contextually targeted text ads.

Search

Online Performance Marketing ran search campaigns using keywords like [daily deals], [deal of the day], and [daily online deals] to capture the existing marketing of "wallet out" customers read to sign up and make purchases.

Banner ads

In the Display network, the client used banner-sized image ads on very high-traffic sites, such as

- Woot.com
- Coupons.com
- Yelp
- YouTube

The banner ads were also used for remarketing on the Display network (see Chapter 17).

Contextually targeted text ads

Shelley also used contextual targeting in the Display network by finding sites by general topics not necessarily tightly connecting to daily deals. She segmented these placements so she could show with text ads for her client's specific product and service offerings that were relevant to the sites on which they appeared. The text ads showed up on sites such as

- ✔ Yelp
- ✔ Restaurants.com
- ✔ Google Maps
- ✔ Mashable

The results

After running the client's ads on the Display network, Online Performance Marketing was able to achieve a conversion rate of 24%, taking into account both conversions and view-through conversions. And by targeting the right sites and keeping an eye on their metrics, they were able to achieve a CPA of $9.20 — $5.80 less than the maximum allowed. The numbers in Figure 19-4 aren't as robust, since the view-through conversions aren't included by Google, and need to be factored in manually.

Figure 19-4: Aggressive targeting in both Search and Display networks generated brand awareness and conversions.

Campaign	Budget	Status	Clicks	Impr.	CTR	Avg. CPC	Cost	Conv. (many-per-click)	Cost / conv. (many-per-click)	Conv. rate (many-per-click)	View-through Conv.
Display Image Ads	$300.00/day	Eligible	15,207	15,717,343	0.10%	$2.47	$37,582.42	1,706	$22.03	11.22%	1,801
Remarketing-Display	$200.00/day	Eligible	5,481	2,681,238	0.20%	$1.11	$6,063.83	449	$13.51	8.19%	1,646
Display Text ads	$200.00/day	Eligible	3,740	4,711,317	0.08%	$2.57	$9,626.76	189	$50.94	5.05%	0
Total - all filtered campaigns			24,428	23,109,898	0.11%	$2.18	$53,273.01	2,344	$22.73	9.60%	3,447

View-through conversions occur when someone views an image ad in the Display network and doesn't click it, but converts via some other channel within the following 30 days. In other words, if you see a big banner ad for "XeroShoe.com" but don't click it, and then a few days later you remember the name, decide to check it out, and buy a pair, the banner ad would generate a view-through conversion.

But the AdWords CPA data tell only half the story. Through the banner advertising, they were also able to increase brand awareness, which was measured in terms of the number of searches for the client's brand name. This, in turn, increased traffic to the client's site and lowered the overall CPA for their whole online marketing strategy. Their analytics data reflected this steady increase in organic traffic to their site on their brand-name keyword (see Figure 19-5).

Figure 19-5:
Increased
brand
awareness
through
aggressive
Display
network
advertis-
ing drove
brand-name
keyword
searches.

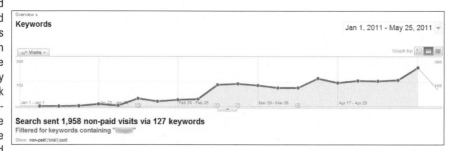

Shelley cautions, "When running ads on the Google Display network, looking at the hard numbers such as conversions, cost, and view-through conversions can be a bit misleading. You must factor in the role Display plays in driving brand awareness and additional non-paid traffic to your site. It works on many levels. Using both banners and text ads, the power of Display can be utilized for brand awareness and direct response."

Cloning Campaigns for More and Better Traffic

The problem

A client of ours (itSM Solutions; www.itsmsolutions.com), provides IT service management training for some of the world's biggest organizations. With low search volume centered around just a few keywords and lots of competitors for that traffic, they needed to optimize bidding for search and take advantage of the untapped potential of the Display network. When we started working with them, their account consisted of a single campaign that included search and display, and geo-targeted pretty much every country on Earth.

The solution

We focused on two things after we took over the AdWords account. We separated Search and Display traffic into their own campaigns, and we restricted traffic by geographic location and funneled the two best regions into their own campaigns.

The resultsPhase 1: Separating Search from Display

One of the first things we did was separate Search from Display traffic by cloning the original campaign (see Chapter 16). Now we could allocate budget to each network individually and adjust ad copy based on the difference responses of each traffic stream.

Table 19-4 shows the difference that occurred in the week immediately following this change. The first week shows the metrics for the original campaign, and the second week combines the two new campaigns, Search and Display.

Table 19-4	More Conversions through Campaign Cloning			
Week	**Impr.**	**Clicks**	**CTR**	**Avg. CPC**
3/7/2011	699,698	1,206	0.17%	$0.60
3/14/2011	1,606,475	1,767	0.11%	$0.66
Week	**Cost**	**Conversions**	**Cost/Conv.**	**Conv.rate**
3/7/2011	$722.29	29	$24.91	2.40%
3/14/2011	$1,162.43	46	$25.27	2.60%

At first glance, this may not seem like a wonderful change. After all, CTR decreased, and average CPC increased. But the important columns are the three on the right. Increasing Display traffic generated almost 60 percent more conversions, at an only slightly higher cost per conversion. And that was before any bid optimization or ad testing.

Think of AdWords as a big gumball machine: Every time you put in $25, you get a conversion. If your conversions are worth $50 each, how many times do you want to put in $25? The answer should be, as many times as you possibly can. Allowing the Display network its own campaign and budget instantly increased the rate at which itSM could exchange $25 for conversions.

Phase 2: Separating traffic by geographic region

After getting such a gratifying return on the first change, we were emboldened to split campaigns further based on geo-targeting. We discovered by analyzing the data in the Dimensions tab (see Chapter 13) that two regions were providing the highest quantities and quality of traffic: the United States and Asia. We split the Search and Display campaigns as follows:

- ✔ Search USA
- ✔ Search Asia
- ✔ Display USA
- ✔ Display Asia

We increased the total budget so that each campaign had a fair chance to prove its worth. Table 19-5 compares the week of March 14, 2011 (the last row of the previous table) with the week of April 4, after the geographic campaign cloning had a couple of weeks to run.

Table 19-5	Cheaper Conversions through Geotargeting			
Week	*Impr.*	*Clicks*	*CTR*	*Avg. CPC*
3/14/2011	1,606,475	1,767	0.11%	$0.66
4/4/2011	1,115,196	1,647	0.15%	$0.61
Week	*Cost*	*Conversions*	*Cost/Conv.*	*Conv.rate*
3/14/2011	$1,162.43	46	$25.27	2.60%
4/4/2011	$1,008.70	56	$18.01	3.40%

Although impressions are down significantly, clicks are down only slightly because of the improved CTR. The average CPC is lower — and most importantly, the number of conversions has increased by 22 percent thanks to a 31 percent boost in the conversion rate. Because we hadn't touched the website at this point, the improved conversion numbers were entirely the result of attracting more highly qualified traffic.

Adding Sitelinks to Ads to Improve CTR

The problem

A client came to us wanting more clicks. This client sells a product to a very niche audience, so it was crucial to make the most of every impression. With initial CTRs of 3.93% in one campaign and 5.90% in another, we weren't dealing with an unappealing ad (those are always the easiest to improve). And for most of their keywords, they had no ad competition, so there was no way to be "more" compelling and relevant. Before we began split testing ad copy, we wanted to find a simpler and quicker way to increase website traffic from the same ad.

The solution

We wondered whether making the ad bigger and more authoritative-looking would boost CTR. The natural choice was to include the Ad Sitelink extension, which adds up to four additional text links below the ad as long as the keywords' Max CPC and Quality Scores are high enough for Google. (See Chapter 8 for more about ad extensions.)

The results

Sitelinks produced instant increases in CTR, at a much higher level than is typical by simply improving the ad message. In one campaign, the average CTR increased from 3.93% to 6.57% when sitelinks were present. In a second campaign, the increase was greater, from 5.90% to a whopping 14.57%.

Interestingly, the sitelinks did not increase CTR by getting clicked themselves. When we segmented the data by click type, we found that the sitelinks received much lower CTRs than the headlines. Instead of providing greater relevance, the sitelinks appear to have worked by increasing the size and authoritative look of the ad.

Getting Cheap and Hungry Traffic by Bidding on Your Own Brand Name

The problem

Christian Bedard of `www.calimacil.com` sells high-end and high-quality foam swords for live action role-playing aficionados. With such a targeted niche, Christian thought he had tapped out all the potential keywords in the swords, shields, and live action weapons department. How could he generate more traffic when there didn't seem to be any?

The solution

Christian discovered a clever AdWords strategy not from one of his competitors, but from Dell Computers. While searching for a Dell machine, he noticed that the company was bidding on its own brand name, even though the entire first page of Google search results was about Dell Computers. Happy to borrow promising ideas wherever he could find them, Christian bid on the keyword [Calimacil] and headlined the ad "Calimacil Official Site." (See Figure 19-6.)

One of the smartest things you can do as an AdWords advertiser is notice what works on you while you're searching. Most innovation is just borrowing a good idea from somewhere else and applying it where it has never been applied before.

Figure 19-6:
An effective ad that capitalizes on searches for their own brand name.

Even though the Calimacil listing comes up at the top of the organic listings for the keyword [Calimacil], the ad and organic listing combined generate more traffic and sales than just the top organic listing by itself. Rather than cannibalize the free clicks, the sponsored link reinforces Calimacil's domination of the page. The ad's CTR is 44% in French-speaking territories and 19% in English. The two campaigns have almost identical cost per conversion, around $5.80 Canadian.

Un-muddying the Testing Waters: A Website Optimizer Cautionary Tale

The challenge

A client with a lead generation business model wanted to improve the effectiveness of its landing pages using Website Optimizer testing. While initial tests showed significant improvements in some page variations, after about a month, the differences disappeared, and all the pages seemed to perform about the same. This was very confusing.

The client knew that testing to improve conversion rates is one of the most powerful strategies for online success, but with the ambiguous results, it wasn't paying off. We had to dig into AdWords data and the account history to find the wrench in the testing works.

The discovery

The client had been buying traffic in its three most profitable markets only: the US, the UK, and Australia. This traffic was converting so well that they decided to get aggressive and bid on clicks in other regions, including the Middle East, the European Union, South America, and Japan. The new international traffic was about 90 percent less expensive on a per-click basis than the original traffic, and even with a much lower conversion rate, the international cost per conversion was about one-half that in the US.

We still didn't have an explanation for the collapse of Website Optimizer testing protocol. Even if the new traffic converted half as well, why would these visitors mess up our testing so badly?

We discovered the answer in a conversation with the client's Chief Operating Officer, who had been monitoring the conversion of leads into actual sales on the back end. Thanks to the specific tracking code we had installed on every click from the new lead source (whew!), he was able to determine that many fewer of these leads were actual prospects, and a large percentage appeared to be fraudulent.

In hindsight, we suspect that the chief culprits were Display network sites whose owners made money every time someone clicked the ads Google displayed on their pages. This turned out to be a very sophisticated form of click fraud because the fake prospects completed the lead capture form as well. Because the conversion rate seemed so good, we weren't alerted to the poor quality of the traffic for the duration of the sales cycle, and therefore kept paying the website owners for this traffic.

When people make money by filling out your opt-in form, it doesn't matter how good or bad your landing page is. That's why testing this traffic led to inconclusive results.

The solution

We turned off the poor-quality traffic streams.

The result

As soon as we eliminated that traffic, conversion rates skyrocketed. Website Optimizer started reflecting the true preferences of its prospects, so the client was able to identify the best converting pages and continue to improve them. As an added bonus, the sales staff appreciated not having to deal with the bad leads.

Index

Notes

Notes

Apple & Macs

iPad For Dummies
978-0-470-58027-1

iPhone For Dummies,
4th Edition
978-0-470-87870-5

MacBook For Dummies, 3rd
Edition
978-0-470-76918-8

Mac OS X Snow Leopard For
Dummies
978-0-470-43543-4

Business

Bookkeeping For Dummies
978-0-7645-9848-7

Job Interviews
For Dummies,
3rd Edition
978-0-470-17748-8

Resumes For Dummies,
5th Edition
978-0-470-08037-5

Starting an
Online Business
For Dummies,
6th Edition
978-0-470-60210-2

Stock Investing
For Dummies,
3rd Edition
978-0-470-40114-9

Successful
Time Management
For Dummies
978-0-470-29034-7

Computer Hardware

BlackBerry
For Dummies,
4th Edition
978-0-470-60700-8

Computers For Seniors
For Dummies,
2nd Edition
978-0-470-53483-0

PCs For Dummies,
Windows
7 Edition
978-0-470-46542-4

Laptops For Dummies,
4th Edition
978-0-470-57829-2

Cooking & Entertaining

Cooking Basics
For Dummies,
3rd Edition
978-0-7645-7206-7

Wine For Dummies,
4th Edition
978-0-470-04579-4

Diet & Nutrition

Dieting For Dummies,
2nd Edition
978-0-7645-4149-0

Nutrition For Dummies,
4th Edition
978-0-471-79868-2

Weight Training
For Dummies,
3rd Edition
978-0-471-76845-6

Digital Photography

Digital SLR Cameras &
Photography For Dummies,
3rd Edition
978-0-470-46606-3

Photoshop Elements 8
For Dummies
978-0-470-52967-6

Gardening

Gardening Basics
For Dummies
978-0-470-03749-2

Organic Gardening
For Dummies,
2nd Edition
978-0-470-43067-5

Green/Sustainable

Raising Chickens
For Dummies
978-0-470-46544-8

Green Cleaning
For Dummies
978-0-470-39106-8

Health

Diabetes For Dummies,
3rd Edition
978-0-470-27086-8

Food Allergies
For Dummies
978-0-470-09584-3

Living Gluten-Free
For Dummies,
2nd Edition
978-0-470-58589-4

Hobbies/General

Chess For Dummies,
2nd Edition
978-0-7645-8404-6

Drawing
Cartoons & Comics
For Dummies
978-0-470-42683-8

Knitting For Dummies,
2nd Edition
978-0-470-28747-7

Organizing
For Dummies
978-0-7645-5300-4

Su Doku For Dummies
978-0-470-01892-7

Home Improvement

Home Maintenance
For Dummies,
2nd Edition
978-0-470-43063-7

Home Theater
For Dummies,
3rd Edition
978-0-470-41189-6

Living the
Country Lifestyle
All-in-One
For Dummies
978-0-470-43061-3

Solar Power Your Home
For Dummies,
2nd Edition
978-0-470-59678-4

Available wherever books are sold. For more information or to order direct: U.S. customers visit www.dummies.com or call 1-877-762-2974.
U.K. customers visit www.wileyeurope.com or call (0) 1243 843291. Canadian customers visit www.wiley.ca or call 1-800-567-4797.

Internet

Blogging For Dummies,
3rd Edition
978-0-470-61996-4

eBay For Dummies,
6th Edition
978-0-470-49741-8

Facebook For Dummies,
3rd Edition
978-0-470-87804-0

Web Marketing
For Dummies,
2nd Edition
978-0-470-37181-7

WordPress
For Dummies,
3rd Edition
978-0-470-59274-8

Language & Foreign Language

French For Dummies
978-0-7645-5193-2

Italian Phrases
For Dummies
978-0-7645-7203-6

Spanish For Dummies,
2nd Edition
978-0-470-87855-2

Spanish
For Dummies,
Audio Set
978-0-470-09585-0

Math & Science

Algebra I
For Dummies,
2nd Edition
978-0-470-55964-2

Biology For Dummies,
2nd Edition
978-0-470-59875-7

Calculus For Dummies
978-0-7645-2498-1

Chemistry For Dummies
978-0-7645-5430-8

Microsoft Office

Excel 2010 For Dummies
978-0-470-48953-6

Office 2010 All-in-One
For Dummies
978-0-470-49748-7

Office 2010 For Dummies,
Book + DVD Bundle
978-0-470-62698-6

Word 2010 For Dummies
978-0-470-48772-3

Music

Guitar For Dummies,
2nd Edition
978-0-7645-9904-0

iPod & iTunes For
Dummies, 8th Edition
978-0-470-87871-2

Piano Exercises
For Dummies
978-0-470-38765-8

Parenting & Education

Parenting For Dummies,
2nd Edition
978-0-7645-5418-6

Type 1 Diabetes
For Dummies
978-0-470-17811-9

Pets

Cats For Dummies,
2nd Edition
978-0-7645-5275-5

Dog Training For Dummies,
3rd Edition
978-0-470-60029-0

Puppies For Dummies,
2nd Edition
978-0-470-03717-1

Religion & Inspiration

The Bible For Dummies
978-0-7645-5296-0

Catholicism For Dummies
978-0-7645-5391-2

Women in the Bible
For Dummies
978-0-7645-8475-6

Self-Help & Relationship

Anger Management
For Dummies
978-0-470-03715-7

Overcoming Anxiety
For Dummies,
2nd Edition
978-0-470-57441-6

Sports

Baseball
For Dummies,
3rd Edition
978-0-7645-7537-2

Basketball
For Dummies,
2nd Edition
978-0-7645-5248-9

Golf For Dummies,
3rd Edition
978-0-471-76871-5

Web Development

Web Design
All-in-One
For Dummies
978-0-470-41796-6

Web Sites
Do-It-Yourself
For Dummies,
2nd Edition
978-0-470-56520-9

Windows 7

Windows 7
For Dummies
978-0-470-49743-2

Windows 7
For Dummies,
Book + DVD Bundle
978-0-470-52398-8

Windows 7 All-in-One
For Dummies
978-0-470-48763-1

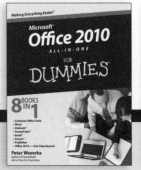
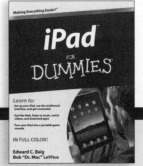
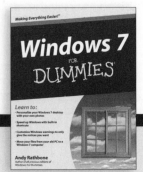

Available wherever books are sold. For more information or to order direct: U.S. customers visit www.dummies.com or call 1-877-762-297
U.K. customers visit www.wileyeurope.com or call (0) 1243 843291. Canadian customers visit www.wiley.ca or call 1-800-567-4797.

DUMMIES.COM®

Wherever you are in life, Dummies makes it easier.

From fashion to Facebook®, wine to Windows®, and everything in between, Dummies makes it easier.

Visit us at Dummies.com

Dummies products make life easier!

DIY • Consumer Electronics •
Crafts • Software • Cookware •
Hobbies • Videos • Music •
Games • and More!

For more information, go to
Dummies.com® and search
the store by category.

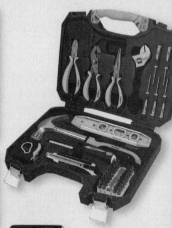

Making everything easier!™